BAR

TATE GALLERY LIVERPOOL CRITICAL FORUM

Acknowledgments
The Editorial Board gratefully acknowledges the advice contributed to the Critical Forum (which initiated this collection of essays) by Penelope Curtis and Lisa Tickner, and is especially indebted to Lisa Tickner for chairing the event. Thanks are also expressed to Sir Alan Bowness and the Trustees of Barbara Hepworth, Nina Gabo Williams and the Trustees of Naum Gabo, and John Taylor of Lund Humphries Ltd., for their invaluable assistance with illustrations.

Previously published in this series
American Abstract Expressionism edited by David Thistlewood. ISBN 0-85323-338-1
Joseph Beuys: Diverging Critiques edited by David Thistlewood. ISBN 0-85323-349-7

Cover illustration
Two Segments and Sphere, 1935–36;
marble; 267 × 267 × 216 mm. Private Collection;

TATE GALLERY LIVERPOOL CRITICAL FORUM SERIES, VOLUME 3

BARBARA HEPWORTH
RECONSIDERED

Editor DAVID THISTLEWOOD
Critical Forum Coordinator ANNE MACPHEE

LIVERPOOL UNIVERSITY PRESS AND TATE GALLERY LIVERPOOL

First published 1996 by
Liverpool University Press
Senate House
Liverpool
L69 3BX
and
Tate Gallery Liverpool
Albert Dock
Liverpool
L3 4BB

British Library Cataloguing-in-Publication Data
A British Library CIP Record is available
ISBN 0-85323-770-0

Set in 11/13pt Linotron 202 Bembo by
Wilmaset Limited, Birkenhead, Wirral
Printed and bound in the European Union by
Henry Ling Limited,
The Dorset Press, Dorchester, UK

CONTENTS

ILLUSTRATIONS

executors of the artist's estate 1980; © Trustees of the Barbara Hepworth Estate/Tate Gallery London.

26 *Spindle Cyclide*. Mathematical model; © Gerd Fischer (published in Fischer, *Mathematical Models*, Wiesbaden, Vieweg, 1986).

27 *Fresnel's Wave Surface*. Mathematical model; © Gerd Fischer (published in Fischer, *Mathematical Models*, Wiesbaden, Vieweg, 1986).

28 *Cubic with an A3 Double Point*. Mathematical model; © Gerd Fischer (published in Fischer, *Mathematical Models*, Wiesbaden, Vieweg, 1986).

29 Barbara Hepworth: *Pelagos*, 1946; wood with colour and strings, 368 × 387 × 330 mm. Tate Gallery, London. Presented by the artist 1964; © Trustees of the Barbara Hepworth Estate/Tate Gallery London.

30 *Minimal Surface with a One-parameter Family of Parabolas*. Mathematical model; © Gerd Fischer (published in Fischer, *Mathematical Models*, Wiesbaden, Vieweg, 1986).

31 Barbara Hepworth: *Drawing*, 1940; graphite on card. Private Collection; © Trustees of the Barbara Hepworth Estate.

32 Naum Gabo: *Construction in Space with a Crystalline Centre*, *c.*1938; perspex and celluloid. Tate Gallery, London; © Nina and Graham Williams/Tate Gallery London.

33 *Example of curve stitching* from Edith L. Somervell (1906) *A Rhythmic Approach to Mathematics* (London, George Philip).

34 Naum Gabo: *Linear Construction in Space No.1*, 1942–49; perspex with nylon monofilament, 613 × 613 × 130 mm. Art Gallery of Ontario, Toronto. Gift of the Volunteer Committee Fund 1986; © Nina and Graham Williams/Art Gallery of Ontario.

35 *Mathematical Model*. Collection L'Institut Henri Poincaré, Paris.

36 Curve stitching of 'A Pair of Opposite Parabolas', from *Boole Curve-Sewing Cards*, designed to accompany Edith L. Somervell (1906) *A Rhythmic Approach to Mathematics* (London, George Philip). Reproduced in complete form in Jon Millington (1989) *Curve Stitching* (Diss, Tarquin Publications), p. 14.

37 Barbara Hepworth: *Reconstruction*, 1947; oil and pencil on board, 343 × 464 mm. Arts Council Collection, South Bank Centre, London; © Trustees of the Barbara Hepworth Estate/Arts Council Collection.

38 Barbara Hepworth: *Concentration of Hands No.1*, 1948; oil and pencil on board, 533 × 400 mm. Collection of the British Council; © Trustees of the Barbara Hepworth Estate/The British Council.

CONTRIBUTORS

ANNE J. BARLOW, Curator of Modern Art and Design, Glasgow Museums and Art Galleries.

PENELOPE CURTIS, Head, Henry Moore Centre for the Study of Sculpture, Leeds.

KATY DEEPWELL, Artist, critic, curator and teacher.

CLAIRE DOHERTY, Exhibitions Coordinator, Ikon Gallery, Birmingham.

MEG DUFF, Librarian, Tate Gallery.

PENNY FLORENCE, Reader, Falmouth School of Art.

ALUN R. GRAVES, Victoria and Albert Museum.

CHRISTINA LODDER and MARTIN HAMMER, Universities of St. Andrews and Edinburgh.

ALEX POTTS, Professor of History of Art, University of Reading.

EMMA ROBERTS, Doctoral Student, University of Liverpool.

CHRIS STEPHENS, Research Assistant, Modern Collection, Tate Gallery London. Doctoral Student, University of Sussex.

DAVID THISTLEWOOD, Professor in History of Art, University of Liverpool.

ANNE WAGNER, Chair and Professor of History of Art, University of California at Berkeley.

Introduction

DAVID THISTLEWOOD

Contested Significance in the Work of Barbara Hepworth: Absolutist and Relativist Interpretations

One of the objectives of the Tate Gallery Liverpool (T.G.L.) is to stimulate new critical responses to art within its purview, which is broadly characterised as art locatable within or in significant relation to the avant-garde 'project'. There is acute realisation that this portmanteau concept is itself being constantly redefined through interventions by the T.G.L. and comparable institutions, and that it is becoming increasingly acceptable to think in terms of multiple avant-garde programmes that do not necessarily cohere. This may be a useful, if grossly simplistic, way of distinguishing between modernist (absolutist) critiques which respected—however tacitly—the notion that all of the great results of experimental creativity since Cubism could be mapped in stable relationship, and postmodernist (relativist) critiques which accept and work with all the fractures and dislocations evident within the critical field and are content with localised patterns of meaning.

The T.G.L. *Critical Forum Series*, of which this is the third volume, is expressly positioned at the interface of these two enterprises, in the sense that it exploits both the T.G.L.'s facility for marshalling consensus knowledge and interpretation in its expositions, and its ability to attract an international field of historians and critics to reflect on the consensus in seminar debate. A typical Critical Forum brings together scholars who are extending and consolidating conventional interpretation, others who are proposing alternatives, and an informed audience of respondents who can be immensely selective and synthetic in their reception of presented views.

Volumes in this series record the resulting collisions of interests. In Volume One it was evident that even a critical field as apparently stable as that of American Abstract Expressionism must sustain dynamic readjustment. Volume Two adopted the reverse of this perspective in recognising that the work of Joseph Beuys—intentionally a site of resistance to the normalising influences which have historicised contemporary art—nevertheless needs a minimum of conventionalising activity to make sense of its dynamically diverging critiques. The aim of the Critical Forum which gave rise to the present volume—following a prime objective of the exhibition which stimulated it, *Barbara Hepworth: a Retrospective*

(T.G.L., 14 September – 4 December 1994)—was to test the application of these principles to a subject so deeply anchored in absolutist interpretation that it had brooked no inflection for over a quarter of a century. And this will be complemented in Volume Four with attention to a subject—Sigmar Polke—whose critiques are dominantly relativist and exhibit virtually no agreement. The first four volumes of the series will therefore have established wide parameters, dealing with attributes ranging from emphatic stability (Hepworth) to emphatic dynamism (Polke), via the general stability of American Abstract Expressionism and the general dynamism of Beuys—properties apparent in critiques of these subjects *prior to Critical Forum engagement.*

The work of Barbara Hepworth, then, was considered a suitable case for Critical Forum attention precisely because it was encumbered with interpretation which had proved resistant to other forms of mediation. Before the T.G.L.'s retrospective, and the record-straightening work of Penelope Curtis and Alan G. Wilkinson in the accompanying catalogue [1], Hepworth seemed about as deeply conventionalised as it was possible to become while retaining avant-garde affiliation. But the retrospective exhibition is not the best medium for positing new meaning: it consolidates a reputation while signalling potential for its revision and enhancement. When it addresses the causes of critical injustice—as clearly was the case in relation to Hepworth—it does so with circumspection so as not to sour a predominantly celebratory occasion. The Critical Forum is not affected by such inhibition, and the event represented in this volume stimulated bluntness on the reasons for Hepworth's previous marginalisation, besides a range of speculation on the most appropriate lines of rehabilitation.

Let me attempt to summarise the circumstances of critical inertia prior to 1994. Firstly there is the default reason that Hepworth's personal archives had remained closed since her death in 1975 out of respect for her wish to be protected from premature scrutiny. Historians are generally unwilling to address restricted fields of evidence. Nevertheless, the T.G.L. exhibition demonstrated what could be accomplished without recourse to Hepworth's main body of papers, and did much to prepare for their *mature* investigation. Secondly, there is the supposition that all that could reasonably have been said about Hepworth had been expressed by Herbert Read, Adrian Stokes and Josef P. Hodin—expert critics and confidants who reported on her work during her lifetime and whose views were blessed with her approval. Now in decent retrospect it may be questioned whether such intimacy may actually have contaminated appreciation, and the Hepworth Critical Forum did indeed address this possibility.

Then there are the number of strategies, deliberately pursued by Hepworth, which appear to have licensed her categorisation as a proto-modernist who, after the mid 1930s, continued to inhabit the modernist fringe. She affirmed her status as a carver in an age of Constructivism: in spite of close association with Constructivists and her repeated devotion to 'Constructive Art', she mainly made objects by reduction of the block. Constructivists—as represented by British exponents who were Hepworth's contemporaries—regarded carving as *necessarily* entailing preconceived anticipation of the form to be attained, and favoured assemblage and spatial construction as the best means of usurping academic conventions [2]. Hepworth's generation founded the Institute of Contemporary Arts, London, which in its early years promoted Constructivism as a great hope for uniting British avant-gardes of art and architecture [3]. The referents here were Naum Gabo's techno-artistry and a Tatlinesque use of unrefined materials and 'unskilled' execution. Hepworth's apparent disregard for such principles identified her as 'old guard' and as a more or less respected elder statesperson when she was still only fifty.

She seemed not to dissent from this perception. She had once been at the very centre of the Cultural International during its brief occupation of Hampstead as a staging post for migrating Europeans; then she had chosen to live and work at the periphery, in St. Ives. Her addressing 'the organic' when other great figures of modern sculpture were working with the detritus of industry and mechanisation, or alternatively pursuing the transcendentally significant object devoid of references beyond itself, suggested a perverse attempt to provincialise the great achievements of the centre. Such misapprehension went unchecked—it was, moreover, strengthened by unfortunate visitations of works on metropolitan audiences, for example the incongruously motorised 'organic' *Turning Forms* at the Festival of Britain in 1951 (Fig. 1), and the deeply melodramatic *Maquette for 'The Unknown Political Prisoner'*, exhibited at the I.C.A. the following year (Fig. 2). Hepworth at this time was in effect exposing her least convincing work to highly focused—and, in the case of the I.C.A., increasingly sophisticated—scrutiny. She

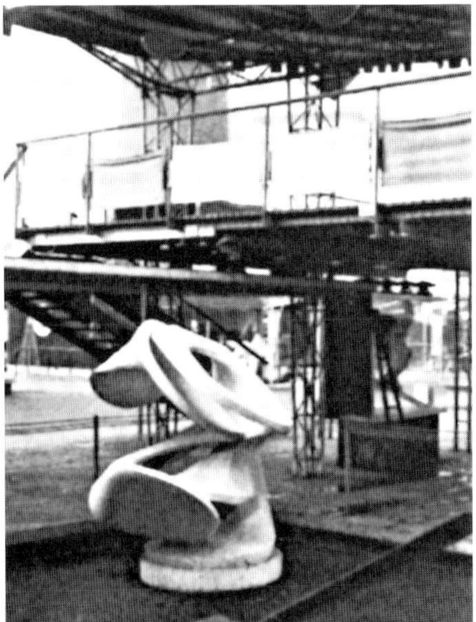

Fig. 1 BARBARA HEPWORTH, *Turning Forms*, 1951 *in situ* at the Festival of Britain © Trustees of the Barbara Hepworth Estate/Tate Gallery London (published in Curtis and Wilkinson, *Barbara Hepworth: A Retrospective*, London, Tate Gallery Publications, 1994)

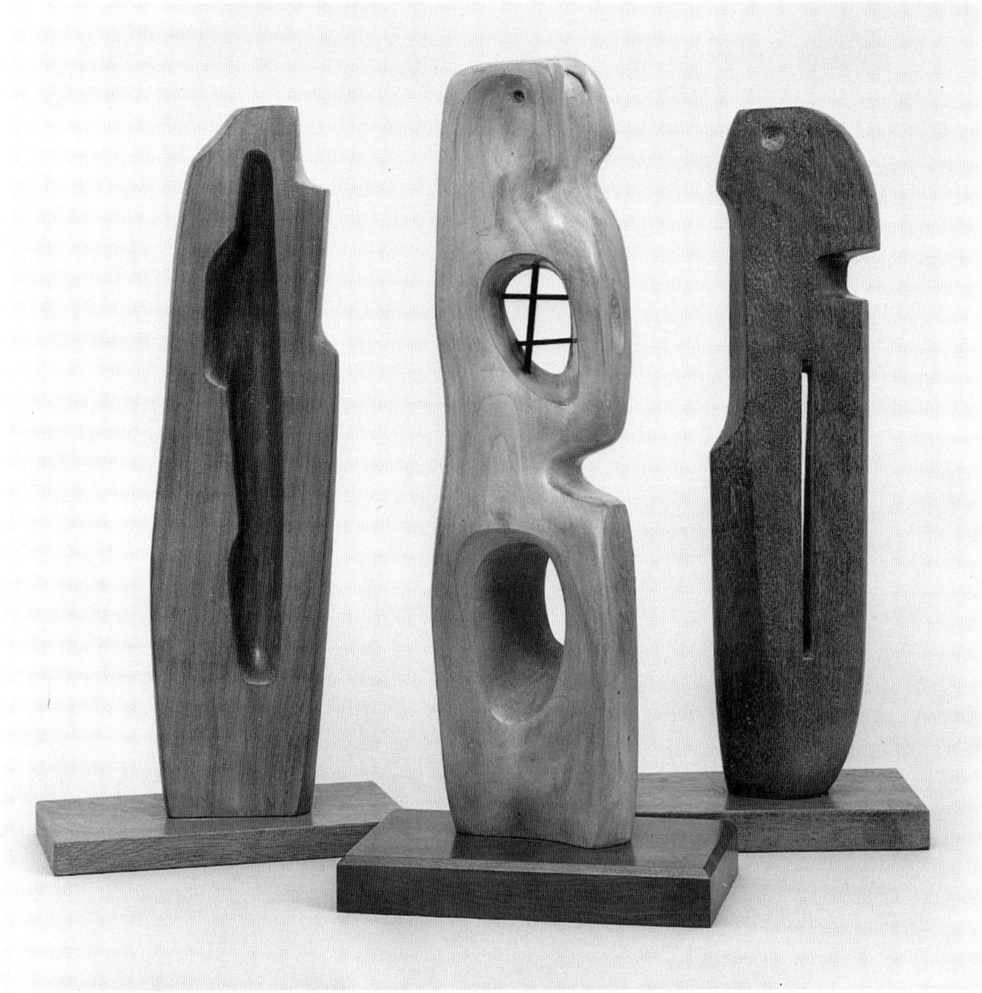

Fig. 2 BARBARA HEPWORTH, *Maquette for 'The Unknown Political Prisoner'*, 1952
© Trustees of the Barbara Hepworth Estate

also appeared to be defending a position of extreme privilege by maintaining the practice—from which she would never generally depart—of using the finest materials, particularly rare woods and stones (even during the war and succeeding austerity), which could not fail to set her apart from all but a handful of other artists.

Throughout the whole of the second half of Hepworth's working life there seems to have been little serious attempt to counter an image of her as an 'ambassadorial artist'—a former revolutionary having found a niche in polite modernism. This injustice was compounded by a number of definitive Hayward Gallery exhibitions—the entirely incidental effects of which were to frame modernism largely to her exclusion in the years just before her death. If her work had then received the re-evaluation which normally gets under way once a major artist's life's work is known to be complete, it would have borne poor comparison with the range of early twentieth century objectives and achievements now being brought into simultaneous focus.

In 1971 the Hayward presented *Art in Revolution: Soviet Art and Design Since 1917*. The historiographic importance of this exhibition is immense, for the prior English literature of Constructivism had tended to maintain aesthetic objectives for application to industrial design. Herbert Read's *Art and Industry* (1934) had suggested this directly with reference to industrially-produced furniture, tools and utensils, carefully presenting examples consistent with the look of the most daring engineering structures of the day [4]. The exhibition *Circle: International Survey of Constructive Art* (1937) and the book of the same title had taken this further, involving artists such as Hepworth in an attempt to popularise Constructivist abstraction by stressing its *normal* presence in the mundane (for example, suburban and leisure environments). The notion that Constructivism was an *application*, the purpose of which signified 'modernisation', survived the Second World War and was strongly embedded in the Festival of Britain—proposing that buildings, furniture, utensils, bric-à-brac, even works of art, could be deconventionalised with the aesthetic impress of science, technology and rational manufacture. The receptive audience could have been forgiven for assuming this intentionality in the radiating and parallel lines of Hepworth's stringed carvings such as *Wave*, 1943 (Fig. 48), and *Pelagos*, 1946 (Fig. 29).

This audience would have considered Hepworth's work safely pigeon-holed: gentle, English, carved abstractions bearing signifiers of an otherwise-vague modernity. Her frequent use of the term 'Constructive Art' to denote her intentionality would have been largely uncontested until the Hayward's *Art in Revolution* showed that Soviet Constructivism had not been remotely interested in conjunctions of conventional techniques and modernistic applications, having been categorically against any *gradual* transition from traditional to industrially-scientific modes of production [5]. In these terms Hepworth's stringed carvings—juxtaposing an Arts and Crafts *intrinsic* aesthetic and a Constructivist *extrinsic* aesthetic—smacked of confused ideology, not to say a fundamental misapprehension of the revolution with which she had identified. Additionally, and equally damning, *Art in Revolution* documented an enterprise dedicated to strict utility and universal technocracy—attributes difficult to associate with life in St. Ives. It may be understandable why a younger generation of industrial constructors—typified, for example, by Anthony Caro, Phillip King or William Tucker—would have been considered more in touch than she with the wellspring of revolutionary sculpture.

Two years before Hepworth died the Hayward mounted a profoundly didactic survey entitled *The Pioneers of Modern Sculpture* [6]. Its purpose was to explain the heroic defining achievements of sculpture between the 1890s and 1918, and to identify ramifications that would constitute the great challenges for sculptors throughout the twentieth century. It was a survey of predominantly western European revolt against traditions culminating in Rodin, and it might have been expected that a firm anchoring for Hepworth's work (her Constructivist references apart) would have been evident here. However, there was nothing in this survey that could have been associated with Hepworth as *originator*. Rather, by intensifying knowledge of seminal works by Brancusi, in particular, it would have suggested a derivative aspect of her work that had not previously been noted except in comparison to Moore. Her *Square Forms (Two Sequences)*, 1963, would have been recognised as closely descendent from Brancusi's *Endless Column*, 1918. Familial likeness would also have been detected as between her oval and spheroid carvings of the kind typified by *Two Forms*, 1936 (illustrated in *Circle* in 1937) (Fig. 19) and Brancusi's *Sculpture for the Blind*, 1916. Even the tendency of her pre-1930 works to conform to the block (Fig. 3) [7] could not now fail to be associated with Brancusi's various versions of *The Kiss*, particularly its third treatment in limestone, 1908, exhibited at the Hayward. And as with Brancusi so with others: Hepworth's appropriation of forms and themes evident in the work of Giacometti—*cf.* Hepworth's *Two Segments and Sphere*, 1935–36 (Fig. 4) and Giacometti's *Suspended Ball*, 1930—is still being commented on today [8].

What then was Hepworth's reputation in the early 1970s, judged in terms of absolutist, modernist criteria? She was exquisitely handicapped with carving; she had misunderstood the Constructivist revolution; she had engaged with others in creative dialogues that came close to emulation. Even the convention that she had participated in Britain's first truly authentic avant-garde was brought into doubt, for just a year before she died the Hayward mounted the exhibition *Vorticism and its Allies* [9] which deprived Hampstead of this particular distinction. In Vorticism there was seen to have been a movement with strong European referents but self-sufficient motivating energies, not simply having reacted to an influx of European ideas. It was unambiguously inorganic in is abstraction, and its intentionality bore respectable comparison to the seminal European events which had been canonised at the Hayward less than a year earlier. There was more than a hint of its having been 'lost' and now rediscovered, and with its rediscovery came the recalling of a 'lost' literature—for example, Horace Shipp's monograph on the painter and sculptor Lawrence Atkinson, whose uncompromisingly austere, geometric compositions predated Hepworth's and Nicholson's by over a decade and yet managed to make them look half-hearted by comparison. *Vorticism and its Allies* stimulated intense interest in the decade which straddled the First World War. Richard Cork, its compiler and presenter, went on to publish his exhaustive study of Vorticism [10] two years later, and the only unfortunate aspect of this admirable achievement was that it took any remaining limelight away from Hampstead at the worst possible moment as far as Hepworth's reconsideration was concerned.

Twenty years later, *Barbara Hepworth: a Retrospective* provided the first *focused* reconsideration. In the critical hiatus various suppositions had taken root: Hepworth's fame was greatly assisted by Moore's achievement and Nicholson's

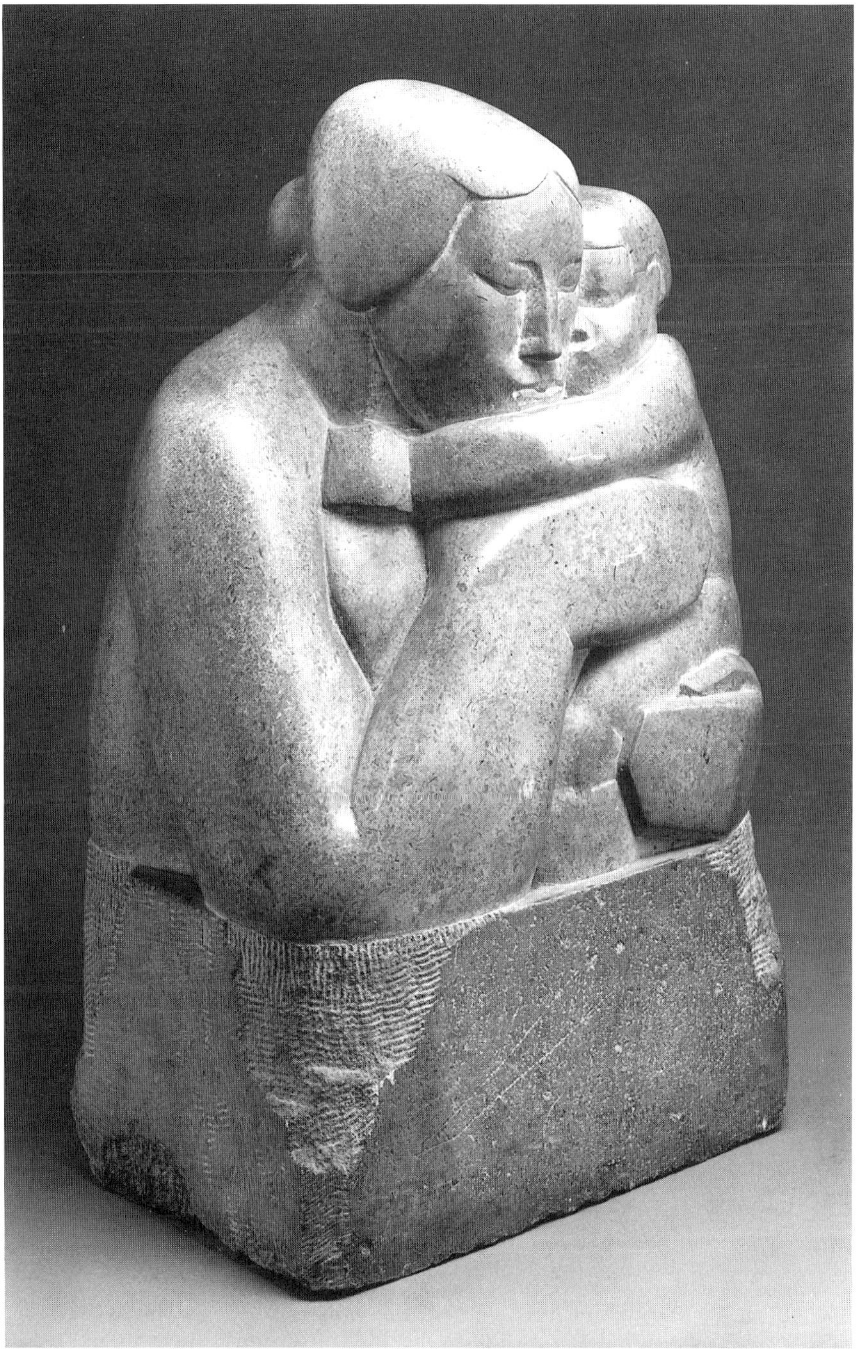

Fig. 3 BARBARA HEPWORTH, *Mother and Child*, 1927 © Trustees of the Barbara Hepworth Estate/Art Gallery of Ontario

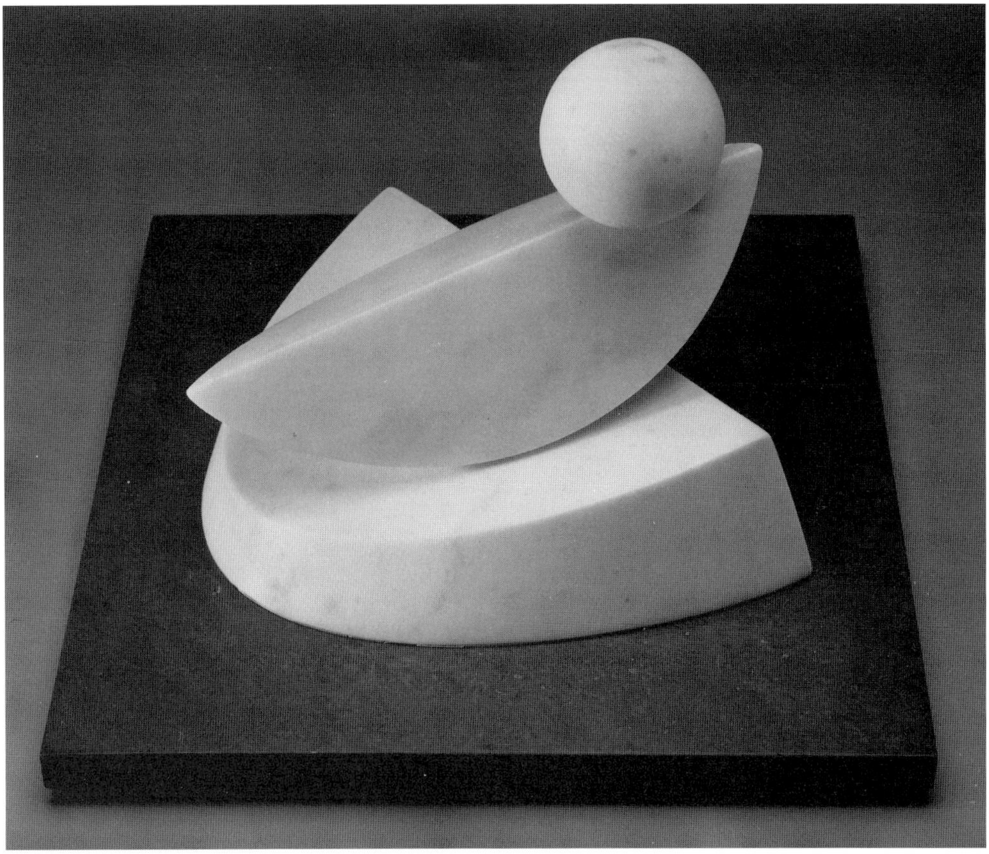

Fig. 4 BARBARA HEPWORTH, *Two Segments and Sphere*, 1935–36 © Trustees of the Barbara Hepworth Estate

guidance; she received unusually kind attention from male critics who invariably were close friends; she was officially approved for promotion abroad because her works conformed to dignified and unchallenging cultural standards the establishment wished to project. The only real questioning of such myths had occurred in studies which dealt with Hepworth incidentally—either as one of many participants in a general field (for example, Charles Harrison's *English Art and Modernism 1900–1939* [11]) or as an associate of other great figures of the period as they each came under scrutiny (for example, in my own critical biography of Herbert Read [12]). Hepworth has been the last of her comparable contemporaries to receive dedicated attention, and it is Harrison who has prepared for this by establishing a number of firm proposals in relation to which other historians may begin to range their detailed investigations. He has posited Hepworth's participation in three distinct 'projects'—one shared with Moore, one with Nicholson (and others), and one pursued alone (which—Harrison does not say, but it may nevertheless be inferred—would continue to dominate Hepworth's work throughout the rest of her life).

Harrison dates the Hepworth-Moore interaction approximately between 1928 and 1932. He identifies it as centred on the figure but with strong secondary references to landscape, as being primarily concerned to press the validity of carving, and as constituting, in effect, a vernacular modernism with direct antecedents in the Arts and Crafts Movement. Harrison maintains that Moore was generally the innovator—principal changes of motif and external influence are first evident in his work and are taken up by Hepworth in manifest assimilation—but he is also clear that there were notable differences of facture, indicating that Hepworth was taking technical initiatives [13].

Harrison then finds what amounts to a major shift in Hepworth's sculpture and her published statements which he associates partly with Nicholson's introduction of European referents (leading to participation in *Abstraction-Création* and knowledge of the works of Brancusi and Giacometti) and partly with Hepworth's involvement in the *Circle* exhibition and the intimate connection with the likes of Naum Gabo that this entailed. The resulting Hepworth-Nicholson 'enterprise' is much more obviously a collaboration and is characterised by austere lifestyle, aesthetic purity, and attempts to frame both a Constructive philosophy of art and a related, supranational ideology penetrating other realms, for example science and politics. Harrison attributes to Hepworth a significant achievement:

> The distinguishing feature of Hepworth's statements in *Abstraction-Création* and *Unit 1* and, by implication from their observable characteristics, of her works after 1934, is that the implicit claims made in the twenties for the universality of 'sculpture' as a form of experience have been annexed to explicit claims made for the universality of 'abstract art' as a form of experience. In Hepworth's works of the mid-thirties, the more avant-garde features of English sculpture of the twenties were thus assimilated into the prevailing ideology of the Modern Movement. [14]

The twin facts that her abstract sculptures, now replete with geometric references, are palpably hand-made, while her writings uncompromisingly extol abstraction, provide a link with the European sculptural avant-garde comparable to Nicholson's achievement in painting.

Finally, Harrison observes how such preoccupations support the emotional content of Hepworth's post-war work, and though his interests here do not project beyond 1939, he provides the basis for extrapolating a useful late critique. What Harrison seems to maintain about Hepworth's later work is that she walks a tightrope between form as generalised type and form as particularised representation. Her works are abstract but hand-made: geometry bearing the marks of individual identity, even—some would say particularly—the visible signs of internalised feelings about people and places. Harrison believes Hepworth courts sentimentality in her desire to infuse her works with

> . . . the kinds of feelings . . . which are really only defensibly introduced into discussion of works of art in the context of a carefully scrutinized analogy. [15]

From this it may be apparent that though Harrison does not entirely applaud Hepworth's later work, his partial appraisal has provided the basis for evaluating her production in its entirety. This three-phase model—exponent of vernacular modernism; exponent of mainstream modernism; moderator of modernism with highly specific feelings about people, places, historic presences, cultural identities and other highly particularised sensations—provided the tacit framework for the diverse contributions to the Hepworth Critical Forum. It is also a model which accommodates what contemporary critics in the 1940s found initially confusing: Hepworth's occasional departure from the abstraction she professed most dearly.

It is interesting that she projected and defended this activity in the arena of Herbert Read's critical writing rather than her own (thus supporting the myth that she needed to be spoken for). In correspondence to Read she wrote:

> . . . Working realistically replenishes one's love for life, humanity and the earth. Working abstractly seems to release one's personality and sharpen the perceptions . . . [16]

In 1948 she drew Read an explanatory diagram [17] which profoundly informed his critique as expressed in *The Philosophy of Modern Art* (1952) and later writings. It is an axial arrangement (Fig. 5) with at one side realism, symbols of the known, figures, hands, eyes, trees, and so forth, and at the other abstraction, symbols of the unknown, including erotic, pre-natal and primitive forms, dream images and childhood imagery. She said her point of address might be at either extremity, but that during the development of a work there might well be autonomous transition. An initially abstract process might materialise recognisable traces—eye-like hollows or similar presentative features—and drawing from observation might liberate formal ideas for abstract carving. Hepworth's account of such abstract working in which she felt 'in the grip of an emotion . . . pursuing the unknown form to hold it', together with her relational diagram of creative impulses, provided Read with evidence for linking Abstraction and Surrealism in productive relationship, and helped complete his great intellectual achievement of accommodating the diverse manifestations of the avant-gardes of his day within a unitary system of relationships. The point here, however, is that this vital insight of Hepworth's came to light only as a result of work on Read and too late to inform Hepworth critiques except by challenging already-ingrained mythologies—in this case the notion that she was a passive recipient of Read's interpretation. But it underlines the need for Hepworth's re-evaluation, validates the extrapolation of Harrison's analysis, and points up the need for mistaken assumptions to be rectified.

The Hepworth Critical Forum was a first assault on this objective. In fact it was

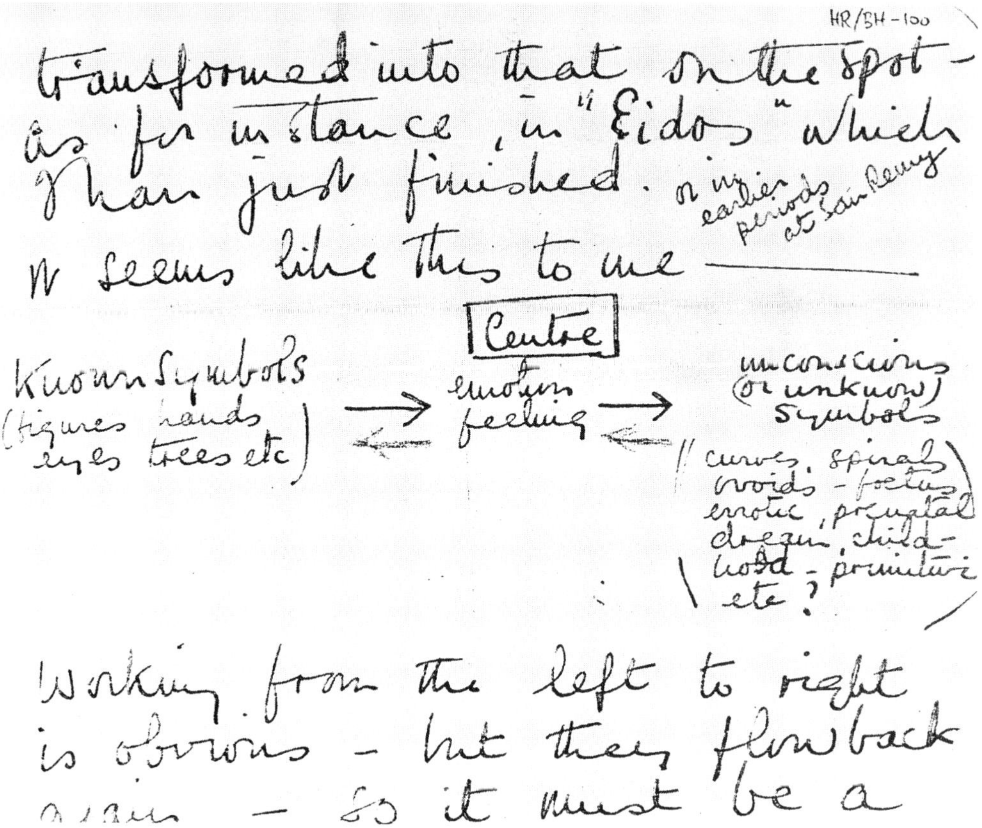

Fig. 5 BARBARA HEPWORTH, *Diagram of the creative sensibility*, 1947 © Trustees of the Barbara Hepworth Estate

two-pronged, indicating that current interest in Hepworth is broadly dedicated to alternative, and to a large extent mutually antagonistic, purposes. One of these is to intensify knowledge of Hepworth within the terms of those absolutist critiques with which she is familiarly associated; the other is to liberate her from such critiques as the means of revising fundamentally the appreciation of her achievements. The critical field as a whole is straining to accommodate both tendencies, and many individual studies also bear evidence of the resulting tensions.

Penny Florence's work, for example, is geared to reconciling Hepworth's great, high-profile success within a male gendered culture and the self-evident fact that she would not have succeeded had she not been perceived as highly originative—in other words, that her success as an individual was achieved in a realm where the prerequisite for success was to be a male individual. This is incapable of resolution without enhancing one part of the received wisdom about Hepworth while fundamentally questioning another part. Hepworth's efforts are historicised in a movement dedicated to cultural—as a prelude to socio-political—universalism, and therefore the successful reception of Hepworth's sculpture in her day is to be understood as recognition of its *potential* universality. Her dalliance with geometric abstraction in the 1930s is entirely understandable in these terms, but her later attention to encapsulating the essences of particular places, mythic presences and emotive landscapes is not—unless a distinction is to be made between two problematics. One of these is an essentially male gendered universalism, hard edged and geometric, and the other a female gendered universalism, spiritual in essence—what Florence calls a 'more fluid imaginary' [18]—perhaps explaining without at all condoning Harrison's charge of sentimentality.

In this view of Hepworth she first competes on men's terms and then gradually transcends all the qualities she had had to assume to make a reputation, taking increasing risks of misinterpretation in a world where female universal values lack a sustaining critique. Here the historians' objectives are to develop critiques that will bring Hepworth's work into fuller understanding while also studying Hepworth precisely in order to develop such critiques. Her works of art are to be seen as 'mediating' between intentionality and critique—Florence posits a number of comparable mediations that Hepworth's works fulfil—which suggests that one of their functions is explicatory. Hepworth's work as having the purpose of illuminating criticism casts unexpected light on her relationship with her critics, inverts one of the main tenets of the very modernism in which she excelled, and may indeed begin to resolve the difficult problem of her supposed emulation of those other (invariably male) artists she admired.

The notion of Hepworth's work informing criticism, rather than (in the context of modernism) the more conventional reverse, is examined closely by Alex Potts in his study of one of Hepworth's earliest published critics, Adrian Stokes. Potts notes that Stokes had already substantially developed his theory of carving as the most legitimate means of making sculpture, and that in effect this concept also for him validated such modern painting as could be said to follow Cézanne's great example of delineating form by 'carving' the shallow pictorial space behind the picture plane. Potts also describes the crucial distinction Stokes observed between carving and modelling—the former involving an inherent respect for previously hidden characteristics within the stone which gradually revealed themselves in response to a respectful reduction of the mass and its infusion with significance, and the latter, amounting to an indecent imposition of creative will upon unresisting material.

Making sculpture, to Stokes, therefore involved two highly gendered problematics, and he promoted carving as the most acceptable address—an address nevertheless explained analogously as 'impregnation' of the block, a disciplined realisation of the potential within, and the eventual birthing of a form bearing the living signs of its material and the specific impress of its carver. Recognising Hepworth as a meritorious carver, Stokes had to execute some deft critical footwork, and here perhaps was the first evidence of her work affecting beneficially an already well-worked theory. Taking advantage of the frequency with which she explored the theme 'Mother and Child', Stokes seemed to discuss this motif while really negotiating her genius. He noted a 'poignancy' not present in other artists' treatment of the same theme, identifying pronounced mother-like psychic charges that seemed unique to her work. In praising this achievement he was really proposing that all her carving epitomised 'post-natal' survival and therefore provided a profound validation of his analogy.

To Anne Wagner, however, Stokes' response to Hepworth's carving does not suggest that his theory was informed by it, but rather that he stopped short of accepting its full ramifications, preferring to deal with it impressionistically so as not to challenge seriously his gendered analogy. She charges Read with similar negligence—in his case, though, with recognising the presence of deep symbolism in Hepworth's work while evading discussion of what it might mean. Wagner contends that Stokes and Read encountered Hepworth's art 'at its most urgently autobiographical moment, in the early 1930s—the moment of her espousal of a special, bodily abstraction' [19]. Her text is that it defeated their critical apprehension, while her subtext is that their inadequate observations conditioned Hepworth critiques for years to come.

This takes the fight to reconstruct Hepworth's intentionality right to the heart of what was formerly considered to be agreed about her work—the notion that she was contributing to a universalist aesthetic in the main period of English modernism. It challenges not only her critics but also Hepworth herself in her belief that she was approaching impersonal ideals. But Wagner validates this objective by proposing that Hepworth's work is a much more accurate register of achievement than that provided by her modernist rhetoric. This poses several questions, not least: Why must Hepworth's art be considered autobiography? and: Is the autobiographic impetus localised, by attachment to some particular episode, or does it permeate the whole of her life's work? The latter is too enormous to be dealt with in her present paper—and is in any case highly complicated, Wagner believes, by the ill-advised nature of Hepworth's published *Pictorial Autobiography*, with its presentation of art and life as effortlessly contiguous. But the former question is exhaustively addressed, leading to the conclusion that in her Mother and Child pieces Hepworth expressed empathetically what her male counterparts could only express mimetically, that she identified with what they could merely idealise, and that in so doing she represented 'ambivalences and ambiguities of the maternal bond and state' not usually associated with this motif. This also, in spite of his priority of engagement, places the supposed emulation of Moore in questionable standing.

The difference with Moore as carver might ultimately reduce to this: Moore did what Read and others said he did—he animated human forms with the vital presence of landscape—while Hepworth animated her works with *human* presence. Wagner believes Hepworth was wrong to profess the primacy of carving for she finds evidence of Hepworth sacrificing certain carving principles for the sake of maternal poignancy. The sacrifice is very slight, but was probably sufficient to sustain inferior comparison with Moore if viewed entirely on Moore's own terms. This may have been the foundation of the consensual assumption that Moore initiated a common enterprise up to the point where Hepworth veered towards geometric abstraction and he towards Surrealism. But in spite of the earliness of this *assumed* dependence, it firmly established the critique of Hepworth as dependant.

In this, Katy Deepwell believes, is the origin of an indisputable fact that Hepworth's and Moore's 'shared' critics treated them differentially—for example tending to quote Moore's own words in order to develop their *potential* meaning in extrapolation, while quoting Hepworth in order to limit meaning to the strictly definable terms of her words. It is as if Moore the initiator were licensed to speculate and be speculated *about*, while Hepworth is entitled merely to confirm expectations. Her words are not interpreted *strategically*, and in order to address this fundamental lack, Deepwell suggests (and in this she differs from Wagner), Hepworth structured her *Pictorial Autobiography* quite deliberately to prove the validity of an 'other' career strategy entirely unrelated to the Moore project by which she had generally been judged. This also necessarily constitutes a critique of Read, the champion of Moore and for whom Moore was the premier artist of his generation. Read judged everyone—Picasso, Brancusi, Arp, and every other significant artist—by criteria he recognised in, or projected upon, the work of Moore.

To Deepwell, the *Pictorial Autobiography*, because of its comprehensive acknowledgement of Read's writings on Hepworth, constitutes an amicable protest against such comparison. What Deepwell now in effect demands is critical analysis undistracted by such matters as Hepworth's personal gratitude to Read, and uncontaminated by the shared vocabulary of Hepworth and Moore which—interpreted as a range of common intentionality—led to the prioritising of Moore. In other words, the *Pictorial Autobiography* courts ambiguity and invites creative recombination: it is an invitation to *extrapolate*. And this extrapolation, according to Deepwell, will naturally foreground Hepworth's insistence on complementarity, rather than competition, with such as Moore—a concept difficult to assimilate to Read's notion of the lone spearheading of the avant-garde.

Josef Hodin offers Deepwell a much better prospect—the identification in Hepworth's work of a 'life-affirming monism' with referents in contemporary science and technology, intellectual thought and philosophy. This indicates how much work there is to be done in this field, for to devotees of Read the privileging of Hodin in this respect will be distinctly questionable. From the 1920s Read had consistently argued the aesthetic significance of science, regarding the General Theory of Relativity as marking a threshold of modern consciousness and promoting Alfred North Whitehead's consolidating theories in the realm of art. When Hodin became associated with the I.C.A. Read, its President, had already built scientific philosophy into its founding principles and begun to ensure that such scientists as D'Arcy Wentworth Thompson, Lancelot Law Whyte, J. Zachary

Young and Anton Ehrenzweig were well represented in its programmes [20]. It is clear that Hodin, as I.C.A. Librarian, would have benefited from this as much as any other member. This is not to say that priority of engagement means greater profundity, but it does give rise to the possibility of an interesting influential chain, with Read's theorising influencing Hepworth and Hepworth's work informing Hodin—with Read receiving tacit, and Hodin explicit, confirmation in Hepworth's aesthetic interrogation of science.

Certainly the impetus provided by Read is highly significant to Anne Barlow, who sees Read as an intermediary between Hepworth and the morphologist Henri Focillon, bringing Focillon's work to her attention before it became available in English translation. Focillon's phrase 'the life of forms' signified to Hepworth, as to Read, a principle of inherent creative energy within forms, the exudation of which both determined shape and also projected beyond external surface, communicating directly with the receptive sensibility. This constituted her definition of 'vitality'—previously a troublesome concept, as Deepwell notes, because of its gendered connotation—and Barlow maintains that this then absolutely characterised Hepworth's rationale:

> The notion of vitality being released through the work as a manifestation of some inner process is evident in the way in which Hepworth viewed the work of art as possessing vitality not through its physical attributes, but rather through its spiritual inner life—an inner force and energy. The work would then continue to 'live' through the very nature of its spatial displacement. [21]

Barlow also notes how compatible this was with certain principles of Christian Science to which Hepworth had been introduced by Ben Nicholson—especially an emphasis on spiritual essences underlying the accidents of surface appearance. And this aligned well, as she also notes, with the biologist Thompson's view of internal energies acting against external force fields to produce specifically unique conformations. Combined and applied to sculpture, these two concepts provided a synthetic analogue which illuminated both the idea of inner structure truly expressed in outer form and the notion of the form as the source of a projected 'life' or 'presence'—precisely the mixture of formalism and animism which increasingly characterised Hepworth's Cornish and later work in general.

Which is why interest in Hepworth is suddenly timely at a juncture where two such critiques are no longer considered mutually-negating: they seem specifically *complementary* in Hepworth. Martin Hammer and Christina Lodder reflect on this complementarity as exemplified in Hepworth's fascination for the science of complex geometry—a fascination distinguished from the formalist preoccupations of other artists by Hepworth's emotional attachment to the principle of uniting art and science to help fulfil a Utopian socialist programme. Hammer and Lodder discuss Hepworth's stringed works, detaching this subject from the conventional dispute as to whether inspiration came from Moore or Gabo, and indeed suggesting that Gabo may have been stimulated by Hepworth's example. In fact what is here sketched out is an idealist enterprise in which the participants all brought stimuli—mathematical models; 'curve stitching' samples—to each other's attention and enjoyed common purchase on the principles they were annexing to their art.

It may have been the case that following such collaboration Hepworth was the least willing to claim ownership of achievement—indeed to have done so would have been contrary to her personal definition of the 'Constructive' project. However, Hammer and Lodder do precisely this on Hepworth's behalf, identifying her deep interest in creating virtual geometric fields in the context of her palpably material objects—a fusing of mathematical and organic form. This may with certainty be considered Hepworth's initiative, which by extension also incorporates the spiritual or animistic. Hammer and Lodder dispute the conventional interpretation of the latter as manifesting a renewed British Romanticism—the insularity of this tendency would have been contrary to Hepworth's internationalism. Instead they posit a mature Hepworthian definition of Abstraction—one in which the object inserts evocations of other places, customs and states of consciousness into the here and now, instead of drawing the spectator into an imaginary environment, the stuff of Romanticism.

In the context of this proposal Hepworth's 'hospital theatre drawings' of the late 1940s are endowed with special significance, pivotal as they are between the more objective abstraction of the 1930s and the more subjective abstraction which followed. Chris Stephens regards these drawings as critical in the sense that they mark and address a number of crises. Among the most obvious of these is Hepworth's dissociation from Constructivism as no longer fulfilling the main purposes of the 'Constructive idea' in art and society, to which she remained deeply committed. The concomitant loss of Gabo's collaboration must have seemed irredeemable. Obvious too is the growing domestic tension in the years prior to separation from Nicholson, and Stephens finds evidence in the 'hospital theatre drawings' of an informed Jungian resolution of responsibilities to family and community comparable to those which, it is presumed, were affecting her marital and public roles during this time.

These are the drawings which prompted Read to identify a 'new phase' [22] in Hepworth's work, stimulating her description of the creative process (Fig. 5) which had such profound effect on Read's paradigm of the avant-garde. Read's immediate interest in them was mainly idiomatic—they provided evidence of a reverse application of what may be termed the 'Mondrian principle' of resolving the figurative into pure formal relationships. For Stephens, however, they are evidence of something Read was fundamentally interested in but appears to have overlooked in them—they 'embody the themes of reintegration and of reconstruction at different levels: the social, ideological and psychological'.

This may reinforce suspicions that Read could not deal adequately with works of acutely representational content, especially if they did not seem to possess (as for example Moore's 'Shelter Drawings' had done) the canonic characteristics of 'drawings for sculpture'. Stephens makes it clear that their strong documentary significance could not possibly have been missed, for in a real sense they celebrate the inauguration of the National Health Service and the deep investment in an equitable sharing of the benefits of scientific medicine that this entailed. There must have been the thought that Hepworth, now bereft of Gabo's guiding influence, was embracing Soviet-type socialist realism—certainly she had not been reticent in promoting anti-fascist, collectivist socio-political ideals. The hospital pictures, Stephens argues:

> . . . in presenting a vision of collective effort in the setting that epitomised the new society, must be seen as celebratory of the flowering of the social reconstruction that . . . the 1945 Labour government promised. The ordered and rationalised style in which they are executed alludes to the ordering of social planning and implies the sense of security that the welfare policies sought to achieve. [23]

They thus focus upon a subject central to the greatest possible commonwealth of interest, reflecting Hepworth's commitment to an art which is active ('vital') at the very heart of the community. They are therefore not to be regarded as a temporary departure from Hepworth's greater project so much as part of the seamless transition which defines it. There is thus the possibility of an illuminating critique featuring phases of denoted interest—the geometric abstractions of the 1930s idealise socialism in contemplative symbols; the 'hospital theatre drawings' attend to socialist ideals in process of fulfilment; and later works reflect on socialist particulars (the *genii loci* of exemplary communities and their relationships with the sustaining landscape).

One of the reasons why genuinely relevant critiques have not been generated, according to Penelope Curtis, is that the record of Hepworth's achievement has been dominated by accounts—carefully constructed by Hepworth and by trusted critics—defending her inclusion within a 'Moore, Nicholson, Gabo' framework. If this is correct it is not surprising that there has been a tendency to generalise about Hepworth in terms of fragments of comparability with the intentionalities of these three. Neither should it be surprising if she were denied recognition as inspirer of a younger generation: inspiration would come direct from its 'true' source. Curtis implies Hepworth's inadvertent complicity here—in striving for recognition 'on equal terms' she failed to inform all but a few individuals of her paramount originality. One of these was E. H. Ramsden, to whom Hepworth opened up more than to any other confidant with the exception of Read. It is highly implicit in Curtis' argument that Ramsden perceived matters to which Read remained unresponsive or indifferent.

Curtis posits the importance of gender to understanding Hepworth, noting, however, that Hepworth parted critical company with Ramsden over the latter's promotion of a taxonomy devoid of gender-laden references. Ramsden wished

Hepworth to relinquish figuration and return to pure formal abstraction. Hepworth resisted, yet as Claire Doherty points out, much of the figuration recognised in Hepworth's late works is either imputed from their titles or from the assumption that women's art is necessarily subjective. There is the strong suggestion here that Hepworth colluded in the attribution to her work of 'expected' feminine qualities, perhaps out of desire to distinguish herself from the Moore-Nicholson-Gabo trinity. As a result she was contaminated with the expected quality of respectful imitation, thus shoring up their reputations and, by extension, confirming the status of a patriarchal modernism. In order to cope with features which bore little relation to her male contemporaries' work, (male) critics invested metaphorical significance in 'motherhood, feminine intuition, warmth, mysticism and ancient rites'. To Doherty these are the principal reasons for Hepworth's relative neglect by feminist critics and historians:

> . . . her achievements were seen to be removed from the endeavours of other women, and therefore she could only be accepted as exceptional to women. She was never celebrated as an example of what women are able to achieve given equal opportunities. [24]

Doherty proposes the basis of a proper—and in effect a dual—critique of Hepworth, with one aspect reflecting on her exploration of space and volume and of quasi-organic properties (in other words, the general preoccupations of her male contemporaries), but with another aspect reflecting on her abilities to *evade* these preoccupations, especially in her late works. Elicited 'strategies' are geared to expressing unrestrained tensions and instabilities which unsettle that prerequisite of the Modernist project, the contemplative gaze. Here seems to be the reason for assumed inferiority: Hepworth, capable of achieving the good Gestalt, ultimately produces works which defy this expectation. But to Doherty it is the badge of Hepworth's clarity of purpose: together with the infusion of her work with polyvalent meanings and signification only now becoming apparent, the 'subversion of the mastery of the gaze' is a defining criterion both of Hepworth and of what Doherty calls *la sculpture féminine*. It is, above all, a reason for regarding Hepworth as an exemplary relativist subject.

So too is something Alun Graves has detected—Hepworth's tendency to subvert the mastery of that defining moment when the work of art is assumed to have been created. Absolutist critiques depend on the convention of the idealised occasion when the work of art enters the cultural realm as a finally perfected thing, and it is at the heart of their logic to propose significant sequences of such occasions as denoting individual artists' 'development' and collective 'progress'. Graves approaches this from a museological standpoint, arguing that in the case of Hepworth it is difficult to determine what precise condition of a particular work is to be the goal of conservation. Hepworth's carvings gradually transmogrify: they crack and deform. She specified applied colouring only vaguely and on at least one occasion confirmed her acceptance of its fading and even change of hue. However, in apparent contradiction, she also tended to cast in bronze those of her carvings which were particularly vulnerable to deformation, thus setting up tensions between works of obviously close identity which nevertheless exhibit differing rates and trajectories of change. They also exhibit confusing materiality, subverting the 'truth to materials' ethic so respected by critics of her own generation. This may be compounded by ideological choice of materials—as for example on a rare occasion when Hepworth used aluminium partly in order to identify with the great faith currently invested in this 'people's material'.

The effect of all of this is to prevent works being firmly locked into chains of significance. The field of Hepworth's production includes not only records of objects changing due to natural and expected processes, but also the results of her annexing earlier stylistic characteristics to later phases of her work, and also the effects of ideological self-contradiction as when she commits revolutionary forms of the 1930s to the civic politeness epitomised by bronze in the late 1950s. It is as if Hepworth anticipated the new museology of the 1990s by maximising the range of 'messages' her works would sustain. The resulting warping of time and intentionality may be considered her strategy for warding off absolutist interpretation, though here we are confronted with the irony of Hepworth's apparent courting of absolutist recognition in what seems to have been her positive wish for comparison with her male contemporaries.

Drastic action may be needed to negotiate this fatal weakness, and the anticipated access to Hepworth's personal papers will not necessarily be of help because they may be expected to confirm her yearning for comparability. Emma Roberts attempts to break the 'Moore-Nicholson-Gabo' stranglehold on Hepworth by comparing her with an artist towards whom she expressed no desired affinity, Mark Rothko. Rothko was chosen because he was Hepworth's exact contemporary (they were born in the same year and died within three years of one another) and thus he may be assumed to have shared her general *Zeitgeistiges* referents. There is also a perceptible circumstantial chain linking him to Hepworth by means of those European artists and teachers who emigrated to North America via Hampstead, particularly Walter Gropius. There are thus the smallest possible grounds for this comparison, the great virtue of which lies in the fact that they share little *declared* intentionality. Allowing the subjects 'Hepworth' and 'Rothko' to collide in theoretical discussion is a highly speculative exercise, but it is a collision which shakes out tentative proposals about Hepworth which would not otherwise occur due to her default grounding in grossly familiar comparators. Roberts here is not attempting to prove influence or dependence (she also speculates on connections with Wassily Kandinsky, whose work Hepworth reputedly could not stand) but rather to remove Hepworth from the realm of conventional discussion where automatic assumptions prevail.

As will be evident in the following essays, the Hepworth Critical Forum has revealed and stimulated a wide spectrum of enquiry, ranging from the re-evaluation of Hepworth within conventional paradigms to the renegotiation of her achievements within newly perceived or newly posited structures of relationship. The general message is that we may learn much more about Hepworth by respecting multiple critiques than by pursuing the lost cause of absolutism. Appreciation of Hepworth, so long handicapped by respect for her evident desire for a place within the modernist pantheon, is totally revitalised by recognition that her work ultimately evades this fate. She may yet become accepted as one of a growing number of antecedent 'postmodernists': a relativist before her time.

NOTES AND REFERENCES

1 CURTIS, PENELOPE and WILKINSON, ALAN G. (1994) *Barbara Hepworth: a Retrospective* (Liverpool, Tate Gallery Liverpool).

2 See GRIEVE, ALASTAIR (1981) 'Constructivism after the Second World War', in: NAIRNE, SANDY and SEROTA, NICHOLAS (Eds) (1981) *British Sculpture in the Twentieth Century* (London, Whitechapel Art Gallery), pp. 155–65.

3 See THISTLEWOOD, DAVID (1990) 'The Independent Group and Art Education in Britain 1950–65', in: ROBBINS, D. (Ed) *The Independent Group: Post-War Britain and the Aesthetics of Plenty* (Cambridge, Mass. and London, MIT Press), pp. 212–20.

4 Underlying this most obvious message was the tacit proposal, much more consistent with Soviet Constructivism, that broadcasting, replete with propaganda masts, aerial devices and recording and transmission equipment which generally seemed the hybridised products of science and art, would become the engine of the twentieth century economy. READ, HERBERT (1934) *Art and Industry: the Principles of Industrial Design* (London, Faber).

5 See FRAMPTON, KENNETH (1971) 'Notes on a Lost Avant-Garde', in *Art in Revolution: Soviet Art and Design since 1917* (London, Arts Council) (pp. 21–29), p. 21. Catalogue of the exhibition of the same title, Hayward Gallery, 26 Feb.–18 Apr. 1971.

6 *Pioneers of Modern Sculpture*, Hayward Gallery, 20 July–23 Sept. 1973.

7 As noted by Curtis in CURTIS, PENELOPE (1994) 'Barbara Hepworth and the Avant-Garde of the 1920s', in: Curtis and Wilkinson (n. 1) (pp. 11–28), p. 25.

8 See WILKINSON, ALAN G. (1994) 'The 1930s: "Constructive Forms and Poetic Sculpture" ', in: Curtis and Wilkinson (n. 1) (pp. 31–69), pp. 60–61.

9 *Vorticism and its Allies*, Hayward Gallery, 27 March–2 June 1974.

10 CORK, RICHARD (1976) *Vorticism and Abstract Art in the First Machine Age. Vol. I: Origins and Development; Vol. II: Synthesis and Decline* (London, Gordon Fraser).

11 HARRISON, CHARLES (1981) *English Art and Modernism 1900–1939* (London, Allen Lane; Bloomington, Indiana University Press).

12 THISTLEWOOD, DAVID (1984) *Herbert Read: Formless and Form: an Introduction to his Aesthetics* (London, Routledge & Kegan Paul). See especially a discussion of Hepworth's decisive influence on Read's paradigmatic theory of modernism, pp. 96–98.

13 Harrison (n. 11), p. 229.

14 *Ibid.*, p. 268.

15 *Ibid.*, p. 269.

16 Letter HEPWORTH to Herbert Read, 14 May 1944; Lot 48/61, Sir Herbert Read Archive, University of Victoria, B.C.

17 Letter HEPWORTH to Herbert Read, 6 March 1948; Lot 48/61, Sir Herbert Read Archive, University of Victoria, B.C.

18 FLORENCE, PENNY: this volume, p. 26.

19 WAGNER, ANNE: this volume, p. 59.

20 See Thistlewood (n. 12), Chapter 6, pp. 126–48. See also THISTLEWOOD, DAVID (1982) 'Organic Art and the Popularisation of a Scientific Philosophy', *British Journal of*

Aesthetics Vol. 22, No. 4, Autumn, pp. 311–21.

21 BARLOW, ANNE: this volume, p. 105.

22 READ, HERBERT (1948) 'Barbara Hepworth: a New Phase', *The Listener* Vol. 39, No. 1002, 8 April, p. 592.

23 STEPHENS, CHRIS: this volume, p. 141.

24 DOHERTY, CLAIRE: this volume, p. 164.

PENNY FLORENCE

Barbara Hepworth: the Odd Man Out? Preliminary Thoughts about a Public Artist

> Sexual difference also corresponds to the possibility of different perceptions and creations. [1]

> . . . the theories and practices of modernity, when taken up by female voices, become strangely and irresistibly subversive, promising new questions and answers . . . [2]

BETWEEN THEN AND NOW

Hepworth fulfilled many public commissions [3], was an active contributor to the artistic debates of her time, and believed with an informed understanding in a social function of art. A full assessment of her ideas and achievements as a public artist will have to take account of all of her work in the public domain including her writing and opera designs, while not simply assimilating them to each other. Of the latter, on which she worked with Tippett in 1954–55, for example, she said:

> I think *The Midsummer Marriage* asked, both in its allegorical meaning and its symbolism, for a new discipline; also for a new tradition, perhaps related to the formality of Greek theatre or of the Mystery Plays . . . the composer can find a new form which will in the future be full of meaning for our society. [4]

What follows is a preliminary outline of some of the main issues and problems involved in understanding Hepworth's achievements as a public woman.

Hepworth's approach to art today seems remarkably confident and unproblematic. Neither her self-conception as an artist nor her work is easily assessed in the highly contested context of contemporary art practices and theory. The revisionist discourses of art history, whether 'new', 'social-historical' or 'feminist', have not recently centred on the kinds of issue she herself was preoccupied with, nor on critical questions that relate in a clear or obvious way to her thinking and practice [5]. On questions of gender, she seems to veer between denial and evasiveness. Hepworth appears an odd man out, a disruptive historical presence. Our contemporary 'world scene' is already far from that of even her late years up to her death in 1975, both in political realities and conceptualisations, so that the idealistic internationalism she shared with many fellow Western modernist artists early in the twentieth century demands of those who would understand her an effort of historical imagination as great as that required of seemingly far more distant ancestors. This is, of course, true to varying degrees of many. What makes Hepworth particularly resistant today to either feminist or modernist categorisation is itself something of a paradox, since it derives partly from the uncompromising pursuit of strongly held ideals in art and politics. But the philosophies and subject positions underlying such beliefs are now very much under scrutiny. Few commentators in either Western culture or any other can be currently well placed to read sympathetically remarks such as:

> . . . we all felt the fast growing understanding of art round the world and the international language which had been created. [6]

If account is taken of her position as a woman, the matter becomes still more refractory. Few women have so successfully and seemingly unproblematically inhabited the central and public arena of recent culture as she. What is to be learned from this? What kind of public sculptor was she? How did she invent a language for herself, both in terms of sculpture, or art practice in general, and theory? Hepworth is a courageous and important example of a woman artist who refused to be contained within the feminine spaces women have been allowed. For this reason, even if there were no other, her position in the history of modernism requires reassessment. I think it probable that such reappraisal will contribute to developing understandings of modernism that both articulate its silent spaces and change understandings of its self-articulation, partly because it will have to go beyond definitional strategies that prevent women entering and functioning within contemporary and historical discourses other than as honorary males. This is despite what looks like her complicity with such discourses; but before taking this at face value it is worth remembering that contemporary abstract work by women still seems to require the double-edged gender card to be played before it can either be exhibited or understood [7], and the reassessment of modernism in the light of women's marginalised cultural production is far from complete [8]. Hepworth surely has a major role to play in this paradoxical and problematic revisioning.

BETWEEN THE ABSTRACT, THE FEMALE AND HUMAN RELATIONS

Exploring 'the public Hepworth' thus raises a number of issues, and there is space here only to suggest a beginning. Gender is both crucial and troublesome because public culture is not in this society 'female' culture, even in the limited sense of 'made by women'. The aim here is to offer some ways into understanding the art and the semiotic gesture of a woman who transgresses the border between public and private spaces to intervene in the masculine public discourse as subject. Such conceptual groundwork is essential before it will be possible to deal directly and adequately with her socio-politics as public woman artist, and so this last remains beyond the scope of the present essay.

Moving in this way towards a gendered understanding of her work and her professional strategies will have to take account, for example, of her claims of 'universality' without reinstating the 'universal subject' that continues to be under critical scrutiny not only in relation to modernism, but as one of the prime cultural issues of our time. In the light of such fundamental debates, is it demonstrable, for example, that in Hepworth's self-positioning she performs a radical displacement of female subjectivity in semiosis of the kind that Irigaray might be understood to enact in language—what has been called 'miming mimesis' [9]? How might such displacement of the phallic economy 'through repetition and catachresis' be articulated in relation to sculpture, a repetition which, rather than confirming the origin as origin, reinserts what was systematically excluded? It looks possible in the following example, from her *Pictorial Autobiography*, where Hepworth's words about her work in Cornwall in the 1950s are placed next to *Curved Form with Inner Form (Anima)*, creating an intertext in which the insertion of the sculptor–spectator anticipates later preoccupations with 'inside–outside'.

> I became more and more preoccupied with the inside and outside of forms as I had been in the late 1930s, but on a bigger scale. I wanted to make forms to stand on hillsides and through which to look to the sea. Forms to lie down in, or forms to climb through. I would go out at night to see the effect of moonlight and then wait for the rising sun and make notes as to what happened then. [10]

While it would be questionable to read an ovoid form as necessarily female, the preoccupation with an exploration of bodies within bodies, 'forms to lie down in', irresistibly suggests the womb, and thus the female. Yet the evocation of the womb remains implicit, and in its exploration of the figure in the landscape, the sculptor and the sculpture, visual framing, the work pushes beyond the mother and child relation—which nevertheless remains the underlying pattern—towards the general idea of a particular relatedness. The title *Curved Form with Inner Form* stresses the abstract, while the subtitle (*Anima*) at least raises the possibility of gender. Taken together, these movements both suggest and erase gender. But it leaves a trace. What this tension between the bracketed feminine and the proposed abstraction suggests is the possibility, or reinsertion, of a gendered movement towards the universal. It starts very clearly from the body, a body which is not a self-contained unit, but rather one which is already in a mutually defining relationship with what is outside.

What kind of 'abstraction' is this? How does the current disputatious scrutiny of claims to 'universal' symbolisations help elucidate her work and assess its historical significance? How far is the female universalising movement, inevitably one of displacement in this culture, analogous to Salman Rushdie's contention that the experience of dislocation can create a concretisation of the artist's specific viewpoint that renders it universal? Hepworth's observation—'I hope to discover some absolute essence in sculptural terms, giving the quality of human relationships'—is in some ways contradictory if viewed according to some accounts of abstraction in art, since an 'absolute essence in sculptural terms' would not concern human relationships. It sits uneasily, for example, with T. E. Hulme's geometry of the machine as distinct from the 'accidental details of existing things' [11], with Fry's privileging of form, or indeed Maurice Denis' nineteenth century view of the formal abstraction that is any painting, the flat surface and colour that any image 'is' before it 'represents' [12].

Of course 'abstraction' is a contested term, and the point here is not to become embroiled in terminology [13]. It is rather to effect a retrospective intercalation towards a variform sense of abstraction as rich as it was in that crucial decade of early abstract painting leading up to 1920 when Hepworth won her scholarship to Leeds School of Art. My interest here, as in the art of that decade, has less to do with 'the abstracted', the 'non-objective' or 'non-representational' than it has with a changed economy of relations with the external world, with time, space and subjectivity. It is perhaps to turn to advantage modernism's massively disruptive intervention in the art of the past, so that instead of loss, it becomes an opportunity for revisioning.

Abstraction does not have to be seen only in terms of an art of self-sufficiency, distant from the social world [14]. As a necessary preliminary to considering Hepworth as a public sculptor, it is this more fluid imaginary I want to consider, because Hepworth is an important instance of a woman who managed to inhabit both woman's time and that of the masculine subject, and to sustain that contradiction throughout a long and prolific artistic career. It may have become less comprehensible because of limited interpretations of modernism and the history of her historical moment. Certainly, at a glance, Hepworth was eloquent both on paper and in form in ways that can be read simply as high modernism:

> The sculptor must search with passionate intensity for the underlying principle of the organisation of mass and tension, the meaning of gesture and the structure of rhythm . . .

But then she goes on:

> . . . in making my abstract drawings I am most often aware of those human values which dominate the structure and meaning of abstract forms. [15]

Those drawings are among the most apparently discrete works, yet again it is something she calls 'human values' that determines not only their meaning but also their structure. To understand this thoroughly is to historicise those human values in Hepworth, not as pertaining to some simple universal female, but as produced out of specific female experience, with which they have a spatio-temporal relationship.

Hepworth's conceptualisation of space, which, of course, ultimately concerns both time and the subject, may be approached through her well-known intense interest in the figure in the landscape. This has been associated specifically with the verticals of Cornwall's standing stones and abandoned mining chimneys [16]. Such remains are a kind of metaphor for a way of viewing her relationship to place and space, and especially to landscape, since they embody a temporal tension around a return of the human to the natural, a liminal space-between. The landscape is not entirely natural, the standing stones and chimneys are not at all natural; but their location in the landscape renders them part of it and subject to the same forces of change. Hepworth reproduces a bodily relationship with the artefact and with the sun and moon, sea and tide, cloud and wind 'which change the depth of shadow on forms' and which 'have governed my life for a long time' [17].

Remembering the importance to Hepworth of carving as process, Herbert Read observed: 'Carving is an extension of the telluric forces that mould the landscape' [18]. Hepworth's interest clearly pertains to the natural in some sense, but in tension with the sculptor's own positioning especially here in relation to light. 'Telluric' could imply an unthinking and earthbound process of inhuman forces; Hepworth's carving may seek a relationship with such forces, but it is not one of identity.

> I used colour and strings . . . the strings were the tension I felt between myself and the sea, the wind or the hills. [19]

It is a conception of enfolding, yet not of enclosure:

> . . . now I had a studio workroom looking straight towards the horizon of the sea and enfolded (but with always the escape for the eye straight out to the Atlantic) by the arms of land to the left and right of me. I have used this idea in 'Pelagos' 1946. [20]

Both this enfolding and that of *Curved Form with Inner Form*, discussed above, may usefully be seen in the light of Irigaray's contention that

> The *relationship between the envelope and the thing* represents one of the aporia, of not the aporia, of Aristotelianism and the philosophical systems that derive from it. [21]

Irigaray is discussing how in her view the 'mother woman' is reduced to a thing, 'a place deprived of a place of its own'. Escape from the dialectic which renders her the place of an other who is incapable of separating from her/it would entail a double self-enveloping as a woman and as a mother, requiring 'a complete change in our conception of time and space' [22]. Irigaray goes on with a characteristically ironic play on Freud and female morphology in which buccal space is associated with the foetal and points towards a new and gendered relation between 'form, matter, interval and limit' [23]. Irigaray's mental economy brings into question the relation of the tactile to the visual [24], and in Hepworth's view, through sculpture, light becomes an extension of what she calls 'the stereognostic sensibility', the mental apprehension of form by touch.

> Light gives full play to our tactile perceptions through the experience of our eyes, and the vitality of forms is revealed by the interplay between space and volume. [25]

These ideas are again articulated with reference to the inside-outside relationship, for Hepworth is most drawn to the effects of light when this is 'in special accord':

> . . . as for instance a nut in its shell or a child in the womb, or when one senses the architecture of bones in the human figure. [26]

Hepworth's 'sensible transcendental' traces in her work the corporeality of an artist-mother without circumscribing it to exclusive reference. *Three Forms*, 1935 (Fig. 20), made the year after giving birth to triplets, evinces this movement where, in Hepworth's words, her work had become 'more formal and all traces of naturalism had disappeared' [27]. Without privileging the artist's maternity it may be seen to inflect the various other works with the same title that were to follow, their place in the modulations of space, form and thematics in her work—the many other works that explore different aspects of number.

The kind of disruption this signals is a subtext to Katie Campbell's *Nine Meditations on Three Forms*, a response to this work published in the catalogue to *Writing on the Wall*, the Tate Gallery London's 1993 exhibition, which was the gallery's first gender-explicit show. Campbell's nine sections almost ricochet between questions of form and abstraction (the number three, the stone, the relationships of round objects in space, scale) and questions of the body (femaleness, motherhood, childhood, anthropomorphisation):

> . . . the symbolic absence which is its own presence . . . the absence which links, the link which separates . . . [28]

Between these shifting points, issues of representation and interpretation hang suspended. New dimensions are needed for women to create their own space out of that appropriated, in Irigaray's words, in an 'obscure sort of commemoration' to a nostalgia for 'the first and ultimate dwelling place' [29].

BETWEEN CORNWALL AND NEW YORK

Single Form (Chûn Quoit), 1961 (Fig. 6) is one of the thematic series to which *Single Form*, 1963 (Fig. 7) belongs, the memorial to Hepworth's friend, Secretary General Dag Hammarskjöld, placed outside the United Nations building in New York. Hammacher notes the change in the larger piece, compared with one of its predecessors—from a small concavity to a hole (what he calls a valley and an eye)—

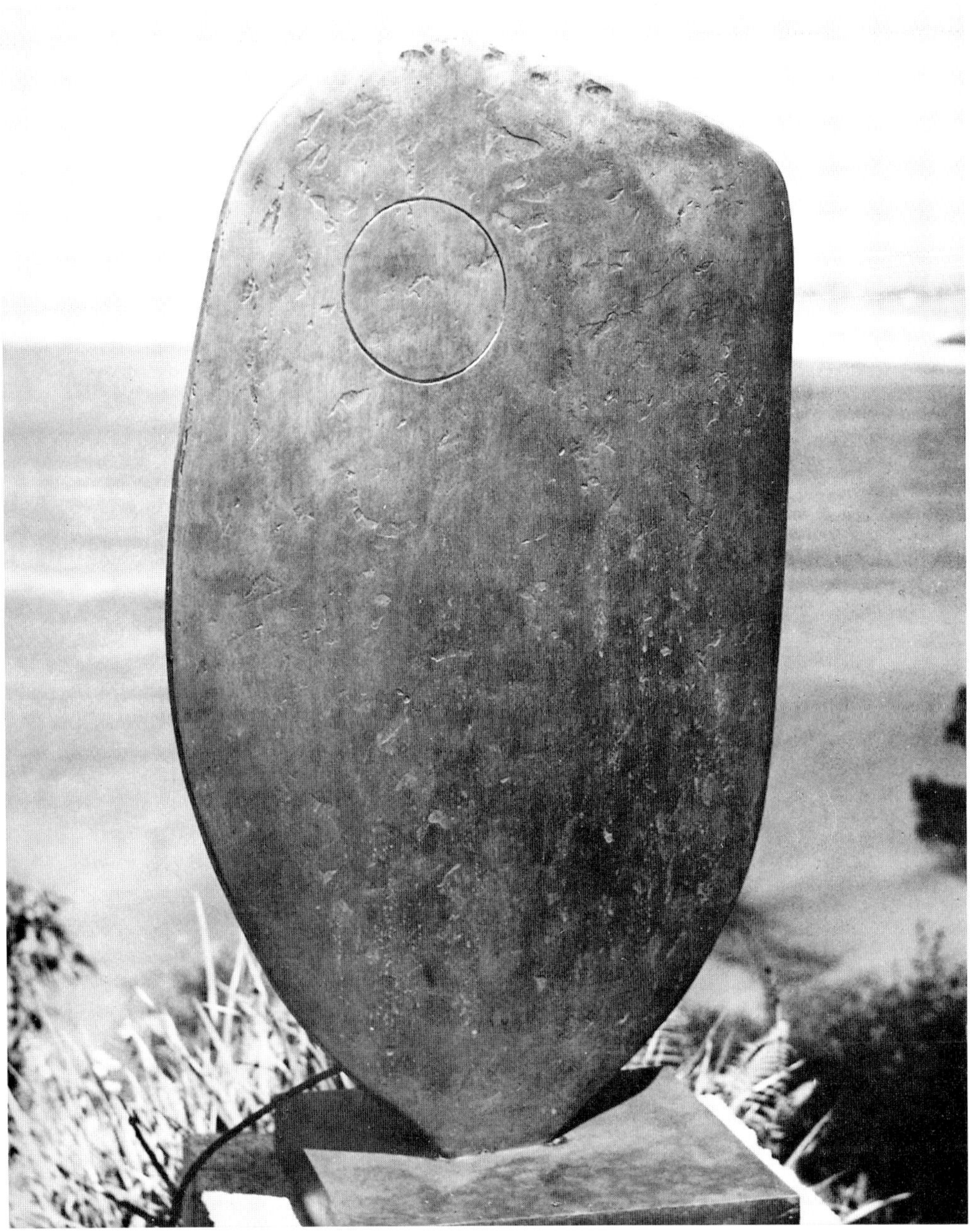

Fig. 6 BARBARA HEPWORTH, *Single Form (Chûn Quoit)*, 1961 © Trustees of the Barbara Hepworth Estate (published in Bowness, *The Complete Sculpture of Barbara Hepworth 1960–69*, London, Lund Humphries, 1971)

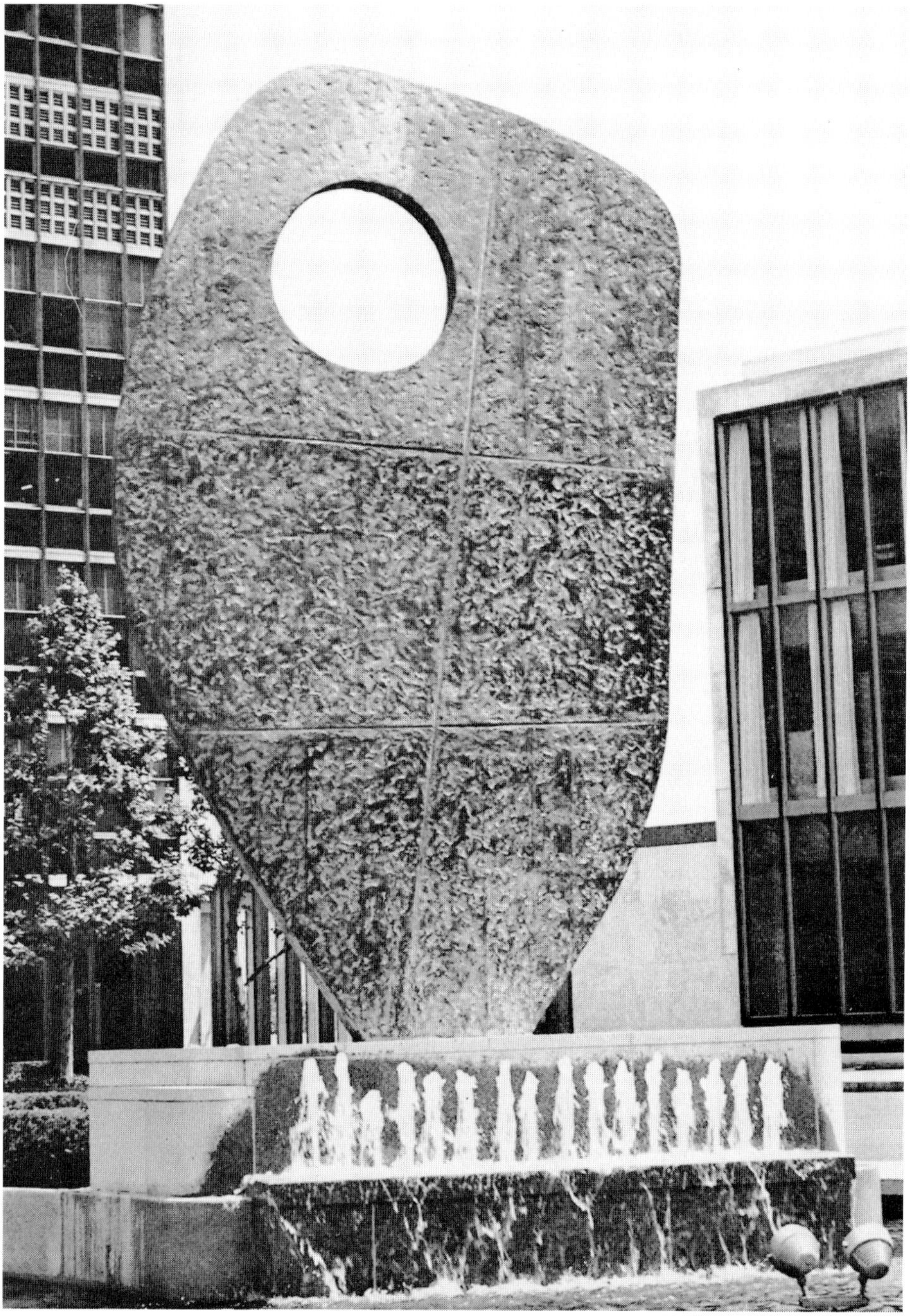

Fig. 7 BARBARA HEPWORTH, *Single Form*, 1963 (memorial to Dag Hammarskjöld) © Trustees of the Barbara Hepworth Estate (published in Bowness, *The Complete Sculpture of Barbara Hepworth 1960–69*, London, Lund Humphries, 1971)

and how it 'sets up a tension with all the edges, a tension that is resolved by the perfect clarity of the circular cavity' [30]. Again, the spatial tension is between the internal and the border, the exact definition and its equiponderant beyond. Hammacher recalls Bernal's impression of the early neolithic in relation to Hepworth's 'Single Form' themes [31], and with words that resonate with Irigaray's 'obscure sort of commemoration' goes on to say:

> He might have quoted the Old Testament in which Jews like Jacob raise a neolithic stone as a memorial on the spot where, sleeping, they had received their heavenly visions. [32]

Whether or not this is a coded reference both to the Jewish benefactor Jacob Blaustein, whose generosity had financed the project [33], and to the ideals of the United Nations in establishing a world order in which the Holocaust would be inconceivable, the work poses questions of historical time and space. What kind of geopolitical and historical gesture is constituted in the transposition of a piece finely balanced between a modern female subject in a remote landscape and prehistory into the quintessential modern cityscape of New York? And not only into New York, but into its highly symbolic political location outside the United Nations building.

It is, of course, personal, a memorial to a friend, but such a friendship between public figures is imbued with wider meaning, as Hepworth was well aware: she felt it 'professionally and historically necessary' to announce the dedication of the work at a particular moment, and wrote of her need to retain her focus (and therefore not visit New York at that point) 'knowing how Dag was thinking about world ideas and about ideas in sculpture' [34]. The location of sculpture in the landscape seems to occupy a whole different physical and semiotic space to that located in an architectural setting. Does relocation from one to the other pose a whole different set of relationships, or extend the reach of those already set in tension? The pierced form in Penwith relates to colour as well as to space:

> . . . sculpture in landscape and the essential quality of light in relation to sculpture which induced a new way of piercing the forms to contain colour. [35]

The architectural is inextricable from an historicised 'present', the quotidian either of a specific cultural past or of the contemporary, while the landscape setting may more readily refer to natural cycles or time in the abstract. Perhaps colour may be a linkage or balancing agent between them, constitutive of a liminal site [36]. The American architect Peter Eisenmann points towards a paradox of architecture which Hepworth mobilises:

> . . . in order to reinvent a site . . . the idea of site must be freed from its traditional places, histories, and systems of meaning. This involves the dislocation of the traditional interpretation of its elements. [37]

BETWEEN TIME AND SPACE

In order to understand Hepworth's work as gendered, it seems to me that conceptualisations of the abstract must be brought back into time, or if not into time, into some relation with the idea of time. Like the universal, it must be reconceptualised beyond a bipolar relation with particular representation or location.

Moving on from Klee's observation, that the point of painting is to spatialise perception and to make time simultaneous, Irigaray explores the need for the psychoanalytic process to locate the subject in a reformulated understanding of history, to 'establish perspectives between present-past-future'. She offers painting as an answer to the distortion in psychoanalysis arising from the difference in 'the speed of transmission and perception between sound and light' [38]. There is a sense in which I see this dislocation as a crucial problem, not only for psychoanalysis, or indeed for painting, but for Western culture, certainly since the late nineteenth century, partly because the conceptualisation of how space and time relate in the imaginary is fundamental to signification; it underlies the definitional split in the received idea of the sign as visual or aural [39]. This is one way of reinserting the problematics of gender, since women's cultural time differs from men's if only because it has begun to be recorded comparatively late. That is, it has been seriously narrativised and thus shifted into discourse and the realm of the aural sign at a different point in history [40]. In non-literate cultures there is less likely to be this temporal gender imbalance in culture or representation; in what is fast becoming a world culture of variform media its reproduction is exponential.

Hepworth's work spans half a century of a culture which has come to be characterised in terms of a 'mainstream', 'dominant' or 'central' body, and—in a variety of senses—its 'alternative' 'oppositional' 'avant-garde'. Such nominations are all indicative of spatial or temporal disjunction; the alternative is an elsewhere to the central, the avant-garde ambiguously ahead of the mainstream in time or space. Another word to describe this intercalation might be corrugation, since it gives equal space to either part. Gender inserts into this spatio-temporal derangement as non-essential and promiscuous, and as corporeal and disruptive. By now many scholars have demonstrated that women have been assigned to what has been perceived as the secondary or dependent part of this grossly weighted structure, together with an amalgam of varying elements assigned to them as female or feminine. Hepworth, as woman and cultural producer, fits easily into neither a gendered nor an ungendered analysis.

BETWEEN WRITTEN AND MATERIAL TRACE

An important part of Hepworth's public persona is her writing. Since the intertextuality between an artist's writing, theorising and their principal media is never simple, and since Hepworth's is particularly interesting and innovative, reading it requires discrimination. Her *Pictorial Autobiography*, like most of her published writing, is deceptive in its simplicity and apparent transparency. While the book was not produced single-handedly, it was developed in close co-operation with her, and though she wanted 'more work than life' [41], it contains a great deal of intimate detail, down to pictures of her children and family pets, indicating a blurring of the line between work and life.

She was a gifted writer, and clearly wrote for 'the public'; a public assumed to take art and the importance of the artist both seriously and for granted. Although not all of her writing is yet in the public domain, she was among the first to put her work as a sculptor into discourse, not only through autobiography but also, for example, through articles, critic-friends and the group *Unit One*. The contexts of publication, and the kinds of meanings she was trying to produce, require scrutiny. Her formative years were in an age of artistic manifestos, and if the *Futurist Manifesto of Painters* and the *Technical Manifesto of Futurist Paintings* were a little early in 1910, the *Vorticist Manifesto* in the inaugural issue of *Blast* in 1914, the first *De Stijl Manifesto* in 1917, and Breton's *Surrealist Manifestos* of the 1920s were all examples of a new kind of mobilisation of the word by visual artists.

This is not the place to go into her writing in depth, but work to be done clearly requires assessment of it as modernist prose, perhaps in the light of other women modernists, particularly those with either a central and articulated relationship with Cornwall, like Virginia Woolf, H. D. and Mary Butts [42], or with an innovative understanding of the artistic and physical body, such as Gertrude Stein. Here in her 'autobiographical' work as elsewhere, Hepworth presents a challenge to received understandings, in this case of how a woman artist can symbolise her woman's life experience as integrated with that of a very public artist with a politicised sense of artistic mission. Yet the straightforward application of her prose to her sculpture remains problematic; for instance, her attempt to distance herself from Moore by placing him on the 'surrealist side' and herself on the 'constructive side' [43] may be more useful as a commentary on the limitations of those categories and on her frustration with repeated comparisons with Moore that tended to overshadow and distort her work. Hepworth's work seems to me to challenge any opposition of 'biomorphic abstraction' to constructivism.

BETWEEN ARTIST AND PUBLIC

Hepworth, then, adopted specific strategies to influence her position in the art world and her relation to her public. It is certainly true that there was a need for a directly interventionist stance, but her diplomacy makes it far from simple to assess. She has still had her due neither from mainstream art historians nor from feminists, despite recognition in her lifetime. At her death in 1975, *The Guardian* said of her 'She was probably the most significant woman artist in the history of art to this day'. This is quite a sweeping claim—not the history of British art, or of modern art, but the history of all art. Is this the accolade it seems to be—

or the poisoned chalice? Does the presence of the qualifier 'woman' before 'artist' undermine what has been called her 'leading role in the revitalising of what had almost become a moribund art', that of sculpture [44]?

Where, now, is her place in contemporary debates over crucial instabilities within modernism, whether explicitly gendered or not, in which her work must surely figure [45]? It would appear that if her seeming gender-neutrality has made her readily assimilable into one version of modernism, it has made her suffer from another kind of invisibility, de-sexed through her success in Christine Battersby's wittily dubbed 'Virility School of Creativity' [46]. Feminism works within many contradictions, of which a necessarily reactive element is one, and it has tended to reproduce some of the same values as that which it opposes, as reaction will. This has made Hepworth's achievements as a woman difficult to see, and has left undeveloped understandings of what is involved in the few but significant cases of female success in, and accommodation to, the masculine tradition. Bridget Riley would be another example, and she also does not enjoy the current feminist popularity of, say, Frida Kahlo or Hannah Hoch.

Understandings of the female as confined to the private and the small-scale obscure matters on several levels. Although the view of the obituary writer already cited betrays such assumptions, the tools to demonstrate how they operate are still being developed. His view was:

> In her later years [her sculpture] sometimes tended towards the monumental . . . It may be doubted whether [this] suited her special gifts best. At any rate, she returned often to making smaller pieces . . . and it is in these that her artistic character seems most persuasively expressed. [47]

Given modernism's complicity with masculinist discourse, and with 'woman's' inscription into it as ground, we are brought directly up against that woman whom Gayatri Spivak proposes as she 'whom we strictly, historically, geo-politically, *cannot imagine*, as literal referent'. To deal with her, the name 'woman' must be split, to create a decolonised space in which as the 'gendered subaltern' [48] women become active in naming, not merely the named.

BETWEEN GENDER, RACE AND PLACE

Contemporary Western artists of non-European origin are forced to invent strategies that enable them to articulate their complex location. Thus an artist like Anish Kapoor neither aims at nor refuses Indian elements. Similarly, recognition of their distinctive place in the history of modernism is constantly threatened with erasure because it is a place that by definition disrupts Western incorporation of Oriental and African art into its semiotic systems. Women of colour have faced the conjunction of gender and race directly, while white women have yet to develop ways of understanding their/our position in this respect [49].

In her essay 'Barbara Hepworth and the Avant-garde of the 1920s', Penelope

Curtis looks at Hepworth's introduction to carving within a context in which carving was 'characterised by its presentation within the non-Western tradition' [50]. Curtis establishes connections between Hepworth and African and Chinese art in particular, noting that

> . . . one of her few stated concerns about Christian Science was that 'it cuts out all the warmth, creativeness, humanness of the negro carvings' because [Christian] 'science will not admit the necessity of sex harmony'. [51]

How far this, taken together with other statements and her actual practice, can be equated with the widespread enthusiasm for 'the primitive' [52], and the historical as well as the cross-cultural positioning this entailed, requires elucidation in the light of her politics as well as her gender. A white woman who admires early Italian art and thinks that

> . . . Beethoven, Bach, Cézanne and Picasso, negro carvings, all give infinitely because of their life force . . . [53]

is specifically positioned within modernism, and cannot be assumed to articulate the same as a white man who seeks a return to 'the primitive' or to seek out an ideal beginning from which to reshape his history.

BETWEEN SELF-/AND/REPRESENTATION

Class and place complicate the issue further. They may usefully be framed here as concerning the point at which public presentation, representation and self-representation collide.

To begin with self-representation, the problem with Hepworth's personal vision as that of a white, middle class woman and that same vision as 'public' or 'universal' evinces what Gayatri Spivak has called a 'fractured semiotic field'. In explaining her use of the idea, as part of addressing the problems of cultural self-representation, Spivak takes care not to reduce the world to a semiotic field. She points out—and it is an interview I quote from, hence to some extent the discursiveness—that

> . . . there are collections of axioms in the socius, depending on your position within the socius, and these axioms are by no means unified all over the globe . . . when a writer writes, she doesn't just write in English or French, she also writes in these so-called sign-systems . . . With respect to the notion of fracture, . . . the way in which semiotic fields are tapped for cultural self-representation . . . always covers over the dislocation between the kinds of axiomatics that are being used, and whatever it is in the 'culture' that constitutes the hidden agenda of the suppression of ideological production. [54]

While the notion of fracture overlaps with the understanding that signs carry different meanings according to the moment and place of their deployment and reception, it is more original and exact than this, and more precisely relevant to modernism and its self-representation. The idea is clarified in Spivak's example of the American Fourth of July picnic, translatable to the 'folk' festivals of various kinds in the U.K. as approximations, particularly the Cornish festivals that are currently enjoying a revival. At the Fourth of July picnics, the U.S.A. 'represents itself as engaging in independent commodity production', whereas it is an example of 'micro-electronic capitalism' [55]. Thus Cornwall represents itself at its festivals as a craft-based agricultural and fishing economy, whereas it is an exploited and impoverished region of the same micro-electronic capitalism. This is the fracture, which is always Utopian or directed towards some 'golden age'; by representing itself in this way the U.S.A., or the dominant culture, betrays signs of its hidden agenda. The self-representation here is as something the U.S.A. is not, and it covers a nexus of socio-economic relations.

The specifics of Barbara Hepworth's position as 'female' may be opened up through comparison with that of the painter Alfred Wallis as 'Cornish'—he was in fact born in Devon—in that they are portrayed, and to some extent portrayed themselves, as something they were not. Though I would not want to push any comparison between them too far, it does demonstrate some of the contradictions of how Hepworth is placed, for her oblique position in straddling the semiotic fracture tends towards its exposure. She is both othered by and part of the conceptual framework that attributes interpretative power to the modernist art of the metropolis, one which can make sense of 'the remote places' Wallis stands for—though it, too, came from a self-positioning marginal to the art of the day and forms part of a fragmentation whose effects we continue to experience.

Her name must appear on the list of now-established names who prove his worth—Nicholson, Hepworth, Hampstead-based critics Herbert Read and Adrian Stokes, they all collected him, as Tooby points out:

> . . . alongside other naive or 'primitive' artists, as part of the discussion of the general importance of this art to modernism. [56]

But women, too, are structurally in Wallis' position, exemplified as the intuitive, the naive, that which is native to dominant Western nurture. How else can Hepworth maintain the modernist fiction, other than by seeking to cover the nexus of socio-economic relations that threatens to push its way through the gender-based nexus she seems, at first, to disprove? Is it going too far to wonder whether this fracture in the semiotic field may connect in a way the artists may well not have sought with Cornwall as 'natural environment'—which, of course, it is not? Arguably even at the turn of the twentieth century there were very few such left. Consider Jean Rouche's ethnographic film of the Dogon people, and Surrealist film, part of the mutually transformative encounter into which this mythical 'natural' inserts.

The political idealism of the modernists is well known, but the kinds of subsequent theoretical developments I have been indicating provide clear ways in which their totalising internationalism, and their incorporation of the 'natural' and the 'primitive', both may be questioned and gendered. Even at the time Fascism was appropriating 'wilderness' to its ideological purposes, Alpinism would ensure the building of a formidable national will, uplifted by the study of wild nature [57]. Without hypostatising the external world, it is important to establish with some exactitude what the modernists' quest has to do with Cornwall, how it is that Wallis' art was not seen as 'Cornish', but rather as 'natural', and what these fractures in the semiotic field tell us about the awkward presence of Hepworth, the odd man out. Hepworth is homogenised or sidelined; in the same gesture, Cornwall is reduced to a 'background'. But the natural environment is much more than a *tabula rasa*, and its relationship to cultural self definitions is both complex and mutable. It can be used by women, their allies and their antagonists, as an illusory, extra-cultural space, a seeming-beyond to masculinist culture. That Cornwall is no such place in actuality need not mean that it has no imaginative significance in its envisioning.

BETWEEN PERSONAL MUSEUM AND PUBLIC GALLERY

The opening in June 1993 of the new Tate Gallery at St. Ives was a welcome development that throws into relief the difficulties of accommodating a gendered understanding of Hepworth to the context of the kinds of work and values embodied in major public collections. The Gallery is located a few hundred yards away from the Barbara Hepworth Museum and Garden, which was opened in 1975, the year after the artist's death. Hepworth at the Tate Gallery St. Ives, Porthmeor, reads rather differently from Hepworth in the Museum at Barnoon Hill.

The point is not that the setting of her work either at the new gallery or at the museum is inappropriate in itself, but rather to suggest that each should refer to the other in such a way as to mobilise their differences to cast light on the kinds of problematic Hepworth's public presence raises.

This is the blurb from both the leaflet *Information for Visitors* about the Hepworth Museum, and the larger gallery's regular calendar:

> The Barbara Hepworth Museum and Sculpture Garden is an integral element of the Tate Gallery at St Ives. In her will, she asked her executors to investigate the possibility of 'establishing a permanent exhibition of some of my works in the Trewyn Studio and its garden.' The Museum is unique in this country. The small house, her working studios and the lush secluded garden she created provide a remarkable insight into her vision of the world.

The Barbara Hepworth museum is clearly not an integral part of the Tate Gallery in anything other than broad administrative control, which is not in itself a problem, and so far there has thankfully been no attempt to conform the studio-museum to the style of the gallery.

The presentation of the museum is, however, problematic in its personalisation and domestication of Hepworth's monumental and abstract art. This is in contrast to the universalising gestures that characterise the displays in the larger museum. The publicity for the museum emphasises the house, studios and garden over the work. There is no direct reference to the substantial collection of sculptures from large to small scale, as opposed to the Tate's permanent display of three sculptures and one painting. Nor is the visitor alerted to the range of historical material the artist left behind, which not only documents her own artistic development, but also that of the modernist movement in Britain of which she was one of the leading figures. The Tate now has a great opportunity in the task of making its presentation of Hepworth expressive of a coherent approach to her challenge to the gendered division between public and private, and to the relation of modernism to Cornwall on the one hand and the global context to which it aspired on the other. Such re-visioning would contribute to tackling the historical difficulties of curating all those whose work has been either marginalised or distorted [58].

The Tate in Cornwall has a privileged and vital role to play in developing understandings of the contradictions inherent in the multiplicity of semiotic fields it traverses. A monument to monolithic modernism is the last thing that will serve as a fitting memorial to Barbara Hepworth. It is also the last thing St. Ives needs. It would have kept the modernists away for a start.

NOTES AND REFERENCES

1 IRIGARAY, LUCE (1992) *Sexes and Genealogies* (New York and Chichester, Columbia University Press), p. 164.

2 JARDINE, ALICE (1985) *Gynesis. Configurations of Woman and Modernity* (Ithaca and London, Cornell University Press), p. 258.

3 See 'Chronology of Public Commissions', in: CURTIS, PENELOPE and WILKINSON, ALAN G. (1994) *Barbara Hepworth: a Retrospective* (Liverpool, Tate Gallery Liverpool), pp. 152–56. Public support for her work was not as great as for the men of her generation and stature, however, and it only appears considerable if a double gender standard is applied.

4 HEPWORTH, BARBARA (1970, 1985, 1993) *A Pictorial Autobiography* (London, Tate Gallery Publications), p. 68.

5 Emphasis on the purely visual and the gaze, for example, or on linguistics-based semiosis, or again on the 'oppositional'.

6 Hepworth (n. 4), pp. 34, 76.

7 In reviewing the recent MoMA show of *Women Artists and Minimalism*, Johanna Drucker raises pertinent issues, including that of 'women wresting from the past production of art history a recognition of their position in that history—not merely as retrospective writing—but as a background against which current work can be understood'. See DRUCKER, JOHANNA (1994) 'Sense and Sensibility: Women Artists and Minimalism in the Nineties', *Third Text* 27, Summer, p. 103.

8 Jardine (n. 2) explores what this historical work might imply. She lists some of the tasks to be done in her Afterword (p. 263). For an elaboration of her neologism 'gynesis', 'the putting into discourse of "woman" ', see pp. 25–26. Hepworth's position did figure in an

early feminist historical debate in which Carol Duncan challenged the essay NEMSER, CINDY (1973) 'Art Talk: Conversations with 12 Woman Artists', *Feminist Art Journal* Vol. 2, No. 2. One of the twelve was Hepworth. Nemser's piece was itself a response to Linda Nochlin's well-known ironic question, 'Why are there no great woman artists?' Duncan interrogates Nemser's values, in particular her outrage that Hepworth among others has been denied 'the power and prestige of their top male colleagues'. DUNCAN, CAROL (1993) *The Aesthetics of Power* (Cambridge, Cambridge University Press), p. 123. According to Duncan, Nemser remains within the terms of orthodox art criticism, still using the art-historical lens which 'dims or filters out lived experience' (*ibid.*, p. 124) and failing to take account of the ambivalent and awkward relationships between artists, critics and capitalism (*ibid.*, p. 130).

9 Butler explores this interpretation of Irigaray in BUTLER, JUDITH (1993) *Bodies that Matter: On the Discursive Limits of 'Sex'* (New York and London, Routledge), p. 45, further developing the analysis of 'performativity' in her earlier book *Gender Trouble*. Readers of Irigaray will be aware of her theoretical presence in this essay, particularly her thinking on the necessity for, and possibility of, women's differentiated social and symbolic representation. I have in mind here her observation: 'The transition to a new age in turn necessitates a new perception and a new conception of *time and space*, our *occupation of place*, and the different *envelopes known as identity*. It assumes and entails an evolution and transformation of forms, of the relationship of *matter* to *form* and of the *between* the two.' Irigaray (n. 1), p. 167. There is a fascinating discussion of varying, recent re-articulations of the Platonic feminine as inscriptional space in the first chapter of *Bodies that Matter*. Butler explores the implications in various writers of the threat to systematicity that erupts because that which is excluded from the form/matter binary is also produced by it (p. 39)—exclusion, according to Irigaray, that 'is the differentiating relation between masculine and feminine, where the masculine occupies both terms of the binary opposition, and the feminine cannot be said to be an intelligible term at all' (*op. cit.*).

10 Hepworth (n. 4), p. 80. See also below (n. 23).

11 Quoted in BROWN, DAVID (1980) 'Early Abstract Art in Britain', catalogue of the exhibition *Abstraction: Towards a New Art* (London, Tate Gallery) Feb.–April 1980, p. 105.

12 According to Denis a painting is, before being a warhorse or a nude or whatever, 'essentiellement une surface plane recouverte de couleurs en un certain ordre assemblées' (essentially a flat surface covered with colours arranged in a particular order). DENIS, MAURICE (1964) *Du Symbolisme au Classicisme: Théories* (Paris, Hermann), p. 33. While the issues raised in this way of looking change in relation to sculpture, the underlying viewpoint applies equally to either medium.

13 My position would not be fundamentally at odds with that of Meyer Schapiro in his 1937 essay on the 'Nature of Abstract Art', partly itself a critique of Barr's dehistoricised language of absolutes and pure, contentless form. SCHAPIRO, MEYER (1978) *Modern Art in the Nineteenth and Twentieth Centuries* (London, Chatto & Windus), pp. 185–211. It is for a detailed pursuit of the implications of gender in his 'immense, historically developed, capacity to hold the world in mind' (p. 195) that I am arguing.

14 Suzi Gablik traces this version of abstraction in her indictment of the art world. GABLIK, SUZI (1988) *Has Modernism Failed?* (London and New York, Thames & Hudson), pp. 20ff. Certainly in a poet such as Mallarmé, the abstract is a terrifying aporia, not an optimistic aesthetic of 'progress'. I admire much of what Gablik says, but regret that her analysis is actually close to gender denying; for example, she praises Lucy Lippard's 1983 book *Overlay* for its commitment to radicalism without taking up its feminism in any way, despite feminism's theorised espousal of many of the same concerns (*Ibid.*, p. 26). Lippard, however, though her book was written in the south west of England and

includes many references to its prehistoric sites, including the Men an Tol, for example, makes no mention of Hepworth. Such silences are perhaps indicative of the depth and intransigence of the problem of properly gendering history.

15 Hepworth (n. 4), p. 108.

16 WILKINSON, ALAN, in: Curtis and Wilkinson (n. 3), p. 79.

17 Hepworth (n. 4), p. 81.

18 *Ibid.*, p. 104.

19 Quoted in Curtis and Wilkinson (n. 3), back cover.

20 See READ, HERBERT (1952) 'Introduction', *Barbara Hepworth: Carvings and Drawings* (London, Lund Humphries), p. 76, quoted by Wilkinson in: Curtis and Wilkinson (n. 3), p. 81.

21 Irigaray (n. 1), p. 169.

22 *Ibid.*

23 My understanding of buccal space and the formation of both subjectivity and perception owes much to the work of Elizabeth Grosz; in the context of a discussion of Merleau-Ponty, she observes how 'the mouth is a primordial link or bridge connecting perceptions from the inside and the outside of the body. There is a gradual shift from such contact perception to more distance-oriented perception . . .' GROSZ, ELIZABETH (1994) *Volatile Bodies* (Bloomington, Indiana University Press), p. 92.

24 'In opposition to Merleau-Ponty, Irigaray claims that the map provided by the tactile is not congruous with that provided by the visual . . . although it is clear that there is some interchange between them.' *Ibid.*, p. 105.

25 Hepworth (n. 4), p. 27.

26 *Ibid.*

27 *Ibid.*, p. 37.

28 CAMPBELL, KATIE (1991) 'Nine Meditations on Three Forms', in: COLLINS, J. and LINDNER, E. (Eds) *Writing on the Wall: Women Writers on Women Artists* (London, Weidenfeld & Nicholson), p. 52.

29 Irigaray (n. 1), p. 170.

30 Hammacher illustrates the version in walnut of 1961 without any reference in its title to Chûn. HAMMACHER, A. M. (1968, 1987) *Barbara Hepworth* (London, Thames & Hudson). The bronze, in which the round is neither concavity nor hole, but a line, has '(Chûn Quoit)' as its subtitle and is illustrated in Curtis and Wilkinson (n. 3), p. 105. Wilkinson draws attention to Bowness' information that titles were sometimes casually assigned. To my mind this does not make them arbitrary. Hepworth gives an account of the project in Hepworth (n. 4), pp. 94–98, including three pictures of the work *in situ* and the text of her address at the unveiling in which she said 'Throughout my work on the "Single Form" I have kept in mind Dag Hammarskjöld's ideas of human and aesthetic ideology'. *Ibid.*, p. 96.

31 Bernal's Foreword to Hepworth's 1937 Catalogue is quoted in full in Hepworth (n. 4), p. 36.

32 Hammacher (n. 30), p. 164.

33 Curtis and Wilkinson (n. 3), p. 155.

34 *Ibid.* According to Hammacher, Hepworth visited the site several times. Hammacher (n. 30), p. 166. While it is clear that careful consideration was given to its exact position from the beginning, it appears that she had not revisited the site since 1959, two years earlier. Curtis and Wilkinson (n. 3), p. 155.

35 Curtis and Wilkinson (n. 3), p. 81.

36 I have Irigaray's suggestive essay 'Flesh Colours', Irigaray (n. 1), pp. 153–65, in mind here, though her elliptical remarks may not be directly assimilable into this notion of colour and spatiality.

37 Quoted in GOLDBLATT, DAVID (1991) 'The Dislocation of the Architectural Self', *Journal of Aesthetics and Art Criticism* Vol. 49, No. 4, p. 383.

38 Irigaray (n. 1), p. 155.

39 See FLORENCE, PENNY (1986) *Mallarmé, Manet and Redon: Visual and Aural Signs and the Generation of Meaning* (Cambridge and New York, Cambridge University Press). See also FLORENCE, PENNY (1992) 'Remembrance of Space-Time', *Journal of the Institute of Romance Studies* Vol. 1, No. 1.

40 Jardine outlines how crucial the opposition between space and time has been to the master narratives of the West. Jardine (n. 2), pp. 24 - 25. How it has been put into question within the sign through self-referential art, the best of which is to some extent distorted

by theories of art for art's sake, has been a particular interest of mine (n. 39). Jardine is particularly useful in her gendering of this self-questioning process through her idea of 'gynesis'. There is an interesting and important debate between Krauss and Bryson (bringing others in) about the direct application of linguistic models to visual semiotics. BRYSON, HOLLY and MOXLEY (Eds) (1992) *Visual Theory* (Oxford, Blackwell; Cambridge, Polity), pp. 79–100.

41 There is a note on the latter by Alan Bowness opposite the contents page of the 1993 edition, in which he recounts the book's genesis from an idea by the publisher Anthony Adams, its first publication in 1970 and his own preparation of the last section for a new edition after Hepworth's death.

42 Mary Butts (1890–1937) was a highly regarded avant-garde prose writer, admired by Pound and Ford, who requires reassessment. Her last years were spent at Sennen Cove, the westerly tip of the Penwith peninsular. H.D., the American poet Hilda Doolittle, knew D.H. and Frieda Lawrence during their time at Higher Tregerthen, near Zennor, Penwith, during the First World War (1917). H.D. shared Hepworth's enthusiasm for the Greek landscape (explicit in titles for sculpture and in Hepworth (n. 4), p. 71 and saw in the Cornish landscape a strange land of 'subtle psychic reverberations'. 'The whole place was out of this world . . . it was not England . . . the Greek words went with the texture of the stones here.' H.D. (1984) *Bid Me to Live* (London, Virago), p. 162. I am grateful to Diana Collecott for her work on H.D. in Cornwall.

43 Wilkinson, in: Curtis and Wilkinson (n. 3), p. 145.

44 Hepworth (n. 4), p. 136.

45 Careful analysis of the trajectory of Hepworth criticism remains important work to be done. A superficial glance reveals only six entries in the British Library copyright list of publications, for example, most of them either exhibition catalogues or autobiographical. Though Hepworth's name is present in histories of modern sculpture in Britain, it does tend to be in lists rather than in substantive analyses, and not as often as is readily defensible. The index to READ, HERBERT (1964, 1992) *A Concise History of Modern Sculpture* (London, Thames & Hudson), while it mentions Henry Moore 32 times, gives Hepworth seven mentions, only two of which are sustained. Not only do these two overlap, but they concern her tributes to Brancusi which, Read tells us, 'must be quoted if only because it reveals history at the moment of its making' (p. 94). The history to which he refers is, in this account, being witnessed, not made, by Hepworth.

46 Battersby was referring in an article in the generalist magazine *Everywoman* to the 'band of mid-century males' like Picasso, Jackson Pollock, Norman Mailer, Henry Miller who postured against the earlier idea of genius as a feminine male. Genius, their stance insists, requires balls. See also her more serious book BATTERSBY, CHRISTINE (1989) *Gender and Genius: Towards a Feminist Aesthetics* (London, The Women's Press).

47 Hepworth (n. 4), p. 356.

48 SPIVAK, GAYATRI (1989) 'Feminism and Deconstruction, Again', in: BRENNAN, T. (Ed) *Between Feminism and Psychoanalysis* (London, Routledge).

49 See for example Roberts on Rasheed Araeen. ROBERTS, JOHN (1987) 'Postmodernism and the Critique of Ethnicity', in: *From Modernism to Postmodernism. Rasheed Araeen. A Retrospective: 1959–1987* (Birmingham, Ikon Gallery). I am grateful to Sarah Patel for drawing my attention to this piece and to other British Asian debates.

50 Curtis, in: Curtis and Wilkinson (n. 3), p. 11.

51 *Ibid.*, p. 28.

52 'In the 1920s some writers on modern art sought to make a connection with cultures untainted by the European post-Renaissance tradition . . . Nicholson said [this] was part of a search to go back to something with solid foundations at a time of economic and political turmoil in the aftermath of the First World War. "One was wanting to get right back to the beginning and then take one step forward at a time on a firm basis".' TOOBY, MICHAEL (1993) *The Tate St Ives: An Illustrated Companion* (London, Tate Gallery Publications), p. 21.

53 HEPWORTH, BARBARA (1932) *Interview in The Studio*, reproduced in Hepworth (n. 4), p. 27.

54 SPIVAK, GAYATRI (1990) *The Post-Colonial Critic* (London and New York, Routledge & Kegan Paul), pp. 52–53.

55 *Ibid.*, p. 53.

56 Tooby (n. 52), p. 28.

57 See the reviews in *The Times Higher Education Supplement*, 11 March 1994, p. 18, of recent developments in geopolitics. Dennis Cosgrove points out how nature and landscape function as signifiers in European cultures and national identities.

58 Damisch discusses the historical role of the museum and points out its contribution to the establishment of an hierarchisation of difference, from the regional to the global. DAMISCH, HUBERT (1989) 'Le Musée à l'Heure de sa Disponibilité technique', in: *L'Art Contemporain et le Musée*, special edition of *Les Cahiers du Musée National de l'Art Moderne* (Paris, Centre Georges Pompidou), pp. 25–26.

ALEX POTTS

Carving and the Engendering of Sculpture: Adrian Stokes on Barbara Hepworth

The essay on Barbara Hepworth that Adrian Stokes published in *The Spectator* in November 1933 [1] is a somewhat disturbed and incoherent piece of writing, but the more interesting precisely for this. The force of his exceptionally eloquent encounter with the highly charged work Hepworth produced in the early 1930s [2] comes from the insistent contradictions it keeps throwing up. Stokes was fascinated, one might even say lured, by Hepworth's work, but he could not get a grip on his response to it. It was not that it challenged the new sculptural aesthetic he was developing at the time, and which he elaborated in his book *Stones of Rimini* published the following year [3]. Far from it. The problem was that Hepworth's small stone figures resonated so vividly for him. Here was a modern sculpture that seemed literally to embody his ideal of a carving aesthetic. But it did not do so quite on his terms. The incoherencies openly exposed in his writing indicate that at some level he recognised this to be the case. Momentarily he seems to have yielded to unnegotiable tensions surfacing in his response to Hepworth's work that he was better able to mediate in his more considered historical and theoretical writings. These included not only *Stones of Rimini*, but another publication on Italian Renaissance stone work that had just appeared the previous year, *The Quattro Cento*.

One of the problems for Stokes was the very literalness of Hepworth's apparent realisation of his carving ideal. What he meant by carving was not so much the actual sculpting activity as an approach to making art opposed to the all-pervasive subjectivism of modern culture that he associated with modelling. Carving for him represented an objective approach where the artist did not just mould matter to a desired form, but instead allowed the material qualities of the object being fashioned to play a determining role. Sculptural metaphor functioned to give substance and concreteness to this aesthetic ideal. But the carving activity Stokes had in mind was one that could most readily be assimilated to painting, namely relief carving. Indeed carving for him involved an enlivening of surface that was different in kind from the plastic activity of fashioning free-standing solid shapes in blocks of matter [4]. The latter process, even when imagined as the carving away of a block to reveal the form the artist had imagined within it, as in traditional conceptions of Michelangelo's sculptural practice, was for him in essence a modelling activity, the imposing of a subjectively imagined shape or form on the material to hand [5]. The work was not generated, as with carving, through a give and take between the artist's projective phantasy and the objectively given surface s/he was working over.

In his pronouncements on the fate of the carving ideal he saw embodied in certain masterpieces of stone architecture and relief carving of fifteenth-century Italy, Stokes envisaged its possible return within modern culture as metaphor rather than palpable reality. The carving ideal was being reactivated, according to him, in the virtual spaces of modern painting, not in the literally carved objects of modern sculpture. When he wrote about the return of a true carving ideal in his essay on Henry Moore, published at the same time as the one on Hepworth, it was not modern sculpture he had in mind but modern painting:

> . . . it was a carving approach to the canvas that underlay the modern movement in painting. The sculptors, though they have concentrated upon actual carving almost exclusively, have shown a far less pure carving conception in their work: for they have sought to make of the block something as simple and integral as a lump of clay: possibly because natural stone is losing its use and importance . . . even stone can now be manufactured (we are overwhelmed by moulding, manufacture). [6]

The works by Moore he singled out were those in concrete, for Stokes the material *par excellence* of a modern plastic imagination that was indifferent to the distinctive substance of the materials it used to realise its conceptions. When he defined the essence of Moore's work, he stressed 'how intense has been the plastic aim behind his conception of carving'.

It is important to realise that this marginalising of the literal sculptural object in favour of the ostensiveness of painting did not make Stokes an old fogy but, on the contrary, very much put him in the mainstream of modernist visual aesthetics. He shared with the high modernists a privileging of optical effect over palpable objecthood. His conception of the visual essence of visual art—form realised in space and apprehended instantaneously—had a lot in common with the formal aesthetics of Clement Greenberg and Michael Fried [7].

Like Fried, Stokes located the basis of a fully realised experience of a work in a sense of spatiality that was purely optical and existed outside time. He explicitly contrasted this instantaneous visual experience of space with a more impure plastic one involving the changing tactile exploration of an object or environment in real space and time. As he put it in *The Quattro Cento*:

> I consider that in painting and architecture, and even in sculpture, the appeal should be first and primarily to the eye; that is to say the appeal should be such that the eye, with the assistance of previous tactile experience in materials and textures, would be able largely to synthesise the successive element in the tactile part of the appeal, and cause it to be something immediate as vision itself. [8]

Even when he was talking about sculpture, carving for him was to be imagined, not as a cutting away of the block to fashion a free-standing object, but as a subtle modulating of its surface. For Stokes the virtual materialisation of space on the surface of Cézanne's paintings constituted the most compelling realisation of the carving ideal in modern times—just as Cubist painting functioned as a paradigm for the artistic embodiment of form in the high modernist aesthetic. The effect of objectivity achieved in both cases was quite different in kind from the literal three-dimensionality and presence that distinguish free-standing sculpture. Stokes' idea of carving thus can hardly be identified in any straightforward way with the cult of direct carving and truth to materials that dominated modern sculpture during the late 1920s and early 1930s [9].

What happened when Stokes responded to Hepworth's 'unstressed rounded [stone] shapes', then, inevitably involved contradictions even at a purely formal level. What he had to say was more telling than anything in his conceptually more coherent representation of Henry Moore as yet another powerful modern modeller. It was not Moore's work but Hepworth's which presented itself to him as that impossible ideal—a modern realisation of true carving in sculpture. Momentarily seduced into taking his sculptural metaphor at face value, he was forced to confront contradictions he evaded elsewhere. The issue, then, was not in any way the vulnerability of Hepworth's small-scale stone carvings in the face of his masculine phantasising; on the contrary, these works' powerful wooing of and resistance to the phantasies embodied in his carving ideal exposed the precariousness of this ideal.

Almost at the very outset of Stokes' essay on Hepworth, an unmediated tension opens up between the femininity of 'unstressed rounded shapes', of a surface seemingly fashioned through caressing and rubbing, rather than cutting, and a very masculine 'steadiness of shape' and 'solid and vital repose'. There follows an even more vivid disparity in Stokes' characterisation of the artist's engagement with her materials. On the one hand she is the 'true [masculine] carver [who] attacks his material so that it may bear a vivifying or plastic fruit'. On the other hand, she also 'woos the block'. One of the difficulties is the assumption Stokes keeps hidden here that for him a convincing free standing modern sculpture is not a carving of surface, but a plastic creation in which the artist imposes shape on a lump of matter [10].

But there is a further rather more intractable issue involved, namely that Stokes was trying to imagine carving as somehow encompassing both a non-aggressive feminised interaction of the artist with his or her materials, and a masculine assertiveness and mastery. The relation between viewer and work, or between artist and object, envisioned in his notion of carving is both a kind of symbiosis and a confrontation. At the same time the object presents itself either as willing to yield and be penetrated or as hard and resistant. At one moment Stokes suggests that Hepworth's work is limited by a lingering over the more feminine aspect of carving. Not only she, but the other 'advanced carvers' of the time who were men, all 'approach the block with such gravity that more ebullient, more masculine, forms evade them'.

If we wished to make Stokes' figure of speech more literal, we could say that there is here a wooing of the block that stops short of impregnation. But set against this is Stokes' statement that Hepworth's distinctive—and hence at some level distinctively feminine—intervention is to create mother and child groups of 'surer poignancy', whose 'shapes of stone' get beyond this 'trifle too stolid a feeling in our modern carving' to something more 'ebullient', something 'spectacular' not achieved by her male contemporaries. Yet not quite, or not in any consistent way. For Stokes qualifies:

> A man would have made the group more pointed: no man could have treated this composition with such pure complacence.

The result is a tangle that Stokes could not undo. He then literally gives up.

> Her carving is astonishingly mature [he concludes] whereas the appreciation and critique of sculpture remains fatuous.

There is undoubtedly a self-awareness here regarding the fix he got himself into trying to make sense of Hepworth's work. But the contradictions involved were for him pretty significant, not fatuous. They were rooted in powerful sexual tensions inherent in his larger theory of carving, that this particular woman's vital and intriguing and also perplexing and awkward mother and child groups momentarily brought into focus.

Stokes' conception of artistic creativity, whether modelling or carving, envisaged a masculine force activating female matter so as to give birth to a new male progeny. The carver might begin the process by wooing the female block. But he still had to effect a radical, one might say violent, transfiguration that involved no less a rupture than the work of the modeller who brazenly made the material on which he worked submit to his will. Female matter had to be transformed into a masculine object, exuding not just vitality but a hard objectivity. There was in all this a lingering contradiction that Stokes was not in a position to recognise—namely that his conception of carving effectively presented the objectivity of the finished work as anchored in the solid material substance of the maternal block.

The gendering of Stokes' visual aesthetic emerges very nakedly in the following passage of *The Quattro Cento*. Here, where the residues of his youthful commitment to Ezra Pound's hard edged and vitalist conception of artistic creativity are still very overt [11], Stokes has not yet distinguished carving from modelling. The privileged place of the male figure in the two great schools of sculpture in Western art, that of classical Greece and the Italian Quattrocento, he explains:

> . . . shows a predominance in sculptural phantasy of a feeling for spatial value alone [which later became for him the optical essence of carving], of a feeling for mass, for material as being the fruitful female block that will

> give birth to the most active shapes full of prolific sap. From the stone comes a new, near fearless, energy. [Note how it comes from the stone, it is not just implanted there.] And to push this phantasy further, since the architect's building is female, set on the earth like Giorgione's woman by the running stream, the sculptor's attendant statuary are her lovers and sons rather than her daughters or a mere projection of herself. But only sculptors with a passion for the material, stone, will keep so close to this primary phantasy. [12]

There is a level at which Hepworth's early mother and child groups might almost seem to embody Stokes' sexualised mythology of sculptural creativity. But for this to work, Hepworth had to become the 'male' artist who made the mother block give birth to the vital solid forms of the son. To give Stokes his due, he knew this could not quite be. The phantasy might seem suspect if taken too much at face value. The mythology of generation it evoked was a decidedly archaic one that had dominated pre-Enlightenment views of human anatomy, one in which the woman's body was conceived as a negative echo of the man's and functioned largely as passive receptacle for his procreative power [13]. Stokes, who at this point was entering analysis with Melanie Klein, was enough in tune with feminine counter-narratives to such macho phantasy not to push it too far. Indeed his conception of carving, once distinguished systematically from modelling where the artist's will simply forced inert material into the mould it desired, introduced a feminine moment, a mothering, giving birth, into the story of artistic creation.

Modelling for Stokes came to be associated with naked sexual domination, and represented an act of violation in a double sense—firstly through the idea of the artist forcing his conception onto his materials without any intermediate moment of wooing, and secondly through the violence of the associated image of giving birth. As Stokes imagined it, the modeller wresting the figure he had conceived from within the block performed an act analogous to ripping the child from the womb [14]. The creative act he envisaged with carving, by contrast, was a gradual process more akin to natural childbirth that mitigated any suggestions of a violent cutting away of the finished shape from its containing block [15]. But even in this case, there had to be a moment of rupture when the sculpture suddenly came alive through a sharpening of form and polishing of stone in the very final stages of creation, that Stokes likened to 'slapping the new-born infant to make it breathe'. A sudden, and in some way violent, transfiguration of the female block had to occur for it to give forth its male progeny.

In only one of the Hepworth mother and child groups which might have attracted Stokes' attention is any marked distinction evident between a firm round male child stone and a more amorphous enveloping mother block—*Figure (Mother and Child)*, 1933 (Fig. 8) [16]. In the other groups, nothing compels us to envisage the child as anything but of the same substance, in other words of the same gender, as the mother. Stokes simultaneously recognised and disavowed this. The

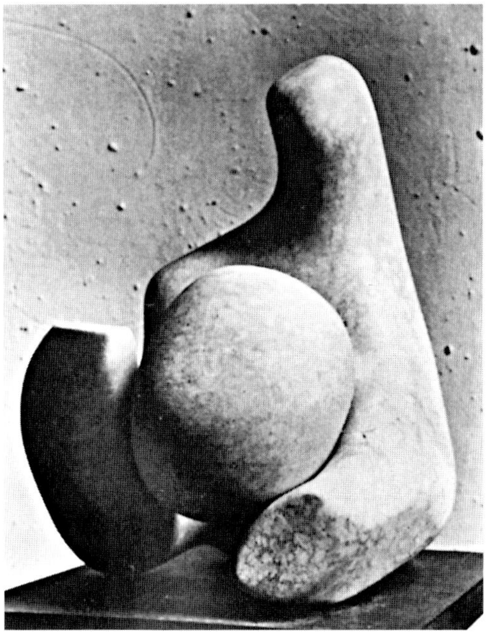

Fig. 8 BARBARA HEPWORTH, *Figure (Mother and Child)*, 1933 © Trustees of the Barbara Hepworth Estate/Tate Gallery London (published in Curtis and Wilkinson, *Barbara Hepworth: A Retrospective*, London, Tate Gallery Publications, 1994)

problems involved are compounded by the fact that in sculpted images of mother and child such as these, the mother has just as much to be the artist's creation as the child, has the same claim to being an 'ebullient masculine' form emerging from the 'female' block. If anything, in Hepworth's mother and child groups, the mother block is the more solid and powerful form, giving anchorage to the child.

What emerges most insistently in Stokes' response to Hepworth's mother and child groups, however, is the 'poignancy' he detects in them. He may describe the child stone as being 'of the block yet separate, beyond the womb yet of her being', but it is the sense of separation that for him dominates, the 'poignancy' of two discrete forms that cannot be recombined as one. Stokes' fixation on the separation between mother and child is quite in tune with any credible reading we might offer of the conception of these works. In some, for example *Mother and Child*, 1934 (Fig. 9), the mother may seem warmly to embrace, or threaten to envelop, the child, depending upon how we wish to load the implied mother-infant bond. At the same time, there is the insistent and irreparably literal fact of the child stone's autonomous identity—it can never be reintegrated with the mother, except in the viewer's phantasy. In one group at least, the grey alabaster *Mother and Child*, 1934 (Fig. 10), in the Tate, there is even a certain suggestion of a pulling away of one form from the other.

In any account of how an artist transforms an inert and indifferent lump of matter into an object that carries a psychic charge, there is going to be a moment of rupture, a moment of enforced splitting, even if, as with the readymade, no physical process of shaping has taken place. In the phantasies elicited by such a

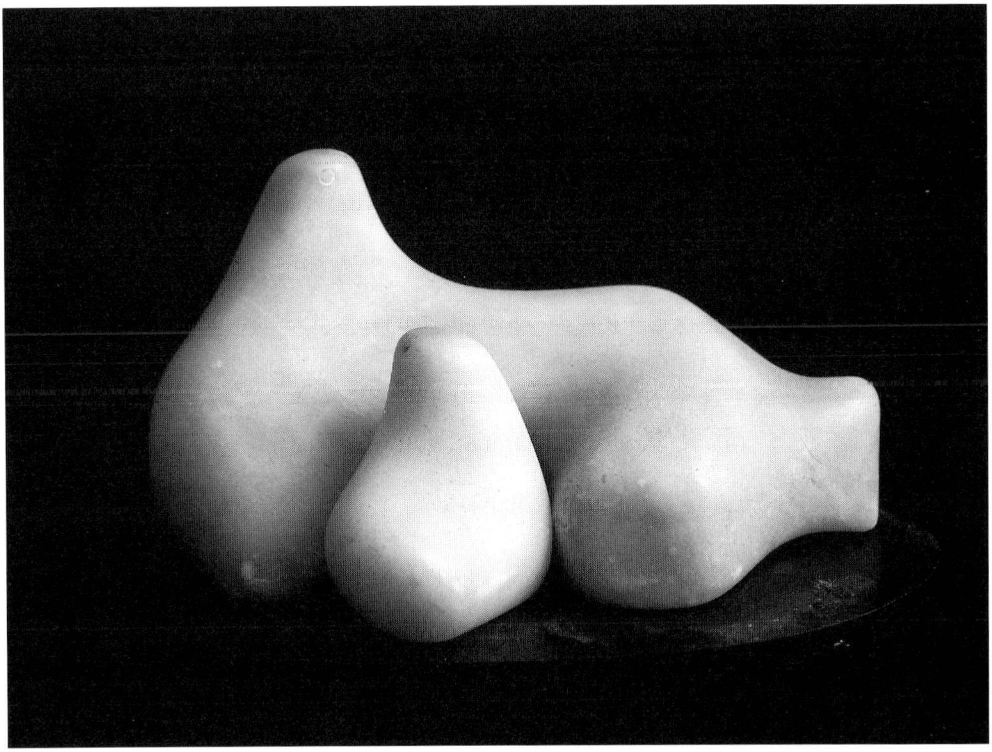

Fig. 9 BARBARA HEPWORTH, *Mother and Child*, 1934 © Trustees of the Barbara Hepworth Estate

splitting, ideas of artistic creativity inevitably mingle with ideas of giving birth and engendering. This psychic and ideological minefield was one Stokes wished simultaneously to explore and to render less explosive through his theory of carving, but he could never render it safe.

Stokes was seeking a model for imagining the making of a work of art where the artist's engagement with concrete objects in the external world achieved a kind of transfiguration without conflict and violent resistance, and without any too-overt dominating and subjugating. But he would not do without the idea of some radical alteration being forced by the artist onto his or her materials. A conventional 'male' power politics of subject–object relations could not be entirely annulled without, in his view, annulling the life of the work of art, any more than could the poignancy of an ineradicable alienation between creator and object. The phantasy of overcoming this ideologically and psychically loaded divide between creative subject and created object—permeating, as Stokes himself insisted, the whole fabric of experience in the modern world—could not be evaded in art [17]. A true symbiosis between the objective autonomy of the artwork and the subjectivity of the creating artist was an impossibility—made all the more evident by the free-standing sculpture's literal identity as isolated thing confronting the artist.

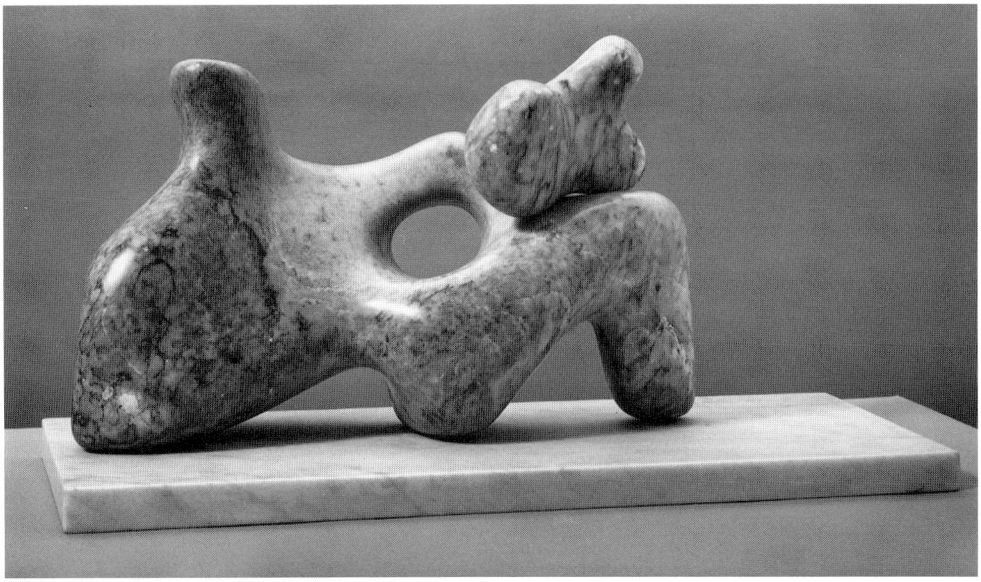

Fig. 10 BARBARA HEPWORTH, *Mother and Child*, 1934 © Trustees of the Barbara Hepworth Estate/Tate Gallery London

The impossibility was not just the problem of a narrowly male phantasy. I should like to close by citing one of those rare moments in Hepworth's writing where the mythology of effortlessly free creativity falters to reveal something of the irreducible conflict which fuels her more compelling work [18]. The passage in question refers to her experiences drawing in an operating theatre in the late 1940s (Fig. 37–41):

> A particularly beautiful example of the difference between physical and spiritual animation can be observed in a delicate operation on the human hand by a great surgeon. The anatomy of the unconscious hand exposed and manipulated by the conscious hand with the scalpel, expresses vividly the creative inspiration of superb co-ordination between hand and spirit in contrast to the unconscious mechanism. The basic tenderness of the large and small form, or mother and child, proclaims a rhythm of composition which is in contrast to the slapping and pushing of tired mother and frustrated child through faults in our way of living and unresolved social conditions. [19]

But the slapping and pushing are an unavoidable and ever-recurring reality, no less than the violence of the surgeon's making an incision into the body and sewing it up again—or the cutting and carving and piercing and stringing together of blocks of stone and wood in which Hepworth apparently so delighted [20].

NOTES AND REFERENCES

1 Stokes' essay on Barbara Hepworth is reprinted in STOKES, ADRIAN (1978) *The Critical Writings of Adrian Stokes* Vol. II (London, Thames & Hudson), pp. 309–10. Unless indicated otherwise, this is the source for the commentary by Stokes quoted here.

2 I was excited to find when I gave this paper at the Hepworth conference in 1994 that issues with which I had been trying to grapple in Stokes' text had such clear affinities with those which Anne Wagner was exploring in her particularly fine and compelling interpretation of Hepworth's sculpture of the early 1930s ('Miss Hepworth's Stone *is* a Mother', pp. 53–74, this volume). Her discussion makes an entirely convincing case for the unusual density and charge of Hepworth's mother and child groups from the period. For my part, this helped give substance to the conviction that the conjuncture between these particular sculptures by Hepworth and Stokes' complexly invested aesthetic of carving had sparked off something unusually significant.

3 STOKES, ADRIAN (1934, 1969) *Stones of Rimini* (London, Faber; New York, Schoken), particularly pp. 109–26.

4 See for example *ibid.*, p. 153. All the examples of carving he analyses in this book are relief carvings. Cf. the passage in his (1937) 'Colour and Form': 'Carving creates a face for the stone, as agriculture for the earth, and as man for woman . . .'. *Critical Writings* (n. 1) Vol. II, p. 22.

5 *Stones of Rimini* (n. 3), pp. 108, 119–20. See also STOKES, ADRIAN (1932, 1968) *The Quattro Cento: a Different Conception of the Italian Renaissance* (London, Faber; New York, Schoken), pp. 159–64.

6 *Critical Writings* (n. 1) Vol. II, p. 312. Compare also *Stones of Rimini* (n. 3), p. 166. Of the contemporary art on which Stokes commented, it was not sculpture but Ben Nicholson's painting that exemplified most unproblematically his aesthetic of carving. *Critical Writings* (n. 1) Vol. II, p. 306.

7 The painterly bias of Greenberg's view of sculpture is very evident in the revised version of GREENBERG, CLEMENT (1949) 'The New Sculpture'—reproduced in: GREENBERG, CLEMENT (1986) *Collected Writings* Vol. II (Chicago, University of Chicago Press), pp. 314–19—that Greenberg prepared for (1961) *Art and Culture* (Boston, Beacon Press); see particularly p. 144. See also Fried's now classic response to the challenge offered to the optical purism of his modernist aesthetic through the focus on the literal three dimensional object in Minimalist art: FRIED, MICHAEL (1967) 'Art and Objecthood', *Artforum*, June, reprinted in BATTCOCK, G. (Ed) (1968) *Minimal Art* (New York, Dutton), pp. 116–47.

8 *The Quattro Cento* (n. 5), pp. 28–29, note 1. See also *Stones of Rimini* (n. 3), pp. 119–20. Compare Fried's strikingly similar account of an optical experience of artistic form that can suspend time in 'Art and Objecthood' (n. 7), pp. 145–46.

9 See the discussion in CURTIS, PENELOPE (1994) 'Barbara Hepworth and the Avant-Garde of the 1920s', in: CURTIS, PENELOPE and WILKINSON, ALAN G. (1994) *Barbara Hepworth: a Retrospective* (Liverpool, Tate Gallery Liverpool), p. 14.

10 See n. 4.

11 The significant role played by Pound's aesthetic in Stokes' early thinking about art was brought home to me in a fascinating talk given by Richard Read, 'Art Criticism versus Poetry: Pater and the Anti-Poundian Modernism of Stokes' Pisanello', at a conference on Walter Pater held at the University of Kent at Canterbury in 1994. Read revealed that the most overtly Poundian section of Stokes' early essay on Pisanello, dating from 1930, had been omitted (or censored?) in the version published in the standard modern edition of his *Critical Writings* (n. 1).

12 *The Quattro Cento* (n. 5), p. 132. Compare also *Stones of Rimini* (n. 3) p. 110. On the latter passage see Anne Wagner's essay in this volume 'Miss Hepworth's Stone *Is* a Mother', p. xx, note 8.

13 See LACQUEUR, T. (1990) *Making Sex: Body and Gender from the Greeks to Freud* (Cambridge, Mass. and London, Harvard University Press), particularly pp. 58 ff.

14 *Stones of Rimini* (n. 3), p. 126.

15 *Ibid.*, p. 112.

16 This sculpture, which was shown in the Hepworth exhibition at the Lefevre Galleries that Stokes was reviewing, seems to have played a key role in Stokes' view of her work.

17 In his earlier writing, Stokes discussed the sense of alienation between inner self and outer object in the modern world primarily in terms of an indifference to the concrete materiality of things produced by industrialised manufacture. *Stones of Rimini* (n. 3), pp. 163ff. In his later writing he took a broader, more richly articulated sociological view of the phenomenon. See for example section 7 of STOKES, ADRIAN (1951) *Smooth and Rough* (London, Faber) reproduced in: *Critical Writings* (n. 1) Vol. II, pp. 248ff. See also Part II of STOKES, ADRIAN (1965, 1966) *The Invitation in Art* (London, Tavistock; New York, Chilmark Press), reproduced in: *Critical Writings* (n. 1) Vol. II, pp. 280ff.

18 There is one interesting passage where Hepworth does talk explicitly about having to negotiate an hiatus between inner phantasy and outer object, precisely the syndrome Stokes was seeking to resolve with his notion of carving: 'I used colour and string in many of the carvings of this time [1940s]. The colour in the concavities plunged me into the depth of water, caves, or shadows deeper than the carved concavities themselves. The strings were the tension I felt between myself and the sea, the wind or the hills'. See the section relating to the years 1939–46 in: (1952) *Barbara Hepworth: Carvings and Drawings* (London, Lund Humphries).

19 1946–49 section, *Carvings and Drawings* (n. 18).

20 Consider for example the following comments by Hepworth, all quoted in Curtis and Wilkinson (n. 9): 'I had felt the most intense pleasure in piercing the stone' (p. 37); 'The carving and piercing of such a form seem to open up an infinite variety of continuous curves in the third dimension changing in accordance with the degree of penetration of the material' (p. 82); 'I like to carve the hard surface' (p. 102); and, to Ben Nicholson, 'You never liked arrogant sculpture nor fierce forms—but I do' (p. 138).

ANNE M. WAGNER

'Miss Hepworth's Stone *Is* a Mother'

Barbara Hepworth began her autobiography where most autobiographies start, at the beginning. 'I was the firstborn', she wrote. As a statement of origins the phrase seems unexceptionable. it seeks no controversy, and brooks no denial. Yet however declarative, it is also clearly incomplete; it is only the beginning of the story, after all. I shall let Alan Bowness, writing in an introductory note to the most recent edition of the autobiography (he dated his contribution 'July 1993'), pick up the thread:

> Barbara began, but found she had neither time nor inclination to write a long text, and so the concept of a pictorial autobiography was born. She looked out some family photographs, but this made the book too personal for her tastes, so she asked me to help. I added the art historical material, and this helped to give the book a more rounded character—more work than life, which was what she wanted. [1]

If 'more work than life' *is* what Hepworth wanted, she has got it, yet Hepworth studies have paid a certain price for that art-historical rounding out. Let me try to explain what I mean. The *Pictorial Autobiography* does make a special, perhaps unprecedented mix between two modes. Photographs of the artist and her dogs, cats, babies, studios, spouses and friends, are there flanked by sculptures and texts and documents, with that second set of images—the sculptures and texts and documents—acting as a kind of art-historical leaven: they are the ingredients of a 'profession', as supplied by a professional, after all. And while there are connections among the various images, the looseness—the banality—of the main organising principle seems to function to keep the personal rather firmly under control. It is never more than an image, a way-station on a smooth route from life to work. On one page is the artist with her tools, on the next a photograph of a sculpture: then that same photograph is shown being put to prompt use, illustrating the pages of a book or catalogue. Thus the sculptor's life and work enter 'art' and 'art history'; it happened, we learn, with very little fuss or ado.

The logic of these illustrations seems, in its elisions, much like that of the too-brief written text. Take for example these phrases: 'This was a wonderfully happy time. My son Paul was born, and, with him in his cot, or on a rug at my feet, my carving developed and strengthened' [2]. What could be simpler? Read next to the photographs these phrases flank—illustrations entitled 'With son Paul' and

'Carving of *Infant*, Burmese wood'—they direct us to a happy and inevitable conclusion. The transition from the 'life' to 'art' domain is made easy through omission, and again the illustrations pick up the slack. We see that the infant Paul, whether tucked up in his crib or wriggling on his rug, was not just a talisman or tutelary deity; he was a subject for art, from which a small deity might be fashioned, fat legs, round head and all (Fig. 11). But the context also insists that what the work stands for or means concerns only its role in the 'development' and 'strengthening' of Hepworth's art.

The odd and remarkable thing about Hepworth's reputation is that the *Pictorial Autobiography*, far from sparking speculation about the personal resonances of her art, seems to have forestalled it. This is 'self-curating' (as it is called nowadays) at its most efficient—though 'assisted self-curating' might actually be the better term. We continue to get 'more works than life': the two seem mostly to cohabit in criticism in a familiar, even conventional way. Stylistic changes and influences still sit cheek by jowl with the other circumstances of Hepworth's life, their deeper connections, like those among the photographs, still largely unexplored. The result is that while we may know something about the artist's trips to Happisburgh and Paris and St. Rémy, or recognise that there is a question as to who first pierced the sculptural block, we know much less about what these events have to do with what or how her art might be said to mean in other than formal or narrowly historical terms.

In the light of this lacuna, it seems ironic that the *Autobiography* reprints, as visual objects in their own right, two texts—the only texts—which speak with some authority to suggest that her sculpture—or some of it, at least—can be seen to have meanings rather different in kind and scope. One is the brief foreword written by Herbert Read for the catalogue of her 1932 show at Arthur Tooth's. The other, a year later, was Adrian Stokes' review of her Lefevre Gallery show—certainly the most notorious review he wrote [3].

Maybe once turned into pictures, Read's and Stokes' words seemed no longer to signify. But if they were to be given some credit as texts, I think that the balance between work and life would have to be totted up anew. While nothing could wipe clean our sense of these authors' real interest in Hepworth's formal revisions of her art—their conviction that her work demonstrated, to borrow Read's terms, the 'two essential principles of sculpture: the organisation of masses in expressive relation and the revelation of the potentialities of the sculptured material' [4]—interest or conviction alone is not a guarantee of particularly original thought. As Penelope Curtis has shown, this was the contemporary critic's catechism where new sculpture was concerned [5]. So let me cite Read a bit further to find a more venturesome thesis:

> Beyond these essentials [he continued] so appealing to our immediate senses, there is a fantasy which should awaken subtler delight in the imagination and memory.

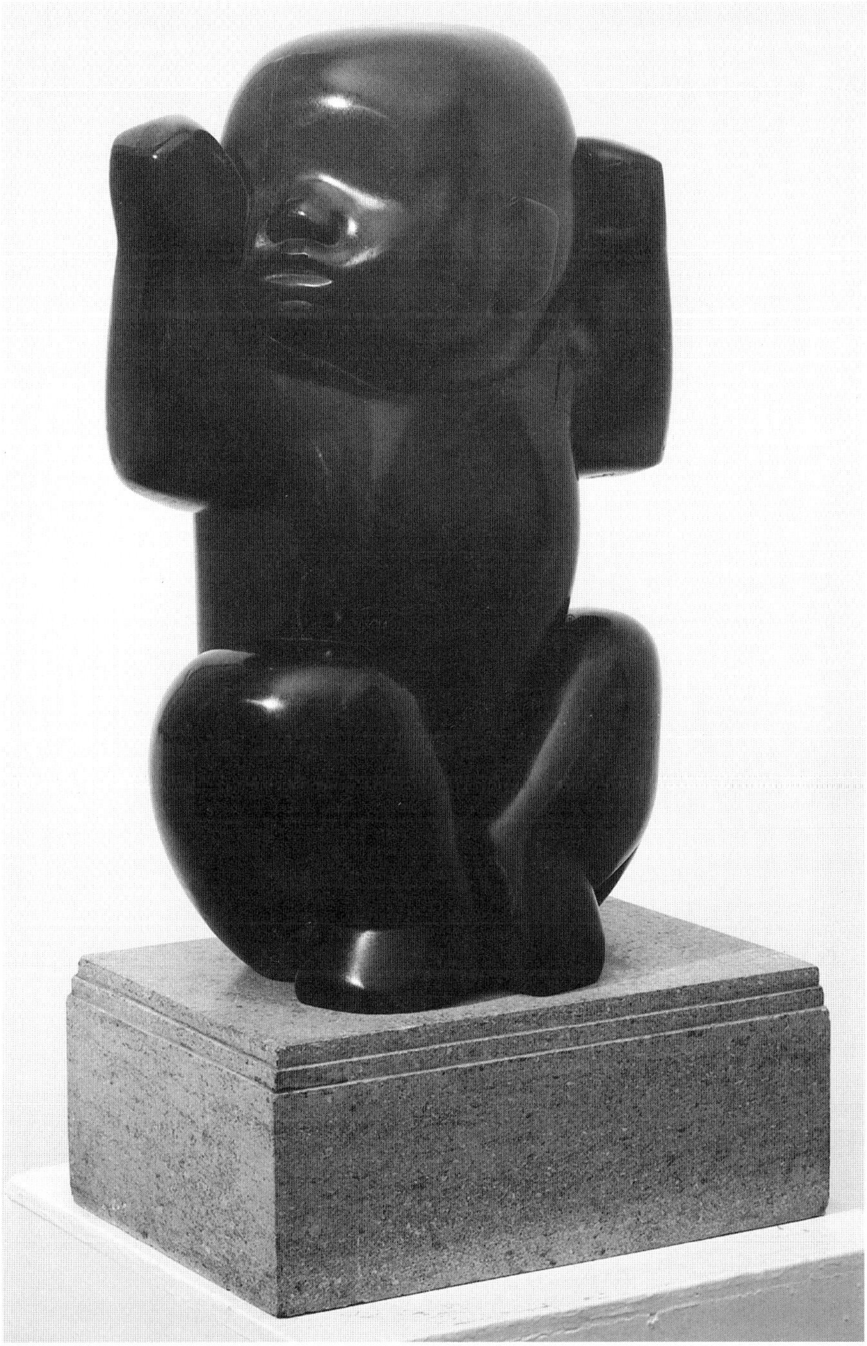

Fig. 11 BARBARA HEPWORTH, *Infant*, 1929 © Trustees of the Barbara Hepworth Estate/Tate Gallery London

'Should' here seems the operative word, for it quickly occurred to Read that the offer of fantasy might well not arouse in readers the anticipated sensation of 'subtler delight'. So he elaborated, bent on reassurance, though not quite succeeding:

> . . . that some of Miss Hepworth's creative conceptions should recede into a symbolic world of abstractions is not a feature that should deter the disinterested spectator; art is a servant (and a redeeming sanction) in any sphere of the human spirit—and not least in this marginal world between consciousness and unconsciousness from which emerge strange images of universal appeal. [6]

Could the spectator, however impartial, feel much bucked up? We read a Read who betrays odd uncertainty about aspects of this art: above all about the way it seems to slip away from its vaunted immediacy—from sculptural materiality and the senses—to enter an elusive nether world of abstraction and symbol, a realm somewhere on the psychic margin. The viewer may well be deterred, not least because Read's assertion of art's positive role in all this—the willingness and ability of its strange images to provide redemption and universal appeal—has to be taken mainly on faith.

Remember that Read is writing about abstract art, but not in the abstract. He is aiming to address the workings of Hepworth's art in 1932—he was speaking of works like *Profile* and *Two Heads*, two works carved that year and visible in the Arthur Tooth show. As the author of a 1925 essay, 'Psychoanalysis and the Critic', he knew what his terms meant (by then he had read Freud, Jung and Adler, as well as Ernest Jones) and cannot have used them casually [7]. On the contrary, Read's usage is more purposeful than casual: he had long since put his faith in the sub-Freudian notion that, as he put it:

> . . . the artist is initially by tendency a neurotic, but . . . in becoming an artist he as it were escapes the ultimate fate of his tendency and through art finds his way back to reality. [8]

To grasp neurosis, Read followed an Adlerian adage:

> . . . every neurosis can be understood as an attempt to free oneself from a feeling of inferiority in order to gain a feeling of superiority. [9]

Such hybrid views became the main tenets of Read's notion of art as social therapy—meanwhile a catalogue puff was hardly the appropriate place for real analysis of Hepworth's neuroses, the 'marginal symbolic' world from which art comes: surely this is one reason he made do with suggestions and generalities.

That another reading of Hepworth's work was once possible, however briefly, is further attested by the response of Adrian Stokes. 'Miss Hepworth's Carving' is still the single most suggestive piece of writing on Hepworth—so much so that I cannot hope to do it justice here [10]. I cannot hope, for a start, to make it emerge with much particularity as a piece of writing by Stokes—that is, with at least some of its protocols and commitments having been supplied by his emerging critical project, rather than by Hepworth's art. By this date Stokes had already begun, as he said, 'to write of stone', to 'exhibit stones the opposite of barren' and to find in carving the great organising principle of his aesthetic, to which modelling, its counterpart and sometime antithesis, would only ever play a subordinated role [11]. Carving would be paired in his mind with Melanie Klein's notion of the depressive position, in which the ego achieves a certain measure of integration. By these lights the carver, to use Richard Wollheim's words:

> . . . in respecting the integrity and the separateness of the stone, celebrates the whole object with which he characteristically enters into relation and also the integrated ego that he projects. [12]

In 1933, however, Stokes was still in the early stages of his analysis with Klein, while Klein's own work had thus far concentrated on mapping the stages in the infant's fraught incorporation of a relationship to the maternal body, first as part, then as whole. By 1933, in other words, aesthetics and psychoanalysis had not yet been—could not have been—so sweepingly synthesised. Both are present in Stokes' essay, to be sure; it is just that they do not yet make a consistent theoretical whole.

To address Hepworth's carving in the singular—carving, not carvings—made of the term the principle of her art; it meant, for a start, that Stokes speaks only of 'stone shapes', ignoring her work in wood. And in those shapes he senses a 'vast certainty' which stems from their evident belonging to a particular substance—they are stone–shapes, once again. In the rubbed form, however thinned and flattened, a deep and incontrovertible roundness can still be seen: an echo of nature, it is the note which, paradoxically, the subtractive work of the carver is able to sound. Carving, in other words, engineers through its absences a contradictory return to natural form and value, and embodies them to and for vision. 'The stone', Stokes wrote, 'through the medium of the figure, has come to life' [13].

Life and birth and infancy were for Stokes 'the underlying subject' of Hepworth's art in 1933, as indeed they were, to his mind, where all great carving was concerned. In the case of Hepworth, he was clearly thinking most of the lost alabaster *Figure (Mother and Child)* (Fig. 8). And I believe he was also thinking of Klein, whose work on the maternal imaginary had already been begun.

> This is the child which the mother owns with all her weight, a child that is of the block yet separate, beyond her womb yet of her being . . . It is not a matter of a mother and child group represented in stone. Miss Hepworth's stone *is* a mother, her huge pebble its child. A man would have made the group more pointed: no man could have treated this composition with such a pure complacence.

Stokes' interpretative conviction is absolute and specialised; I say this in the knowledge that the reviews in *The Listener* and *The New Statesman and Nation* saw fit to mention neither mother nor child—even though in the former the self-same group is actually reproduced [14].

I do not think that either Hepworth or Stokes would have been long detained by the problems that arise when his description is backed up against another of his contemporary accounts of the carver, the block, and their progeny. For perhaps it now goes without saying that carving and modelling are gendered, in Stokes' lexicon, so as to echo another, more familiar order. 'Man, in his male aspect', Stokes wrote in *The Stones of Rimini* (in press in November 1933, the book appeared in January 1934):

> . . . is the cultivator or carver of woman who, in her female aspect, moulds her products as does the earth. We see both the ultimate distinction and the necessary interaction between carving and moulding in their widest senses. The stone block is female, the plastic figures that emerge from it are her children, the proof of the carver's love for the stone. [15]

The problem arises because while Hepworth was said to be a carver, she was also a woman—the risk was that she might only merit the modeller's rank [16]. Even though Hepworth herself was sure both that she carved and that she did so from a certain bodily compulsion, her unforgettable formula, 'A sculptor carves because he must', declares these convictions—and the paradox which results from their espousal [17]. Her urges as a carver could nevertheless not logically be thought to play the necessary fertilising role. Her 'love for the stone' would apparently demand parthenogenesis to get results; based on principles of similitude, rather than difference, it would be narcissistic at best. There might even be a certain auto-eroticism involved. Though not according to Hepworth, I hasten to add. When asked why she went in for direct carving rather than modelling, she replied:

> I have always preferred direct carving to modelling because I like the resistance of the hard material and feel happier working that way. Carving is more adapted to the expression of the accumulative idea of experience . . . [18]

Note that if the block is here still understood as female, then this woman's pleasure comes from working away at the resistance of a feminine-coded thing—at least I shall later argue this case.

Lodged at the interpretative heart of Stokes' essay on Hepworth are traces of this predicament concerning gender. There is the carver to account for; there is the mother; and there is the child. These are all key terms for Stokes, if in different ways. Yet used in this particular context to speak of Hepworth and her work, they are immediately and awkwardly conflated, since she herself is carver, mother, and (necessarily) child. (Remember that it is Stokes who invents the Kleinian adage 'The Infant is mother to the Man' to name the determinant continuities between adult and child [19]. We might usefully rephrase it for our purposes: 'The Infant is mother to the Woman'—and even, 'to the Mother'.) What is more, were these conflations to be pursued and understood as having an objective, material site, they would overlap in (or on) Hepworth's body, since it is simultaneously that of the sculptor, the female, the mother, and the child.

I think that Stokes' essay betrays a certain anxiety about these conflations at its interpretative heart, in the kinds of assertions it uses, and in the contradictions it aims to refute. Let me give the key sentences again:

> In this case at least the abstractions employed enforce a vast certainty. It is not a matter of a mother and child group represented in stone. Miss Hepworth's stone *is* a mother, her huge pebble its child.

Is it not Stokes' language, more than Hepworth's abstraction, that is aiming to enforce certainty? That emphatic *is* ('Miss Hepworth's stone *is* a mother') insists on a literal meaning that otherwise would be hard to secure.

Miss Hepworth's stone *is* a mother. The phrase should be the equivalent to something like 'Juliet is the sun', but the insistent *is* (it is the *is* of identity) literalises the metaphor and in so doing puts the brakes on the free play of its meanings. As a result, what William Empson calls the 'pregnancy' of metaphor is terminated, and its potential circuitry of meaning effectively closed down [20].

Why? In discouraging imagination as to what the stone and mother might mean, to say nothing of what they might mean for Hepworth, Stokes seems to me to be doing nothing so much as fending off a more thoroughgoing Kleinian reading of her art. Rather like Read, he stands at the margin of interpretation, unwilling or unable to ruffle the surface of his need for 'vast certainty' and 'pure complacence' as the terms of her achievement. This was his definition of carving: he would not admit it did not really apply to Hepworth's art (at least not when its imagery is seen in a Kleinian light). Yet also like Read he knew that something else, however inadmissible, was afoot.

Might it not be salutary to take Read and Stokes seriously? To see their uncertainty and insistence as having something—however backhanded—to say about Hepworth's art? Such a resolution would have at the very least the purpose of offering an antidote to the normalising impulses which have had her life and art so firmly in their grasp.

So here is my central hypothesis. Both Stokes and Read encountered Hepworth's art at its most urgently autobiographical moment, in the early 1930s—the moment of her espousal of a special, bodily abstraction. They wrote of it, in other words, at just the juncture when its maker was carving a set of objects with quite particular weight and resonance where fantasy and symbol, maternity and infancy are concerned. Looking at these works—at their sheer formal extremity—it is safe to say that their maker seems to have laid claim to a whole spectrum of resistances, including those of the block, both identifying them, and identifying *with* them, in a notably original way.

Why should this add up to autobiography? For a start, it is claimed as such by the artist herself, written onto the surface of the stone as a telling inscription: I am speaking of Hepworth's practice, in the early 1930s, of transcribing into the stone a precisely delineated profile, a real auto-graph. This is also an art-world move, of course: an identification of her art with the painting of Picasso, and of her sculpted forms with his painted women of the late 1920s—with the 1927 *Seated Woman*, for example (Fig. 12). The analogy speaks, it would seem, to the odd disjointed ponderousness and presence which, in both cases, characterise their range of form. But it is also a usage with a source and reference that come much closer to home: Ben Nicholson had adopted the same device himself to depict Hepworth in a series of works done around 1932. In them, her profile serves as a metaphor for art. *1932 (profile-Venetian red)* (Fig. 13) is a good example: it uses both oil and pencil on canvas, but privileges the latter, taking it as the vehicle to trace her features and make their elusive contour emerge (paradoxically) as the focus of the whole. While the profiles differ from one image to the next, it is certain that Hepworth is always meant to be depicted, and love recorded; it is as if Nicholson is updating the story of Dibutades, the Corinthian maiden who invented drawing for just this purpose [21]. Moreover, in a 1932 photogram—a self-portrait in her as yet unpublished archives—Hepworth herself adopts a parallel strategy, staging an opposition between the omissions of the cloudy outlined profile and the particularity of the realist trace, the strands of her hair. Both effects were the result of a single process—she laid her head on a piece of photographic paper, then exposed it to light—but the impact of the work *as a portrait* is lodged in the profiled line.

To claim that for Hepworth carving, at least at this moment in her career, involved an act of self-inscription—an identification with the stone—is a way of beginning to think of these works as representations of female bodies—even, perhaps, as representations of a single one. That the terms of the identification are both fragile—mere traces—and in a real sense provided—or borrowed—from Picasso's art, does not undermine that claim: how else, out of what materials, we might well ask, do most self-identifications come about? Nor is it to be expected that the sign and the body marked by it necessarily cohere to form a unified whole. Hepworth's incised conventions—those provided symbols for female personhood—mostly fail to discipline the stone curves and swellings on which they sit. We read past the inscriptions to bodily meanings the profiled trace can neither contain nor obscure. And we discover that her stones are remarkable for the range and consistency of their concerns. What can be known or said of the female body exactly? For which of its real or imagined properties can a sculptural embodiment plausibly be found? To what realm of the viewer's experience or understanding should that embodiment aim to appeal? These are the kinds of questions which should accumulate around Hepworth's carvings of the early 1930s—between 1931 and 1934, she made about twenty-five in all. They are also, I submit, the kinds of questions which gave them rise.

Such a judgment needs specific interpretations to back it up. Let me provide

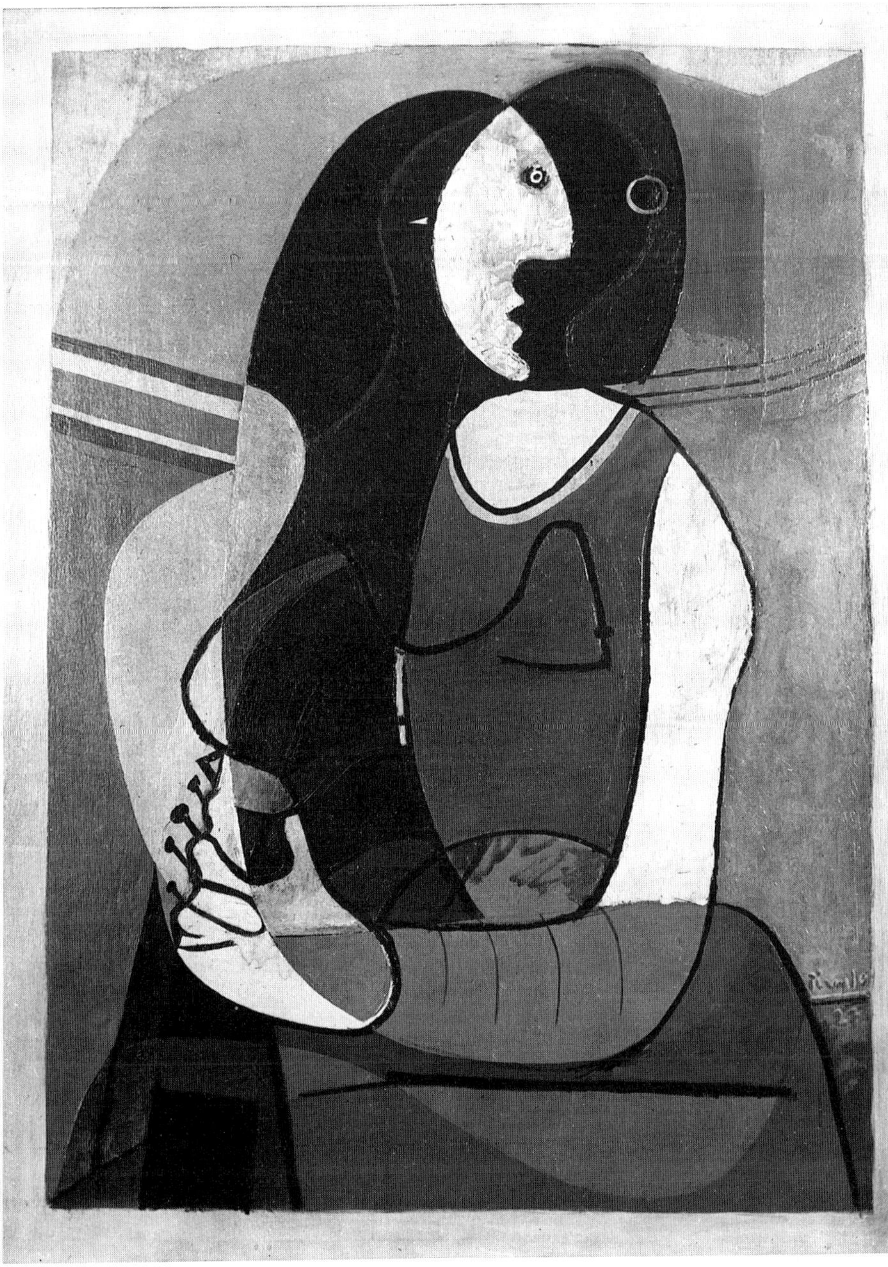

Fig. 12 PABLO PICASSO, *Seated Woman*, 1927 © The Museum of Modern Art, New York/Succession Picasso/DACS 1996

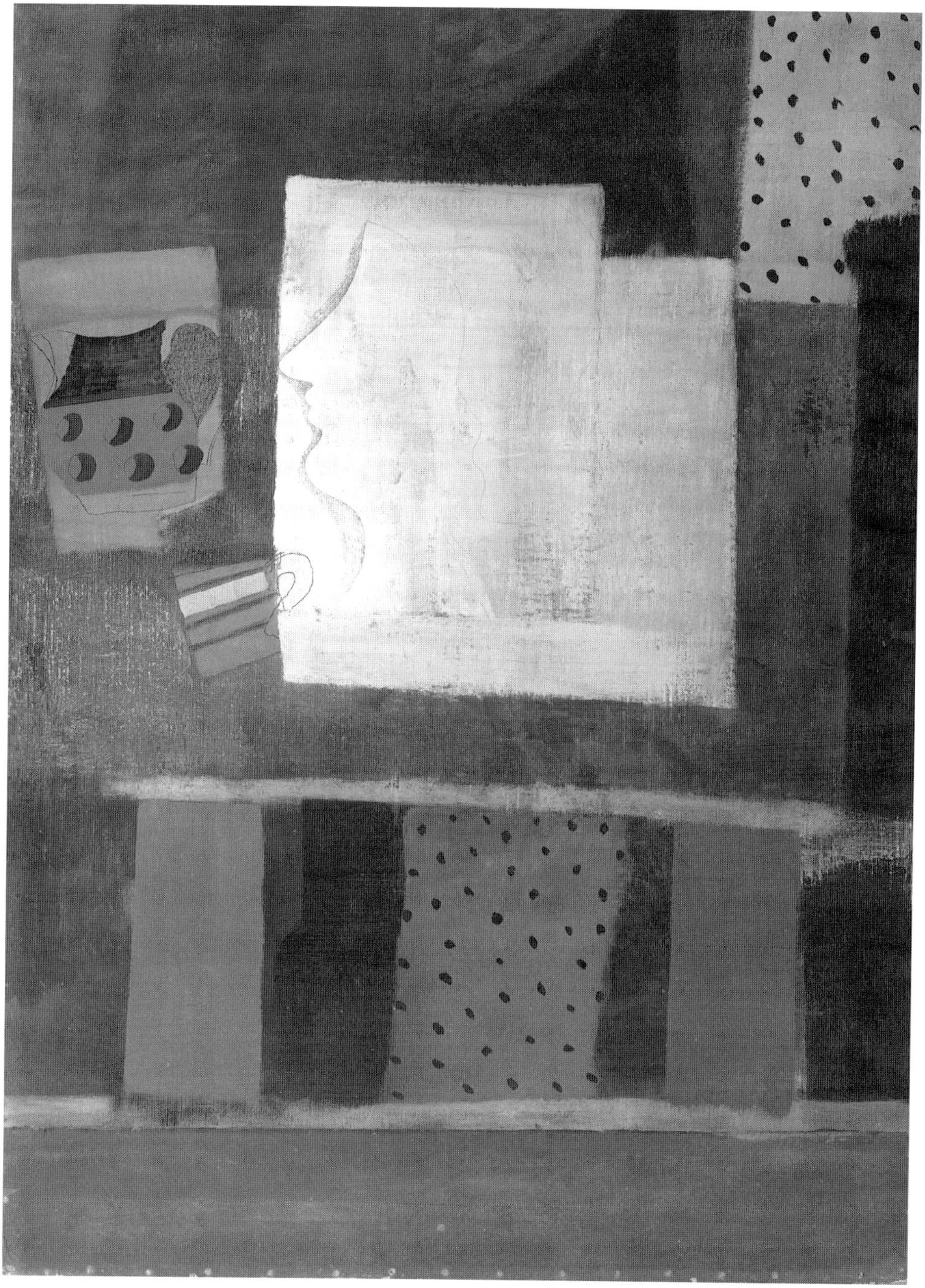

Fig. 13 BEN NICHOLSON, *1932 (profile-Venetian red)*, 1932 © Angela Verren-Taunt.

them for at least a few of the sculptures in question—the 'symbolic' and 'maternal' works on which Read's and Stokes' responses were based. Take, for two examples, *Figure* and *Reclining Figure* (Fig. 14), both alabasters done at just this time. Each proposes a notion of the body as singular—the *Figure* is a miniature monolith, after all, its parts kept within a continuous contour—and that sense of unity is maintained even given the greater complexity of the other work. Convexities and concavities are linked in loosely matching pairings, formal correspondences which seem to urge the sensation of a dense and continuous whole—a whole in each instance that by virtue of its very density can be understood to have no contents. Instead it is reassuringly all of a piece.

This rhetoric of dense coherence is repeated in other figures, but the forms of those repetitions—as in *Sculpture with Profile* (1932) and *Carving* (1933), for example—have something important to say on their own. It is that Hepworth's proposal concerning the female body announces more than its coherence and unity. It is a body which can be as abrupt as it is unified, can seem as stunted as it is continuous. It becomes less a body than an object—and a threatening one at that. Hepworth seems to have sought out her figures' analogies to other bodies and objects—to primitive weapons and the phallus and to phallic weapons. In one signal instance—the uncanny *Two Forms* (Fig. 15)—far from being contained, the

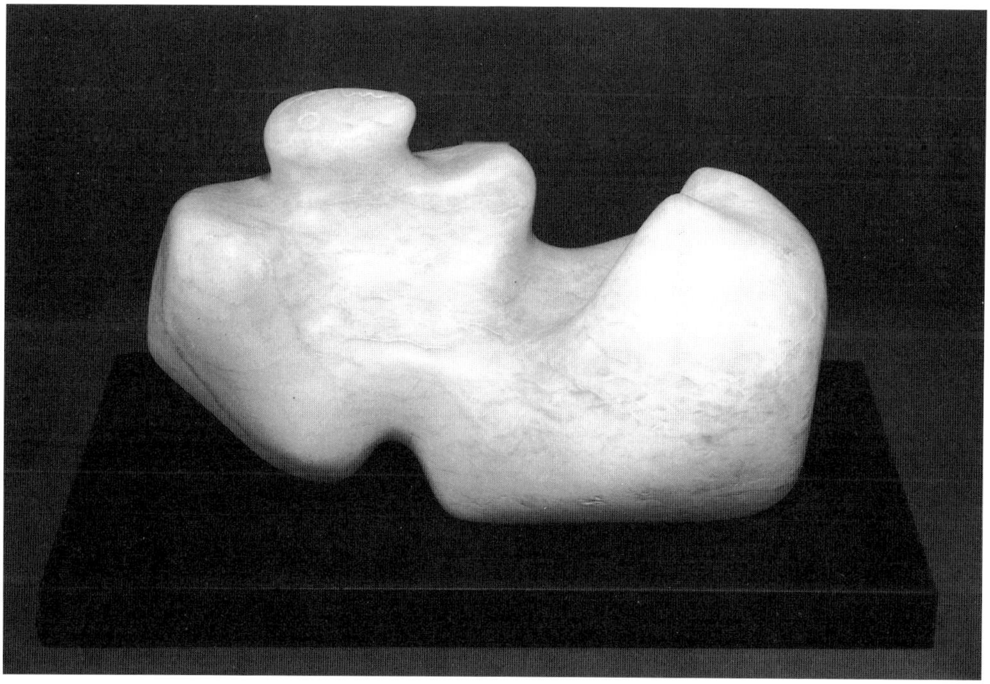

Fig. 14 BARBARA HEPWORTH, *Reclining Figure*, 1933 © Trustees of the Barbara Hepworth Estate/Hirshhorn Museum and Sculpture Garden, Smithsonian Institution (photo: Lee Stalsworth)

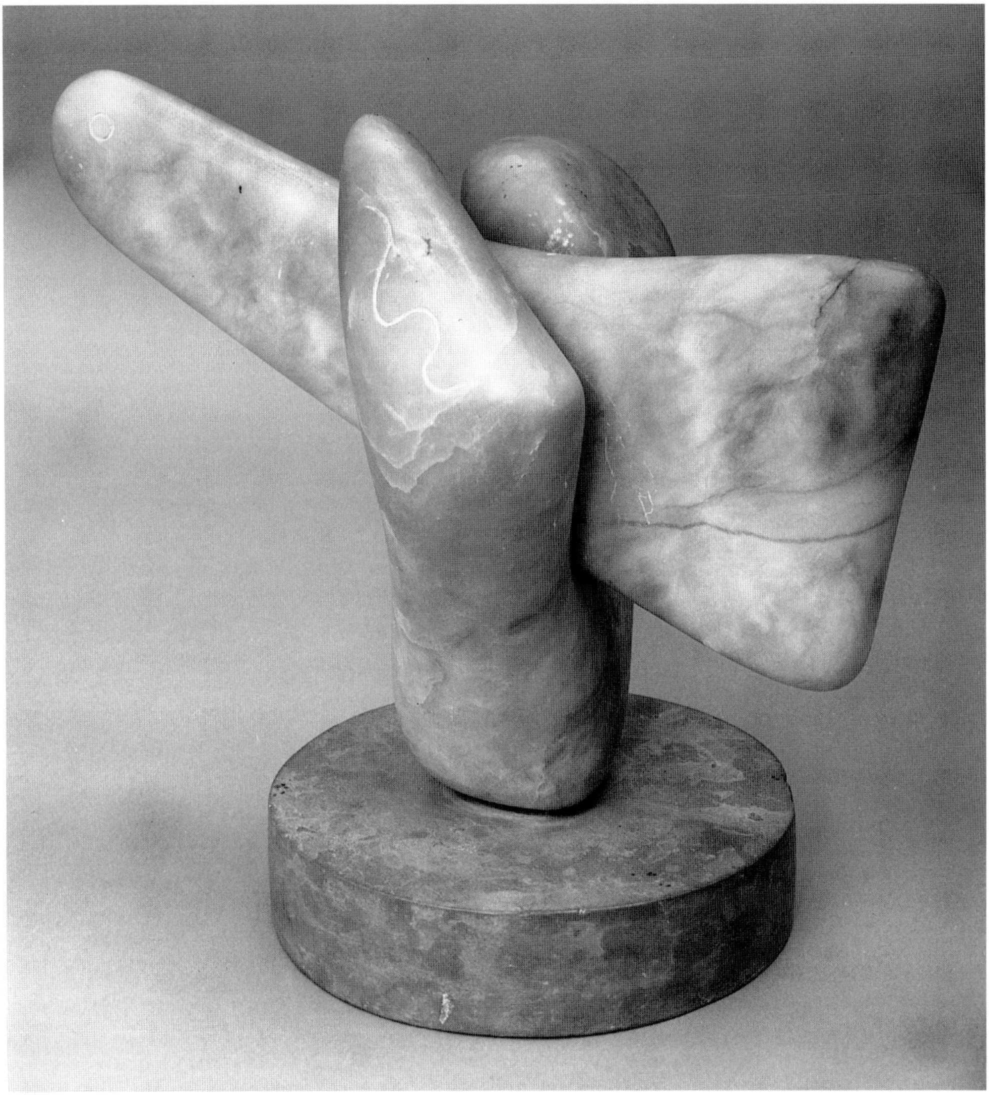

Fig. 15 BARBARA HEPWORTH, *Two Forms*, 1933 © Trustees of the Barbara Hepworth Estate

body has split into parts, amputees or fragments which mime a grotesque and fruitless intercourse.

Much of this bluntness and incompletion survives even in the shapes which Stokes, remember, took to be most complacent: the works Hepworth called *Compositions*, the pieces which have come by now to be known mostly as 'Mother and Child'. I think Stokes was wrong about their tone. Granted that in them the artist was concerned with principles and degrees of closeness and separation between two forms, and consequently with the kinds of relationships and analogies which might be established between them. The result, however, is that ideas of unity, of part and whole, inside and out, are put under even greater investigative stress. This is the case with the white marble *Figure* of 1933, for example, in which the stone widens out to form a carefully rounded base. There seem to be real nuances here, clefts and curves in the stone which demonstrate that the main issue is not the essential or material principles of the medium (a dowel was used to keep the thing upright). The message is the thing: mother and child are held together in a single block. Their relationship is a fundamental identity—they are made materially closer than the linkage signalled by the sign for a hand scratched in the stone—but it is achieved by sacrificing the structural probity of the whole. The 'carving' ethos, in other words, does not speak to the real instability of the work.

When the 'mother' and 'child' are separated, as they are in the piece Stokes took as his main example, that resolution does not serve to ease the discomfort of the forms. The pebble sits heavily on the limbs of the mother stone, pinioning them with its weight, and 'her' limbs themselves seem painfully extended, elongated only to be abruptly curtailed. And that sense of distressing incompletion persists, even when, in an alabaster 1934 *Mother and Child*, principles of complementarity and analogy have been convincingly secured (Fig. 9). The degree of likeness between the two forms, and the pleasure to be taken in their shapes still do not entirely displace the awkward knowledge of the larger body as an amputated form. Desire for these shapes soon seems regressive, a return to some founding category of form: to faeces as much as to a pebble, to the redundancy of the mirror more than to adequately individuated selves.

If further evidence is needed of Hepworth's enquiry into the related and separable status of the maternal and infant body, it is provided by two drawings that the 1994 Hepworth retrospective made public for the first time [22]. The two sheets come to us as studies for sculpture by virtue of their subject matter, and also because one places three of its figures on sketchy bases. The other sees its figures from different points of view, giving them both a front and side, thus projecting for them a place in three dimensions. Both are convincingly dated *c*.1932. But if they are studies for sculpture they are nonetheless imagined in a notably hypothetical way. The drawings operate under the sign of Surrealism, as much as of sculpture: that the surreal means Picasso is clear from the strangely tusked figure in the upper right of the smaller sheet. This figure seems to have served to license Hepworth's further speculations about the female form: hence the other sketches, which expand and amplify its forms. In them the body is overlaid with circles of various densities and scales: navel and breasts and wombs both full and empty proliferate; they are sometimes contained within the basic scaffolding of the body, and sometimes pull against or out from the figural core.

Such speculations are continued in a different way on the other sheet. Here the overlap concerns the intimate relationship between the bodies of mother and child. They are all too easily conflated. In the two sketches at upper left and centre, the child may actually be within the mother's body; its organs seem like hers, its parts hook up and into her core. I think it was to put that risky visual possibility to rest that Hepworth then drew the more reassuring profile view, one which serves finally and decisively to prise them apart.

In the kinds of emphases I have built into my interpretations—emphases on the ways in which Hepworth's carvings present an experience of parts and wholes, and on the ways those experiences might be seen to be charged in various measure with pleasure and discomfiture—I have been consciously employing a vocabulary indebted to the theories of Melanie Klein. My use of this language may have something of a rough and ready flavour; it is not yet the same thing as a fully-fledged Kleinian analysis of her art; indeed, examples of such interpretations are still rather few and far between. Yet reading Klein has offered me the only tools I have so far encountered to make more than superficial sense of Hepworth's art—to speak to its intensity, above all. This is why I want to draw attention to the various ways Hepworth's works stand for the female body, symbolising not merely the whole body but its parts or fragments as separable sites and sources of visual response. These are bodies made into objects which may present dangers or threats, or themselves be threatened. Together they act as answers to a series of founding questions about the female form. What are its contents and boundaries? What does it hold or do? How might it best be joined to other bodies and forms? That the limits of Hepworth's bodies are not those of biology, however, does not mean that they are wildly inclusive in their referential range. They add up to a testing and verification of a limited range of fantasmatic fears and hopes concerning the female body's presence, its contents and its voids. Their tone is simultaneously investigative and intimate—their hand-sized scale sees to that—yet for all their variety, I do not see their tone or purpose as involving much sense of play.

Nowhere are these purposes more evident than in Hepworth's various efforts to pierce the stone. They began in 1931 with the destroyed *Abstraction*, a casualty of World War II [23]. It is a work which has the status of a demonstration: the form is pierced—the form is a body, needless to say—and with eminently reassuring results. Look, there is nothing inside, no babies or faeces or penis: out of the absence will come a reassuring w/hole. The resistances of the (feminine) block have been made to yield to the most basic possible inquiry about its contents; as a result, the practice of sculpture was no longer to be quite the same.

It is a tribute to Hepworth's powers as an artist that the hole in the block was so promptly and satisfyingly incorporated into sculpture, as in the Tate Gallery's 1934 alabaster *Mother and Child* (Fig. 10). The hole was made aesthetically whole, rather than remaining the wilful, even compulsive gesture it first seemed to be. We can still trace the stages in that process—for example, the eventual alignment of the hole with the space under the breasts, in the 1933 *Figure*, and its use, in the 1932–33 lignum vitae *Seated Figure*, to detach arm from torso [24]. The Tate *Mother and Child* profits from and revises both these works. To discover how a hole might paradoxically leave a body aesthetically intact is to offer a practical and material demonstration of one's successful integration of the emotions and issues involved.

It is only on reflection or, perhaps, on seeing the work in the flesh (so to speak) that the tense balance of all of this becomes clear. The form of the baby is not really balanced; it has been glued into its precarious place on the mother's knee.

When Stokes wrote so insistently, 'Miss Hepworth's stone *is* a mother', the phrase was, among other things, a way of *not* writing 'Miss Hepworth is a mother', which of course she then was and would soon be again (her son Paul had been born in 1929; triplets appeared in October 1934). As was Klein herself, I might add; this may be one reason that the analyst brought to her professional work a salutary lack of concern with prescribing maternal duties and obligations, especially of a kind it would be hard for a professional woman to meet [25]. She focused instead on the needs, hostilities and aggressions of infantile structuring of an internal fantasy world, and even when faced with a particularly damaged child, as in the case of the near-autistic little Dick, remarks only in passing that 'though he had every care, no real love was lavished on him, his mother's feeling being from the very beginning cold' [26]. Klein's purpose in analysis was to deal with circumstances, rather than judge them, to provide a set of symbols which her young patients could use to advance towards integration and personhood. Those symbols, she thought, never lost their force.

But to stick with Hepworth: the imagery of her work seems to back up the Kleinian claim. It seems clear that by 1934 she did arrive at symbols which both aesthetically and personally might be said to mark a fragile resolution. That year's carvings achieve a kind of management of the recalcitrant topics they had explored: she had worked away at 'resistances' with some success. Yet exactly how this success connects with her decision, a month after the birth of her triplets, to place them in the care of nursing sisters, seems unclear. She did so to keep on carving, replacing one bodily obligation for another: remember her declaration, 'The sculptor carves because he must'. And the domestic change coincided with a stylistic one: the body was summarily banished from her art for more than a decade—on this she and her critics have always been agreed.

We might call Hepworth's decision a personal one. Maternal duties conflicted with artistic ones so she took the steps necessary to realign them. It seems that she saw the triplets once a week until their return home at the age of two; Paul meantime spent much of his time with his father, John Skeaping. Yet though personal, these child-care arrangements also have a social dimension; after all, maternity has always sparked—and continues to spark as hotly as ever—public concern and attention in the modern state. In this particular instance, the intersection is mimed with breathtaking directness. Has it ever been noticed that Stokes' 1933 *Spectator* column ran next to the week's broadcast schedule for BBC Radio? Half an hour on November planting and Bartok playing Bach and programmes scrutinising 'The National Character—[by] A Parson' and 'My Place in Commerce: by a Colliery Undermanager'. On Friday, the day the *Spectator* appeared, was a broadcast billed as: 'Common Sense and Infant Feeding: By a Doctor. These practical health talks have an interest not only for mothers of young babies but for those who are in any way trying to influence or educate public opinion on these lines'.

Public opinion evidently needed considerable influencing, given that in the 1930s the birth rate in Great Britain hit an all-time low: 1933 saw only 14.4 births per thousand, against 25 per thousand thirteen years earlier [27]. By then officials had given up promoting childbirth as a means to increase the capital of the state, since the population had proved so unwilling to oblige [28]. More characteristic of social policy were the many instances of governmental—not to say patriarchal—interest in infant feeding and maternal bonding, reproductive concerns which assert their broad relationship and relevance to the public good. These were concerns with which, let it be said, middle class women aligned themselves: they took up the cause of bringing them to the working class. All these efforts—even the radio doctor's practical chats—represent the climate in which Hepworth left infant feeding to others so as to be able to negotiate her female, professional and maternal roles. And she gave body to the complexity of those issues by yoking them to various formal concerns. The 'resistance of the block', she called them, but other resistances, which concern the objective and fantasmatic guises of the female body—of that body as mother—are tackled there as well.

The risks in speaking of personal circumstance in addressing art and artists are several: the speaker may seem somehow to sit in judgment on the past, or to cast representation as the direct reflection of a maker's 'personal' concerns. This is not my purpose. I do not think Hepworth's motivations or imagery *mirror* the personal; in any case the personal is only legible as art if it is given artistic form. Nor was the fact that Hepworth was herself a mother single-handedly able to make of maternity a culturally valuable, culturally negotiable theme. The interest in sculpting mothers and infants was widespread in the 1920s and '30s; the old theme (paradoxically) became a vehicle for the new. Henry Moore's preoccupation with the topic predates that of Hepworth by some five years; it goes back at least to 1922, the year of a now-lost *Mother and Child* [29]. And from the outset his work aimed determinedly at its revitalisation, proposing new bodies and bodily relationships. At first these were positively pneumatic, pumped full of confidence that mother and child can be animated and integrated anew, given specially weighty stature and an unaccustomed force. His work stands as the best demonstration, if not the only one, that the topic Hepworth took up in her carved bodies was not merely or simply personal in its purpose and charge. On the contrary, it was a central metaphor, gauging prosperity, imperium and their reproduction, on the one hand, and on the other indexing artistic value and ambition. I remember in this context how much an imagery of birth haunts Stokes' writing: when the carver polishes stone, he 'slaps the newborn infant to make it breathe'; when the modeller unmoulds his figure, it is like ripping it from a womb [30]. What is remarkable is not that such metaphors flourish, however, but that at this particular moment in history—around 1930 in England—they take on such uncanny, and *pace* Read, such desublimated life.

That special vitality, I am suggesting, is not limited to Hepworth's art. In demonstration of that claim, let me produce a work by Moore: a cast concrete figure of 1927, it represents a suckling child (Fig. 16). The mother, we might say, has been reduced to a mere object, and a purely Kleinian one at that—she is a single breast at which the infant pulls. The side view makes it clear that she is only that breast: indications of other forms—the much flattened second breast and chest wall—are elliptical at best. But this very absence of the mother—her reduction to her best part—presents the viewer with an unexpected result. Viewer and mother become one—the elision is unavoidable—and now together make up a special, unprecedented whole. And the child's dependence on this hybrid mother/viewer is notably urgent and demanding; there is none of the improbable erectness and independence Hepworth attributes to her *Infant* (Fig. 11) despite his suckling state [31].

I think that Moore quickly backed off from this remarkable conception, and

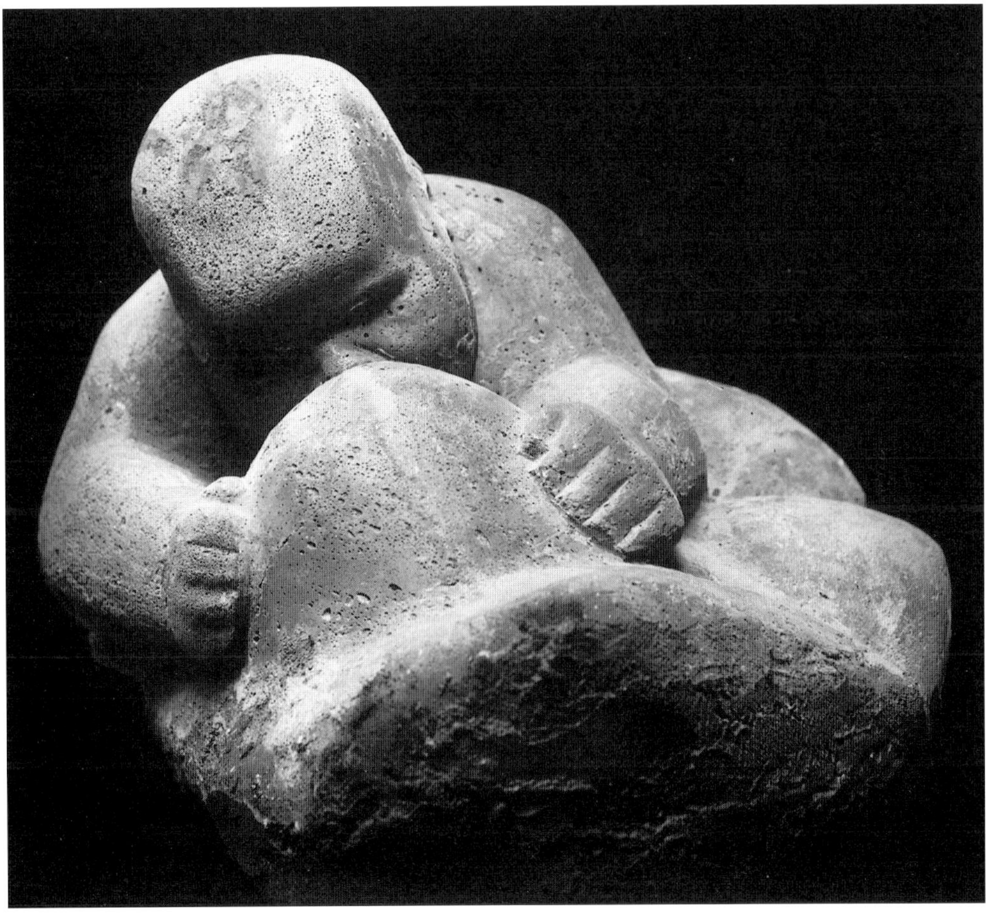

Fig. 16 HENRY MOORE, *Suckling Child*, 1927 © The Henry Moore Foundation

from its circuitry of identifications above all. The loss of the mother's body and its simultaneous relocation in and as that of the viewer seem to have needed reconsideration: the rethinking involved both hyperbole and, ultimately, considerable toning down. When in a drawing of about 1930 he returned to the figure of the suckling child, he did so under the sign of his first conception—he drew a small reprise of it at the lower right—but as sketched now it is caricatural and disturbing (Fig. 17) [32]. Its eyes are bizarrely emphasised as if to deflect, rather than attract, the gaze, and in the sketch pencilled just above it, which imagines a second version of the group, this same feature contributes to a distressing, quasi-foetal formlessness. The infant's body is now entered by one nipple (indeed by the line of the breast as a whole), while that same nipple also stands for a second eye. The mode is hyperbolic, as I say, and in the sculpture that followed this sheet, a small alabaster work of 1930, bizarrerie has been put aside in favour of another kind of formlessness [33]. Now the careful uniformity of the whole, in which the smooth surfaces of both breast and infant are rubbed to a glowing similitude,

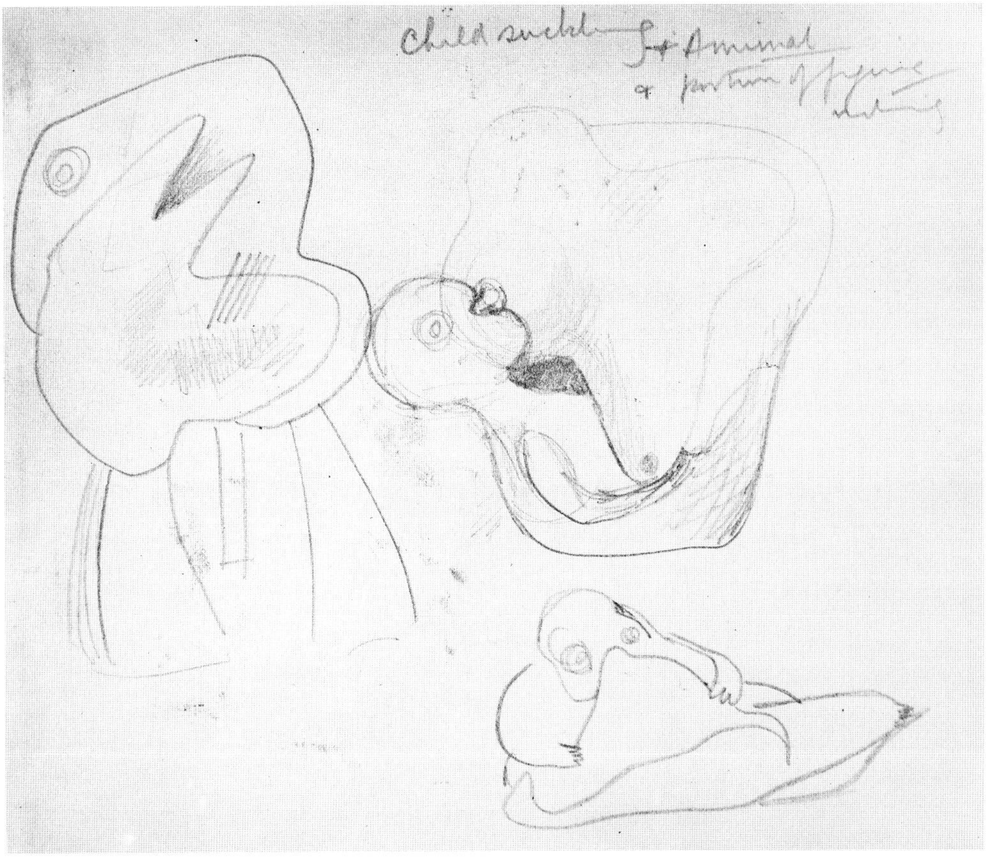

Fig. 17 HENRY MOORE, *Ideas for Sculpture: Page from No.1 Drawing Book*, 1930–31

arrests any desire for identification on the viewer's part. The soft skin works instead to objectify the work, while affecting a kind of aesthetic completion. Moore meant to make of the new group an independent artistic whole, to give it a kind of euphony of treatment declarative of its nurturing theme. This is part of a wider purpose: Moore wanted sculpture to nurture and aimed to produce an art that could be made to play that role.

This is not a purpose I think it right to attribute to Hepworth's art, at least around 1930. Her sculpture of that moment had neither the complacency nor the distance such an ambition seemed to demand. Complacency and distance about what? About the feminine, of course, and the female: about the ways her sculpture might negotiate a topic which her ambitions as an artist made unavoidable, but which by virtue of personal circumstance was inevitably highly charged. Her stance seems to have been edgy and investigative, declarative and mistrustful. Her art is full of proposals about the female body, without achieving much pleasure or comfort with its terms. We might explain the tone of her work by the fact that she was a woman, though our reasoning would not seem forceful or sufficient, since this was self-evidently the case. But if there is satisfaction to be found in this explanation, partial as it is, it lies in the fact that as a woman, Hepworth was able to represent the ambivalences and ambiguities of the maternal bond and state. And she incorporated them in and as sculpture. So much for the femininity of the sculptural block.

Yet I do not think that Hepworth would have been much pleased with my account of her work's achievement. On the contrary, she seems later in life to have been bent on securing a specially untroubled account of her maternal history, so much so that the particular version she offered in the *Pictorial Autobiography* appears purposeful to say the least: hence all those family snaps. Do they not seem to have a case to plead? At the very least they give a vivid idea of the constitutive importance of maternity in the making of this particular sense of a public self. Yet they do so by forgetting or erasing the formative concerns of her sculptural art.

That this topic once had for Hepworth a more vital and complex role to play—that it played a role in the development of her art—is an idea shored up by a work which falls outside the period considered here, the years from 1927 to 1934. A *Mother and Child* of 1954, it is her memorial to her firstborn child, the son called Paul; it is in St. Ives Parish Church (Fig. 18). It makes a notable contrast to the anguished wooden crucifix carved and burned into being by his father, John Skeaping. Though it says nothing particular about Paul, it is evidently meant to index its maker's grief at his loss [34]. For Hepworth, by contrast, all the affect and interest the subject once carried have long since been laid to rest. Her work is an exercise in archaism, its drapery as flat and linear as a Hellenistic imitation of a distant Hellenic past. The group seems uttered as if by rote, as if feeling could not be allowed to find its way back into its folds. Its very flatness throws into high relief the fact that both motherhood and carving had once had a profoundly different status for Hepworth. A sculptor and a mother, she first conceived of

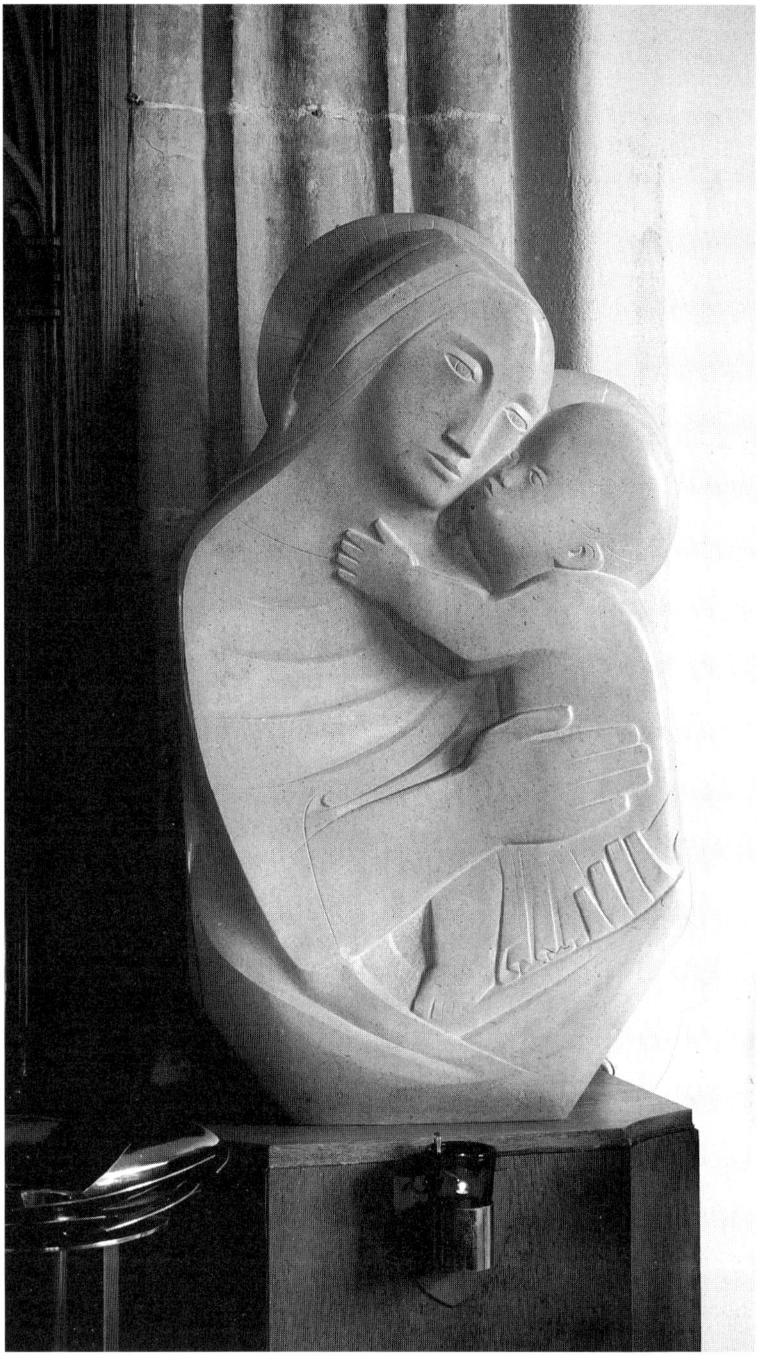

Fig. 18 BARBARA HEPWORTH, *Madonna and Child*, 1954 © Trustees of the Barbara Hepworth Estate

sculpture and 'mother' as demanding more original—and more troubling—forms, and she did so at a moment of what we might call over-valuation of the maternal by both her profession and her state. Her work took shape as an Imaginary of the body, as the infant might envision it—or better, as a mother who was once an infant might feel it—given her purpose of regrounding sculpture as an advanced and authentic art. In such circumstances Hepworth conjured a body that could be and contain everything, and nothing at all—little wonder she did not go on.

NOTES AND REFERENCES

1 BOWNESS, ALAN (1993) 'A note on the 1993 edition', in *Barbara Hepworth: a Pictorial Autobiography* (London, Tate Gallery Publications), unpag. [p. 4]. First published in 1970, revised 1978.
2 *Ibid.*, p. 17.
3 READ, HERBERT (1932) 'Foreword', *Carvings by Barbara Hepworth. Paintings by Ben Nicholson* (London, Arthur Tooth & Sons), 9 November–3 December; see *Pictorial Autobiography*, p. 21. STOKES, ADRIAN (1933) 'Art: Miss Hepworth's Carving', *The Spectator*, 3 November, p. 621; see *Pictorial Autobiography*, p. 29. Also reprinted in STOKES, ADRIAN (1978) *The Critical Writings of Adrian Stokes: Volume 1, 1930–37* (London, Thames and Hudson) pp. 309–10.
4 Read (n. 3).
5 CURTIS, PENELOPE (1994) 'Barbara Hepworth and the Avant-Garde of the 1920s', in: CURTIS, PENELOPE and WILKINSON, ALAN G. (1994) *Barbara Hepworth: a Retrospective* (Liverpool, Tate Gallery Liverpool), pp. 11–30.
6 Read (n. 3). Note that Read is not the only critic to suggest that the 1932 Tooth show might dismay its public. In his review, Paul Nash produced a brief vignette of a Tooth employee, one Mr. Keene, 'imploring a lady and gentleman, obviously slightly suffering from shock, to abandon at once any idea of looking in the work before them for anything they expected to find'. NASH, PAUL (1932) 'Goings On: a Painter and a Sculptor', *The Weekend Review*, 19 November, p. 613.
7 READ, HERBERT (1924–25) 'Psychoanalysis and the Critic', *The Criterion* Vol. III, pp. 214–30. Note that Read included as number 4 in the questionnaire he prepared to stimulate the Unit One artists to reflect on their art and intentions, the straightforward query 'Have you studied the theories of Freud?'. See READ, HERBERT (1934) 'Introduction', *Unit 1. The Modern Movement in English Architecture, Painting and Sculpture* (London, Cassell and Co. Ltd.), p. 14.
8 Read, 'Psychoanalysis' (n. 7), p. 225.
9 *Ibid.*, p. 224. Read is citing ADLER, ALFRED (1924) *The Practice and Theory of Individual Psychology* (English edition, London), p. 23.
10 See Alex Potts' study, 'Carving and the Engendering of Sculpture: Adrian Stokes on Barbara Hepworth' (this volume) for direct and helpful attention to Stokes' text.
11 WOLLHEIM, RICHARD (Ed) (1972) *The Image in Form: Selected Writings of Adrian Stokes* (Harmondsworth, Penguin), p. 36. From *The Quattro Cento*, 1932, pp. 7–8.
12 *Ibid.*, p. 27.
13 STOKES, ADRIAN (1934) *The Stones of Rimini* (London, Faber), p. 110.
14 BERTRAM, ANTHONY (1933) 'Artists Indoors', *The Listener* Vol. X, No. 251, 1 November, pp. 660–61; repro. p. 661. See also (1933) 'Plays and Pictures', *The New Statesman and Nation*, 4 November, p. 551.
15 Stokes (n. 13).
16 Despite the differences in our interpretations, my discussion acknowledges with interest TICKNER, LISA (1993) 'Now and Then: the Hieratic Head of Ezra Pound', *Oxford Art Journal* Vol. 16, No. 2, p. 59.
17 HEPWORTH, BARBARA (1932) 'The Aim of the Modern Artist', *The Studio* No. 2, p. 322.
18 *Ibid.*
19 STOKES, ADRIAN (1965) *The Invitation in Art* (London, Tavistock), p. 4.
20 As cited in CAVELL, STANLEY (1969)

Must We Mean What We Say? A Book of Essays (Cambridge, Cambridge University Press), p. 122, n. 3.

21 Nicholson evidently identified his uses of Hepworth's profile with his reflections on the relative status of drawing and painting, and their claims to address the real. Indeed, it seems safe to claim that he used his images of her as a means for that reflection.

22 For reproductions of these works, see Curtis and Wilkinson (n. 5), Figs 88, 92, pp. 49–50.

23 In HARRISON, CHARLES (1981) *English Art and Modernism. 1900–1939* (London and Bloomington, Allen Lane and Indiana University Press), p. 266, Harrison points convincingly to the evidence of its importance to Hepworth's view of her sculptural achievement.

24 For illustrations of these works, see HODIN, J. P. (1961) *Barbara Hepworth* (Boston, Boston Book and Art Shop), nos. 46, 47.

25 This is the hypothesis of DOANE, JANICE and HODGES, DEVON (1992) *From Klein to Kristeva: Psychoanalytic Feminism and the Search for the 'Good Enough' Mother* (Ann Arbor, The University of Michigan Press), p. 18.

26 MITCHELL, J. (Ed) (1986) *The Selected Melanie Klein* (Harmondsworth, Penguin), p. 100.

27 THANE, PAT (1991) 'Visions of Gender in the Making of the British Welfare State', in: BOCK, G. and THANE, P. (Eds) (1991) *Maternity and Gender Policies: Women and the Rise of the European Welfare State* (London, Routledge), p. 100.

28 For histories of pronatalism in England see DAVIN, ANNA (1978) 'Imperialism and Motherhood', *History Workshop Journal* No. 5, Spring, pp. 9–65, and LEWIS, JANE (1980) *The Politics of Motherhood: Child and Maternal Welfare in England 1900–1939* (London and Montreal, Croom Helm and McGill-Queen's University Press).

29 SYLVESTER, DAVID (Ed) (1957) *Henry Moore; Vol. One: Sculpture and Drawing 1921–1948*; 4th edition (London, Lund Humphries), No. 3.

30 Stokes (n. 13), pp. 112, 126. Note that in both of these usages the 'female' block (so-called) is almost instantly elided—it [she] is subordinated to the sculptural product—to the 'child'.

31 I thank Lisa Tickner and Beth Dungan for conversations about Hepworth's *Infant*.

32 The drawing was published in MITCHINSON, DAVID (1972) *Henry Moore: Unpublished Drawings* (New York, Abrams), Pl. 86. Mitchinson reproduces (Pl. 85) another closely related sheet from the same sketchbook, which is dated 1930–31. The same sheet, along with another from the same notebook (the 'No. 1 Drawing Book') is discussed by WILKINSON, ALAN G. (1977) *The Drawings of Henry Moore* (London, Tate Gallery with Art Gallery of Ontario), pp. 83–84.

33 For a reproduction of this work see Sylvester (n. 29), No. 96. The 1927 cast concrete *Suckling Child* is No. 42.

34 For a reproduction of this work see SKEAPING, JOHN (1977) *Drawn from Life: an Autobiography* (London, Collins), p. 128.

KATY DEEPWELL

Hepworth and her Critics

Two feminist anthologies on women artists have recently reproduced large sections of Barbara Hepworth's writing from *Carvings and Drawings* (1952) and *A Pictorial Autobiography* (1970). In both Mara Witzling's *Voicing Our Visions* (1992) and Susan A. Waller's *Women Artists in the Modern Era* (1991) [1], Hepworth's words reappear in a new context among statements from other notable women artists in the twentieth century. While this re-presentation is to be applauded for providing renewed access to her writing and introducing new audiences to what she had to say about her life and work, it, at the same time, alters the reading of her work, emphasising, perhaps, access to an authentic female subject speaking about her life and work.

Feminism has rightly sought not only to recover the ways in which the personal can be read as political but also to problematise and reconceive the relationships between the personal and the political. Within a feminist context, the reprinting of Hepworth's words underlines the presence of a female authorial voice, speaking of her life and struggles as a woman. Yet the selection and presentation of the extracts do not draw attention to the politics surrounding the production of these autobiographical statements. While feminism has succeeded in bringing women's experiences and activities back into view and in making women's work visible in a culture where it is frequently marginalised, devalued or neglected, it needs also to attend to and problematise the necessary (even empowering) representation of autobiography as a form of 'truth' [2] in a culture where women's words are readily dismissed as 'personal' rather than analysed for their theoretical or philosophical content. Autobiography as a form never reveals the pure presence of the subject, in spite of its claims to do so. Not only are its forms highly conventionalised and codified narratives from birth to the present day, but it presents the history of its own subject as moving relentlessly towards its present position. The disjunction across time between the months or years in which the work is conceived and written as opposed to the selective past life experiences which the seemingly-present narrating voice of the author claims to represent serves to illustrate this point.

In Hepworth's case the reproduction and repetition of the artist's statements are not confined to feminist accounts. In the criticism published during her lifetime, it is remarkable how often her own published statements are quoted in the work of male critics. The way in which this is done is referred to in the analysis of male critics of Hepworth which follows: but it is rarely the starting point for further discussion. More often her statements are used to settle an argument, to close down upon the potential meaning(s) in what she has to say. If feminism emphasises her voice in terms of her struggle as a woman to realise her potential as an artist, male critics quote her statements to define and designate their view of the limits to her artistic practice. What interests me in particular are the ways in which Hepworth's recourse to artist's statement and autobiography can be seen as an intervention in the critical discourse on her work: a strategy she adopted to resituate her work and open up its theoretical and philosophical tropes for analysis—a strategy which was not always successful.

I want to begin by resituating the production of *A Pictorial Autobiography* as part of a set of strategies which I believe Barbara Hepworth adopted to speak positively about her ideas and artistic practice while at the same time negotiating and mediating the effects of the (then) familiar critical stereotypes about women artists. This is contingent upon a shift in the reading of her autobiographical writings and artist's statements not as manifesting the 'pure presence' of a fixed subject but as the result of negotiated, highly mediated and historically contingent representations of 'self' designed to meet particular envisaged or imagined audiences. For obviously and inevitably any autobiography constructs a retrospective and highly selective narrative of a subject's life, but it is also produced within a set of historical determinations which frame and structure the emphases of that narrative.

A Pictorial Autobiography [3], published in 1970, is structured as a chronological narrative in four sections: childhood and youth; years with Ben Nicholson; St. Ives; and 'A New Decade'—a reference to the 1960s which draw to a close as the book ends. The narrative of the book is structured as much by the careful juxtaposition of the photographs and facsimiles as what is written in the text—this is why reproduction of the text alone makes nonsense (no-sense) of the statements constructed within the book. The author's narrative is arranged between and around photographs. These comprise not just a sequence of works but different views of the artist among friends on her 'working holidays' and at work in her studio, with members of her family, at official functions in her honour, her pets, and the significant places in the artist's life—for example her school, Yorkshire and Cornish landscapes, and her different studios. Another dimension within the collage effect of the book is the reproduction of reviews, catalogues, frontispieces, telegrams awarding prizes, and statements written in her own hand about either pieces of work or speeches offered at award ceremonies. Through the text and juxtaposed images, the steady progress of her career as a productive and celebrated artist forms the dominant narrative. The message is overwhelmingly one of the negotiation of career and family, combining art production *with* motherhood, the possession of a strong work ethic combined with a passionate dedication to sculpture as manifesting life's fundamental values.

Hepworth's own 'authorial' text glosses over many extremely difficult periods in her life as much as it constructs her own version of events. The final section becomes almost entirely a series of statements about her artistic practice and philosophy rather than a description of her reactions to the procession of events and awards which are represented in the photos and facsimiles. The time-span of her two marriages frames and completes the first two sections of the book. References to Ben Nicholson's former wife and family disappear from view in the book, reduced to the reproduction of a *Seven and Five* catalogue where the work of Winifred (exhibiting as Dacre and not Nicholson) is reproduced on page 32. The point is that it is not that Hepworth is obliged to reveal all but that we should be aware of the highly selective emphases within her own account of herself.

In both sections, the end of each marriage is succeeded by a new phase of artistic endeavour which includes meeting new and important people in both her artistic and creative life. The first section, for example, ends with the defiant statement that:

> Friends and relations always said to me, that it was impossible to be dedicated to any art and enjoy marriage and children. This is untrue, as I had nearly thirty years of wonderful family life: but I will confess that the dictates of work are as compelling for a woman as a man. Not competitively, but as complementary and this is only just being realised. [4]

Tempting though it is to see this as the statement of a strong, heroic woman, and as a precedent for the 'modern superwoman', these statements are calculated broadsides against the predominance of the view during her lifetime, particularly during her training in the 1920s and manifesting itself again in the teaching practices of a younger generation of male sculptors like Reg Butler [5], that to combine marriage and career was impossible and that being a wife and mother is incompatible with any creative life for a woman as an artist. Hepworth was well aware of discrimination within the art world against women artists, and much of her practice and statements are constituted in defiance of these prejudices. This was a point made by many male critics who wrote enthusiastically about her practice. As Bryan Robertson suggested in her 1962 retrospective catalogue at the Whitechapel Art Gallery:

> There is an unspoken, undeclared conspiracy in most art circles against the idea of a woman artist, though this absurd and unfair attitude has changed considerably in recent years. [6]

As Penelope Curtis' research indicates, Barbara Hepworth was very conscious that this book had a job to do:

> Its main use was to put beyond dispute certain dates. My dates have been much altered by writers on Henry Moore. And of course, apart from being a woman, it has not been easy always having great bears breathing down one's neck. [7]

Hepworth's consciousness of the distortion occurring in the work of writers on Henry Moore included her awareness of the writing-out of her own role in English Modernism in the 1930s, and of the influence of her own work on younger generations of artists who emerged in the 1950s. This was coupled with her concern about the lack of serious critical attention to her own work. In the 1960s, the majority of criticism on Hepworth was produced by Alan Bowness, Bryan Robertson and Edwin Mullins [8].

Though *A Pictorial Autobiography* is dedicated to her friends Nancy and Fred Halliday, the narrative generated by the reproduction of reviews and catalogue essays carries a carefully staged tribute to her relationship with Herbert Read who died in 1968 when the book was in process of being written. Read is mentioned only twice in the text—as defining the 'nest of gentle artists' [9] in Hampstead in the 1930s, and in the last section in a somewhat isolated paragraph from the rest of the text, where she wrote:

> I can't say much about Herbert Read. Henry Moore, Naum Gabo and Ben Nicholson have spoken so well from all our hearts. Herbert was my first sponsor and friend. For some years before his death we shared a common illness and suffering and had the same surgeons. Without him there is an awful blank. On 18 June 1968 I wrote a poem . . . in both praise and anguish. His great courage and understanding helped me so much. [10]

However, the facsimiles produce references to the majority of texts which Read wrote about her work, including the 1932 Tooth's catalogue introduction with Ben Nicholson (p. 21); others for Bankfield Museum, Halifax in 1944 (p. 46); the British Council in 1950 (frontispiece only, p. 57); her exhibition at Galerie Chalette, New York in 1959 (p. 79); Marlborough Gerson Gallery, New York in 1966 (p. 104); as well as an article for *The Listener* in 1948 (p. 51). Included also are references to Read's introduction to her book *Carvings and Drawings* (frontispiece, p. 63); her article for the book he edited, *Unit One* in 1934 (p. 30); a press cutting about a portrait of Read by Patrick Heron which both Hepworth and Moore donated to the National Portrait Gallery; and finally and most significantly, at the second last page of the book, a full page reproduction of a magazine article with his photograph and the beginning of the text of his last public speech.

It is not just the proximity of Read's death which led to the production of the book in this way, but the adoption of a deliberate strategy to re-emphasise Hepworth's relationship to Read. Although Read was not the only critic to write repeatedly and at length on Hepworth's work, he is the only critic to receive such attention within the reproductions in *A Pictorial Autobiography*. 1968 was a highly significant year for Hepworth in terms of national recognition and awards, and these events are also documented at the end of the book. She became one of only five women during her lifetime to be given a major retrospective at the Tate; she was awarded an Hon. D.Litt by Oxford University; became a Bard of Cornwall; and received the Freedom of the Borough of St. Ives—all in recognition of a lifetime of achievement. The narrative sub-text on Read would suggest that this was a particularly significant relationship which Hepworth (and Bowness who assisted her in its production) decided to emphasise. At the particular moment of its production, Hepworth chose to right the 'wrongs', the distortion produced by Moore scholars, by highlighting her own relationship to Read, and there is, I believe, a very cruel irony in that this seals a perception of Hepworth within a Read/Moore paradigm which has actually closed down upon curatorial and scholarly attention to Hepworth after her death, rather than initiating further research.

For with the exception of several short reviews of her work for Parisian magazines in 1938, 1939 and 1959, and the reproduction of short passages of discussion in his numerous publications on contemporary British art, the majority of Read's writing on Hepworth is referred to in *A Pictorial Autobiography*. Read's publications presented Hepworth's work to predominantly English-speaking audiences, but it was a promotion which consistently linked her to her immediate contemporaries, Moore and Nicholson. Her inclusion in Herbert Read's books—from *Art Now* (1933) to *Contemporary British Art* (1966)—is generally at the same point in the argument where Henry Moore or Ben Nicholson are discussed. Hepworth is significantly the only woman artist on whom Read wrote repeatedly and at any length in his entire prolific output, although the volume of writing on Hepworth is meagre when compared to that on Moore.

As is well-known, Read did much to establish Moore's relative importance as an English sculptor, creating a critical framework for understanding his work—even going so far as to write the artist's early statements for publication [11]. Read also wrote the majority of the catalogues for the numerous and highly successful British Council tours of Moore's work. As has often been noted, Moore was Read's most significant example of the development of contemporary modernist sculpture [12]. However the effect of using Moore as the 'norm' in Read's writing about Hepworth has not been fully explored or analysed in terms of gender.

One can see this very quickly by assessing the type of references to Hepworth in literature on Moore, as opposed to the referencing of Moore in any discussion on Hepworth. In Read's (and Donald Hall's) biographies of Moore, for example, references to Hepworth are confined to the repetition of a few facts: they both came from Yorkshire to study at the Royal College of Art [13]; both spent time studying in Italy on scholarships [14]; Moore was several years older and—it is therefore always implied—Hepworth's intellectual and artistic senior [15]; they lived near one another in Hampstead in the 1930s; and Moore briefly moved into the Hepworth-Nicholson studio in 1939 when they left for St. Ives, until it was bombed in October 1940 [16].

Discussion of Hepworth's work by comparison with Moore's is neatly avoided in the majority of Moore biographies. This reproduces an inherent bias in Moore scholarship—that Moore owes nothing to Hepworth and comparisons with her work are irrelevant. Read's comments on Moore have been instrumental here, firstly in establishing that Hepworth was significantly younger (therefore Moore must claim seniority in age and professionalism); and secondly, that her work is derivative of Moore (because of the age gap their relationship must have been one of teacher and pupil). Where it is acknowledged that the two artists were peers, any real exchange of ideas between them is recognised in the context of the 'gentle nest', and more often than not it is argued that its mature significance can only be found in Moore's work. Hepworth is thus always presented as less deserving of the attention given to Moore.

By contrast, in accounts of Hepworth's work where comparisons to Moore are made, they are made to establish the significance of her work by comparison to his, outlining what it is she shares or potentially develops in parallel with his work. Here, the same points recur as significant: the influence of the landscape, particularly the Yorkshire landscape, on each of them (as children since neither worked there during adult life) [17]; their absorption in the qualities of the sculptor's materials and the use of carving in the 1930s (in line with Read's understanding of the project of the modern artist); the fact that both established pierced forms in their work in the 1930s and employed strings in their sculptures of the early 1940s [18]. These latter 'innovations' are often credited to Hepworth in accounts of her own work, but the absence of any reference to Hepworth's work in accounts of Moore's work has perpetuated the damaging illusion that Hepworth's claims to such 'originality' must be derivative and based on false retrospection, or lacking in any real aesthetic significance.

When one focuses on what Read said rather than repeating the implications or framework which his views established, what is interesting is the problem or difficulties Read had in actually engaging with Hepworth's work on any critical level and the ways this severely limited his writing. The arguments he seeks to pursue are deeply ambivalent and often marked by a refusal to praise or name what she has produced in terms of artistic achievement [19]. Read's statements are never openly negative, just ambivalent and damning because of their faint praise, which is only noticeable when one compares his words on Hepworth to those on Moore. His writings are characterised by a noticeable deferral to either extended quotations from other sources or the artist's own words.

A comparison between Read's contributions on Moore and Hepworth in *A Letter to a Young Painter* (1962) illustrates this point. The piece on Hepworth is a reprint of the 1959 Galerie Chalette essay and that on Moore was initially written in 1961 [20]. In 1959 Read felt able to describe Hepworth's achievement as 'secure', the result of a 'sense of fulfilment', but the piece in which this is written is foreworded by his own remarks that he initially wanted to refuse this writing commission as he felt he had little to say, and the convention of introducing the artist's work to an audience felt rather stale. This is an extraordinary statement from such a prolific and committed advocate of English Modernism! No such hesitancy marks his discussion of Moore in the same volume, whom he consistently and emphatically names as an international figure. Read makes liberal allusions to Moore's genius, to his international importance, to his inheritance from Ruskin and from Michelangelo—that is, to both a specifically English and a grand European tradition of sculpture. When it comes to his discussion of Hepworth, reproduced in the same volume, Read is unable to make such comparisons: we are offered instead observations on the modern artistic dilemma (with reference to Nolde), the ancient Chinese philosophy of Chuang-Tzu, and references to her two nearest contemporaries, Moore and Nicholson. Read does not attempt to comment critically on Hepworth's words which he liberally quotes, nor does he engage in criticism of the work itself.

Robert Burstow has also identified differentiated use of vocabulary by Read in the 1950s to classify the two artists' achievements, but asserts that this is marked by both a refusal to identify this distinction in terms of gender alone and a repetition of 1950s conceptions of appropriate models for feminine achievement. Read, Burstow argues:

> . . . used the sculptors' own words to distinguish between their ideals. Hepworth's desire for a 'sense of mystery', 'loveliness' and 'some universal or abstract vision of beauty', Read valued less highly than Moore's desire for 'power' and 'vitality', although he resisted any simple explanation of this in terms of their gender. [21]

As Burstow notes, and I hope my own arguments are making clear, Hepworth was well aware of the consequences of this system of recognition, as Read refused to recognise her own contribution as a 'parent' to a younger generation of post-war British sculptors [22]. Read does, contrary to Burstow's assertion above, make gender explicit in this distinction between her 'sense of mystery' and Moore's 'explicit disclaimer of beauty' in his introduction to Hepworth's *Carvings and Drawings*, though he frames it in terms of Jungian theories, balancing anima and animus:

> But if these qualities can be sufficiently differentiated as ideals, it must not then be supposed that one is sentimental or feminine, the other realistic or masculine. What one might venture to suggest is that they represent the components of the psyche which Jung had differentiated as the anima and the animus. According to this hypothesis, we all carry in us an image of the other sex, 'the precipitate of all human experience pertaining to the opposite sex', as we tend to project everything that is latent and undifferentiated in the psyche . . . But the projection of images from the unconscious is never direct (except in dream or trance); the woman has to disguise her animus in feminine attributes (loveliness) the man his anima in masculine attributes (vitality and virility). In each case the secret power of the projected image comes from this state of tension, this sexual ambiguity or dialectic. [23]

Read's conception of sexual ambiguity or dialectic, however, has the unfortunate consequence of reinforcing the notion that a woman can only succeed as an artist if she embraces or is conscious of her psychic masculinity—i.e. acts like a man but remains ultimately predominantly female! What significantly disappears from view is the fact that all the terms in this distinction emerged out of a shared vocabulary. Amongst both participants and reviewers in *Seven and Five* exhibitions, 'vitality' had been a key term in distinguishing both ambition and its realisation in particular works.

'Vitality' was a critical term used by reviewers to distinguish the strengths of the men in contrast to the women in the group, as well as being internalised as a standard by both the male and female artists involved. J. M. Richards, reviewing the last *Seven and Five* show in 1935, argued that Nicholson's work could be distinguished for his 'vital concentration', Moore was the 'most vital' sculptor, while Hepworth appears as 'following Ben Nicholson's lead' but in such a way that 'the necessary vitality does not seem to have survived the change' [24]. This underlines the point that Read's choice of words to describe Hepworth's and Moore's project repeats the sexist bias within critical practice in the 1930s.

'Vitality' was also internalised as the mark of elusive genius by many women artists. Frances Hodgkins, a member of the Seven and Five Society until it became exclusively devoted to showing abstract work, wrote to her mother in 1924 (a decade earlier) of her position as both woman, modernist, and expatriate:

> New Zealanders like myself cannot help becoming de-nationalised—they have no country—it is sad but true . . . Art is like that—it absorbs your whole life and being. Few women can do it successfully. It requires enormous vitality. That is my conception of genius—vitality. [25]

Ironically the elusive quality of 'vitality' in a woman was what attracted Nicholson to Hepworth, as he wrote in a letter to his first wife, Winifred, in 1932, that Barbara's

> . . . understanding of life is profound and vital . . . She is a bigger artist than any man or woman I have met. Frances [Hodgkins] is a very real artist—so is Harry [Henry Moore] and Kit [Christopher Wood] as a person not in his painting, I don't feel that same about David [David Jones]—his point of view is not yet vital. [26]

Hepworth's own statement in *Circle* makes clear that she did not regard 'vitality' as a physical attribute, the province of one gender rather than the other, but as a spiritual power. This is quite different from the reduction of her approach to 'loveliness' which Read's analysis suggests.

> When we say that a great sculpture has vision, power, vitality, scale, poise, form or beauty, we are not speaking of physical attributes. Vitality is not a physical, organic attribute of sculpture—it is a spiritual inner life. Power is

> not male power or physical capacity—it is an inner force and energy. Form realisation is not just any three-dimensional mass—it is the chosen perfected form, of perfect size and shape for the sculptural embodiment of the idea. Vision is not sight—it is the perception of the mind. It is the discernment of the reality of life, a piercing of the superficial surfaces of material existence that gives a work of art its own life and purpose and significant power . . . A vital work has perfect co-ordination between conception and realization; but actual physical contours do not limit a perfected idea. [27]

'Vitality' here is 'spiritual vitality' not masculine strength or genius. It is neither a physical attribute of the artist, nor of the sculpture and as such is not gendered. Possession of this quality is in the realisation and conception of the idea and as such it is a quality which women do not automatically or necessarily lack. Hepworth's argument is pitched against the 'negative' lack which contemporary critical reviewing practices (executed overwhelmingly by men) routinely ascribed to women's work. In the 1930s she used the terms 'power' and 'vitality' regularly in her own published statements, divorcing them from the gendered bias found in the discourse of Read. Unlike Read's discourse on Moore, Hepworth's use of these terms is never explicitly linked to conceptions of 'Englishness', 'genius' and 'vision'.

Another of Hepworth's own statements from *Carvings and Drawings* articulates her continued awareness of the positioning of women in critical discourse:

> I have never understood why the word feminine is considered to be a compliment to one's sex if one is a woman, but has a derogatory meaning when applied to anything else. The feminine point of view is a complementary one to the masculine. Perhaps in the visual arts, many women have been intimidated by the false idea of competing with the masculine. There is no question of competition. The woman's approach presents a different emphasis. [28]

Hepworth's insistence on a complementary, not a competitive, model did not sit comfortably with Read's deliberate privileging of 'Englishness', 'genius', 'vision' and 'vitality' for Moore and his paradigm of modern British sculpture. It is also significant that it is not until the 1950s that Hepworth began to comment critically on women's position and the 'derogatory feminine'. This is after her own children had grown up and left home, when her own reputation had been established by several international showings at Venice and São Paulo and by several major retrospectives, and when critical interest had for a time shifted to the new post-war generation of artists including Lynn Chadwick and Eduardo Paolozzi.

Gender asymmetry was prominent in the critical debate about the relative merits of each sculptor early in the 1930s and was not peculiar to Read. Moore and Hepworth's names were linked through their individual participation in a series of group exhibitions. In the majority of publications these two sculptors' names and statements appear among others in publications such as *Circle*, *Unit One*, *The London Gallery Bulletin*, and *Abstraction-Création* [29]. The two artists never showed together except in the context of these larger group exhibitions, where what marked any point of comparison between them was the fact that they were both sculptors. Hepworth was one of the few women sculptors to take part in abstract exhibitions and publications; though we should not forget the constructions of Eileen Holding, or the paintings of Winifred Dacre/Nicholson, Jessica Dismorr, Mainie Jellett, Evie Hone, Paule Vezelay, Sophie Taeuber-Arp, and Marlow Moss.

When their work was contrasted directly in the 1930s, Moore was frequently identified as the English sculptor involved in biomorphic abstraction/Surrealism while Hepworth was positioned as abstract/Constructivist, and described as cold or emotional/intuitive [30]. Moore was frequently declared an English genius—owing much to the landscape, humanistic images of women and Surrealism; Hepworth was seen as more abstract, daringly modern. Her work was characterised as very experimental with an eye to continental Constructivism and suffused with the search for absolute values [31].

Geoffrey Grigson's 'Comment on England' in *Axis* in 1935, for example, summarises these two sculptors' projects in the context of Nash, Wadsworth, Nicholson, Jackson and Piper. Hepworth is identified as a sculptor 'more of the single image' and 'a viable abstractionist, more constricted and more exclusively (though in quality more slightly) emotional' whereas Moore is a 'multiform inventive artist, abstraction-surrealism nearly in control'. Grigson nevertheless identifies Moore and Wyndham Lewis as

> . . . the only English artists of maturity in control of enough imaginative power to settle themselves actively between the new preraphaelites of *Minotaure* and the unconscious nihilists of extreme geometric abstraction . . . [32]

both of which are identified as in opposition to the 'etiolated cliquish amateurism' and 'home-bred formalism' of Bloomsbury.

Opportunities for critics to review Moore's and Hepworth's work in isolation, on the basis of contemporary art exhibitions, were actually very few. Their simultaneous solo exhibitions in 1935 and in 1947 were rare opportunities for such a critical comparison. In both cases, Hepworth was showing at the Lefevre and Moore at the Leicester Galleries. Amongst the handful of comparative reviews, significantly, most critics praise Moore while criticising Hepworth. More significant still, it is also in this literature that the criticism of Hepworth's work is ever explicitly negative or derogatory—and these reviews were not selected for reproduction in *A Pictorial Autobiography*. Negative criticism of Hepworth by comparison with Moore centred on the identification of invention as opposed to influence. Moore was credited by Hugh Gordon Porteus in 1935 as being 'the first to turn Arp's toy into a work of art' and his ability to adapt a new idea and supersede his initial influence is used to credit him with the term 'genius' [33]. While Porteus notes that 'It seems likely that work by Barbara Hepworth suggested to Moore the possibilities of this new game', Hepworth's work was derided as being derivative:

> Take away from Barbara Hepworth all that she owes Moore, and nothing would remain but a solitary clutch of Brancusi eggs, with a few Arp scraps . . . Where Moore's forms are linked by an intangible bond of sympathy, attraction of opposite magnetic poles, Barbara Hepworth's are as deliberately based on similarity of forms, magnetic repulsion. Each unit is a highly individualised, haughty, feminine, enclosed lump, spurning its neighbour with a tacit *noli me tangere*. [34]

Such distinctions rely upon the contrasts against which they are made: they should not be read literally as qualities or attributes inherent to the artist or the work discussed. Porteus constructed his claims in 1935 about Moore's inventiveness not only against a woman sculptor but also against Epstein as an 'older semitic genius'. A great deal could be said about the centrality of 'Englishness' to the construction of critical discourse on Moore because nationality is noticeably absent from all critical discussion of Hepworth's work. Along with the term 'genius', it is specifically absent from Read's discussion of her. However, other writers do identify her work as a product of genius and however much she or they discuss the importance of specific landscapes, Cornish or Mediterranean, or the landscape of her Yorkshire upbringing, these are not used to locate her as a product of English culture nor to place her in a nationalistic framework [35]. Another way of conceiving of this is that Hepworth represents a model derived from European modernism which transcends specific nationality in Europe.

Gendered distinctions are far from absent in the writings of the majority of male critics who wrote about Hepworth between the 1930s and the 1960s. Read's work may have become the dominant model in retrospect, but his value system (in terms of the privileging of Moore) was not shared by his contemporaries in these decades. Most of those who did write about Hepworth also wrote about Moore, but the gendered distinctions were not always made in the same way—as examples from William Gibson in the 1940s, David Lewis in the 1950s and J. P. Hodin throughout this period indicate.

William Gibson, writing in 1947, identified a clear model of contrasting and complementary characteristics in each sculptor's work, and—while again attempting not to reduce the equation to gender alone—gender is interpreted through 'temperament' to become the distinguishing factor [36]. Gibson characterises Hepworth as moving from figuration to geometrical abstraction while Moore, after experimenting with abstraction, has returned to 'distortions of the human figure'.

> It is as though either artist at a particular moment tried the other's recipe and found it unsuited to his own temperament. Furthermore, they both have shown certain personal characteristics, evident even in their earlier work, which indicate a natural difference of temperament between them. [37]

Gibson pursues this distinction between Hepworth's 'unrepresentational style', comparing it to Moore's 'degree of naturalism' and contrasting its 'formal' interest with Moore's 'dramatic' interest; her 'delicate adjustment of curved surface and edge' with the 'gestural', 'unfinished' quality of Moore's work [38]. Gibson is openly critical of Moore's project for the ambiguity it creates because it relies on the representational element to gain the spectator's response while concentrating on formal distortions. Highlighting one particular sculpture Moore had recently shown, Gibson shows how this can produce a substantial misreading of the subject 'translated' by the work. The acceptability of Moore's form of modernism, coupled with Read's promotion which emphasised its 'monumental', humanist subjects retaining a 'representational' element, is undoubtedly what contributed to Moore's success in Britain. Comparatively Gibson describes the boldness of Hepworth's abstraction as moving away from a monumental, static, compact conception of sculpture towards experimentation with balance, a configuration in space in which the negative space within the sculpture is as suggestive as the carved form of the sculpture itself. Gibson offers a model of separate development for these two artists' projects but marks it as a 'natural' distinction, which by extension of his argument I take to mean an innate, biological difference—a sex difference defined in his characterisation of the two artists' temperaments. Underlying the argument is the unstated but obvious point that Moore's object is 'Woman' whereas Hepworth's arises from consideration of the bodily experience of 'being a woman'.

David Lewis' article in 1955 links these two artists in terms of their similar backgrounds and preoccupation with carving but rapidly distinguishes their projects as different responses to both the observation of nature and their perception of the inequality of forces and conflicts in the natural and human world [39]. Lewis characterises Moore as a 'realist rather than an idealist', a 'tragic artist' whose response is at best a form of passive and defiant resistance to the disequilibrium observed in nature:

> . . . a figure by Moore gives us a sculptural contrast of particular meaning and a controlled yet tremendous power. [40]

Hepworth, by contrast, has a different response, she refuses to accept the reflection of conflict as inevitable and her carving is

> . . . intended as an object in which a fact of integration takes place. It is a meeting place where a fact of living concordance occurs between

> innumerable separate forces: form, light, colour, rhythm, space, environment. [41]

Hepworth is here credited with developing new formal relationships which integrate modern formal principles abstracted initially from a natural 'truth', observing the natural world, but developed into a new form of 'human truth', the language of abstract form.

Another position again can be found in the work of J. P. Hodin, the only other critic besides Read to have written about Hepworth repeatedly over the course of several decades. Hodin began writing reviews of her work in 1948 and continued until 1966. His criticism was largely for art journals published in Belgium, Austria, the Netherlands, Germany and Italy, but he also wrote the catalogue for her successful showing at the São Paulo Bienal in 1959, for her British Council tour of Scandinavia in 1964–1965 and for a show in Zurich in 1960. Hodin's criticism did much to introduce and promote Hepworth's work in Europe, especially the Netherlands, and at the São Paulo Bienal. As a result of Hodin's critical attention, Hepworth was shown more widely in the Netherlands and earlier than Moore—the only anomaly in the pattern of Hepworth's continuous recognition after Moore in exhibitions in national and international art institutions. With respect to Hodin's writing it is also significant that the São Paulo Bienal marks the most successful celebration of her international stature.

Hodin also wrote about Henry Moore's work, both in the context of trends in modern sculpture and individually. His first essay on Moore was published in 1947 in *Palatten*, a Norwegian art magazine, and he produced two extended studies of his work—one in 1956 (as part of the 'Modern Sculptors' series) and the other a monograph in 1963 published in Buenos Aires [42].

In *The Dilemma of Being Modern* Hodin argued that 'abstract art is the expression of idealism of a time which is in a state of transition and of crisis' and that:

> The abstract artist does not rebel against his age but against certain of his shortcomings and tradition-bound errors and he does so because he believes in the new vistas that constructive scientific thought is opening up for mankind. [43]

Hodin's approach endorses Hepworth's position as expressed in 1937 in *Circle* and also found in her interview in *The Studio* in 1946, of a passionate affirmation of life and ideas in her work:

> A constructive work is an embodiment of freedom itself and is unconsciously perceived even by those who are consciously against it. The desire to live is the strongest universal emotion, it springs from the depths of our unconscious sensibility—and the desire to give life is our most potent, constructive, conscious expression of this intuition. [44]

Unlike Read, Hodin appears to have acknowledged the significance of Hepworth's work as the resolution of what he identified as a basic conflict in modern art between two essentially different approaches: formalist and expressionist. This underlies the clearly different treatment of both artists in Hodin's writing, but his words make clear the significance of Hepworth's work as carrying a life-affirming monism, a reverence for life which could answer what he identified as the dilemma of being modern:

> . . . unless we glorify life's forms in their ultimate significance, unless we reconcile emotionalism and analytical cerebralism in line, colour and handwriting with the finality of life's formative processes, we shall not create an art which is congenial to the wholeness of life. [45]

Perhaps the differences in approach of Hodin and Read are most apparent by juxtaposing two characterisations of their philosophy. David Thistlewood has argued that in Read's modernist paradigm:

> . . . the artist had to empathise (i) with subject-matter (whether phenomenal or noumenal), (ii) with the nature of materials (respecting their legitimate form) and (iii) with organic nature (permitting creative concepts to evolve naturally rather than constraining them with a false aesthetic). [46]

In strong contrast, K. Mitchells has characterised Hodin's critical project as one where the quest for the 'meaning' of the work of art lay:

> . . . in the framework of contemporary culture and ideology and its meaning as artistically expressed philosophical statement about the mysteries of life and creation, as philosophy in paint, in stone, in tone, in rhythm. [47]

One way to characterise these different approaches between Read and Hodin would be in terms of a British versus European perspective. Read emphasised the artist's relationship and reactions to materials in contrast to Hodin's emphasis upon their relationship to developments in European intellectual thought and philosophy. Another way of emphasising this contrast would be in terms of a practical versus spiritual/moral discipline which it is the critic's role to interpret. The modernist paradigm for scholarship in Read's work emphasises that the function of art is determined by the use art has to different societies rather than, in Hodin, where art is seen in the context of a history of ideas and emphasis is placed upon how modern science and technology affect modern art. In Hodin, the artist's project is determined through analysis of developments in contemporary philosophy/literature/psychology. Hodin was also critical of nationalism as the grounds for promoting or grounding an understanding of any artist, which by my extension of his argument includes Read's framework for promoting Moore [48].

Hodin's work is a very useful counter-example to Read, for he did not share Read's perceptions of Moore's work as a superior project. Unlike Read's characterisation of her as 'Other' to a masculine 'norm', Hodin places Hepworth's work at the centre of a resolution to the modern artistic dilemma which he defines. Hodin's comparisons with Moore take on a completely different inflection as a result. Nevertheless his account tends to emphasise reading Hepworth as an 'idealist', or, as Edwin Mullins calls her, 'an exultant optimist' [49], placing Moore by contrast as a 'realist'. For example, Hodin argued that when Hepworth pierced through the stone in 1932:

> A new function of space was discovered and she explored its possibilities with unfailing enthusiasm. But she did not and does not now use concavities and holes in the same sense as Henry Moore. Hers is a classical, a static conception; his is basically organic, nature-bound, romantic. Whereas the hole in a work of Barbara Hepworth pierces straight through a figure, Moore is inclined to widen and to wind through it. In reducing mass, he often diminishes the figure to a shell covering, as it were, the most important messages, the secret of within. Endless new aesthetic possibilities appeared to Barbara Hepworth of exploiting the music and the rhythm of lines created by light and shadow and by the boundaries where form and space meet. [50]

Hodin contrasts Hepworth's project—as classical, static, seeking and attaining 'absolute beauty'—with Moore's, that of an expressive sculptor possessing 'a biological formative will' in our technical age [51]. In the section on Moore, Hodin quotes liberally from Moore, including tautological statements like: 'A real sculptor must be a man with the mental equipment of the sculptor' and 'Purely abstract thinking is a matter of taste and design, it is not sculpture' and

> . . . I pierced an abstract geometrical form because I felt strongly its inadequacy. The hole might be a mouth, and the two points look like the small eyes of a skate; here the will to express the organic is manifest. [52]

These quotations reinforce the continuing representational bent in Moore's work as opposed to Hepworth's.

What is a useful emphasis within the different framework that Hodin established is the opening up of a different set of coordinates for evaluating Hepworth, one engaged in linking philosophy, science and society in a way in which Read's reduction of Hepworth to a search for 'loveliness' and the 'feminine' or to 'truth to materials' cannot accommodate. Hepworth's reactions to nature and the relationship of sculpture, sculptor and landscape can be re-read through this model in a way which avoids the stereotyping of her work as an 'eternal feminine' and begins to open up her philosophy and politics. Thus one could position Hepworth, not so much as marking an assimilable femininity or as 'woman', through a model of complementarity which is wholly unthreatening to the dominant critical ethos, but as marking women's entry into modernist discourse, introducing a destabilising point of difference—women's experiences/perspectives. It might also open up ways of reconceiving Hepworth's stress on the distinctive perspective of women's experience of the world—as a critique of philosophical, scientific and political 'truths'. Perhaps it will allow us to re-emphasise her ideas emerging from bodily experience and the relationships of physical sensation she embodied in abstraction within a broader understanding of this as parallelling human/political relationships. In *Carvings and Drawings* she wrote:

> From the sculptor's point of view one can either be the spectator of the object or the object itself. For a few years I became the object. I was the figure in the landscape and every sculpture contained to a greater or lesser degree the ever changing forms and contours embodying my own response to a given position within the landscape. [53]

Perhaps it may enable us to conceive of the movements from the string sculptures in the 1940s where she identified the strings as 'the tension I felt between myself and the sea, the wind or the hill' [54] to the work in the 1960s which she positions as a new exploration of her ideas from the 1930s, once she had the money, studio space and assistants to realise them.

> I find it easier now I'm more free to make forms and move them around. I don't feel so personally involved—I'm not exactly the sculpture in the landscape any more. I think of works as objects which rise out of the land or the sea, mysteriously. You can't make a sculpture without it being a thing—a creature, a figure, a fetish . . . It's something you experience through your senses, but it's also a life-giving, purposeful force. [55]

Edwin Mullins identifies this as a move from a two-partite formula 'fusion of "I" and object' to a three-partite formula: 'the "I", an object, a landscape'. He continues:

> The object is no longer mainly a projection of the 'I' but possesses a mysterious life of its own—also for its maker. Its existence and that of the 'I', producing the image-object, are two, and it presents a concrete presence *vis-à-vis* the third element, the landscape, as well. 'I' returns to spiritual/ritualistic. [56]

Perhaps we can see this as a move from the extreme internalisation and identification with 'Woman' as object in the 1940s into women's experience of the world becoming the subject. As Hepworth wrote to Mullins:

> This is not an optical sensation: it's a matter of physical relationship. [57]

NOTES AND REFERENCES

1 WITZLING, MARA S. (1992) *Voicing our Visions: Writings by Women Artists* (London, Women's Press), pp. 270–87 includes extracts from HEPWORTH, BARBARA (1970) *A Pictorial Autobiography* (New York, Praeger); interviews in *The Studio* Vol. 132, No. 645, October 1946; Hepworth's statement for READ, HERBERT (Ed) (1934) *Unit One: the Modern Movement in English Architecture, Painting and Sculpture* (London, Cassell); and 'Greek Diary' in KERN, W. (Ed) (1965) *J. P. Hodin: European Critic* (London, Cory, Adams & McKay); along with other short extracts. WALLER, SUSAN A. (1991) *Women Artists in the Modern Era: a Documentary History* (Metuchen, N.J. and London, Scarecrow Press) reproduces extracts from (1952) Barbara Hepworth: *Carvings and Drawings* (London, Lund Humphries), pp. 339–50.

2 See GILMORE, LEIGH (1994) *Autobiographics: a Feminist Theory of Women's Self-Representation* (Icatha, Cornell University Press), esp. Ch. 2, pp. 65–86.

3 HEPWORTH, BARBARA (1970) *A Pictorial Autobiography* (New York, Praeger and Moonraker Press). A similar argument could also be developed for *Carvings and Drawings* (n. 1) as a consolidation of Hepworth's views after the 1950 Venice Biennale.

4 *Ibid.*, p. 17.

5 See DEEPWELL, KATY (1994) 'A Fair Field and No Favour: Women Artists in Britain between the Wars', in: OLDFIELD, S. (Ed) (1994) *This Working-Day World: Women's Lives and Culture(s) in Britain, 1914–1945* (London, Taylor and Francis), pp. 141–55. See also Reg Butler's remarks on 'frustrated maternity' (1962) quoted in PARKER, R. and POLLOCK, G. (1981) *Old Mistresses: Women, Art and Ideology* (London, Routledge and Kegan Paul), pp. 6–7.

6 ROBERTSON, BRYAN (1962) 'Introduction', *Barbara Hepworth: an Exhibition of Sculpture from 1952–1962* (London, Whitechapel Art Gallery) unpag.

7 Letter Hepworth to Nicholson, 31 May 1970, quoted by Penelope Curtis in: CURTIS, PENELOPE and WILKINSON, ALAN G. (1994) *Barbara Hepworth: a Retrospective* (Liverpool, Tate Gallery Liverpool), p. 147.

8 Alan Bowness compiled her 1961 British Council exhibition catalogue, and wrote both *Barbara Hepworth: Drawings from a Sculptor's Landscape* (1965), and *The Complete Sculpture of Barbara Hepworth, 1960–1969* (London, Lund Humphries, 1971). Bryan Robertson wrote the catalogue essay for Hepworth's 1962 retrospective at the Whitechapel Art Gallery and reviewed her work in both *The Spectator* (1967, 1968) and *The Observer* (1964). Edwin Mullins reviewed her work several times in *The Sunday Telegraph*, wrote catalogue notes on her work for Coventry Cathedral's exhibition of British sculpture in 1968, and catalogues for her exhibitions at City Art Gallery, Portsmouth and Hakone Museum, Japan, 1970.

9 *Pictorial Autobiography*. Reproduced in Witzling (n. 1), p. 280.

10 *Ibid.*, p. 115. The poem is not reproduced.

11 THISTLEWOOD, DAVID (1993) 'Herbert Read's Paradigm: a British Vision of Modernism', in: READ, BENEDICT and THISTLEWOOD, DAVID (Eds) *Herbert Read: a British Vision of World Art* (Leeds City Art Gallery/Henry Moore Foundation and London, Lund Humphries), p. 77.

12 *Ibid.*

13 READ, HERBERT (1965) *Henry Moore: a Study of his Life and Work* (London, Thames & Hudson), p. 32. See also HALL, DONALD (1966) *Henry Moore: the Life and Work of a Great Sculptor* (London, Gollancz), p. 41.

14 Hall (n. 13), p. 59.

15 Read (n. 13), p. 32.

16 Read (n. 13), p. 83. Hall (n. 13), p. 106.

17 See HODIN, JOSEF P. (1961) *Barbara Hepworth* (London, Lund Humphries).

18 See HAMMACHER, A. M. (1959) *Barbara Hepworth* (London, Zwemmer). See also WILKINSON, ALAN (1994) 'The 1930s: Constructive Form and Poetic Sculpture', in: Curtis and Wilkinson (n. 7), pp. 31–78.

19 READ, HERBERT (1966) 'Introduction' in *Barbara Hepworth* (New York, Marlborough-

Gerson Gallery) reproduced in *Pictorial Autobiography* (n. 3), p. 104. His most praiseworthy comment is that Hepworth has been 'greatly honoured in her own country and her fame is now worldwide' but his choice of words make clear that his own writing or value judgments about her work have not contributed to her acclaim.

20 READ, HERBERT (1962) *A Letter to a Young Painter* (London, Thames & Hudson), pp. 120–27, 151–71.

21 BURSTOW, ROBERT (1993) 'The Geometry of Fear: Herbert Read and British Modern Sculpture after the Second World War', in: Read and Thistlewood (n. 11), p. 122.

22 *Ibid.*, p. 123.

23 READ, HERBERT (1952) 'Introduction', in: *Carvings and Drawings* (n. 1), p. ix.

24 RICHARDS, J. M. (1935) 'London Shows: Ben Nicholson at the Lefevre; 7 & 5 at Zwemmer's', *Axis: A Quarterly Review of Contemporary 'Abstract' Painting and Sculpture* No. 4, November, pp. 21, 24.

25 McCORMICK, E. H. (1969) 'Frances Hodgkins: a Pictorial Biography' *Ascent*, Commemorative Issue December 1969, p. 8.

26 Letter, B. NICHOLSON to W. Nicholson, 7 March 1932. Tate Gallery Archive.

27 HEPWORTH, BARBARA (1937) 'Sculpture', in: MARTIN, J. L., NICHOLSON, B. and GABO, N. (Eds) (1937) *Circle: International Survey of Constructive Art* (London, Faber), p. 113.

28 '1949–1952', in: *Carvings and Drawings* (n. 1), reproduced in Waller (n. 1), pp. 349–50.

29 *Circle* (n. 27); *Unit One* (n. 1); 'Living Art in England', *The London Gallery Bulletin* Jan.–Feb. 1939; *Abstraction-Création* No. 2, 1933 and No. 3, 1934.

30 'Nothing could be more remote from humankind than these superbly cold, calm, faceless works in an abstract idiom. And again, we may remark the contrast with Moore, whose figures are saturated by human feeling and personality.' HERON, PATRICK (1951) *B. Hepworth: Sculpture and Drawings* (Wakefield City Art Gallery) exhibition catalogue. unpag.

31 E.g. 'Living Art in England' (n. 29).

32 GRIGSON, GEOFFREY (1935) 'Comment on England', *Axis: A Quarterly Review of Contemporary 'Abstract' Painting and Sculpture*, January, pp. 9–10.

33 PORTEUS, HUGH GORDON (1935) 'New Planets', *Axis: A Quarterly Review of Contemporary 'Abstract' Painting and Sculpture* No. 3, pp. 22–23. A very similar line is taken in Wyndham Lewis' review of Hepworth and Moore in *The Listener*, 17 October 1946, p. 506.

34 Porteus (n. 33), p. 22.

35 E.g. Hammacher (n. 18).

36 GIBSON, W. (1947) 'Art: Two English Sculptors', *Britain Today* No. 129, January, pp. 30–31.

37 *Ibid.*, p. 30.

38 *Ibid.*

39 LEWIS, D. (1955) 'Moore and Hepworth', *College Art Journal*, Summer, pp. 314–319.

40 *Ibid.*, p. 319.

41 *Ibid.*

42 Hodin is relatively neglected today but he came to live in Britain in 1944. From 1949 to 1954, he was Director of Studies and librarian at the Institute of Contemporary Arts, London, and remained after 1954 on the I.C.A. board while continuing his long career as a European-wide art critic (from the mid-1930s), writing for and editing a large number of European art magazines. His work was preoccupied with introducing artists abroad to different national audiences in the spirit of international exchange. See VANEK, VLADIMIR (1965) 'J. P. Hodin: a Biographical Study', in: Kern (n. 1), esp. pp. 83–104.

43 HODIN, J. P. (1956) 'Barbara Hepworth: the Meaning of Abstract Art', in: *The Dilemma of Being Modern: Essays on Art and Literature* (London, Routledge & Kegan Paul), p. 130.

44 Hepworth, in *Circle* (n. 27), p. 116.

45 MITCHELLS, K. (1965) 'Art Criticism and Weltanschauung: the Cultural and Philosophical Background of J. P. Hodin's Writings', in: Kern (n. 1), p. 127.

46 Thistlewood (n. 11), p. 77.

47 Mitchells (n. 45), p. 123.

48 Vanek (n. 42), pp. 103–04.

49 MULLINS, E. (1970) *Barbara Hepworth* (London, British Council) exhibition cata-

logue, Hakone Open Air Museum, Japan, unpag.

50 Hodin (n. 43), p. 132.

51 *Ibid.*, p. 104.

52 *Ibid.*, pp. 104–05. In BOWNESS, A. (1971) *The Complete Sculpture of Barbara Hepworth 1960–1969* (London, Lund Humphries), Hepworth states 'I am always concerned with the human relationship' (p. 13)—i.e. physical relationships of human scale—and 'All my life through I've wanted to put a form on a form on a form as an offering' (p. 13).

53 *Carvings and Drawings* (n. 1), p. 19.

54 Bowness (n. 52), p. 14.

55 Mitchells (n. 45), p. 127.

56 MULLINS, E. (1972) 'Introduction', *B. Hepworth: Family of Man: Recent Carvings* (London, Marlborough Fine Art), April–May, p. 9.

57 Mullins (n. 49).

ANNE J. BARLOW

Barbara Hepworth and Science

INTRODUCTION

In her book *Barbara Hepworth: A Memoir* [1], Margaret Gardiner states that the relationship between art and science was a constant preoccupation of Hepworth's. The strength of this statement suggests that this aspect of her work is one which may have been largely overlooked in criticism to date. Unfortunately Margaret Gardiner does not expand upon her statement, and evidence of Hepworth's interest has to be found from other sources. References to science are made in Hepworth's own writings and in comments on her work by critics and friends. For the period covered by this paper—the 1930s and 1940s [2]—Hepworth's correspondence with Margaret Gardiner, the physicist and crystallographer J. D. Bernal, and the critic Herbert Read can be seen to offer most insight into her views. These remain the principal sources for the research to date—particularly as the dearth of Hepworth's own writings from this period in the Hepworth archive prevents a more comprehensive analysis of this aspect of her work [3].

Despite these circumstances, it is possible to establish from the available material that Hepworth's interest in science existed on two levels; firstly her concern about the social function of science in relation to that of art, and secondly, her interest in the way in which artists and scientists approached an understanding of form. These levels of interest can be seen to be interrelated, and an attempt will be made here to highlight some points of contact between them. It is not intended that this approach should supersede existing interpretations, but it will be argued that it can be seen as a valuable perspective on her work.

CONTEXTS

When considering a statement such as Gardiner's, one should start by questioning what was meant by the term 'science' within the context of the 1930s and 1940s in England. The term in its most general sense was used to refer to several disciplines, including physics, chemistry, biology, mathematics and psychology. Although the nature of their approach differs, it can generally be said that these different branches of science attempt to understand and interpret nature (including the study of humanity). It should also be remembered that these disciplines would have encompassed a variety of often opposing theories or philosophies. The use of the general term 'science' in connection with Hepworth's work therefore has little meaning unless it is clear which of these disciplines or philosophies found parallels in her work.

To assess the nature of Hepworth's knowledge of scientific thoughts or developments in the early to mid 1930s, it is useful to consider her contact with scientists (and artists) who may have affected her emerging views on the nature of the relationship between the two fields. In *Experiments in Totality*, Sibyl Moholy-Nagy recollects that Hepworth was part of a London circle which included Herbert Read, Jack Pritchard, Julian Huxley, Jim Crowther, J. D. Bernal, Henry Moore and Ben Nicholson [4]. Discussions within such an 'art and science' group are likely to have raised Hepworth's awareness of current scientific thought, as would her links with European artists, both through her visits to Europe in the early 1930s [5] and subsequently through her increased contact with them after their arrival in England in the late 1930s.

Artists such as Naum Gabo, whose notions of the relationship between art and science were more developed than those of most British artists, could well have proved enlightening contacts. Hepworth's friendship with Herbert Read, in particular, appears to have been important in developing notions within the artistic community of the relation between art and science in the 1930s. Read's association with artists in London at this time (particularly Hepworth and Gabo) has been shown by David Thistlewood to have influenced the development of Read's theories on this subject [6]. Following her move to St. Ives with Ben Nicholson in 1939, Hepworth continued to maintain contact with Read and also Bernal (who carried out secret war work in Cornwall).

THE SOCIAL FUNCTION OF ART AND SCIENCE

Hepworth's views on the social function of art and science are evident in her letters to Margaret Gardiner [7]. In these letters, Hepworth expressed concern that the speed of progress in science alone could be detrimental to society, and implied that the potential social value of art and science was dependent on their developing at a similar pace. She referred to the impact of new technology during the Second World War as an example of the dangers of a lack of synchronism between the two:

> It seems to me that unless we fight like the devil for every human and creative value our senses cannot survive the cold power of a machine age. [8]

This feeling seems to have informed her definition of cultural progress as the 'acceptance and understanding of the machine age' [9] which should follow *only* from a full knowledge of its 'benefits and detriment to man, both biologically and psychologically . . .' [10]. The knowledge gained from a fuller understanding of all man's needs—moral, social and emotional—could then be taken into account and used constructively. Of her own position, she states:

> I should consider myself an imbecile to accept each new discovery as good in itself because it's new or scientific . . . [11]

Hepworth reinforced her views on the relationship between art and the 'machine age' in a letter to Read in May 1944, in response to his draft essay on Henry Moore's sculpture. Read had pointed to the fact that constructive art was sometimes perceived to be linked to the machine, and Hepworth was at pains to stress that this could result in the reader's misapprehension of constructive art. In the letter, she described the machine as being the result of a 'collective function with its own laws', unlike the work of art which was produced as a result of both the 'heart and the emotions' [12]. Rather than accept a significant impact of the forms of technology on art, Hepworth even seemed to suggest that art may have influenced the evolution of certain design concepts, relating the evolution of the shape of the Spitfire aircraft to the 'pure lines' of Brancusi's sculpture.

Within a wider context the publication *Circle: International Survey of Constructive Art* (1937) [13], to which Hepworth contributed, is an important document of contemporary views on the role of art and science in society. Although primarily concerned with clarifying the definitions and aims of 'constructive' art, the publication contained a number of references to the perceived social function of art and science. Differences of opinion on the exact nature of this function are apparent, but contributors shared the view that the widening gulf between the two fields was detrimental to society. For most writers in *Circle*, both artists and scientists had an obligation to address this problem. It is not the purpose of this essay to question the validity of this position, nor to dwell on whether *Circle* represented (from both a scientific and an artistic perspective) an overly idealistic view. What is important is that the publication provides a context for Hepworth's views by 1937. Her comments on the social function of art in her essay are, however, somewhat opaque and require interpretation:

> It is the sculptor's work fully to comprehend the world of space and form, to project his individual understanding of his own life and time as it is related universally in this particular extension of thought, and to keep alive this special side of existence. A clear social solution can only be achieved when there is a full consciousness in the realm of thought and when every section constitutes an inherent part of the whole. [14]

This consciousness for Hepworth seems, in part, to be one of 'form consciousness':

> The consciousness and understanding of volume and mass, laws of gravity, contour of the earth under our feet, thrusts and stresses of internal structure, space displacement and space volume. [15]

One could find links here with the Hegelian view that the logical outcome of human evolution would be complete consciousness—the 'absolute' mind. If one takes Hepworth's statements in this context, a possible interpretation would be that her ideal would be an improved social order in which people were more aware of their own experience in relation to their own 'time'. This awareness would come from a 'full consciousness' which embodied the kind of understanding implicit in her statements on form consciousness. This consciousness would be expressed and communicated through the form of the work of art itself.

The strength of her convictions about the need for art and science to act from common moral and political grounds can be seen in the way in which her relationship with J. D. Bernal changed from the late 1930s to the mid 1940s. This period was marked by the publication of Bernal's *The Social Function of Science* (1939), C. H. Waddington's *The Scientific Attitude* (1941) and Marcus Brumwell's *This Changing World* (1944). These publications advocated greater collaboration between science and art in order to affect and improve society. This notion, which had gathered increasing momentum from the early 1930s, was very much 'in the air' at the time Margaret Gardiner introduced Bernal to Hepworth.

The value Hepworth placed on Bernal's comments on her work as their friendship developed may well have been aided by their generally shared beliefs in the social function of art and science during this period. Hepworth and Bernal stressed the importance of the social 'utility' of both science and art, but it is interesting to note that this affinity with each other's stance lessened as Bernal's views were increasingly motivated by Marxist doctrine. His belief that art should have direct social utility above all else was seen by Hepworth as 'blind doctrinism' and she commented in a letter to Gardiner after the war:

> I could not ask him to write about my work when he feels the work is useless . . . This is of no importance as far as he or I are concerned personally, but it is of paramount importance in relation to society . . . [16]

It is clear from this that his views on the definitions of social 'utility' by this time had developed to the stage that they were no longer compatible with her own.

AN APPROACH TO FORM—INTUITION OR ANALYSIS?

In looking at the 'formal' aspects of Hepworth's work, it is interesting to consider some of the 'scientific' allusions made both by scientists and art critics. Of those who have commented on her work in relation to science, some have referred to the similarities between the external appearance of Hepworth's sculptural forms and graphic representations of physical phenomena, while others have attempted more in-depth analyses.

An example of the first kind of approach can be seen in Peter Goffin's article published in *Image*, No. 2 (1949). Goffin refers to the similarities between the graphic representation of a pendulum's movement in space and the shape of a carving by Hepworth. He refers to the combination of thought and feeling in what he views as the artistic process, and expresses admiration for Hepworth, who he feels has 'intuitively' understood a particular type of movement in space. He relates this understanding to the artist's awareness of certain fundamental principles and dynamic laws, including the principles of growth, order and balance, and the artist's need to communicate this through a work of art.

The artist's 'intuitive', as opposed to 'analytical', powers were thus seen as the primary means through which artists were able to approximate the scientist's understanding and interpretation of forms. This stance presumably arose from the assumption that it was unlikely for artists to possess an understanding of complex scientific principles. It would, however, be difficult to apply this notion universally, as it implies that intuition was primarily a characteristic of an artistic, as opposed to a scientific, approach. It could be argued that it would be difficult to state that intuition plays no part in scientific research, or that analysis is foreign to particular types of artistic practice; this statement is then perhaps best taken as an indication of the degree to which one or the other is present in the artist's or scientist's approach.

In his article in *Circle* Bernal adopted a similar approach to Goffin in comparing Hepworth's *Two Forms* (Fig. 19) with a graphic interpretation of the equipotential surface of two like charges:

> There is an extraordinary grasp of the unity of a surface which although separated in space and apparently disconnected yet belong together both to the mathematician and the sculptor. [17]

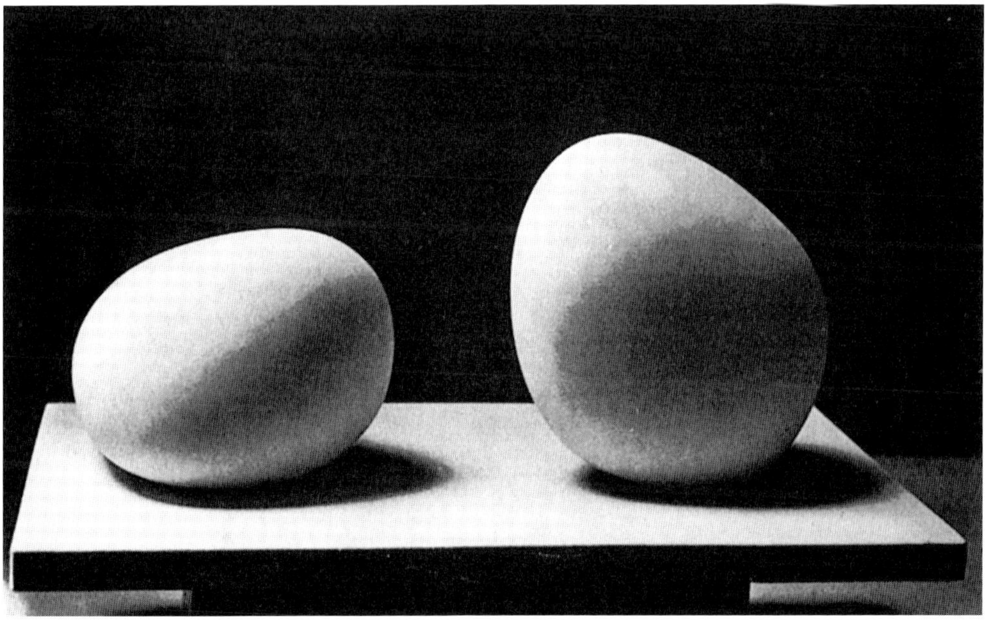

Fig. 19 BARBARA HEPWORTH, *Two Forms*, 1935 © Trustees of the Barbara Hepworth Estate/Art Gallery of Ontario

In referring to this 'extraordinary grasp', Bernal also makes an implicit reference to the role of intuition. It appears that his observation about this aspect of her work was a reasonably accurate one—Hepworth herself reinforced the role of intuition in terms of her own practice and related this to the work of other 'constructive' artists. In a letter to Bernal in the late 1930s she comments:

> . . . we work intuitively whereas you can express it and apply it in constructive criticism because science, surely, does not work as emotionally as painting or sculpture . . . [18]

Hepworth expands on these comments in her statements about the laws underlying both natural and 'artistic' form:

> You always seem to me to be searching for, discovering and applying basic laws and principles . . . It seems to me that we know these laws emotionally and intuitively, learning by our experience and trying to live the sort of life that will most easily enable us to express the laws—that is construction. [19]

An interest in the laws determining both artistic and scientific 'form' can be seen to be one of the more constant aspects of the discussions between Hepworth and Bernal. It is clear in the same letter to Bernal that he had commented on the composition of the sculpture *Three Forms* (1935) (Fig. 20). Hepworth's response to these comments was decidedly welcoming:

> Your criticism is most stimulating because you know exactly when a law has been broken and can apply the principle so that you can make the solution clear . . . When you criticised my carving and said this was wrong and should have been this you were quite right, sculpturally, spatially, and constructively. [20]

Hepworth attributed this perceived 'inadequacy' in her work to a lack of clarity of thought:

> . . . my state of mind when I did it was not sufficiently clear. Consequently the other 2 shapes have not the perfection that was required to solve the third shape . . . [21]

Bernal's perception of her work in this case is particularly interesting, as it shows that he was considered able to ascertain when the laws governing artistic—and not scientific—form had not been fully realised. Their interest in each other's fields was apparently evident from their first meeting. Gardiner noted that Bernal was immediately fascinated by her carvings, whilst Hepworth was intrigued to know more about his explanations of their historic and scientific parallels. An indication of what these 'historic' parallels may have been can be seen in Bernal's introduction to the exhibition of Hepworth's work at the Lefevre Gallery in 1937, when he

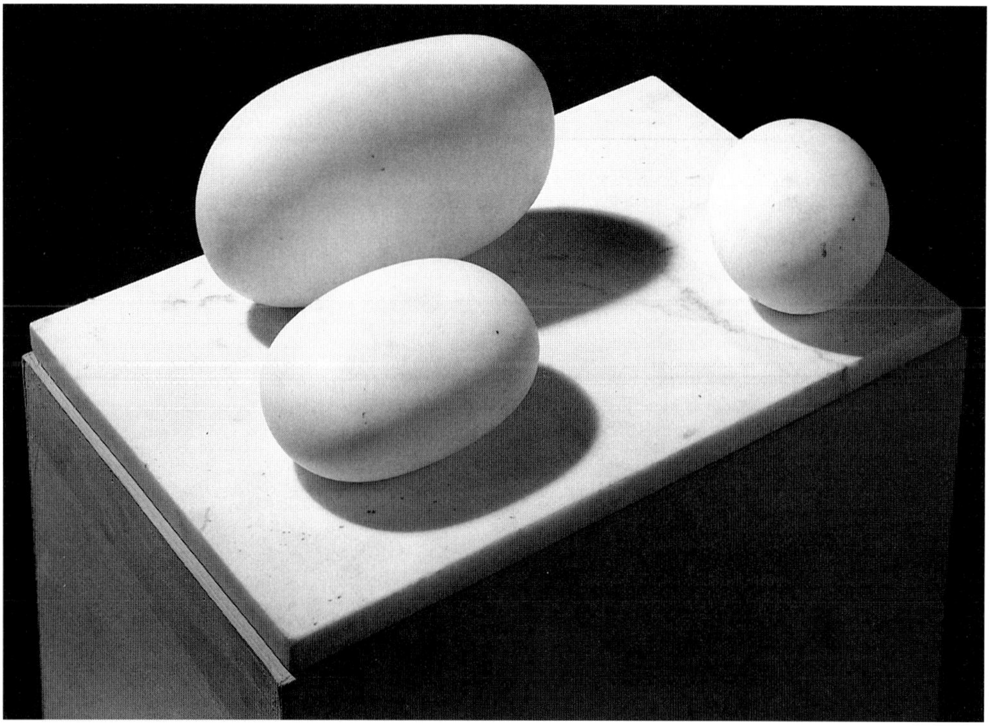

Fig. 20 BARBARA HEPWORTH, *Three Forms*, 1935 © Trustees of the Barbara Hepworth Estate/Tate Gallery London

compared Hepworth's work and neolithic stone monuments. In terms of the scientific parallels, he referred to four of her single forms and stated:

> Though at first sight similar, comparison brings out subtle differences of entasis and change of section. They may indeed be considered to introduce a fourth dimension into sculpture, representing by a surface the movement of a closed curve in time. [22]

Bernal also focused on the simplicity of Hepworth's forms, and noted that there was evidence in her work of a process of reduction. His analysis thus extended beyond the 'superficial' appearance of the forms in his comments on what this process revealed in her work:

> By reducing traditional forms of sculpture it is possible to see the geometry which underlies it . . . [23]

One of the ways in which Hepworth's work may have gone through this process is implied in her own comments in *Circle*:

> Very often, as the thought becomes more free the line is purified, and as principles—the laws which contain lesser laws—are comprehended, the forms become simplified and strengthened. [24]

The use of geometrical forms in constructive art of the late 1920s and 1930s was regarded by some critics as evidence of an interest in the laws which govern the external appearance of natural forms, although this view was by no means the one adopted by critics or the public [25]. A wider context for Hepworth's interest in the laws governing form can be seen in the essays in *Circle*. As Leslie Martin commented in 'The State of Transition':

> It is a matter of common knowledge that in science as in art, the world of 'appearances' has been jettisoned in favour of a world discovered only through the penetration of appearances. [26]

With regard to Hepworth's own work, this notion of the penetration of appearances might be reflected in her piercing of the solid form as early as 1932. Hepworth's comments in *Circle* add another dimension to this:

> Vision is not sight—it is the perception of the mind. It is the discernment of the reality of life, a piercing of the superficial surfaces of material existence, that gives a work of art its own life and purpose and power. [27]

The penetration of the 'superficial surfaces of material existence' can be seen not only to echo contemporary concerns of science, but also certain aspects of Christian Science—with which Hepworth had become familiar primarily through her relationship with Ben Nicholson—especially an emphasis on the 'spiritual', which for Christian Scientists was the perceivable reality beyond the penetration of material appearances, and also the notion in that the spirit manifests itself through 'thought-forms' [28].

Bernal's perception of the geometry underlying the forms in her work can also be seen in the context of the production of images of the internal structure of natural form revealed through micro-photography. Charles Harrison has pointed to the availability of reproductions of these images, referring specifically to Karl Blossfeldt's *Art Forms in Nature* (reissued in English in the early 1930s). Blossfeldt's prints were shown in the Leicester Galleries in 1929, and images of the plates were reproduced in R. Wilenski's *The Meaning of Modern Sculpture* (1932). In terms of expanding artists' knowledge of the internal structure of natural phenomena, and of processes of growth, Harrison also points to the potential influence of D'Arcy Thompson's *On Growth and Form* (reprinted in 1942) which he claims was 'widely consumed among the avant-garde' at that time [29]. The work of Thompson was certainly something with which Henry Moore was familiar by the 1930s, and Thompson's ideas may well have been discussed within the artistic community in London as a result [30]. In addition to absorbing ideas through these wider associations, it is likely that Hepworth had at least second-hand knowledge of the internal structure of natural phenomena as revealed through the process of magnification [31]. Hepworth's interest in the 'internal structure' of form is referred to by Alan Bowness in his comments on her drawing of the late 1930s:

> The kind of drawing associated with such sculptures as the *Pierced Hemisphere* of 1938 . . . is precise, measured, cool, and totally abstract—an examination of crystal structure and a construction of forms within cubes and circles and polyhedrons which reminds one that Barbara Hepworth has always found friends among mathematicians and pure scientists. [32]

Within this context, it is useful to consider in what way such drawings constituted *examinations* of crystal structure.

In his biography of Bernal, Maurice Goldsmith recalls that Hepworth 'loved the visits of Bernal, who would examine her works and explain their mathematical and geometrical forms' [33]. He also refers to a comment made by Marcus Brumwell, who visited Hepworth's studio in St. Ives, that Bernal wrote:

> . . . the equation of part of a sculpture on that part, using delible pencil . . . they both used to clear space on the floor . . . and draw things for each other, both excitedly understanding each other's ideas . . . [34]

But what kind of understanding could Brumwell have meant here? Hammacher has pointed out in his book on Hepworth's life that she 'seemed to have no difficulty at all with mathematics and geometry, including solid geometry' [35]. He also states that Hepworth had 'studied mathematical models in Paris and London in her youth . . .' [36]. Bernal reinforces the 'mathematical' connotations of her work in his reference to Hepworth's crystal drawings as 'the locus of the ultimate intersections of consecutive curves in a system of curves' [37]. Given this dialogue, it is tempting to think that Bernal's study of crystalline forms could in some way have influenced Hepworth's work. Yet if one looks at Hammacher's qualification of this statement, it could be argued that it would be dangerous to take this too literally.

Hammacher observes that Hepworth's response to these models was to 'let the idea lie dormant in her mind until she could use it emotionally, not mathematically'. This is confirmed for Hammacher in the way in which her drawings cannot be read as representations of crystal structures, as some of the forms are 'highly unusual and illogical' [38]. In a letter to Read in May 1944, Hepworth appears to bear out this interpretation:

> . . . I seem to be incapable of starting with an 'idea' or 'subject' and all the shells and bones and crystals I tend to enjoy more with my heart rather than understanding them with my head . . . [39]

The references to mathematics, or scientific models, in her work should then be viewed with these comments in mind. Movement of the human form in space was also an important part of her understanding of dynamic form, and should be taken into account when looking at this aspect of her work. Her interest in the physical manifestations of growth patterns in nature can be seen in her use of crystalline or spiral shapes in her sculpture. It has been shown, however, that these forms did not always relate to existing, perceived forms in nature. Hepworth also referred to the shape of the crystal in her statement about the way in which people interact or move within a particular space, noting:

> . . . the unconscious grouping of people when they are working together, producing a spatial movement that approximates to the structure of spirals in shells or rhythms in crystal structure . . . [40]

These statements allow one to look at the works most commonly ascribed to 'mathematical' influences—the crystal drawings and the stringed works—in a new light. Hepworth's statement about the works which incorporated strings is revealing, as it echoes her comments on the spatial movement relating to the crystalline forms in her work. On a superficial level, these are the works which most visibly echo the forms of the mathematical models she had seen years earlier, in terms of her use of strings to connect two or more points within her sculptures. It could be said that Hepworth benefited from her understanding of the role of the strings in the mathematical models, in that the strings could be seen to represent her greater understanding of lines as directional forces which express tension. Her use of this understanding should, however, be seen in the wider context of her preoccupation with the way in which the human being (in this case herself as an artist) related to the rest of nature, and the natural laws which govern it. Her statements about her use of strings illuminate this:

> I used colour and strings in many of the carvings of this time. The colour in the concavities plunged me into the depths of the water, caves, or shadows deeper than the concavities themselves. The strings were the tension I felt between myself and the sea, the wind and the hills. [41]

It can be seen, therefore, through her dialogue with Bernal, that Hepworth was interested in the scientist's understanding of nature and intrigued to find parallels in their approaches. The extent to which Hepworth would have used a scientist's visual interpretation of this understanding (i.e. mathematical models) as inspiration for the forms in her work is debatable. Her study of forms such as the mathematical models could be viewed rather as a means of enhancing her 'form consciousness' as opposed to an acceptance of them on a purely literal level. However, it can be shown that this 'form consciousness' had other dimensions which should be taken into account.

Hepworth's statements on her work in relation to 'the body' indicate one of these dimensions:

> From a sculptor's point of view one can either be the spectator of the object or the object itself. For a few years I became the object. I was the figure in the landscape and every sculpture contained to a greater or lesser degree the ever-changing forms and contours embodying my own response to a given position in that landscape. [42]

It is interesting here to compare Hepworth's statements with Henri Focillon's *Life of Forms* and the introduction to the new edition of his work by Jean Molina. Molina draws on a statement by A. Leroi-Gourham:

> This code of aesthetic emotions, based on biological properties common to all living creatures, is that of the senses which afford a perception of values and rhythms, or more generally still, from the simplest invertebrates on, a reflexive participation in rhythms and a reaction to variations in values. [43]

Molina compares this to Focillon's own thoughts on form, and remarks:

> Form is therefore not primarily line and colour, it is a dynamic organization that brings into play the concrete texture of the world as the sum of the body's reactions to that which surrounds it. [44]

It is possible to find parallels with this notion in a statement made by Hepworth on her reactions to nature: 'I rarely draw what I see—I draw what I feel in my body' [45].

The links between Hepworth's approach and Focillon's work could therefore merit further investigation, particularly given Hepworth's response to the phrase the 'life of forms' used by Focillon and referred to by Read in an article on Moore. From her letter to Read in May 1944, it is apparent that Hepworth had not yet read Focillon's work, but she expressed great interest in being sent a copy of the book (*La Vie des Formes*, then still untranslated into English).

> I think the greatest impact of pleasure was when I came to 'a life of forms'. These 4 words seem pregnant to me of everything that matters—the full reality of sculpture. Sculpture is 'reality' for me . . . because sculpture has its own intrinsic power . . . natural laws and obeys them and yet rises above them . . . and it seems to me that there is no limitation on this power or vitality . . . It is in the shape itself that sculptural vitality is released and very much in its spatial displacement . . . [46]

The notion of vitality being released through the work as a manifestation of some inner process is evident in the way in which Hepworth viewed the work of art as possessing vitality not through its physical attributes, but rather through its spiritual inner life—an inner force and energy. The work would then continue to 'live' through the very nature of its spatial displacement. Again, one can compare this with Focillon's comment on the vitality of forms:

> They mingle with life, whence they come; they translate into space certain movements of the mind. [47]

The correspondence between Hepworth's work and contemporary scientific philosophical thought is to be investigated further, as is her relationship with Bernal and Read. Nevertheless, the issues raised above show that to make purely superficial comparisons between 'scientific' forms and Hepworth's work can be misleading, and is an approach which does not reveal the depth or complexity of her thoughts on the subject.

NOTES AND REFERENCES

1 GARDINER, MARGARET (1982) *Barbara Hepworth: a Memoir* (Edinburgh, The Salamander Press), p. 28.

2 This paper is part of continuing research into the relationship between art (principally sculpture) and science between 1937 and 1951, the respective dates of the publications MARTIN, J. L., NICHOLSON, B. and GABO, N. (Eds) (1937) *Circle: International Survey of Constructive Art* (London, Faber) and WHYTE, LANCELOT LAW (Ed) (1952) *Aspects of Form* (London, Lund Humphries).

3 According to Sir Alan Bowness, Hepworth did not keep much correspondence from the 1930s and 1940s: it is therefore difficult to obtain original documentation from this period.

4 MOHOLY-NAGY, SIBYL (1950) *Experiment in Totality* (New York, Harpers) [London and Cambridge, Mass., The MIT Press, 1969], p. 135. The members of this 'group' present a range of 'disciplines' from physics and crystallography (J. D. Bernal) and natural science (Julian Huxley) to art (Nicholson, Moore and Hepworth).

5 Hepworth had visited Paris in spring 1933 and met, among others, Brancusi and Arp.

6 The development of Read's theories of 'organicism' (particularly in relation to creativity) are studied in THISTLEWOOD, DAVID (1984) *Herbert Read, Formlessness and Form: an Introduction to his Aesthetics* (London, Routledge & Kegan Paul), in particular the chapter entitled 'Superrealism and Abstraction'.

7 Currently held in the Hepworth archive; reproduced in part in Gardiner (n. 1).

8 *Ibid.*, p. 36.

9 *Ibid.*, p. 54.

10 *Ibid.*

11 *Ibid.*, p. 55.

12 Letter HEPWORTH to Read dated 17 May 1944, 48/61 VlCT. Ref: HR/BH-76, p. 3. Sir Herbert Read Archive, University of Victoria, B.C.

13 *Circle* (n. 2). Reprinted 1971.

14 *Ibid.*, p. 115.

15 *Ibid.*

16 Gardiner (n. 1), p. 54.

17 BERNAL, J. D. (1937) 'Art and the Scientist', in: *Circle* (n. 2), p. 121.

18 Letter HEPWORTH to Bernal [1937–39]. Bernal Archive, University of Cambridge.

19 *Ibid.*

20 *Ibid.*

21 *Ibid.*

22 BERNAL, J. D. (1937) 'Introduction', cat. exhib. *Barbara Hepworth* (London, Alex. Reid & Lefevre), October, p. 2.

23 *Ibid.*

24 HEPWORTH, BARBARA (1937) 'Sculpture', in: *Circle* (n. 2), p. 114.

25 One of the main criticisms by the media was precisely that the forms used by the artists who contributed to *Circle* were too geometrical, cold and mechanical. These works were allied with scientific or mathematical interpretations of form but in a negative manner which seemed rather to deny the links between these geometrical forms and nature and emphasise those with the 'man-made' machine.

26 MARTIN, J. L. (1937) 'The State of Transition', in: *Circle* (n. 2), p. 217.

27 Hepworth (n. 24), p. 113.

28 Hepworth's interest in Christian Science continues to be investigated; some references which have obviously been made to it cannot, however, be explored in more depth as consultation of the relevant part of the Tate Gallery Archive is not yet permitted.

29 HARRISON, CHARLES (1981) *English Art and Modernism 1900–1939* (London, Allen Lane; Bloomington, Indiana University Press), p. 282.

30 As noted in MUNDY, JENNIFER (1986)

Biomorphism, unpublished thesis, University of London.

31 In his study of Bernal's life, Maurice Goldsmith refers to an occasion when Bernal took Ben Nicholson to C. D. Darlington's laboratory to show him the structures of vegetable cells, genes and chromosomes through a microscope. See GOLDSMITH, MAURICE (1980) *Sage: a Life of J. D. Bernal* (London, Hutchinson), p. 225.

32 BOWNESS, ALAN (1966) 'Introduction', *Barbara Hepworth: Drawings from a Sculptor's Landscape* (London, Cory, Adam & Mackay), p. 17.

33 Goldsmith (n. 31), p. 87.

34 *Ibid.*, p. 225.

35 HAMMACHER, A. M. (1958) *Barbara Hepworth* (London, Zwemmer), p. 12.

36 *Ibid.*, p. 76

37 Goldsmith (n. 31), p. 225.

38 Hammacher (n. 35), p. 85.

39 Letter HEPWORTH to Read dated 17 May 1944, 48/61 VICT. Ref. HR/BH-79, p. 6. Sir Herbert Read Archive, University of Victoria, B.C.

40 HEPWORTH, BARBARA (1970, 1985) *A Pictorial Autobiography* (New York, Praeger; London, Tate Gallery), p. 67.

41 (1952) *Barbara Hepworth: Carvings and Drawings* (London, Lund Humphries); Part 4: 'The War, Cornwall, and Artist in Landscape 1939–1946', unpag.

42 *Ibid.*

43 FOCILLON, HENRI (1948) *The Life of Forms* (N.Y., Wittenborn, Schultz Inc.). Revised edition (1989) Trans. MOLINA, JEAN (New York, Urzone), p. 17. Molina quotes from LEROI-GOURHAM, A. (1965) *Le Geste et la Parole: La Memoire et les Rythmes* (Paris, Albin Michel), p. 82.

44 *Ibid.*

45 HEPWORTH, BARBARA, in *Sculptor's Landscape* (n. 32), p. 11.

46 Letter HEPWORTH to Read, dated 17 May 1944, 48/61 VICT. Ref. HR/BH-77, pp. 4–5. Sir Herbert Read Archive, University of Victoria, B.C. Focillon's *La Vie des Formes* was first published in 1934. This would seem to be the version referred to as the first English translation was not published until 1948 (N.Y., Wittenborn, Schultz Inc.).

47 *Life of Forms* (n. 43), p. 60.

MARTIN HAMMER and CHRISTINA LODDER

Hepworth and Gabo: a Constructive Dialogue

In 1952 Barbara Hepworth paid fulsome tribute to the 'profound effect' which Naum Gabo had exerted on the artistic community living in St. Ives:

> His unusual powers of expression in discussion and the exceptional charm of his personality when talking of creative processes seemed to unleash a great energy in all who came near him . . . It is impossible to forget either the extraordinary beauty of his sculptures or the most rare warmth of his nature. [1]

Such remarks inevitably raise the question of whether Hepworth herself may have been stimulated by Gabo's ideas and creative practice.

Gabo moved to England in March 1936 and stayed until November 1946, when he left for America. Throughout these ten years, he and Hepworth were working in close proximity. Before the war they lived a stone's throw apart in North London, ensconced in Herbert Read's proverbial

> . . . 'nest' of gentle artists . . . a spontaneous association of men and women drawn together by common sympathies, shared seriousness and some kind of group criticism. [2]

Gabo was one of a number of émigrés whose contribution and presence were highly valued in this *milieu*. He had previously worked in Russia, Germany and France, but found London

> . . . such a contrast with Paris which was violent, gossipy and full of intrigue and jealousies, which I hated, and London to me was like coming to a place of peace from a place of war . . . [3]

The special intimacy of Gabo's friendship with Ben Nicholson and Hepworth is demonstrated by his asking them to be witnesses at his wedding in 1937. In September 1939, on the outbreak of the Second World War, Hepworth and Nicholson persuaded the Gabos to join them in Cornwall. For the duration of the conflict, they all lived, and tried to carry on working, in the small coastal village of Carbis Bay just outside St. Ives.

The relationship between Hepworth and Gabo clearly encompassed mutual affection, a strong sense of creative kinship and a capacity to communicate with each other as fellow sculptors. In a long letter to Hartley Ramsden in 1943, describing her fundamental sculptural ideas and aspirations, Hepworth referred to such concerns as 'things I usually only talk to Gabo about' [4]. Around the same time she remarked:

> Gabo & I sometimes comfort each other by confiding our secret thoughts about sculpture in relation to life to each other. [5]

Although Gabo was thirteen years older than Hepworth, both were fully-formed artists by 1936. In examining the work they produced over the following years, we shall argue that their creative relationship was one of mutual respect and interchange. This will serve to qualify the accepted generalisation that Gabo was the dominant figure, and that Hepworth admired and was influenced by his work. In fact they probably got to know of each other's work at around the same time, after Gabo settled in Paris in 1933. Hitherto he had been better known in England as the designer of Diaghilev's ballet *La Chatte* than as an avant-garde sculptor [6]. In the mid 1930s, however, Gabo and the English modernists had ample opportunity to meet and to see one another's work [7]. Nicholson and Hepworth were making regular trips to Paris, and Gabo spent three weeks in London in June 1935. Gabo could also have seen Hepworth's sculpture in the *Abstraction-Création* exhibitions and bulletins in 1933–34; both were members of this Paris-based organisation dedicated to promoting abstract art [8].

By early 1936 Ben Nicholson was certainly on friendly terms with Gabo. In January that year he wrote to Herbert Read from Paris about his meetings with artists including Gabo, and reported the latter's surprisingly extravagant enthusiasm for Hepworth's art:

> Gabo is directly in touch with Today & with a very wide & far reaching grasp of life. Potentially, he is one of the most important people working. He seems to hold a very high opinion of Barbara's work—he said her sculpture is the most important being made today either abroad or in England. He then went on to say that in England he also admired Moore's work very much & that he was bound to arrive at something very important but that he had not yet evolved his true idea as Barbara has. [9]

A few months later, in an article on 'Constructive Art' published in *The Listener*, Gabo illustrated Hepworth's *Single Form* (1935) and compared its 'majestic quietness and static harmony' to the classical Hermes of Praxiteles:

> In its plastic content it is more akin . . . than any attempt to imitate the external features of the Greek statue. [10]

Gabo's interest in the work which English artists were producing was clearly one factor in his decision to move to London.

Gabo arrived in time for the London opening of the *Abstract and Concrete* exhibition where non-figurative works by English and European artists were shown together for the first time. Gabo's contribution was his *Circular Relief* from the mid 1920s (Fig. 21). In a construction such as this, the almost machine-like regularity of the forms, the use of synthetic materials, and the emphasis on spatial depth and transparency seem remote from the work of the British sculptors and its concerns with mass and natural materials. The mid 1930s, however, saw significant developments in Gabo's work which brought him closer to the British school. This is particularly apparent in *Stone with a Collar* (Fig. 22), the first construction in which he explored a more irregular language of curvilinear form, and incorporated solid volumes produced by carving. While the collar is made

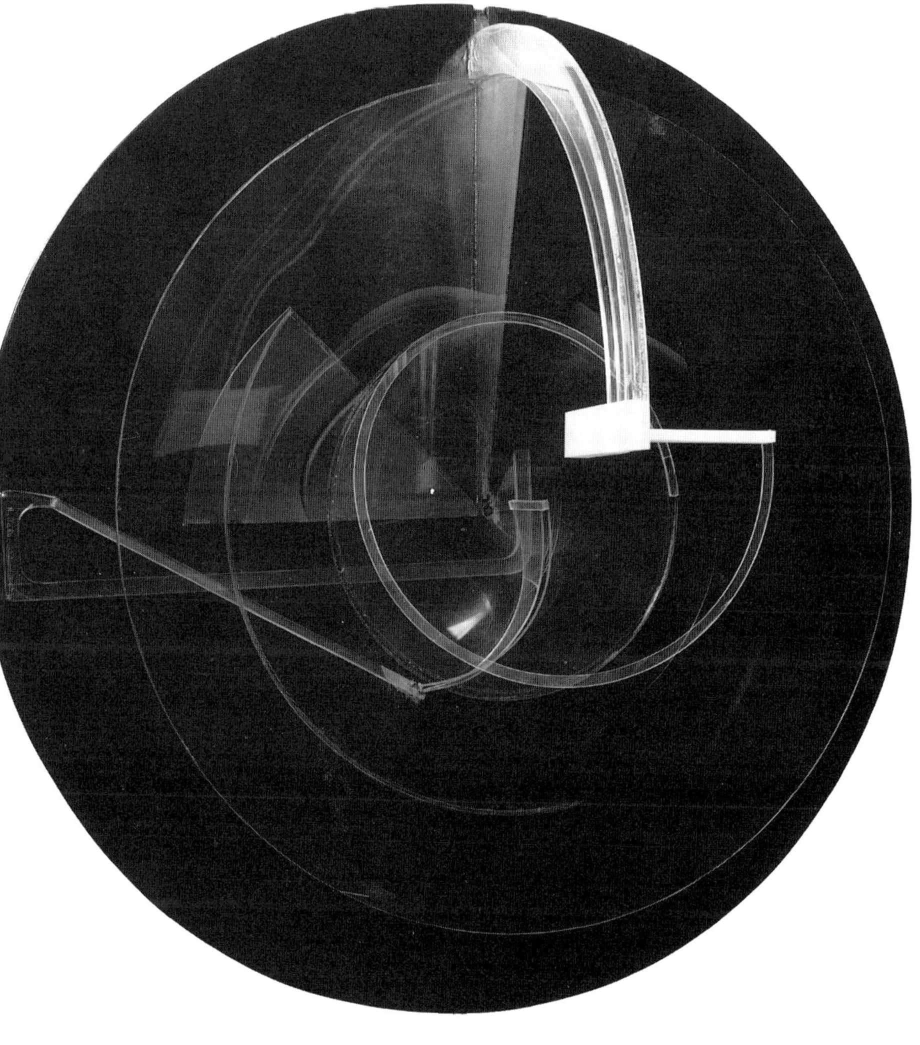

Fig. 21 NAUM GABO, *Circular Relief*, *c.*1925 © Nina and Graham Williams/Tate Gallery London

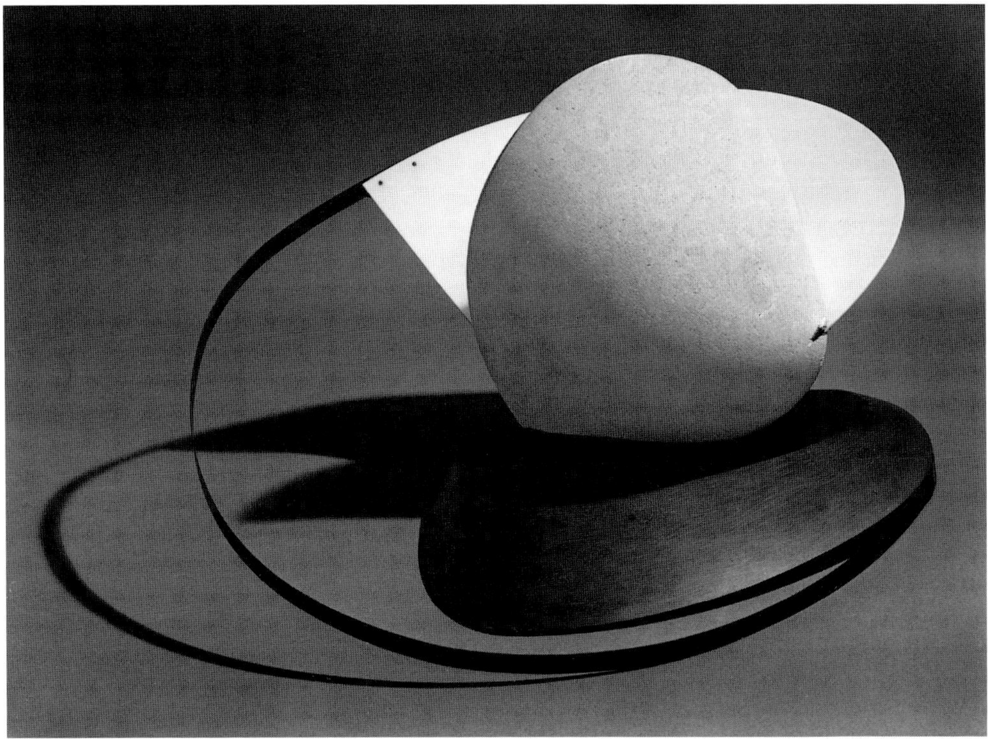

Fig. 22 NAUM GABO, *Stone with a Collar*, 1933 © Nina and Graham Williams/Tate Gallery London

from opaque plastic and the strip from painted metal, the two main elements are carved in contrasting Portland stone and black slate.

The mutual admiration of Gabo and Hepworth can be readily understood if this work is juxtaposed with Hepworth's *Two Segments and Sphere* (Fig. 4). The use of a wedge-like form as an internal base for the construction is common to this work and *Stone with a Collar*. More generally, both explore what Gabo described in his *Listener* article as the tension of latent motion contained within the visual equilibrium of the composition [11].

The affinity between them is, however, evidently coincidental. In experimenting with new materials and forms, Gabo may have been responding to the work of Paris-based sculptors whom Hepworth also admired—most obviously Brancusi and Arp. But *Stone with a Collar* was not entirely a product of Gabo's Parisian period [12]. It can be shown that Gabo had only made a small, rough model before he arrived in Britain. Gabo frequently dated works according to when he had conceived their form, thus he always dated this sculpture to 1933. However, it was first executed as a fully realised sculpture during the second half of 1936, in response to a commission from the painter Winifred Nicholson. At this point Gabo had almost no experience of stone carving, and he would undoubtedly have benefited from talking to Hepworth about technical practicalities and where to obtain tools and materials. To this extent, therefore, the actual creation of *Stone with a Collar* depended upon the English *milieu* in which Gabo now found himself.

It can be argued that *Kinetic Stone Carving*, which was probably begun in London in 1936, shows Gabo directly responding to the approach to materials and form in current British sculpture, although the work has closer affinities with Henry Moore than with Hepworth [13]. Its organic rhythms recall, for instance, Moore's 1936 sculpture illustrated in *Circle* in 1937 [14].

Gabo also shared philosophical ground with his new English friends. This is evident in *Circle*, which he edited together with Nicholson and Leslie Martin. Hepworth too was closely involved in the production of this 'International Survey of Constructive Art'. Broadly speaking, *Circle* sought to present art and architecture as having an active role to play in promoting social change. Gabo made it clear that the ultimate purpose of his own work was not merely to appeal to the aesthetic sense, but also to communicate progressive values by means of artistic metaphor—clarity, order, openness, the priority of the collective over the individual—as embodied in an impersonal technique and the universally accessible forms of geometry. A similar idealism is apparent in Hepworth's article in *Circle* where she rejected the term 'abstract' because it only addressed 'the outer form of a work of art':

> . . . this makes it difficult to use it in relation to the spiritual vitality of inner life which is the real sculpture . . . This is no escapism, no ivory tower, no isolated pleasure in proportion and space—it is an unconscious manner of expressing our belief in a possible life. The language of colour and form is universal and not one for a special class . . . it is a thought which gives the same life, the same expansion, the same universal freedom to everyone. [15]

To this extent, *Circle* epitomised the politicisation of the English intelligentsia in the mid 1930s, reflecting a certain Utopianism which also manifested itself in widespread sympathy for Marxism and the Soviet experiment. Throughout the texts produced by the English core group, the present is characterised as a time of 'transition' (a recurrent term in *Circle*), within a broadly dialectical process of historical development. Thus the 'constructive' impulse to build new structures of knowledge, culture and society is ranged against those forces of destruction and irrationality which have acquired renewed vigour with the growth of fascism. It is assumed that an ideal social order will eventually and inevitably emerge. On this model, the increasing deterioration of European political life in the 1930s could be interpreted in an optimistic light, as the symptom of a terminal process of self-destruction which would usher in the brave new world.

The essay by Gabo which opens *Circle*, 'The Constructive Idea in Art', established this essential paradigm:

> Our century appears in history under the sign of revolutions and disintegration. The revolutions have spared nothing in the edifice of culture . . . The war was only a natural consequence of a disintegration which started long ago . . . But, however long and deep this process may go in its material destruction, it cannot deprive us any more of our optimism about the final outcome, since we see that in the realm of ideas we are now entering on the period of reconstruction.
> We can find . . . support for our optimism in those two domains of our culture where the revolution has been most thorough, namely, in Science and in Art. [16]

He proceeded to construct an explanation of the new art around the proposition that 'the same spiritual state propels artistic and scientific activity at the same time and in the same direction' [17].

In addition to Gabo and Hepworth's essays, the third major contribution to the sculpture section was 'Art and the Scientist' by J. Desmond Bernal, a close friend of both artists. Bernal was an important scientist, specialising in crystallography, as well as a prominent Communist sympathiser, for whom science was, ultimately, 'the chief agent of change in society' [18]. In *Circle* he argued that the radical scientist and artist are confronted with a similar problem—how to be socially progressive within an existing capitalist society which seeks to absorb their labours into its own framework of values and needs:

> Scientists and artists suffer not only from being cut off from one another but being cut off from the most vital part of the life of their times. How to end this isolation and at the same time preserve the integrity of their own work is the main problem of the artist of today. [19]

Bernal also drew a number of specific parallels between current artistic and scientific ideas. Thus in contrast to the Euclidian geometry of past art, modern art had

> . . . evolved many more subtle forms, especially sculpture, which now depends on far more complex curves and surfaces. [20]

Sculptural forms devised by Moore and Hepworth prompted him to refer to 'negative curvature' and to 'an extraordinary intuitive grasp of the unity of a surface' [21]. In more generalised terms, Herbert Read's essay took a similar line:

> Just as surrealism makes use of . . . the knowledge embodied in psychoanalysis, so abstract art makes use of, or proceeds on the basis of, the abstract concepts of physics and dynamics, geometry and mathematics. [22]

Fundamental therefore to *Circle* was the claim that contemporary art and science share a common progressive spirit, and that together artist and scientist might contribute positively to the wider process of social reconstruction. As Hepworth remarked more pithily in a letter:

> I cannot see any hope of stopping this suicidal impulse unless Art & Science stand firm together. [23]

Such ideas provided a theoretical framework for justifying abstract art as a radical project, in opposition to the Soviet Union's official doctrine of socialist realism enunciated and implemented in the early 1930s. Yet how in practice might an artist signify the unity of art and science? Was it possible to go beyond Bernal's 'intuitive grasp' to a more considered translation of scientific ideas into artistic forms? The works which Gabo and Hepworth were producing from around 1936 onwards can to some extent be seen as answers to this problem.

One of the strongest parallels between Gabo and Hepworth from the mid 1930s onwards is their use of overtly mathematical forms, comprising not merely elaborations of regular solids, as in *Three Forms* of 1935 (Fig. 20), but also the more complex kinds of surface evoked by Bernal in *Circle*. One might expect artists to be particularly responsive to the visual manifestations of scientific enquiry, although a great deal of modern theory, especially in physics, does not readily translate into visual images. Geometry, however, provides the most obvious common resource for the artist and the scientist. Indeed, at this point both Gabo and Hepworth seem to have found inspiration in mathematical models, which offered an apparent parallel in the 'objective' world of science to their own aesthetic inventions.

Mathematical models of the kind which fascinated Hepworth and Gabo are extraordinary objects devised to illustrate and teach complex mathematical ideas. Mainly produced in the late 19th century, they were made of diverse materials such as card, metal, plaster; they often had incisions, and sometimes thread was strung around metal frameworks to create three-dimensional parabolic curves.

The incorporation of stringing into sculpture was the most obvious artistic derivation from such mathematical models. Henry Moore acknowledged that he had found 'sculptural possibilities' in the strung models which he had looked at in the Science Museum in London [24]. Subsequently, in 1937, he began to thread strings across the pockets of space in his sculptures [25]. Moore provided the precedent for Hepworth's appropriation of the technique around a year later, although Hammacher reported in 1968 that

> . . . she had studied mathematical models in Paris and London in her youth but let the idea lie dormant in her mind until she could use it emotionally, not mathematically. [26]

Documentary evidence, however, suggests a more recent process of discovery. In December 1935 she wrote to Ben Nicholson:

> John Summerson says there are some marvellous things in a mathematical school in Oxford—sculptural working out of mathematical equations—

> hidden away in a cupboard—I think I shall go to Oxford as soon as I get back from Leeds. [27]

Presumably by 1938 Hepworth too was looking at models in the Science Museum.

Fascination with mathematical models was in fact widespread in the art world in the mid 1930s. They provided the basis for a Moholy-Nagy Constructivist film set in 1936, and were also included in a 1936 show of Surrealist objects [28]. A remarkable set of photographs of individual models produced by Man Ray in 1936 was published in *Cahiers d'Art* [29]. It cannot be proved therefore that Gabo was the unique catalyst for the English artists. Nevertheless Hepworth would surely have been interested in Gabo's exploitation of the sculptural potential of mathematical models at the time of his arrival. He seems to have made a close study of the models during his time in Paris. As Anthony Hill pointed out, the most direct repercussion of this was *Construction in Space: Crystal*, produced in the first half of 1937 [30]. This sculpture was clearly based on a particular example of the type of model with a metal framework and stringing. Gabo elaborated the form in purely sculptural terms and translated the configuration into transparent plastic planes glued together, with the linear pattern incised into the plastic.

To what extent did Hepworth's interest in the models affect her work? The geometric starting point of much of Hepworth's work at this time was acknowledged in titles such as *Holed Polyhedron* (1936), *Pierced Hemisphere* (1937) and *Helicoids in Sphere* (1938) [31]. Mathematical models seem relevant for the latter two works, which epitomise the increasingly curvilinear character of Hepworth's sculpture. *Pierced Hemisphere* loosely recalls the spiralling configuration of 'Riemann surfaces', while *Helicoids in Sphere* seems analogous to the hollowed-out sphere of a model such as 'Steiner's Roman surface' (Fig. 23) [32].

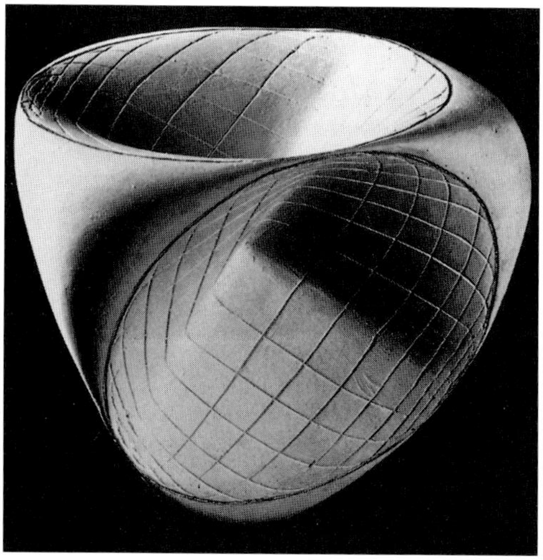

Fig. 23 *Steiner's Roman Surface*, mathematical model © Gerd Fischer (published in Fischer, *Mathematical Models*, Wiesbaden, Vieweg, 1986)

Hepworth's interest here in opening up the surface of a sphere by means of planes of negative curvature marks another parallel with Gabo. Gabo's *Spheric Theme* (Fig. 24) was probably first developed in model form in 1937, and then transposed into a sequence of sculptural variations from 1938 onwards [33]. The configuration results from twisting and joining a pair of circular planes, each with a circular hole at the centre and a single radial incision. Thus the technical processes are quite different, but the final forms are broadly comparable as images of spatial curvature within a spherical form. Gabo too probably found inspiration in mathematical models, although he again chose to use linear striations to emphasise the movement of the planes through space [34].

Hepworth's Cornish sculptures continue to invite comparison with mathematical models. For example, in *Sculpture with Colour* of 1940 (Fig. 25) the oval form and radiating pattern of lines are reminiscent of a 'Spindle cyclide' (Fig. 26) [35]. The 1943 variant also recalls the way in which a section of a hollow hemisphere is

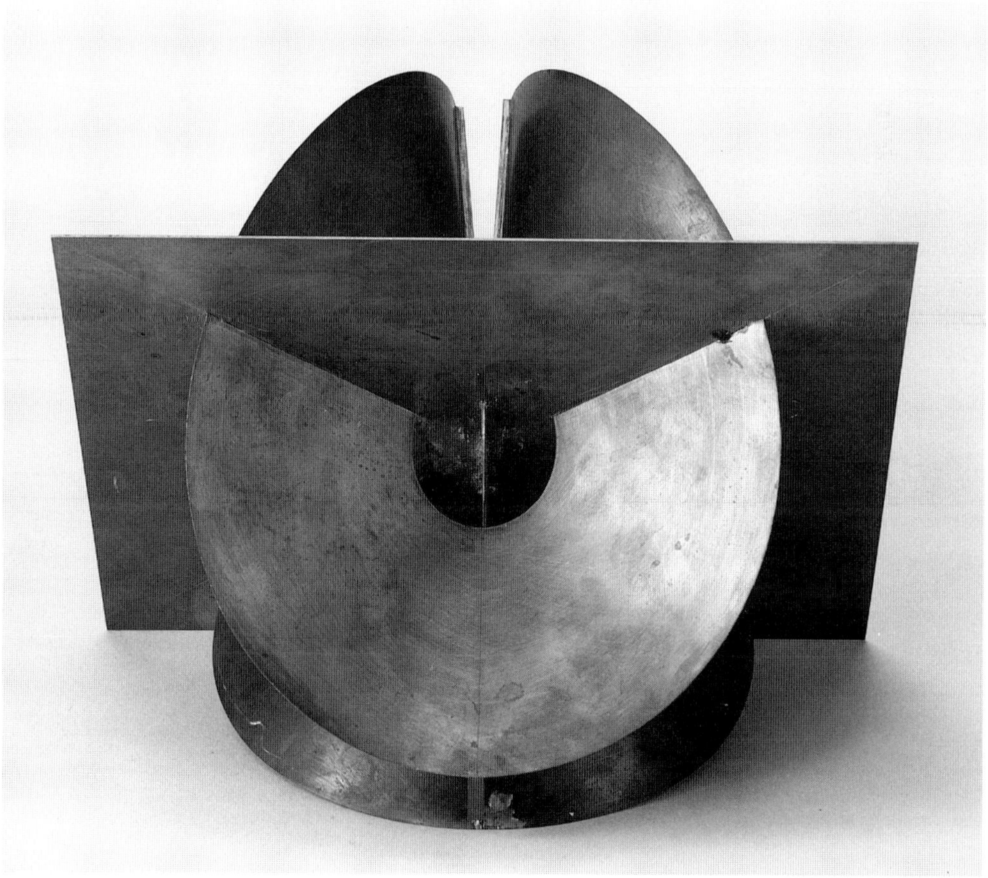

Fig. 24 NAUM GABO, *Spheric Theme (Penetrated Variation)*, *c*.1937–40 © Nina and Graham Williams/Tate Gallery London

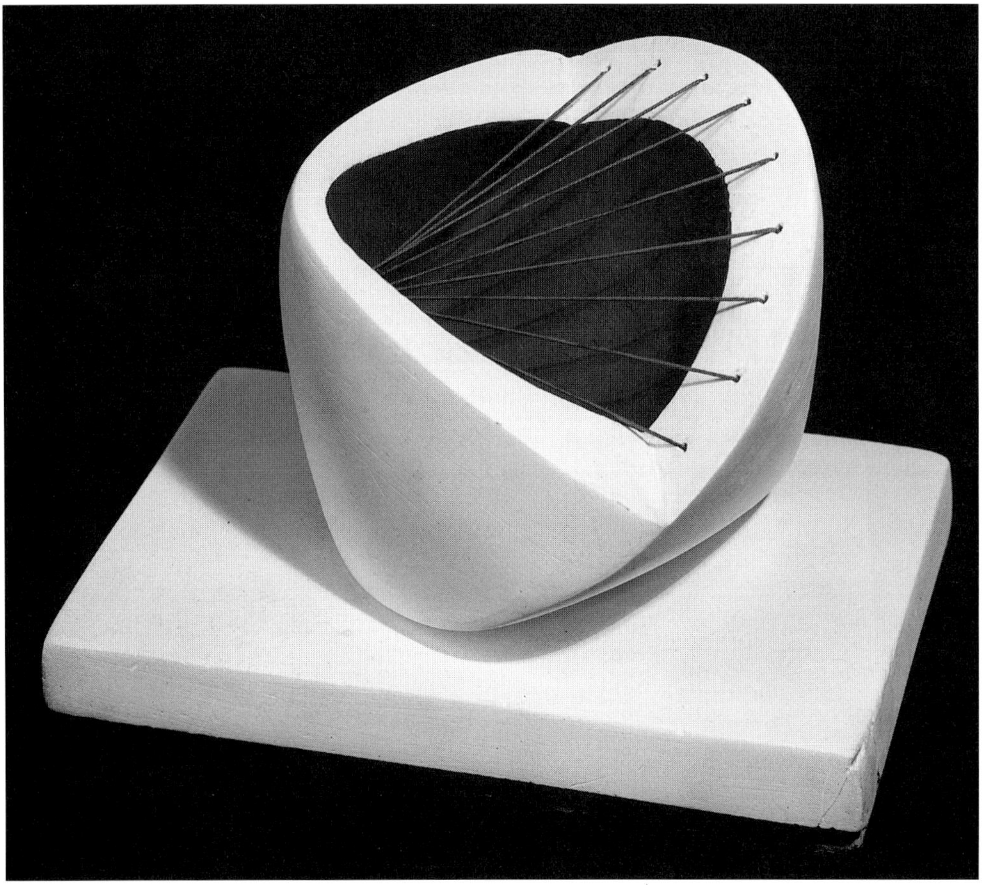

Fig. 25 BARBARA HEPWORTH, *Sculpture with Colour (Deep Blue and Red)*, 1940 © Trustees of the Barbara Hepworth Estate/Tate Gallery London

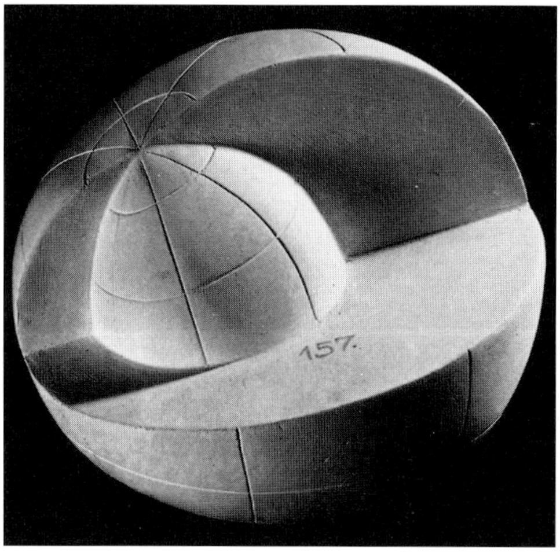

Fig. 26 *Spindle Cyclide*, mathematical model © Gerd Fischer (published in Fischer, *Mathematical Models*, Wiesbaden, Vieweg, 1986)

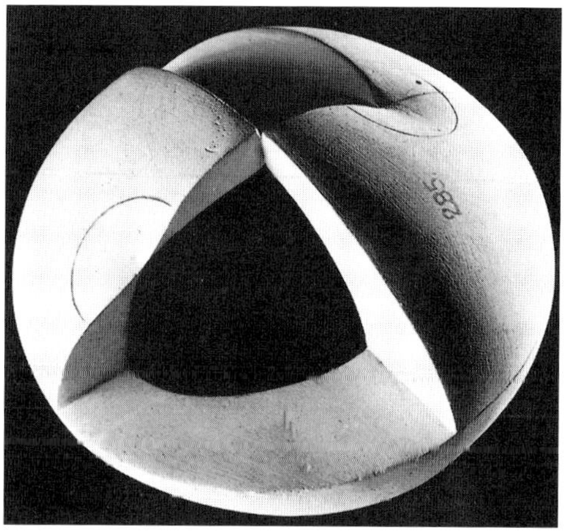

Fig. 27 *Fresnel's Wave Surface*, mathematical model © Gerd Fischer (published in Fischer, *Mathematical Models*, Wiesbaden, Vieweg, 1986)

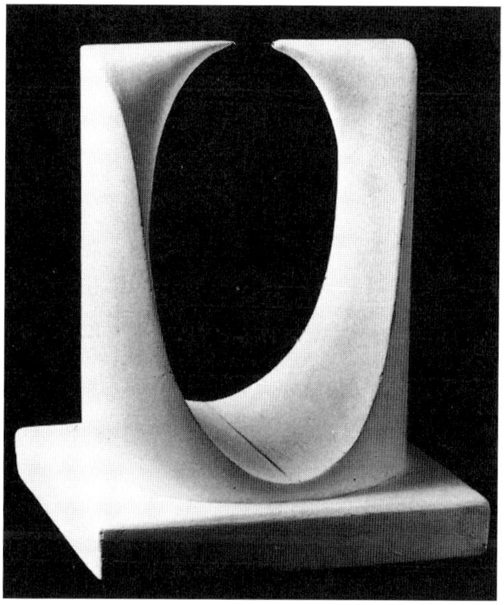

Fig. 28 *Cubic with an A3 Double Point*, mathematical model © Gerd Fischer (published in Fischer, *Mathematical Models*, Wiesbaden, Vieweg, 1986)

cut out to form the opened-out configuration of part of a 'Fresnel's wave surface' (Fig. 27) [36]. Here Hepworth was also using the same material as the model makers, namely white plaster. The model of a 'Cubic with an A3 double point' (Fig. 28) [37] is particularly striking, in visual terms, and seems to have inspired Moore's *Three Points* of 1939–40.

Hepworth's *Wave* (Fig. 48) of 1943 also seems reminiscent of this model, but with the axis of the form turned through 90 degrees. In both sculpture and model, an elliptical pocket of space is defined by a swollen curving plane which has acquired particular tautness from the failure of the tapering edges to meet, as though a continuous surface has sprung open at its thinnest point. Hepworth's twisting apart of the two ends is both sculpturally elegant and suggestive of latent energy. Likewise, the spiral within a sphere in *Pelagos* of 1946 (Fig. 29) recalls the sharp-edged forms encountered in models of a helicoid or a 'minimal surface with a one-parameter family of parabolas' (Fig. 30) [38]. The differentiation between outer and inner surfaces of the models foreshadows the interplay between the grained wooden exterior and the flatly painted interior which Hepworth explored in *Pelagos* and other works of the mid 1940s.

Of course, in each of these comparisons, the differences between the eventual sculptures and the mathematical models are considerable and aesthetically crucial. It was not at all Hepworth's intention to illustrate mathematical concepts. Nevertheless the parallels are close enough, and sufficient in quantity, to warrant the suggestion that mathematical models were an important stimulus for Hepworth. Although her response to them was free and essentially visual, such mathematical allusions would have served to imbue her sculptures with a certain scientific resonance.

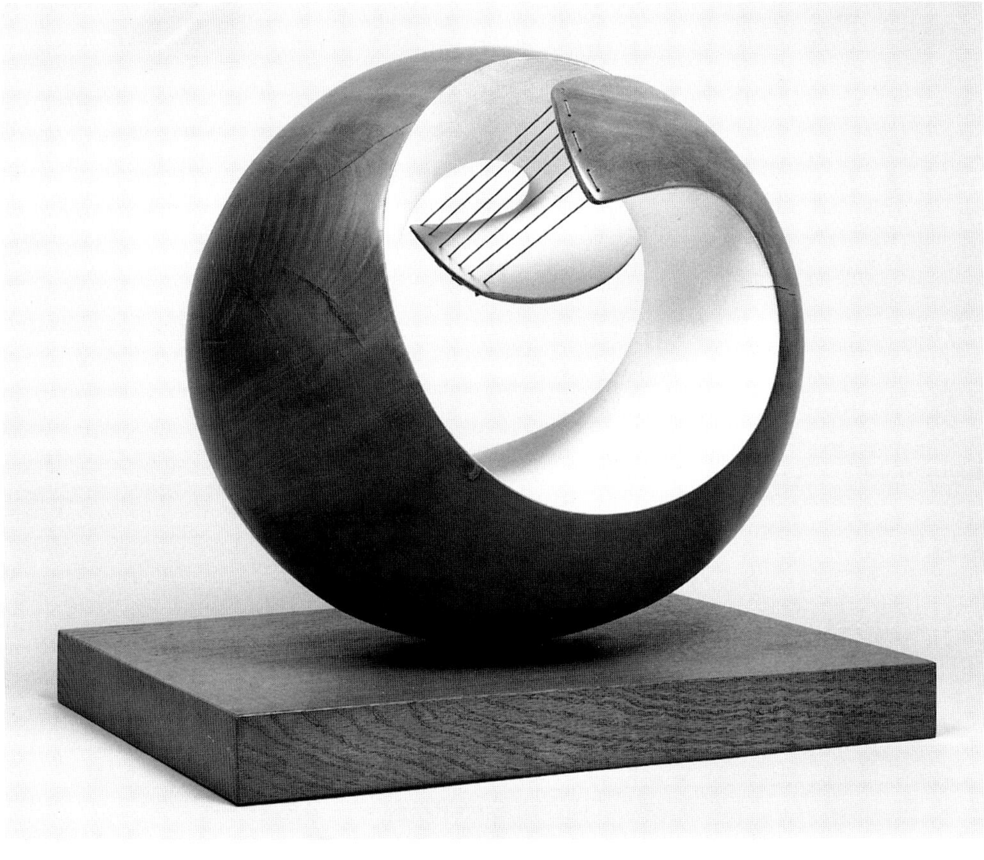

Fig. 29 BARBARA HEPWORTH, *Pelagos*, 1946 © Trustees of the Barbara Hepworth Estate/Tate Gallery London

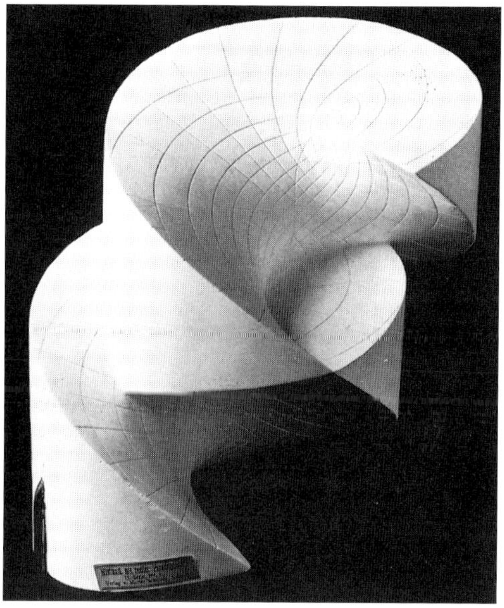

Fig. 30 *Minimal Surface with a One-parameter Family of Parabolas*, mathematical model © Gerd Fischer (published in Fischer, *Mathematical Models*, Wiesbaden, Vieweg, 1986)

Despite their shared mathematical inspiration, there are some enduring distinctions between the sculptures of Gabo and Hepworth, such as the more emphatic solidity and sensuous presence of the materials in the work of the British artist. It was perhaps in the drawings she made in Cornwall from 1940 onwards that Hepworth came closest to the effects of transparency and dematerialisation of form which Gabo sought in his constructions. Indeed, one of the very first of her linear drawings, executed in 1940 (Fig. 31), seems to echo the side view of Gabo's *Construction in Space with Crystalline Centre* (Fig. 32) [39]. Her particular admiration for this Gabo sculpture is conveyed in the beautiful photograph which she took of it, against the backdrop of Carbis Bay [40].

In these drawings Hepworth started with crystalline designs and inserted into them formations of intersecting straight lines which generate parabolic curves, or 'envelopes' in mathematical terminology. In the drawings these read spatially and appear to articulate the internal spaces of imaginary forms with linear threading. This two-dimensional technique is loosely reminiscent not so much of three-dimensional models as of the practice of 'curve-stitching', in which parabolas and other geometric forms are produced by stitching straight lines of coloured thread, at regular intervals, through a pattern of holes in a piece of flat card (Fig. 33). This was a technique dating back to 1906 for teaching children an understanding and love of mathematics [41]. The analogy may not be out of place given that Hepworth herself was running a nursery school at just this time.

Alan Wilkinson has made the obvious and indeed very striking comparison between Hepworth's drawings and Gabo's *Linear Construction No.1* (Fig. 34), the first work in which Gabo explored the possibilities of stringing, as opposed to articulating a plane with linear incisions. Wilkinson implied that this particular

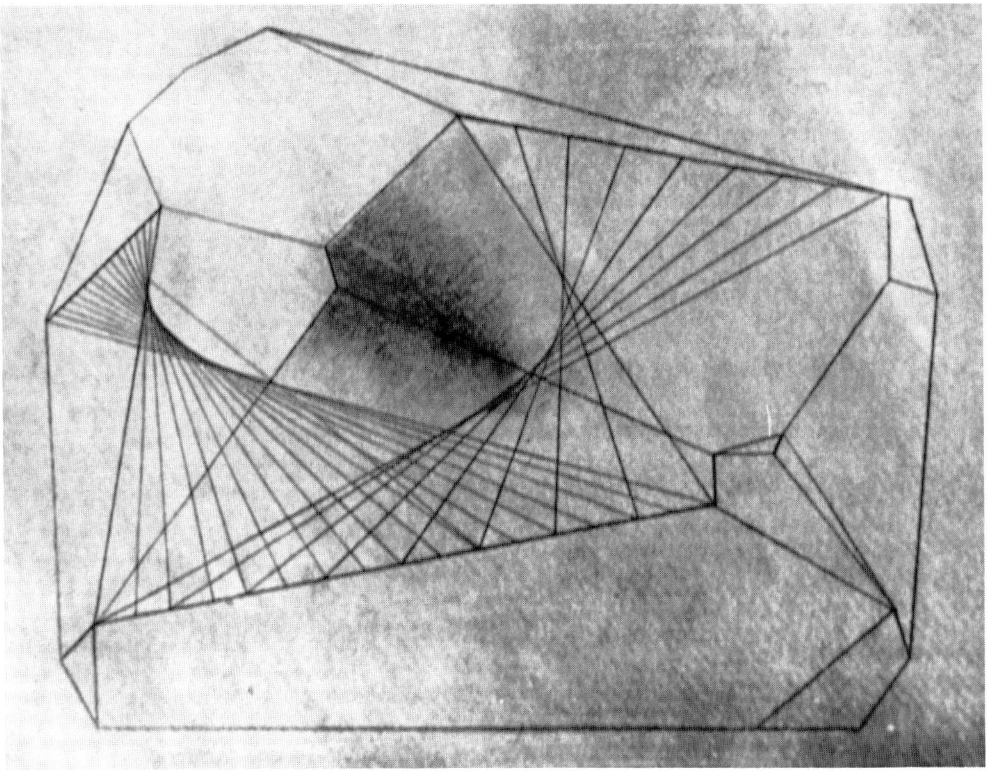

Fig. 31 BARBARA HEPWORTH, *Drawing*, 1940 © Trustees of the Barbara Hepworth Estate

sculpture influenced Hepworth's drawings, on the grounds that Gabo may have first developed this idea around 1938 [42]. Yet the only basis for the early dating of *Linear Construction No.1* is an annotation on one exhibition list of 1965–66 [43]. Contemporary evidence suggests that the work was in fact conceived towards the end of 1942 [44].

A number of factors seem to have contributed to this technical innovation in Gabo's work [45]. At a very practical level, he had by now run out of sheet Perspex, his usual material, and was unable to obtain more since it was all needed for war production. The alternative idea of using stringing was ultimately rooted, of course, in his interest in mathematical models. Indeed, a recollection of one particular model may have suggested a form based on a minimal framework which could be made from small off-cuts of plastic sheeting (Fig. 35). It is likely, however, that the example of Hepworth's current work also acted as a spur to Gabo.

In addition to the fictive stringing of the drawings, actual stringing was used in Hepworth's only sculptural project from the early part of the war, *Sculpture with Colour: Deep Blue and Red* (Fig. 25). She had worked on a small version in 1940 and

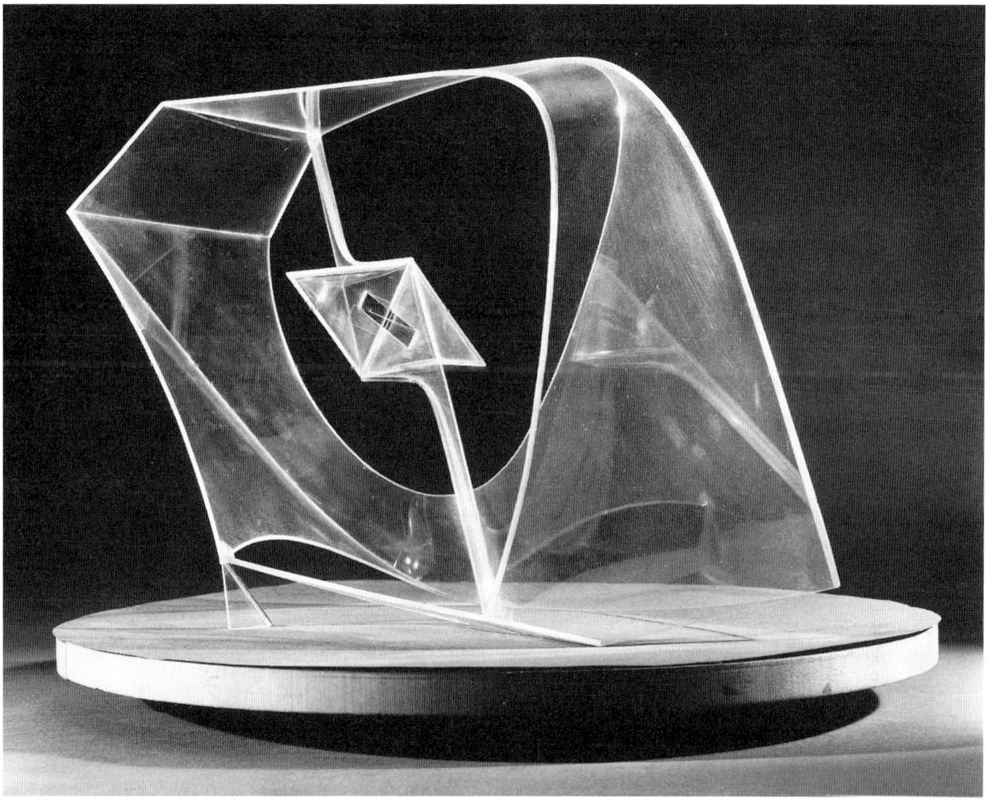

Fig. 32 NAUM GABO, *Construction in Space with a Crystalline Centre*, c.1938 © Nina and Graham Williams/Tate Gallery London

contributed a larger one to the London Museum's exhibition of current British art in Spring 1942, where it was shown alongside Gabo's *Spiral Theme*. Hepworth's use of coloured thread was foreshadowed in mathematical models, and this example was followed by Gabo in his early small models of *Linear Construction No.1*, where red thread was evidently used [46]. Interestingly, Gabo's sculpture could also be viewed as a three-dimensional elaboration of a pattern familiar from curve-stitching, comprising a pair of opposite parabolas. Indeed, an almost identical configuration occurs in one of the most elementary templates intended for children (Fig. 36) [47].

Gabo's use of the stringing technique in *Linear Construction No.1* is ultimately quite different from that of Moore and Hepworth in their sculptures. In the work of the English artists the solid form tends to be dominant. The threads of the stringing are more widely spaced and register as individual linear elements. They serve to articulate an existing spatial structure and to provide formal contrast: of straight line against curvilinear form, open versus opaque, one colour in opposition to others. Gabo, however, finally decided to wind almost colourless, highly

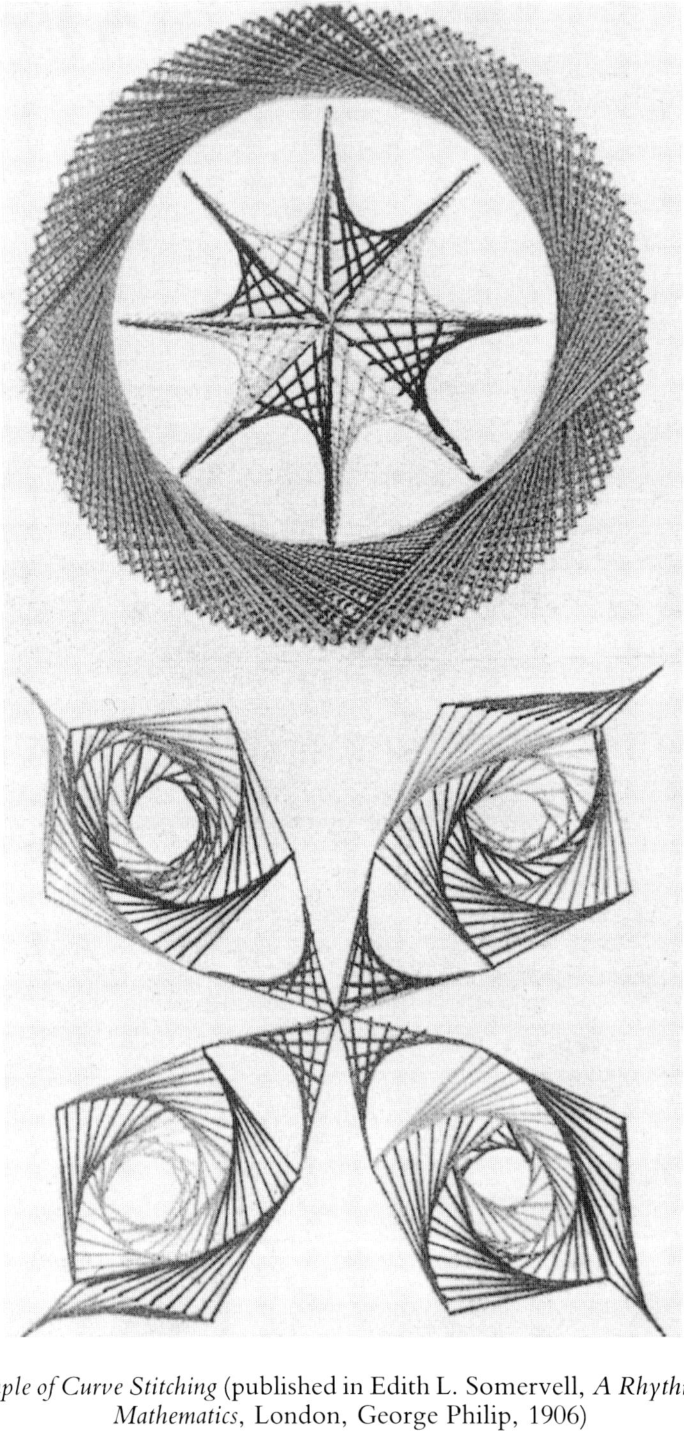

Fig. 33 *Example of Curve Stitching* (published in Edith L. Somervell, *A Rhythmic Approach to Mathematics*, London, George Philip, 1906)

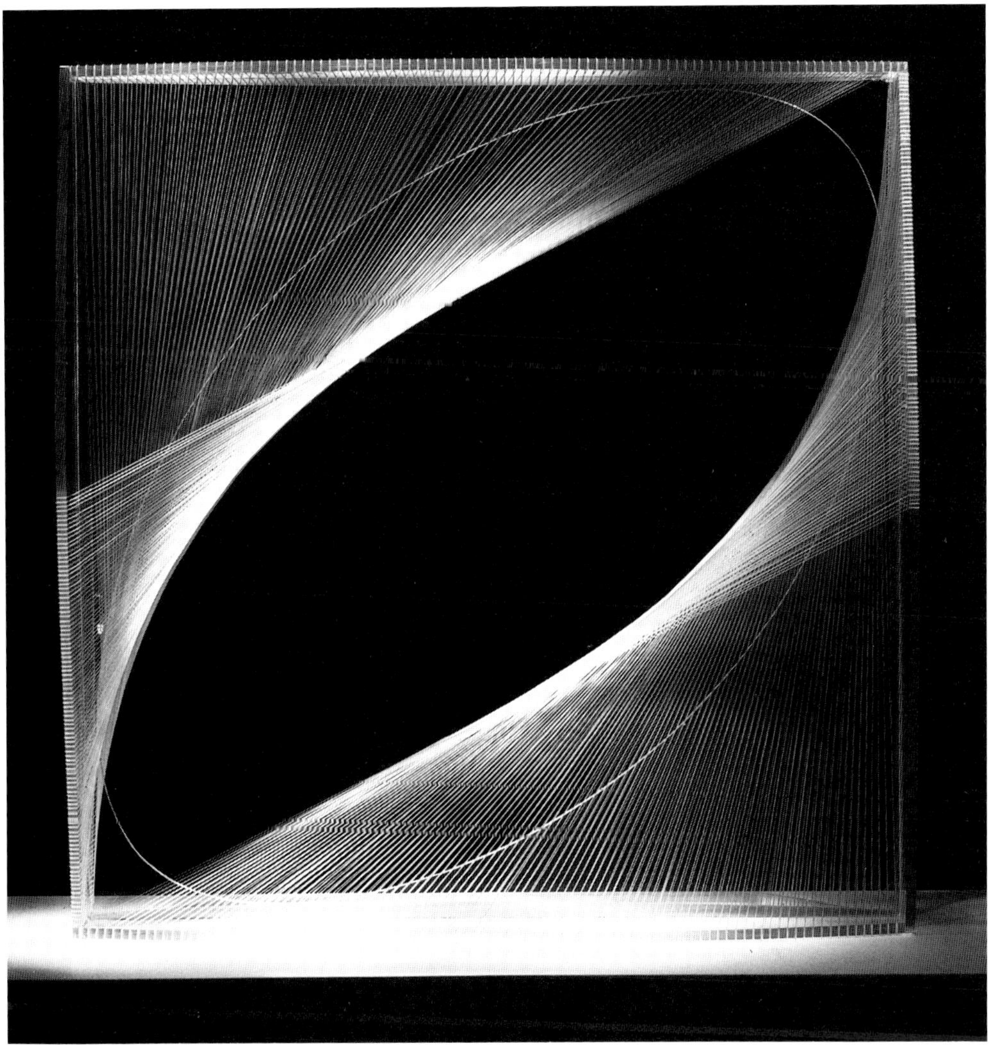

Fig. 34 NAUM GABO, *Linear Construction in Space No.1*, 1942–49 © Nina and Graham Williams/Art Gallery of Ontario

reflective Nylon filament around a more neutral, notched framework of transparent Perspex, and through an open ellipse at the centre. The threads are clustered sufficiently closely together to create the illusion of continuous forms, which are at the same time visibly permeated by space. The curving planes which are generated in this way are taut and elegant, while the inverted repetition of the strung configuration creates a void at the centre of the sculpture which registers strongly as a spatial form in its own right.

Gabo's friendship with Hepworth provides a context not only for the formal language of *Linear Construction No.1*, but also for its underlying conception as,

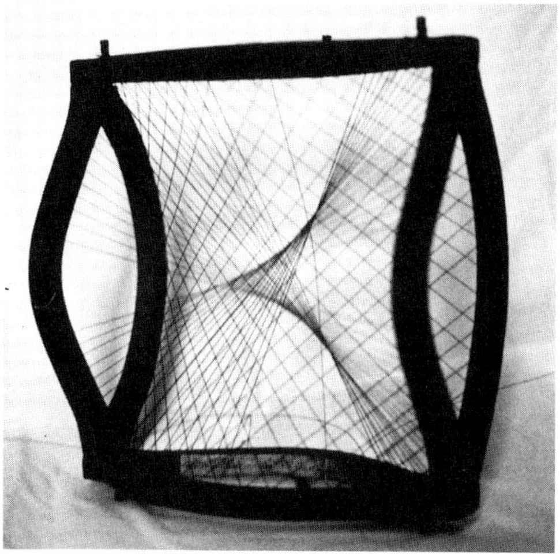

Fig. 35 *Mathematical Model*, Collection L'Institut Henri Poincaré, Paris

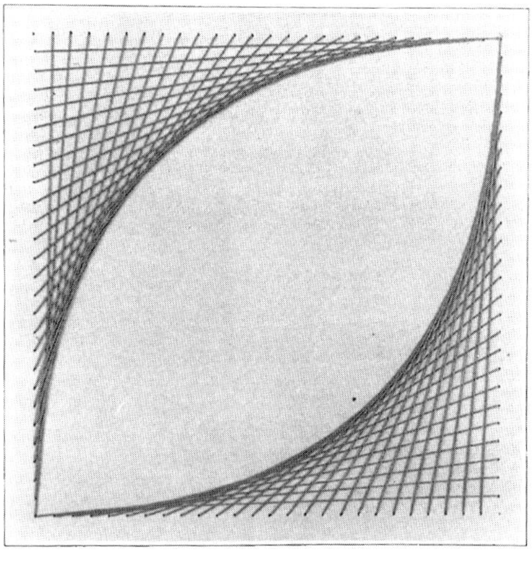

Fig. 36 Curve stitching of 'A Pair of Opposite Parabolas', from *Boole Curve-Sewing Cards* (designed to accompany Edith L. Somervell, *A Rhythmic Approach to Mathematics*, London, George Philip, 1906)

surprisingly perhaps, the basis for a public sculpture. 1942 saw a great deal of discussion in their circle regarding the relationship of the artist and society, and the claims of abstract art to any authentic social relevance. That April, Herbert Read had expressed reservations in print regarding the Constructivists' 'illusion of the transcendence of the work of art' and stated:

> The only real progress is communal progress . . . The work of art is only ratified in the organic ritual of life, and it is only in so far as the constructivist succeeds, not only in constructing these platonic models of reality, but also in modifying the communal environment, that he acquires the full status of a humanist. [48]

The artists at St. Ives clearly perceived this as a challenge, and Hepworth responded to Read as follows:

> I firmly believe that the emotional link is far greater now between society and the artist than at any time since the last war . . . We are . . . quite clear about reconstruction but there is so much to be done—now . . . good art is always socially relevant & the art of the last 30 years has been GOOD & being a part of the revolution it must contain the seed of social critique . . . It is now the time for action—the artists are ready—society not yet. What do you suggest we should do? . . . no ideal is an ideal unless it is practical. [49]

From his own correspondence with Read later in the year it is clear that Gabo initially saw *Linear Construction No.1* not just as a self-contained aesthetic object, but also as the prototype for a large-scale public sculpture. He envisaged it situated in the vicinity of a textile factory, providing a kind of abstract symbol for the technical process of weaving and the possibilities of new synthetic materials [50]. This idea embodied Gabo's practical solution to the problem of the artist's social role. Referring to this construction, he told Read:

> I am trying at the same time to find a way and a more immediate approach to that specific Society in which I think we artists will be compelled to live and work in the not too distant future . . . It is in the end extremely exhausting for an artist to work for nobody in particular. A sculptor is particularly vulnerable at that point. My constructions, in the main, are meant after all for an open space in the new towns . . . It is the professional corporations which will need most of the new sculptures. I am trying to fulfil an order which is not given to me. I am trying to forestall an eventual demand and prevent a probable accusation of ignoring the needs of the community. [51]

Gabo had, in fact, been interested in this kind of public and 'site-specific' sculpture since the 1920s, as a way of integrating his art with the life of the community. In *The Realistic Manifesto* of 1920 he had announced his intention to take his art 'out into the squares and streets' because he believed that, in the new Communist society:

> Art is called upon to accompany man everywhere, wherever his inexhaustible life flows and acts—at the factory bench, at the table, at work, at rest, at play . . . [52]

His return to the idea in 1942, albeit in far more pragmatic terms, can be understood in the context of wartime debates in England, which were fuelled by a mixture of financial desperation and a general climate of looking ahead with optimism to post-war reconstruction [53].

One might argue that Hepworth's discussions with Gabo lay behind the development of her own growing commitment to public sculpture. The idea had been implicit in various maquettes created in London in the late 1930s [54]. It then re-emerged as an aspiration during the latter part of the war and formed the prelude to her involvement in a series of commissions from 1949 onwards, which have been discussed by Penelope Curtis [55]. Gabo likewise was only given opportunities to produce monumental, public sculpture in the post-war years [56].

During the early phase of the war, Hepworth's circumstances enforced a hiatus. When she began carving again in earnest in 1943–44, she also embarked upon a new phase in her art. From now on, there is a greater sense of organic rhythm and of the interpenetration of form and space in her sculptures. As Wilkinson has remarked, in the works of the late 1930s 'the holes are relatively small and are defined by the solid form surrounding them', whereas in works like *Wave* of 1943 'the boundaries between voids and solids dissolve, so that neither space nor form dominates' [57]. Once again, parallels with Gabo's current work suggest themselves. The open curvilinear rhythms of Hepworth's *Oval Sculpture* (1943) recall the paintings from this period, such as *Construction in Depth* of 1944 in which Gabo was exploring more elaborate and multi-layered spatial complexes than seemed possible in the more intractable medium of sculpture.

Wave of 1944 (Fig. 48) may be taken to epitomise the patterns of affinity and difference between Hepworth's and Gabo's work during the latter part of his stay in England. In its rising, open form this sculpture seems specifically indebted to Gabo's *Crystalline Centre* (Fig. 32). Gabo stimulated Hepworth to open up form and to exploit the dynamic potential of taut linear edges. In a sense, it was the example of Gabo's work that enabled Hepworth to make more inventive use at this time of the remarkable configurations which she had observed in mathematical models. The formal contrast and spatial articulation provided by the stringing in the Hepworth is equivalent to the diagonal strut in the Gabo, containing the angular crystalline form which appears almost to hover in space at the core of the construction.

The similarities between these two sculptures go beyond purely formal parallels. Both sculptures embody a fusion of mathematical and organic or natural form. The notion that these two realms, conventionally seen as opposites, were in fact inextricably connected was implicit in scientific investigations such as Bernal's research into the microscopic structure of crystals, and D'Arcy Thompson's *On Growth and Form*, a book widely admired in Gabo and Hepworth's circle, and enthusiastically reviewed by Herbert Read when the second edition appeared in 1941 [58]. The two artists differed, however, in their interpretation of this idea. Gabo's *Crystalline Centre* evokes a scientific imagery of crystalline or atomic structure, a poetic interpretation of the reality behind appearances which had been revealed by microscopic and X-ray technology. The Perspex material removes the work from associations with the empirical world. If the Gabo is radically dematerialised and purely optical in effect, the Hepworth retains an emphasis on the tactile associations of solid form and natural materials. Moreover, *Wave* combines a purely mathematical resonance with suggestions of more familiar visual experience, the essential form and movement of the wave of the sea, and the weathered smoothness and hollowed-out form of objects washed up on the beach [59]. In contemplating the work, one's attention to purely abstract qualities coexists with a more associative reading of natural forms and forces.

Wave illustrates a new departure in Hepworth's work which has often been noted, but never very satisfactorily explained. Her own comments make it sound as though, despite having lived in Cornwall for three years already, she suddenly realised that the landscape was much too beautiful to leave out. In fact a similar reassertion of associations with the natural world is evident in Ben Nicholson's current work and correspondence, and this has been interpreted as an oblique response to the patriotic 'Neo-Romantic' emphasis on reclaiming a distinctively English tradition [60]. In broad terms this seems convincing and could equally apply to Hepworth. It is interesting that Hepworth should have articulated her shifting attitude in the letter to Read of April 1942, cited earlier, where she also mounted a defence of the social purpose of abstract art. In this context she argued that Constructivist art conveyed a profound identification with the inner essence of nature, in contrast to the more superficial process of depicting external appearances:

> Constructivism does not do away with imagery—in fact it contains the most easily understood use of images which are undoubtedly organic in so far as they are the basic forms of the landscape, primary construction, the human figure and so on. They are more elemental than the personal imagery of an individual human being to a particular landscape. [61]

This assimilation of nature also had a very local aspect. Hepworth communicated to Read her positive estimation of the effects of moving to Cornwall from the metropolis:

> . . . we have been decentralised—we are each of us much more a part of a responsible community. For me this two and a half years in this small town has been the most intense and vital time of my life. [62]

One might argue, therefore, that in imbuing her subsequent work, from 1943 onwards, with more immediate associations with the natural world, Hepworth was expressing, in a self-conscious way, her sense of belonging to a specific local community, a community in which human life was particularly tied to the rhythms of nature and the elements. In consciously addressing and articulating a common experience of Cornishness, Hepworth perhaps presented her own distinctive solution to the problem of the alienation of the modernist artist from society at large, the topic of so much agonising between Read, Gabo, Nicholson and herself.

Hepworth gradually came to realise that there were significant differences between her own work and that of the more purist Gabo, who retained a universalist standpoint in every sense. By 1944, like Nicholson, she had decided to stop calling herself a Constructivist, preferring the less programmatic 'Constructive Art' [63]. After Gabo's eventual departure Hepworth reflected on the artistic and temperamental gulf which had opened up between them:

> He may be too deeply wounded about me not wanting to be called 'Constructivist' . . . it's such a religion with him . . . I doubt whether Gabo would like what I do now and in any case it is not important to me what one is called! To Gabo it seems to be important and he does not understand when Ben and I like Picasso, Miró, Klee, Cubism, etc., etc. He hates all that, it is anathema to him—but for me it is pure enjoyment . . . Dear Gabo—I hope one day he'll smile at me again. [64]

In reality, there were all manner of squabbles, aside from such matters of terminology, and Carbis Bay ended up resembling not so much 'a nest of gentle artists' as a nest of vipers. Hepworth reacted against what she came to see as Gabo's aloofness, dogmatism and intolerance. Gabo for his part came to resent what he perceived as Hepworth's stealing of his ideas. In his recent memoirs Sven Berlin has recalled Gabo's public outburst to this effect, and also Gabo's intense irritation on discovering that Hepworth had contrived, as Gabo saw it, to schedule an exhibition at the Lefevre Gallery for October 1946, one month before his own show was due to open [65]. Similar rivalries and disagreements arose between Gabo and Nicholson. In March 1945 Gabo remarked to Herbert Read:

> I hardly see B and B lately and when I see them the room does not get warmer. [66]

Given all the anxieties and frustrations of the war years, and the claustrophobic atmosphere in Carbis Bay, it is hardly surprising that such ambitious and powerful personalities should have ended up bickering. Nevertheless, the argument that such disputes were the determining factor in Gabo's decision to go to America is misguided. His wife Miriam was American and, like Moholy-Nagy, Gropius and many others, he saw the United States as the land of real opportunity for the artist, particularly after the success of his 1938 exhibition in New York. He had in fact been planning to move on from the moment the war began, but kept postponing his departure because of the dangers of submarine attacks on ships in the Atlantic, and then because Miriam became pregnant with Nina, who was born in May 1941. As his diaries indicate, the war generally made Gabo identify more with his Russian and Jewish background than with any English community. If Hepworth ultimately also reasserted her native roots, she could acknowledge to Herbert Read a few years later:

> . . . I have never, since 1942, called myself constructivist (as you know) & therefore I can say that I feel, personally, that of all the 'pulses' of creation this has moved me more profoundly than any other. [67]

NOTES AND REFERENCES

1 (1952) *Barbara Hepworth: Carvings and Drawings* (London, Lund Humphries). Text facing pl. 60.
2 READ, HERBERT (1962) 'A Nest of Gentle Artists', *Apollo*, September, reprinted in READ, BENEDICT and THISTLEWOOD, DAVID (Eds) (1993) *Herbert Read: a British Vision of World Art* (London, Lund Humphries), p. 61.
3 (1969) 'Naum Gabo Talking to Maurice de Sausmarez', in DE SAUSMAREZ, MAURICE (Ed) (1969) *Ben Nicholson: Studio International Special*, p. 23.
4 HEPWORTH, BARBARA (1943) letter to Hartley Ramsden, 4 April, p. 7. Ramsden Papers, Tate Gallery Archive, London.
5 HEPWORTH, BARBARA (n.d. [1943?]) letter to Hartley Ramsden, p. 7. Ramsden Papers, Tate Gallery Archive, London.
6 See GRAY, NICOLETE (1968) 'Barbara Hepworth 1927–1936: the English Background', in: *Barbara Hepworth* (London, Tate Gallery), p. 47. Gabo was not mentioned in the 1933 edition of Herbert Read's *Art Now*.
7 The fullest chronology of Nicholson and Hepworth's activities is provided in LEWISON, JEREMY (1993) *Ben Nicholson* (London, Tate Gallery).
8 Gabo contributed texts and illustrations of his works to *Abstraction-Création: Art Non-Figuratif*, No. 1, 1932, pp. 14, 27; and No. 2, 1933, p. 16. Sculptures by Hepworth were reproduced in *Abstraction-Création: Art Non-Figuratif*, No. 2, 1933, p. 6 and No. 3, 1934, p. 23. Hepworth also contributed to the 'Abstraction-Création' exhibition. She was mentioned in the poster and invitation cards for the second series of exhibitions which took place 2–14 February 1934. See (1978) *Abstraction-Création 1931–1936* (Paris, Musée d'Art Moderne de la Ville de Paris), pp. 42, 51.
9 NICHOLSON, BEN (1936) letter to Herbert Read, 24 January, p. 7, Read Archive, University of Victoria, British Columbia.
10 GABO, NAUM (1936) 'Constructive Art', *The Listener* Vol. 16, No. 408, 4 November, p. 846.
11 *Ibid.*
12 This argument is fully documented in HAMMER, MARTIN and LODDER, CHRISTINA (1997) *Gabo* (London and Newhaven, Yale University Press).
13 SANDERSON, COLIN and LODDER, CHRISTINA (1985) 'Catalogue Raisonné of the Constructions and Sculptures of Naum Gabo', in: NASH, STEVEN A. and MERKERT, JÖRN (Eds) (1985) *Naum Gabo: Sixty Years of Constructivism* (Munich, Prestel Verlag), no. 36.
14 See MARTIN, J. L., NICHOLSON, BEN and GABO, NAUM (Eds) (1937) *Circle: International Survey of Constructive Art* (London, Faber and Faber), pls. 9, 10 in sculpture section. A. M. Hammacher suggested that with *Kinetic Stone Carving* Gabo 'had succumbed for a moment to his English environment'. See HAMMACHER, A. M. (1989) *The Sculpture of Barbara Hepworth* (London, Thames and Hudson), p. 75.
15 HEPWORTH, BARBARA 'Sculpture', in: *Circle* (n. 14), pp. 115–16.
16 GABO, NAUM 'The Constructive Idea in Art', in: *Circle* (n. 14), p. 1.
17 *Ibid.*, p. 2.
18 WERSKEY, GARY (1988) *The Visible College: a Collective Biography of British Scientists and Socialists of the 1930s* (London, Free Association Books), p. 188.
19 BERNAL, J. D. 'Art and the Scientist', in: *Circle* (n. 14), p. 123.
20 *Ibid.*, p. 121.
21 *Ibid.*
22 READ, HERBERT 'The Faculty of Abstraction', in: *Circle* (n. 14), p. 66.
23 HEPWORTH, BARBARA (n.d.) letter to Margaret Gardiner, quoted in GARDINER, MARGARET (1980) *Barbara Hepworth: a Memoir* (Edinburgh, The Salamander Press), p. 28.
24 See COMPTON, SUSAN *et al* (1988) *Henry Moore* (London, Royal Academy of Arts) No. 32, pp. 185–86.
25 *Ibid.*
26 Hammacher (n. 14), p. 76.
27 HEPWORTH, BARBARA (1935) letter to Ben Nicholson, 20 December. Nicholson Papers, Tate Gallery Archive. We are grate-

ful to Penelope Curtis for bringing this to our attention.

28 Moholy-Nagy's design for the H. G. Wells-Alexander Korda film 'The Shape of Things to Come' (London, 1936) is illustrated in: MOHOLY-NAGY, SIBYL (1969) *Moholy-Nagy: Experiment in Totality* (Cambridge, Mass. and London, The MIT Press), pl. 47, p. 128. For installation views of 'L'Exposition des Objets Surréalistes' at the Galerie Charles Ratton, Paris, 1936, see ADES, DAWN (1978) *Dada and Surrealism Reviewed* (London, Arts Council of Great Britain), pp. 322, 450.

29 Some of these are reproduced in FABRE, GLADYS (1990) (Ed) *Arte Abstracto Arte Concreto: Cercle et Carré, Paris 1930* (Valencia, Ivam Centre Julio Gonzalez), pls. 183–88.

30 HILL, ANTHONY (1966) 'Constructivism: the European Phenomenon', *Studio International* Vol. 171, No. 876, April, p. 144. Catalogue Raisonné (n. 13), no. 41.

31 See HODIN, J. P. (1961) *Barbara Hepworth* (London, Lund Humphries), Nos. 88, 93, 109.

32 See FISCHER, GERD (Ed) (1986) *Mathematical Models from the Collections of Universities and Museums* (Braunschweig/Wiesbaden, Friedr. Vieweg & Son), pls. 42–43.

33 Part of the evidence for this dating is the fact that no versions of *Spheric Theme* were included in Gabo's exhibition at the London Gallery in January 1938.

34 For a comparison between *Spheric Theme* and a model of Enneper's Minimal Surface, see CORRADA, MANUEL (1992) 'On Some Vistas Disclosed by Mathematics to the Russian Avant-Garde: Geometry, El Lissitzky and Gabo', *Leonardo* Vol. 25, Nos. 3/4, p. 382.

35 Fischer (n. 32), pl. 73. This represents an example of an inversion of Dupin's cyclides. See also Fischer (n. 32), *Commentary* pp. 28–29.

36 Fischer (n. 32), pl. 38.

37 *Ibid.*, pl. 23.

38 *Ibid.*, pls. 91, 93.

39 *Hepworth: Carvings and Drawings* (n. 1), pl. 61b.

40 Gabo (n. 12), pl. 74 and photographic credits, opp. p. 10.

41 See SOMMERVELL, EDITH L. (1906) *A Rhythmic Approach to Mathematics* (London, George Philip).

42 WILKINSON, ALAN (1994) 'Cornwall and the Sculpture of Landscape: 1939–75', in: CURTIS, PENELOPE and WILKINSON, ALAN (1994) *Barbara Hepworth: a Retrospective* (Liverpool, Tate Gallery Liverpool), p. 80.

43 Catalogue Raisonné (n. 13), no. 48.1. By the mid 1960s Gabo's impulse to assert his own chronological priority in using stringing may have affected his memory.

44 GABO, NAUM (1942) letter to Herbert Read, November. Read Archive, University of Victoria, B.C.

45 The information in this paragraph is documented in Hammer and Lodder (n. 12).

46 Catalogue Raisonné (n. 13), no. 48.

47 See (n.d. [1906?]) *Boole Curve-Sewing Cards. Designed to Accompany 'A Rhythmical Approach to Mathematics by Edith I. Sommervell'* (London, George Philip) Series 1, No. 7. There is a complete set of the cards in the National Library of Scotland, Edinburgh.

48 READ, HERBERT (1942) 'Vulgarity and Impotence', *Horizon* Vol. 5, No. 28, April, p. 275.

49 HEPWORTH, BARBARA (1942) letter to Herbert Read, 8 April. Read Archive, University of Victoria, B.C.

50 GABO, MIRIAM (n.d.) 'Biographical Notes'. Tate Gallery Archive, London, and conversation with the authors.

51 GABO, NAUM (1942) letter to Herbert Read, 7 November. Read Archive, University of Victoria, B.C.

52 See GABO, NAUM and PEVZNER, NOTON [Antoine Pevsner] (1920) *Realisticheskii Manifest* [The Realistic Manifesto] (Moscow, Second State Printing House) reproduced with Gabo's translation in (1957) Gabo: *Constructions, Sculpture, Paintings, Drawings, Engravings* (London, Lund Humphries), insert opposite p. 151 and pp. 151–52. The present quotation is from the authors' own translation.

53 In this connection see GABO, NAUM (1943) 'Prepare for Design', *World Review*, April, pp. 43–49.

54 See Hepworth's remarks concerning her

obsession around 1938–39 with ideas for large works, in: *Barbara Hepworth: a Pictorial Autobiography* (London, Tate Gallery), p. 41.

55 See CURTIS, PENELOPE (1994) 'The Artist in Post-War Britain', in: Curtis and Wilkinson (n. 42), pp. 127ff.

56 The most notable example of Gabo's public sculpture is the Construction erected outside the Bijenkorf Building in Rotterdam in 1957. Catalogue Raisonné (n. 13), no. 67.

57 Wilkinson (n. 42), p. 82.

58 The relationship between D'Arcy Thompson and Gabo was discussed by Martin Hammer and Christina Lodder in 'D'Arcy Thompson's Impact on Modernism', a paper delivered at 'Growth and Form: Art and Science Conference' (Edinburgh, Royal Botanical Garden), November 1993.

59 Patrick Heron's discussion of this aspect of Hepworth's forms remains the most evocative: 'Instead of expanding from the inside, they have been shaped by a wearing away from the outside. Their peculiar beauty, their unique poetic quality, is that of smooth, weather-worn, grooved, fluted or hollowed-out objects such as seashore pebbles and shells, wooden pier stakes, half-burnt logs or rain-washed rock. Like these, her sculpture bears the imprint of vast, impersonal forces . . .'. HERON, PATRICK (1955) *The Changing Forms of Art* (New York, The Noonday Press), p. 217.

60 See BUTTON, VIRGINIA, 'The War Years', in: Lewison (n. 7), pp. 53–62, and the entry on *1941 (painted relief version 1)*, p. 223.

61 HEPWORTH, BARBARA (1942) letter to Herbert Read, 8 April. Read Archive, University of Victoria, B.C.

62 *Ibid.*

63 HEPWORTH, BARBARA (1951) letter to Herbert Read. Read Archive, University of Victoria, B.C.

64 HEPWORTH, BARBARA (n.d. [1946?]) letter to Margaret Gardiner, quoted in Gardiner (n. 23), pp. 45–46.

65 BERLIN, SVEN (1994) *The Coat of Many Colours* (Bristol, Radcliffe), pp. 107–08.

66 GABO, NAUM (1945) letter to Herbert Read, 12 March. Read Archive, University of Victoria, B.C.

67 HEPWORTH, BARBARA (1951) letter to Herbert Read. Read Archive, University of Victoria, B.C.

CHRIS STEPHENS

From Constructivism to Reconstruction: Barbara Hepworth in the 1940s

> Civilization is on the operating table and we sit in the waiting room.
>
> Cyril Connelly [1]

> To create one lasting thing in a lifetime is an affirmation of what we are fighting for . . . there are other things to do—political, social, family—but they must be welded into a coherent wholeness.
>
> Barbara Hepworth [2]

This essay [3] originates from a larger project that seeks to examine and problematise the relationship between the work of so-called 'St. Ives artists' and landscape and place. There is no artist's work for which such a re-examination is more appropriate than the sculpture of Barbara Hepworth. Commentators have taken their lead from Hepworth herself in relating the forms of much of the work she produced in Cornwall to a 'figure in the landscape' source; the work of the post-war period is seen as an inevitable response to Cornwall's powerful landscape. As well as citing 'the remarkable pagan landscape' as a source [4], Hepworth also stresses the importance of the town of St. Ives to her and her work, most clearly in her *Pictorial Autobiography* in which she highlights her position in the social fabric of the town and contrasts the intimacy of its narrow streets with the wider metropolitan spaces of London and New York where her work is consumed. Reciprocally, Hepworth is used to construct a particular 'place-image' for St. Ives, the spaces of which are punctuated by her work. Her public persona and identity as doyen of the local 'art colony' are mapped onto the town by the siting of her sculptures at significant sites: the Guildhall, the library, the church, the Malakoff (a small square overlooking the town and its harbour), the Penwith Gallery and—as a sort of validating signature—at the entrances to blocks of artists' studio-flats built in the 1960s.

In contrast to its more usual construction as a seamless, evolutionary progression [5], the development of Hepworth's work should be seen as interpolated with periods of hesitation and reappraisal. At such moments she might be seen pausing to assess her position and direction, to feel around for the way forward by testing new forms and means of working, sometimes returning to earlier concerns and motifs. A reorientation of her work and its theorisation during and shortly after the Second World War represents one such caesura and is my focus here. I particularly want to examine, rather perversely for an elucidation of the later landscape/figure works, a body of work made up of two-dimensional representations of figures in an interior: the hospital drawings of 1947–49. Whilst clearly discontinuous with most of Hepworth's output, these remarkable images are not inconsistent with her concerns. They will be shown to embody the themes of reintegration and of reconstruction at different levels: the social, ideological and psychological. Around them I shall write a meaning that will reveal them to be made up of layers of metaphorical signification dealing with issues of social organisation, most especially with Hepworth's concerns with her role in society as an artist and as a woman. I would suggest that this interpretation could also be extended to the later landscape/figure pieces, offering a reading of them that exceeds the current essentialist one by seeing the figure-in-the-landscape motif not as a romantic trope but as a metaphor for the social order with which Hepworth was so concerned. In pursuing this line of investigation I shall draw on Hepworth's private writings as well as on the public construction of her and her work, not in order to excavate her conscious intention but to establish a basis or justification for the interpretive tools I shall employ.

In its implication of a precursive marginality, the term 'sculptor's drawings' is inappropriately applied to Hepworth's hospital drawings which are, for the most part, fully finished and independent pieces [6] and which were heavily promoted by Hepworth in exhibitions in London in 1947 and New York in 1948 and in later retrospectives. The drawings derive from the close relationship that developed between Hepworth and orthopaedic surgeon Norman Capener, after he had operated on her daughter Sarah, suffering from osteomyalitis, early in 1944. In 1947 Hepworth accepted Capener's invitation to watch him at work at Exeter's Princess Elizabeth Orthopaedic Hospital, going on to observe over the next two years further operations performed by Capener and ear specialist E. Garnet Passe in Exeter and in London at the National Orthopaedic Hospital and the London Clinic.

The corpus of over one hundred works can be categorised as either studies of details and sketches executed in pencil and crayon, sometimes with wash, on paper, or more finished works of pencil and oil on board, often with a gesso ground. The use of oil wash over gesso gives the pictures a luminosity, enhanced by the scratching and rubbing down of the surface, that is to be seen in a whole body of work produced in England in the 1940s—not least Henry Moore's 'Shelter Drawings'. It is, most particularly, characteristic of work made in St. Ives just after the war where its popularity derived—like Hepworth's subversion of hierarchies of pictorial practice by the use of pencil over oil and gesso—from Ben Nicholson's work of the period.

Some of the pictures show doctors and nurses preparing, ritualistically, for an operation; in others, like *Reconstruction*, 1947 (Fig. 37), *Concentration of Hands No. 1*, 1948 (Fig. 38) and *Fenestration of the Ear No. 4. 'The Microscope'*, 1948 (Fig. 39), the operation is in progress. They consist of groups of varying numbers of figures,

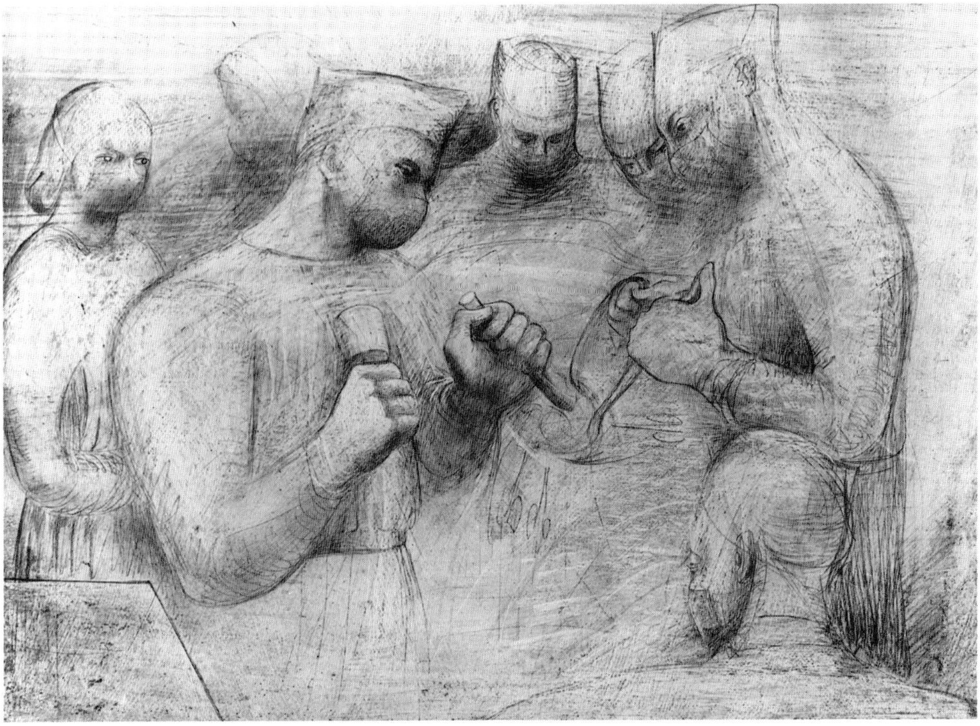

Fig. 37 BARBARA HEPWORTH, *Reconstruction*, 1947 © Trustees of the Barbara Hepworth Estate/Arts Council Collection

sometimes just one; less typical is a painting like *Hands Operating*, 1949 (Fig. 40) which, though study-like, is executed in oil on gesso. A smaller category depicts more complex, self-contained groups—*Hospital Theatre*, 1947 (Fig. 41), for example. Broadly speaking, it is only in this last category that one gets an idea of spatial context—of the room—as the majority of works show figures close-to and tightly composed. Rarely is there anything but the barest suggestion of the patient—perhaps the outline of a hand or the foreshortened, mummy-like form of a body—indeed, at times the composition does not seem to allow sufficient space for the patient within the group.

The works' style clearly draws on Hepworth's knowledge of Italian Renaissance painters—Giotto, Masaccio and Raphael are the most obvious—especially in the formality of composition and the production of voluminous, rounded figures by the use of heavy pencil shading. That shaded delineation of form is concentrated upon the hands and narrow, elongated, Giottesque eyes of the figures, whose gowns and masks otherwise shroud them with a standardised anonymity. They are not, however, as has been suggested [7], de-gendered, for the figures' headwear and the depiction of their eyes and brows distinguishes quite clearly male from female.

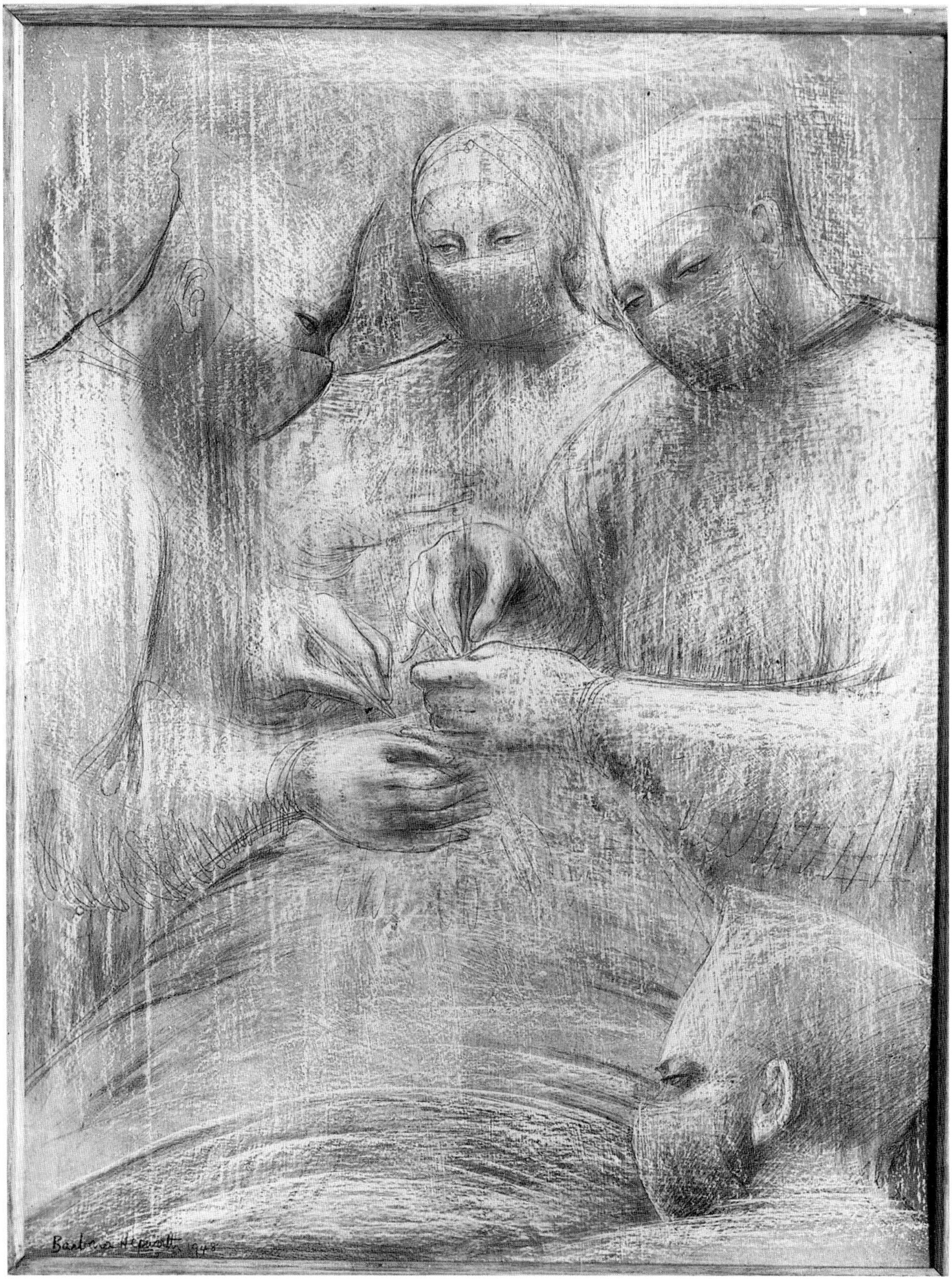

Fig. 38 BARBARA HEPWORTH, *Concentration of Hands No.1*, 1948 © Trustees of the Barbara Hepworth Estate/The British Council

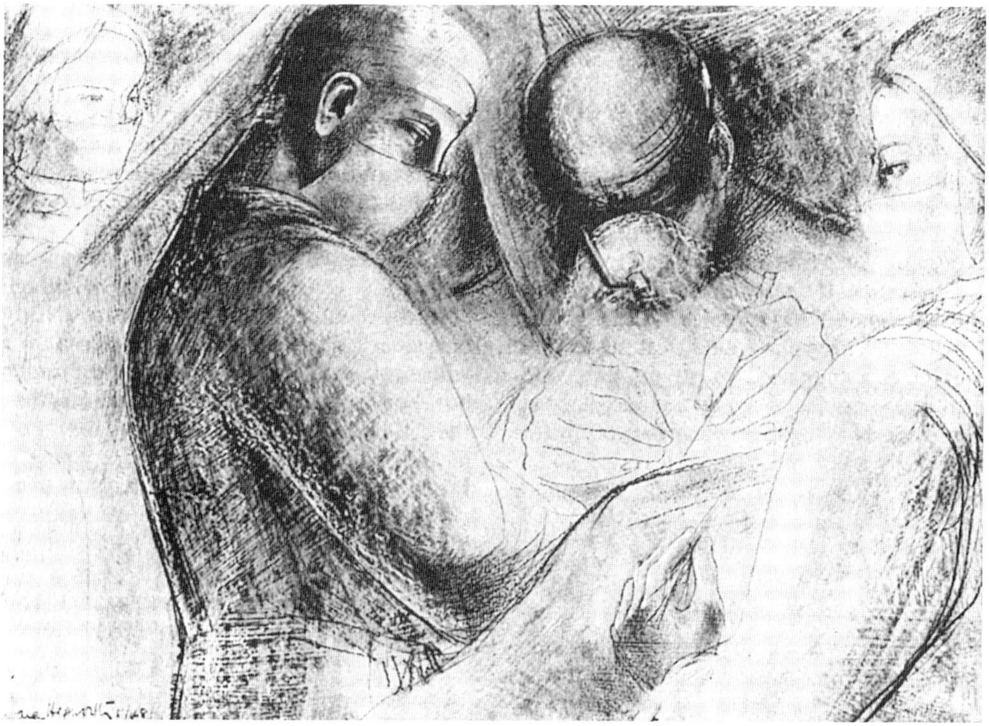

Fig. 39 BARBARA HEPWORTH, *Fenestration of the Ear No. 4: 'The Microscope'*, 1948 © Trustees of the Barbara Hepworth Estate

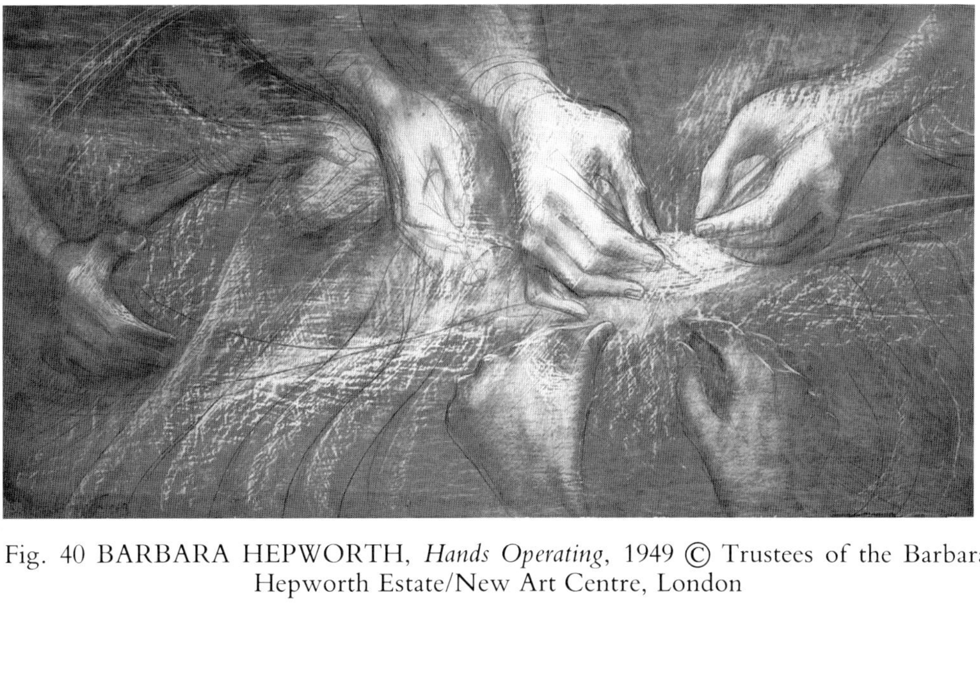

Fig. 40 BARBARA HEPWORTH, *Hands Operating*, 1949 © Trustees of the Barbara Hepworth Estate/New Art Centre, London

Hepworth discussed the scenes these pictures depict in terms of their sense of collective activity and the resultant formal harmony. 'From the moment I entered the operating theatre', she wrote:

> I became completely absorbed by two things: first, the extraordinary beauty of purpose and co-ordination between human beings all dedicated to the saving of a life, and the way that unity of idea and purpose dictated a perfection of concentration, movement, and gesture; and secondly by the way this special grace (grace of mind and body) induced a spontaneous space composition. [8]

In the context of these works, executed at that historical moment, we must see this familiar idealistic rhetoric as having a more material significance.

On 5 July 1948 the National Health Service was inaugurated, offering free health care for everyone in Britain. It was the high point, the most universally approved, of the post-war Labour government's welfare policies. Those policies were the realisation of wartime plans for a more collective society which had become popularly synonymous with the *Beveridge Report* [9] and which had been rapidly integrated into Britain's war aims as the broad-based, anti-Nazi, patriotic front appeared, at least, to merge into a collectivist consensus [10]. For Hepworth, who was among those anxious to get a copy of Beveridge's report as soon as it was published on 1 December 1942, that movement represented the popularisation of her long held vision of society.

The early months of the war had seen Hepworth, geographically marginalised in Carbis Bay, sharing the pessimism of Herbert Read, who warned that, 'all we represent and have fought for is threatened by the most appalling reaction' [11]. In the Spring of 1940, however, Hepworth seems to have recognised that, despite the war, the seeds of hope for a new social order survived. In an echo of her 1934 essay in *Unit One* she told critic E. H. Ramsden that she felt 'we are entering a new phase of existence' [12], and at the same time wrote to Read:

> If there is any virtue in this present war-time destruction it is, I feel, only to be found in its fluid quality—out of which could spring new impulses. [13]

This new found optimism (which Nicholson had never lost) fuelled a concerted rearguard constructivist offensive. In Margaret Mellis' words, Nicholson and Hepworth became obsessed with promoting what they called 'the movement'—its ranks now swollen with younger artists like Mellis herself, Peter Lanyon and John Wells [14]. They laid plans for a new magazine and, with the help of critics like E. H. Ramsden, grasped every opportunity to promote their work and that of their colleagues in exhibitions and publications. In April 1942 Herbert Read was able to write 'so far as constructivism is concerned . . . the column is advancing' [15]. But the most significant instance of the survival of the optimistic spirit of the pre-war period was in the pages of Edward Hulton's popular magazine *World Review*.

The art editor of *World Review*, Marcus Brumwell, director of Stuart's advertising agency and a key figure in the Hepworth-Nicholson circle, also edited a series entitled 'This Changing World', which sought to establish in terms accessible to the average reader if there was 'some common factor behind the contemporary manifestations of thought and life' [16]. The series, in its conjunction of art, science, philosophy and sociology in a unified vision of a future society (contributors included Read, Ramsden, Kathleen Raine, J. D. Bernal, Karl Mannheim, Lewis Mumford and John Summerson), should be seen as continuing the project of *Circle* of 1937 (plans for *Circle 2* were under discussion at the same time).

In his introductory essay Herbert Read identified the optimistic pattern underlying modernity and emphasised its continuity despite the war. Modernist artists, thinkers and scientists, he assured the readers, continued to work, preparing for the post-war period of renewal and its concomitant democratisation of society. 'They may not be in the public eye', he said:

> But the individuals in whom the spirit of modernism is embodied still survive, still work, still create—however obscurely and intermittently. When the cloud of war has passed, they will re-emerge, eager to rebuild the shattered world . . . They will say: our world is in ruins; it needs not only hard work and perseverance to rebuild it, but also skill and vision. We are scientists and we believe we have the skill: we are artists and we believe we have the vision. Let us direct your work and we promise you that out of the ruins a better world will emerge. [17]

The movement towards social reconstruction, of which Keynes and Beveridge were the chief mentors, with its reliance on science and democracy, appeared to coincide with the projections of Brumwell's series and to offer a concrete basis for the ideals of the broad left with which Hepworth identified. 'I happen to be atheist', she stated in 1944, 'and vaguely socialist, *definitely* Left but unformed in doctrine' [18], and she persisted to think about the need for a new theory of socialism, believing that Stalin should not be allowed to invalidate Marxism. She found herself defending the power given to the state over the individual in Beveridge's proposals, an interventionist position which sets her apart from, say, the individualistic disengagement of Herbert Read's anarchism.

The hospital pictures, in presenting a vision of collective effort in the setting that epitomised the new society, must be seen as celebratory of the flowering of the social reconstruction that Beveridge and the 1945 Labour government promised. The ordered and rationalised style in which they are executed alludes to the ordering of social planning and implies the sense of security that the welfare policies sought to achieve. It invests them with the quality that is said to have motivated Aneurin Bevan's policies—serenity. Hepworth's pictures articulate, it could be said, Bevan's

> . . . belief that people have a craving for a design in society, a settled, serene sense of order, not imposed, but co-operatively established. [19]

As well as constructing this sense of serenity—augmented by an almost religious feeling of contemplation—the use of a Renaissance visual language conjures up, of course, an idea of rebirth and renewal appropriate to the context of Reconstruction. However, these works also represent processes of reconstitution at a more subjective level.

Hospital Theatre of 1947 (Fig. 41) is one of the unusually complex compositions. More than in any other of the series, it shows us the room in which the scene is enacted: two double doors mark the limits of two sides of the room, a man is about to leave through one of them; the space between us and the main group is marked out by a table upon which are laid out the surgeon's tools and by two female figures. One of these, in the bottom left hand corner, is close to us and so cut off at the waist by the picture's edge; a little further away the other has her back to us. In

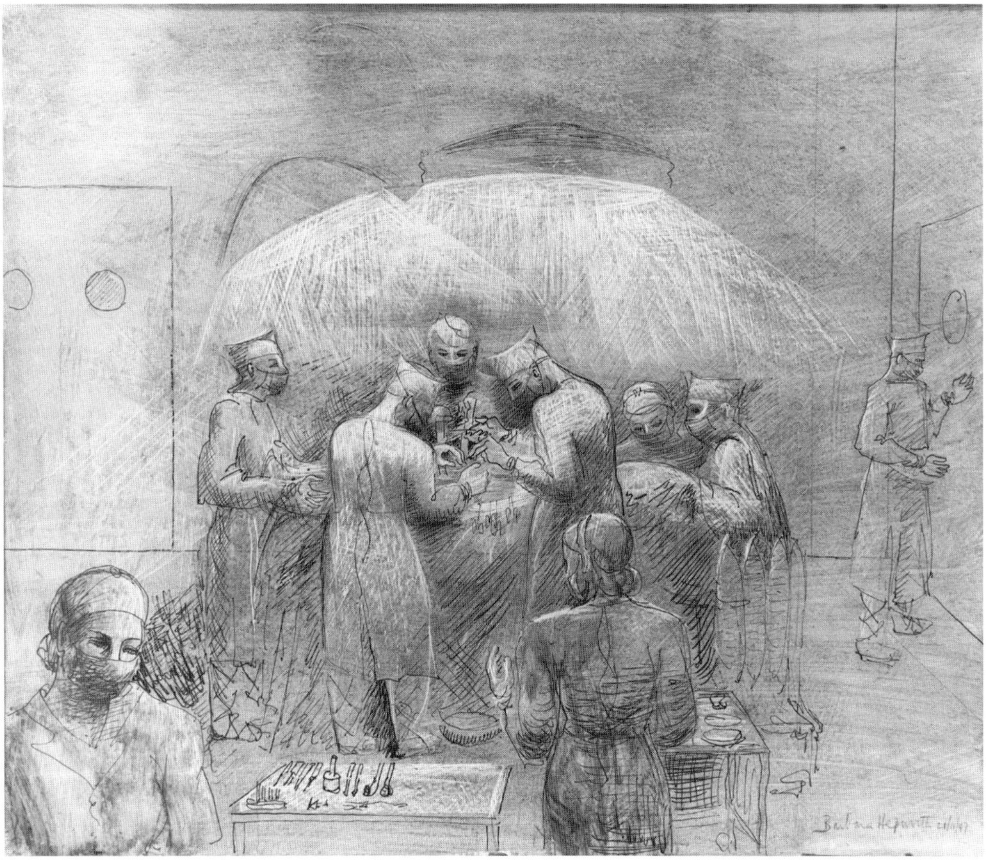

Fig. 41 BARBARA HEPWORTH, *Hospital Theatre*, 1947 © Trustees of the Barbara Hepworth Estate/Art Gallery of Hamilton, Ontario

the middle, the main group of six figures is illuminated from above by two large lamps, the light from which is rendered by the scratching away of the green glaze that covers the whole composition. At the very centre point of this group and of the whole picture, in an uncharacteristically frank allusion to the actual process depicted, an area of bright red pigment signifies the wound, contrasting sharply with the softer tone of the green.

One is reminded of the abstract drawings Hepworth produced during the war—for example, *Forms*, 1941 (Fig. 42). Indeed, it is instructive to think of that group of drawings and the hospital pictures as complementary bodies of work. These wartime drawings (actually as finished as the works in the hospital series) are exercises in the construction of space in two dimensions and in the relationship of colour to form and space. Strong pencil lines define an illusional three-dimensional form at the heart of which is a small area of brightly coloured paint held in tension between the dynamic lines and the tonal, textural surface of the rest of the picture. *Forms* is one of a number of these pieces which contain more than one such image. They relate, of course, to Hepworth's sculpture of the time—as she says, 'they are my sculptures born in the disguise of two dimensions' [20]—and like them their forms are organic.

They belong to a body of works produced in two and three-dimensions by a matrix of artists drawing on Gabo's work—Hepworth, Peter Lanyon and John Wells—that allude to a theme of generation by the description of forms suggestive of crystals, eggs, wombs [21]. This is a reading with which Hepworth would agree: as well as giving some of these drawings organic titles—*Crystals, Stone and Flower*, and so on—she also included these themes when, in 1947, she drew out a scheme of her iconography for Herbert Read. In the centre of the plan (Fig. 5) she wrote, 'Emotion/feeling' with arrows on each side travelling to and from, on the one side, 'known symbols (figures, hands, eyes, trees)', and on the other, 'Unconscious (unknown) symbols (curves, spirals, ovoids-foetus erotic, prenatal, dream, childhood, primitive etc.)' [22].

In these abstract drawings, then, the pencil lines, which either converge to and diverge from a crossing point like the strings of a sculpture, or mark out illusory planes, create the image of an enfolding, womb-like form. The accent of bright colour which articulates the arrangement becomes the embryo and even in the more angular, crystalline pictures it is suggestive of the seed crystal from which the whole has grown. They echo Hepworth's description for Read of her triplets' early drawings of 'egg forms within eggs, folded again and again into a purse and hidden in a secret place' [23]. Hepworth shared Read's interest in children's drawings, and, without doubt, in her mind whilst working on these pictures was the Jungian archetype of the mandala, highlighted by Read in *Education Through Art* [24], which he was researching at the time that she was making them.

In Jungian theory the mandala is 'Formation, Transformation, Eternal Mind's eternal recreation' [25]. It is the 'squaring of the circle' in as much as its concentration on a central point compensates for disorder, for the subject's

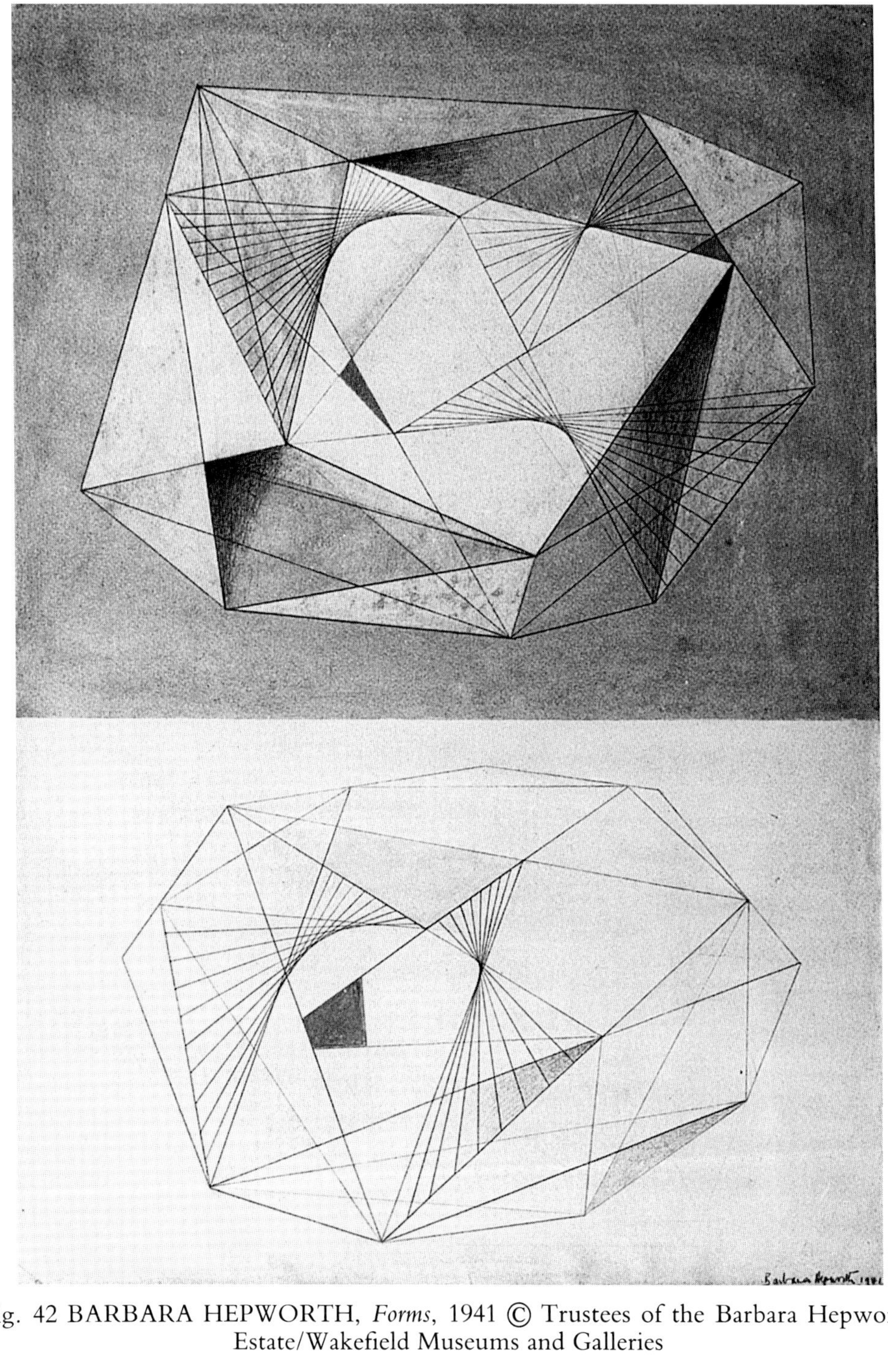

Fig. 42 BARBARA HEPWORTH, *Forms*, 1941 © Trustees of the Barbara Hepworth Estate/Wakefield Museums and Galleries

disorientation. It is an image, then, that acts as a counter to feelings of insecurity and confusion [26]. Such a Jungian notion of restitution might have been a part of the artist's intention, but we can also relate these images to an unconscious process of recreation. This repeated depiction of womb iconography must be related to Melanie Klein's theory of the 'depressive position' and the need therein to make reparation for the phantasied attacks upon the mother's body and its contents (the embryo) that are a part of female ego development [27]. The reparation or reconstitution of the mother, for whose body the womb-like form can be seen as a substitute or a signifier, is a necessary response to the anxiety of 'the loss of love and of the love object' [28]. It is a response most likely to be made manifest at times of insecurity.

The hospital pictures can be said to echo the earlier abstract works in their use of line and colour in composition. The red wound in *Hospital Theatre* equates, as I have suggested, to the coloured embryonic centre of the abstract works. Similarly, in works like *Concentration of Hands* (Fig. 38) the arrangement of forms around a central focus creates a womb-like enclosed space—one articulated by the radiating lines of arms, hands and instruments which, like the string lines of the abstract drawings, draw the composition centripetally into the highlighted focal point. The wound becomes the site of reparation or renewal both in terms of the surgeon's work and in terms of the artist's Kleinian reconstitution of the mother. This is implicit in Hepworth's projection of herself on to the surgeon in her account of one day in the operating theatre:

> I happened to look up into the great lamp above and in the dark hemisphere projecting in the centre was reflected the whole scene—wonderfully distorted in perspective and unrecognisable in a realistic sense and yet giving the whole unity and purpose in a completely poetic way—the periphery of heads with arms and hands radiating far away in great depth to the centre which was the wound—so that when I looked back at the group in front of me one felt all the more keenly the terrific sculptural idea in all the figures in the cubic space of the theatre and I felt *inside* each of them. [29]

The bringing to bear of a Kleinian reading upon the hospital drawings takes on a particularly poignant resonance when one considers Hepworth's relationship to her subject as a mother herself. One could say that the drawings emanate, ultimately, from her experience of her daughter's serious and protracted illness—the threatened loss of the loved object. That was not, however, the only threatened loss or source of insecurity with which Hepworth had to contend during these years. The 1940s saw her having to address the conflict between her ambitions as a professional artist and the expectations of her as a woman and as a mother. In addition, she was compelled to redefine her artistic ideology in terms of her position within Constructivism. The dominating discourse running through both these concerns was the question of the artist's function in society. These conflicts and that question are addressed implicitly or explicitly in the hospital pictures. By looking at that aspect of them I want to suggest that these readings of the drawings as a celebration of a sociopolitical event or as a Kleinian reparation are not alternative interpretations but unite within a single meaning of reconstructive self-definition.

As well as the threat of Sarah's illness, the later 1940s saw the gradual disintegration of the Hepworth-Nicholson domestic structure. Though they did not separate until late 1950, the first signs of tension within their marriage appeared around 1944; certainly by 1946 she saw his departure as a real possibility. The cause of this domestic tension was, it seems clear, a conflict between the expectations of her as a wife and mother and her ambition as an artist. Nicholson believed she was too single-minded and worked too hard, whilst she insisted that she was only absorbed by her work because he was hostile to her as a result of suppressing his jealousy of her work [30]. In short, in the later 1940s the domestic space was, for Hepworth, a site of anxiety and as much a site for gender based professional conflict as was her rivalry with Henry Moore in the public space.

In 1943 Hepworth, and with her Nicholson, announced a wish to be disassociated from Constructivism—a movement they had come to associate with Gabo, Antoine Pevsner *et al*—but not 'the constructive idea', which they saw as an element running through the history of art from Giotto and Masaccio to Cézanne and Mondrian. This break from Gabo, a part of a longer trajectory of progressive disassociation ending in his departure for America in 1946, was precipitated by the fraught plans for a monograph on Constructivism. The motivating forces behind the book (encouraged by Nicholson and Hepworth) were E. H. Ramsden and William Gibson, keeper of the National Gallery, who were to co-write it with Gabo and Read.

Gabo feared that the movement—which he was increasingly treating as having been invented by him and his brother Pevsner—was being hijacked by Nicholson as a nationalistic school. He believed Nicholson and Hepworth were actively suppressing his work and he, in turn, was highly protective of both his ideas and the history of Constructivism—at this time the *Realistic Manifesto* by Gabo and Pevsner had still not been fully translated from the Russian. In retrospect it is clear that there was a great deal of misunderstanding, not least in the British artists' ignorance of the details of that chapter of modernism's history and the significance and intentions of Constructivism (Hepworth, for instance, only learned about 'the two schools in Moscow and how [Gabo] split from the Tatlin, Rodchenko School etc' in May 1944 [31]). In contrast to Gabo, Hepworth and Nicholson proposed a more humanist and organic art, an idea 'with grass roots' [32]. The deliberately archaic style of the hospital drawings might, in this light, be seen as both a re-humanising of Hepworth's art and an evocation of the 'constructive' artists of the past—Giotto, Masaccio, Raphael. Though Hepworth's secession was more of a recognition of existing differences than a change of direction, and her protests of delight at her liberation from the constrictions of Constructivism not withstanding, we might assume that this loss of artistic identity was unsettling.

To return to *Hospital Theatre* (Fig. 41): I want to suggest that it is not fanciful for us to read the foreground figure with her back to us as a representation of the artist herself. The shape of the figure, with its hair tied into a snood (as Hepworth's was whilst working), is somehow reminiscent of Hepworth as we know her from Nicholson's schematic depictions of her from 1932 to 1933 and from photographic representations. Sceptics might like to consider the similar figure on the left in *Reconstruction* (Fig. 37) and the apparently set-apart, delineated face in the top left hand corner of *Fenestration of the Ear No. 4: 'The Microscope'* (Fig. 39). We can read that figure, perhaps, as Hepworth the mother for, whilst she did not of course witness her daughter's operation, it seems legitimate for us to see these drawings as representing the experience of Sarah's illness and treatment if not the event.

Hepworth's inclusion of herself as caring mother might be seen as an attempt to make concrete, or to rationalise, her domestic situation at a time when it was the source of anxiety. The conflict she perceived between her two roles as artist and mother is apparent from her statement to Margaret Gardiner:

> I feel most definitely that when I have got the children safely through to adolescence that a new period will start for me, a period of freedom and activity. [33]

Her self-representation as anxious mother, then, might be seen as a counter to the equivocation she felt in that role in reality. Indeed, during the late 1940s Hepworth produced a number of works addressing the theme of motherhood. They must be seen in the light of her reaction to Moore's much publicised *Madonna and Child* for St. Matthew's, Northampton, which she found profoundly disturbing [34] as aesthetically compromised and emotionally perfidious. In contrast she, as a woman, could identify with the object:

> . . . if I see a woman carrying a child in her arms [she wrote in 1952] it is not so much what I see that affects me, but what I feel within my own body. [35].

The figure in *Hospital Theatre* is, however, ambiguous: her gaze is that of the caring mother but it is also that of the observing artist. Perhaps these works can be seen as an attempt to 'square the circle', to echo Jung's phraseology, of mother/artist in society. Hepworth's theory of the artist's position in society was based upon individuality and equality. She explained to Margaret Gardiner that

> . . . we are much preoccupied (all of us) [Hepworth, Nicholson & Gabo] in thoroughly working out the status of artist to society and that will never be solved by a commission of Fine Arts but only by the artist being allowed to take his place along with other workers. [36]

Or, as Read had put it, 'we must realise that when the day's work is done we are one with the cobblers and tinkers' [37]. Perhaps the democratically standardised figures, including the artist/mother, are intended to allude to this equality of status—each contributing equally to the whole. The artist's role in society was, in Hepworth's thinking, related to a sense of community which she felt she and Nicholson had achieved through their move to Cornwall. Artists, she told Read, must 'become a part of a human community instead of being a minority, de-centralise [geographically] and yet unify' [38]. Does the surgical team not represent such a community?

Hepworth also put her understanding of the artist's relationship with society a slightly different way. In 1942 she wrote to Read (adopting his own terms) that she was working on a

> . . . practical plan for giving the artist a *place* in society—the reorientation of teaching based on the principle that every man is a special kind of artist. [39]

It is this latter idea that is implicit in the concentration in these drawings upon eyes and hands—for Hepworth, signifiers of the artist. Sculpture, to her, was a product of and appeals to the visual and haptic senses and she saw her work emanating from that plane where 'idea and action become one movement' [40]. Hands have repeatedly played a part in the construction of her own artistic persona, from their appearance in *Unit One* in 1934 to David Lewis' description of her feeling an object 'not with fingers but with her palms' in 1985 [41], and most particularly in the casts she made in 1949 of her left hand—her 'thinking hand . . . listening hand' [42]. More broadly speaking, hands as the prosecutors of manual labour signify the union between the artist and other workers as they had in the 1930s when they had been employed as symbols of mutuality. It may be significant that, having had tuition in sculpture from Hepworth, the surgeon in many of these pictures—Norman Capener, who owned one of the casts of Hepworth's hand—entered the *Unknown Political Prisoner* competition with a carving of two hands clasped together.

Ironically, given Hepworth's internal conflicts, the inclusion of the artist/mother figure on an equal basis could be seen to bolster the sexual ideology upon which the *Beveridge Report* and the post-war social structure were predicated. The report, it has been argued, reinforced patriarchy by its assumption of the nuclear family as the basic social unit, its prescription of gender roles and its subordination of women as dependants [43]. It presented marriage 'in terms of the ideologies of domesticity of motherhood' [44]. In the pictures, not only does the caring mother figure reflect patriarchal ideology, the gendered division of labour is also quite apparent. The surgeons are, invariably, male and active while, towards the periphery, the nurses, whose primary function is to attend and look on, are female. Hepworth has encapsulated Elizabeth Wilson's description of the state's definition of femininity and its realisation in welfarism:

> Woman is above all Mother, and with this vocation go all the virtues of femininity: submission, nurturence, passivity . . . The 'feminine' client of the social services waits patiently at clinics, social security offices, and housing departments, to be ministered to by the paternal authority figure, doctor or civil servant, sometimes by the nurturent yet firm model of femininity provided by nurse or social worker. [45]

It may be that Hepworth's signification of this gendering of roles was not unwitting. Around this time she told E. H. Ramsden that she pitied young wives with babies because, she felt, 'if life is going this way (chore after chore) for women—it's not really worth living' [46].

A similar patriarchal subtext is discernible in Hepworth's 1948 depiction of Herbert Read as *The Poet Reading to his Children* (Leeds City Art Gallery). The family is depicted as an organic unit dominated and balanced compositionally by the father figure, whilst the mother's absence is enabled by the embodiment of femininity in the morphology of the group itself. On the other hand, it may be that Hepworth is subverting established gender roles by depicting the father as nurturer. Informed by her knowledge of Jung's theory of the animus/anima archetypes, a dialectic of the masculine and feminine was, undoubtedly, intrinsic to her understanding of the 'constructive idea' in its broad, social sense.

> The feminine point of view [she wrote in 1952] is a complementary one to the masculine . . . There is no question of competition. The woman's approach presents a different emphasis. [47]

Whilst recognising difference, she opposed the qualitative distinction of male and female work and asserted her belief that 'the only way for women to get an equal square deal with men is to openly fight as women' [48]. The family, like the surgical team, acts as a metaphor for a view of a collective, sexually equal society—a view reinforced by Hepworth's interest in the idea of the Gestalt. That interest is reflected in the stylistic characteristics of both the Read picture and the hospital subjects in which formal distinctions and detailed features are subjugated to an overall compositional harmony.

Hepworth's inclusion of her own body in the hospital drawings positions her, as artist and mother, as part of the medical team. The ambiguity of the figures (are they self-portraits or merely nurses?) buttresses that idea. This is consistent with her thoughts on the artist and society, the artist's observing and controlling gaze brings order to and interprets the scene. The standardisation of figures implies that this rationalising role of the artist is an equally important part of the action depicted. Even if we do not choose to see these figures as representations of the artist, she locates herself—and us, as artist and viewer are both visual consumers of the scene—within the picture. The arrangement of the figures in *Reconstruction* and in *Concentration of Hands No. 1*, for example, positions the viewer as a part of the composition; we join with the peripheral figures of the pictures as observers of the operation. By being seen only in part or from the side, figures such as the nurse cut off by the right hand edge of *Fenestration of the Ear No. 4* or that at the bottom right hand corner of *Reconstruction* draw us into the circle and position us as of their group.

In his review of these drawings, Read drew attention to the spectating figures: playing on their 'theatre' setting, he described 'the patient faces of the nurses, who stand in the wings like a Greek chorus' [49]. Their choric function is not simply one of observing the action but also of mediating between the scene depicted and the viewer. Whether signifying the artist or not, the figure on the left of *Reconstruction* certainly brings to mind the Albertian device of the commentator 'who admonishes and points out to us what is happening . . . or invites us to weep or to laugh with them' [50], and so serves to unite all the more strongly our space with that of the picture. The Albertian reference locates Hepworth in the constructive tradition that she and Nicholson saw running through Piero and Raphael. Whilst Hepworth has not of course followed Alberti to the letter, the pictures' compositional style is consistent with what Norman Bryson has said about Albertian perspective: it

> . . . assumes the viewer not simply as an ambient witness . . . but as a physical presence . . . [it] *incarnates* the viewer. [51]

A figure like that of the nurse to the rear of *Concentration of Hands* seems deliberately to invite comparison with ourselves; her gaze echoes our own. Nurse, artist and viewer, then, become equal and necessary components in a harmonious figure composition. By extending that thesis from the level of composition to that of content, one can read these works as an essay on citizenship. The surgical team is an embodiment of the harmonious collective effort of an ideal society, or perhaps of an idealistic view of contemporary society at that moment. Hepworth not only illustrates within the pictures her position as artist (and mother) in that society, but enacts it through the rationalisation of society that the pictures represent. More than that, by using a compositional technique that

> . . . return[s] the gaze upon itself . . . [and] changes the viewer himself into a representation, an object or spectacle before his own vision . . . [52]

and thus by making us necessary components in the composition, the works prescribe a function for us within society. One might say that, in a period of decreasing individuality, they become mediations between the state and the individual.

To conclude, the hospital pictures can be seen as representing different forms of reconstruction or restitution that embody an attempt at figuring subjective and social integration. It should be emphasised that, whilst coincident with Hepworth's intention up to a certain unidentifiable point, the meanings I have written are generated, in a deconstructive sense, from the works in themselves. The use of Hepworth's own writings is not intended to suggest, necessarily, an authorial intentionality but to provide a historical and biographical validation for the conceptual tools brought to bear upon the works. The aim has not been simply to show how Hepworth sought to represent her desire for a 'coherent wholeness' as quoted at the top of the essay, but to go further to suggest ways in which these works are invested with ideological significance beyond that intention. An obvious example is their reproduction, in spite of her belief, of patriarchy.

This reading of the pictures provides an opportunity to write around the later sculptures a meaning that reaches beyond the essentialist formal interpretation posited by Hepworth and reiterated by successive commentators. In Hepworth's terms the sculptures are 'reality—not illusion like painting' [53], and as such incarnate the viewer all the more. The viewer enters into a physical as well as scopic relationship with the sculpture such that s/he becomes a part of the work. The invitation to enter into such a relationship is clear in *The Cosdon Head*, 1949 (Birmingham Museums and Art Gallery), which can be seen as transitional between the hospital drawings and the organic sculptures of the 1950s. In a refrain of her work of the early 1930s, Hepworth has incised an eye and a hand on one side of the head. Does the hand belong to the same figure as the head? Or is it applied affectionately by another? Is it the sculptor's left hand—her 'thinking hand . . . listening hand'? By suggesting her own hand, the artist stresses the interchange between the sculptural object and the artist/spectator: rather than an image of a head, the sculpture becomes an image of a human relationship or interaction.

Hepworth's vision of society, informed by her knowledge of Jung and Gestalt theory as well as by socialism, was based on a belief in the collective effort of individuals, including artists and mothers, regardless of class or gender. In the post-war years that theory was seen increasingly in terms of small communities—exemplified by her continued residence and civic position in St. Ives—rather than a socialist state. One can argue that for Hepworth the landscape, which came to inform much of her sculpture after the war, acts as symbol for that community. Like the hospital pictures, then, the figure-in-the-landscape carvings might be read as metaphors for the relationship of the individual to the community.

NOTES AND REFERENCES

1 Quoted in SINCLAIR, ANDREW (1989) *War Like a Wasp: the Lost Decade of the Forties* (London, Hamish Hamilton), p. 33.

2 Quoted in GARDINER, MARGARET (1982) *Barbara Hepworth: a Memoir* (Edinburgh, Salamander Press) reprint 1994 (London, Lund Humphries), p. 58.

3 I am indebted to Dr. David Mellor and Neil Sharp for their comments on a draft of this essay and to Sally Festing and Michael Tooby for help with gathering material for it.

4 HEPWORTH, BARBARA (1952) in: *Barbara Hepworth: Carvings and Drawings* (London, Lund Humphries), unpag., section 4.

5 Hepworth established this evolutionary construct in *Carvings and Drawings* (n. 4), and it is followed in, for instance, HAMMACHER, A. M. (1959) *Barbara Hepworth* (London, Zwemmer) and HODIN, JOSEF P. (1961) *Barbara Hepworth* (London, Lund Humphries).

6 For information on the series I draw on The Tate St. Ives' Information Sheet for their Study Display 1: *Barbara Hepworth, 'The*

Fenestration of the Ear', 1993, and on BOWNESS, PAUL (1985) 'Operation Drawings of Dame Barbara Hepworth', *British Medical Journal*, 21–28 December, pp. 291, 1788–89.

7 In, for instance, Bowness (n. 6).

8 Reproduced in *Carvings and Drawings* (n. 4).

9 BEVERIDGE, WILLIAM (1942) *Social Insurance and Allied Services* (London, HMSO).

10 On this see MORGAN, DAVID and EVANS, MARY (1993) *The Battle for Britain: Citizenship and Ideology in the Second World War* (London, Routledge).

11 Letter READ, HERBERT to Ben Nicholson, n.d. [Christmas 1939]. Papers of Ben Nicholson; Tate Gallery Archive, London.

12 Letter HEPWORTH to E. H. Ramsden, 7 May [1940]. Papers of E. H. Ramsden & Margot Eates; Tate Gallery Archive, London.

13 Letter HEPWORTH to Herbert Read, 2 May 1940. Sir Herbert Read Archive, University of Victoria, B.C.

14 MELLIS, MARGARET, interviewed by the author, 13 March 1993.

15 READ, HERBERT (1942) 'Vulgarity and Impotence: Speculations on the Present State of the Arts', *Horizon* Vol. 5, No. 28, April, p. 267.

16 READ, HERBERT (1941) 'Threshold of a New Age: Renaissance or Decadence', *World Review*, June, p. 25.

17 *Ibid.*, p. 29.

18 Letter HEPWORTH to E. H. Ramsden, n.d. [August 1944]. Papers of E. H. Ramsden & Margot Eates; Tate Gallery Archive, London.

19 FOOT, MICHAEL (1973) *Aneurin Bevan, a Biography, Vol Two: 1945–1960* (London, Davis Poynter), p. 105.

20 Letter HEPWORTH to E. H. Ramsden, n.d. [1943]. Papers of E. H. Ramsden & Margot Eates; Tate Gallery Archive, London.

21 *Cf.* Anne Wagner's reference to the womb-like forms in Hepworth's earlier drawings; this publication.

22 Letter HEPWORTH to Herbert Read, 6 March 1947. Sir Herbert Read Archive, University of Victoria, B.C.

23 Letter HEPWORTH to Herbert Read, 15 January 1941. Sir Herbert Read Archive, University of Victoria, B.C.

24 READ, HERBERT (1943) *Education through Art* (London, Faber).

25 GOETHE, *Faust, Part Two*, quoted by C. G. Jung, in: JUNG, CARL GUSTAV (1965) *Memories, Dreams, Reflections*, trans. Richard and Clara Williams (London, Vintage), p. 186.

26 See 'Mandalas', in: READ, HERBERT and HULL, R. (Eds) *The Collected Works of C. G. Jung* Vol. 9i (London, Routledge), paras. 713–18.

27 See, for example, KLEIN, MELANIE (1981) 'Infantile Anxiety Situations Reflected in a Work of Art and in the Creative Impulse', in: KLEIN, MELANIE (1981) *Love, Guilt and Reparation & Other Works 1921–45* (London, Hogarth Press).

28 *Ibid.*

29 Letter HEPWORTH to Herbert Read, 6 March 1947. Sir Herbert Read Archive, University of Victoria, B.C.

30 Letter HEPWORTH to E. H. Ramsden, n.d. [September 1950]. Papers of E. H. Ramsden & Margot Eates; Tate Gallery Archive, London.

31 Letter HEPWORTH to Herbert Read, 17 May 1944. Sir Herbert Read Archive, University of Victoria, B.C.

32 Letter NICHOLSON, BEN to Herbert Read, n.d. Papers of Ben Nicholson; Tate Gallery Archive, London.

33 Gardiner (n. 2), p. 25.

34 *Ibid.*, p. 57.

35 Reproduced in: (1954) *Barbara Hepworth: a Retrospective Exhibition of Carvings from 1927 to 1954* (London, Whitechapel Art Gallery), p. 27.

36 Gardiner (n. 2), p. 51.

37 Read (n. 16), p. 29.

38 Letter HEPWORTH to Herbert Read, 8 April 1942. Sir Herbert Read Archive, University of Victoria, B.C.

39 Ibid. Also cited by Penelope Curtis, in: CURTIS, PENELOPE and WILKINSON, ALAN G. (1994) *Barbara Hepworth: a Retrospective* (Liverpool, Tate Gallery Liverpool), p. 125.

40 Letter HEPWORTH to E. H. Ramsden, n.d.

[1944]. Papers of E. H. Ramsden & Margot Eates; Tate Gallery Archive, London.

41 LEWIS, DAVID (1985) *St. Ives 1939–64* (London, Tate Gallery), p. 18.

42 HEPWORTH, BARBARA (1970, 1985) *A Pictorial Autobiography* (New York, Praeger; London, Tate Gallery), p. 79.

43 See MEASOR, LYNDA and WILLIAMSON, VALERIE (1992) 'Vital work to do: The Implications of the Report for Women', in: JACOBS, JOHN (Ed) (1992) *Beveridge 1942–1992* (London, Whiting & Birch).

44 BLAND, LUCY, McCABE, TRISHA and MORT, FRANK (1979) 'Sexuality and Reproduction', in: BARRETT, MICHELE *et al* (Eds) (1979) *Ideology and Cultural Production* (London, Croom Helm), p. 88.

45 WILSON, ELIZABETH (1977) *Women and the Welfare State* (London, Tavistock), pp. 7–8.

46 Letter HEPWORTH to E. H. Ramsden, 10 January [1948]. Papers of E. H. Ramsden & Margot Eates; Tate Gallery Archive, London.

47 Hepworth (n. 35), p. 27.

48 Letter HEPWORTH to E. H. Ramsden, n.d. [1943]. Papers of E. H. Ramsden & Margot Eates; Tate Gallery Archive, London.

49 READ, HERBERT (1948) 'Barbara Hepworth: a New Phase', *The Listener*, 8 April, p. 592.

50 ALBERTI, LEON BATTISTA, *On Painting*, trans. (1966) John R. Spencer (New Haven, Princeton University Press), p. 78.

51 BRYSON, NORMAN (1983) *Vision in Painting: the Logic of the Gaze* (New Haven, Princeton University Press), p. 106.

52 *Ibid.*

53 Letter HEPWORTH to Herbert Read, 14 May [1944]. Sir Herbert Read Archive, University of Victoria, B.C.

PENELOPE CURTIS

What is Left Unsaid

Sometimes, after working on an exhibition for a long time, and especially on one for the Tate, one suddenly realises that one hasn't said what one most wanted to say. Essays are written to fit particular slots in a catalogue, the leaflet has to be a comprehensive general introduction, even one's preface gets published under another name. So it's nice to have another chance.

What then was it that I left unsaid in the various texts that accompanied *Barbara Hepworth: a Retrospective*? While I wanted to make clear in the exhibition's presentation that it should be regarded, before anything else, as an opportunity for a fresh look at Hepworth, there were things I felt ready to say *then*. In the texts I contributed to the catalogue I chose two areas outside that in which Hepworth is normally positioned, seeing this as the most direct way to bring some new material to bear. Crucially, this decision involved missing the opportunity to focus on the work itself, and particularly the work of the central period of her career, the 1930s and 1940s.

The catalogue had been finished six months earlier. Now that the works had arrived and were installed, I wanted to see what the exhibition itself would do in initiating debate about Hepworth's work. The selection was not far from what I had hoped it would be; though it would have been quite possible to choose a similarly large exhibition which made Hepworth look repetitive and stereotyped, I believe that this selection brought out near the best of Hepworth. It provided an opportunity to begin to look at an artist who had been oddly neglected during the previous twenty-five years. To what extent this opportunity is accepted remains to be seen, but the Critical Forum seminar was deliberately intended to begin this process, by presenting more 'voices' than had been possible in the catalogue [1].

Some would argue that if there has been little interest in Hepworth's work in recent years, then this is a clear indication that her work is not very interesting. But I can't agree. Hepworth's work does have a hold on its audience, if only to the extent that so many people can describe a typical piece. This is an interesting phenomenon, but one that has hardly been critically addressed. Apart from the fact that Hepworth's work has not been presented in any depth, we have lacked a framework in which to discuss it. The conventional framework 'Moore, Nicholson, Gabo' is not only outmoded, it is also worn out. There has been very little satisfactory writing about Hepworth's *sculpture*, and what I have written in the catalogue hardly begins to discuss the work itself. Nevertheless I can go some way in defending this approach, in that I do now believe that it will only be by wresting

Hepworth free from the discourse in which she has been placed up to now that we can start to look afresh at her achievement. Though it is also arguable that the impossibility of seeing her archives has served as a pretext—for surely if people really wanted to work on Hepworth, they would have done so—I have to assume that the lack of access to this material has genuinely precluded a development in our understanding. What I want to see tackled is the characterisation of Hepworth's works, and I believe that this will necessarily involve a better understanding of the artist who made them.

There has been a tendency to infer from Hepworth's work that she was a cool and disciplined person. However, if we were able to start instead with the person, we might be persuaded to discard this traditional reading, and infer from her personality that her work is about passion and zeal. We haven't done this, and can't do it, because we have little access to Hepworth as a person. What she let out were carefully modulated accounts in her own voice, or in those of a few trusted spokespersons.

I have, however, had the chance to catch unguarded glimpses of Hepworth through her correspondence with Ben Nicholson, with Herbert Read, and with a number of other correspondents. I am usually disinclined to get involved in discussions of an artist's character, but it may be that in Hepworth's case some kind of corrective is necessary. Though I know that many of those who have met her did not take to her, in her letters she comes over very well. She is both passionate and precise. She is extremely loyal to friends and to causes, energetic in making sure the right thing is done, intelligent but realistic. She cares about the detail as much as the wider cause, and one perceives the place of the detail within the lifestyle as a whole. She delighted, for instance, in the improvement in functional design she witnessed during the 1940s—from utility clothes to pencil sharpeners. But Hepworth was always concerned not to let the detail take over, and it is clear that one of the greatest problems of her late life was the imbalance and intrusion that her success brought with it. I would like to have communicated some of this passion—this commitment to real life and its variety—that I find in Hepworth, and to start to break down the conventional assessment of her work—and of her—as cool and restrained.

Why do reviews of the last fifty years concur in this reading of Hepworth? Must we reach the conclusion that it is because men find something unsettling about a woman who not only makes large sculptures, but also makes them abstract, and has four children? It may well be that critics are less accustomed to discussing sculpture, and that when they have had to do so they have found too-ready a comparison with Moore and his continuing figuration. Has their experience of a clarity of purpose and personal ambition, which they rarely encountered in a woman, affected their interpretation of her work? Certainly much of the more hackneyed criticism begins in this vein—'Mother of triplets finishes her Festival statue'; 'Woman wins Major Award'; 'Fragile Figure with Strong Hands'; 'Tiny Woman wields hammer'—and one can find countless examples of such reviews.

Hepworth inevitably had no time for this kind of journalism, and particularly hated being called a sculptress.

To look at Hepworth as a woman sculptor through reviews which focus on her gender is unrevealing. One is tempted to share Hepworth's own impatience with this kind of approach and leave it at that. Her unwillingness to pursue the question of gender is well known, and tends to be unquestioningly accepted. But this acceptance has tended to obscure a well-hidden concern on Hepworth's part. When occasional comments on gender are glimpsed, they reveal a deep-seated belief in the significance of her sex, and make important reading. They would aid a defence of the view that an understanding of the person—of the woman—could help us to read her work. Hepworth could only allow herself to discuss the issue when she was in company she trusted, and it becomes more evident after the war. This must be due to her position in St. Ives, which was very different to that in London; but whether one takes it as indicating independence or isolation is debatable, and whether one interprets a new readiness to talk about gender as a sign of thwarted ambition, or as a sign of a greater openness, is similarly open to question. But when Hepworth does talk in this way, her observations hit a strikingly contemporary note.

Watching her triplets—two girls and one boy—grow up led Hepworth to acquire a deep belief in the influence of conventional expectations on the development of girls. She shared her experience of running a small drawing class for children with Herbert Read and told him how the drawings had helped her to develop her

> . . . theories about women—how they are born and how affected by what the world demands of them and produces in them from the age of 1 week by the current and past attitude socially and sexually. [2]

Her regular correspondence with Read encouraged her to think in psychoanalytic terms. In her letters to him she opens up as she rarely does, and talks about the importance of the mother-child relationship, and about daring to use the right words to describe sculpture.

> The words which most describe the true forces of sculpture are words which we are only just beginning to use again. The sort of amnesia which has existed for centuries brought us very low—the myth, the image, the fetish, the magic of form and light, mass and space, touch and sight as related to the act of living and going right back to the strength of the child sucking at the breast are themselves almost painful (and provoke great resistance) to a society which finds it easier to swallow quack medicine than to live bravely. [3]

In attempting to explain how, for her, realism and abstraction felt the same, Hepworth drew Read a diagram (Fig. 5) associating these tendencies with the vocabulary she felt was lacking in contemporary critiques.

In 1943 she wrote to Read about always being omitted from British Council exhibitions. The immediate cause of her outburst was the exhibition of Contemporary British Art at the Toledo Museum of Art: this time she felt 'there isn't any excuse for not including me' while recognising in herself her tendency to provide the Council with excuses:

> . . . up till now I have thought of various reasons for this omission—such as
> (1) being a woman
> (2) being abstract
> (3) being young
> (4) being a wife and mother etc. etc. [4]

One is struck by the fact that in her public correspondence with the Arts Council, Hepworth makes a point of fighting for a second commission at the Festival of Britain, and gives as her particular reason the fact that she wanted to work with Jane Drew:

> . . . it would give me especial pleasure to work with another woman on a scheme which is peculiarly sympathetic to me. [5]

As I have noted, there is a paucity of satisfactory writing on Hepworth's work. One of the exceptions is the writing of E. H. Ramsden. Ramsden was close to Hepworth in the 1940s, and wrote a number of key texts in this period which are among the most particular to the artist. Ramsden was much stricter than Hepworth about being defined by gender, and many of her readers will always have assumed she was a man. E. H. Ramsden the writer—a.k.a Hartley Ramsden the artist—died in 1994, and I should like to draw attention to the importance of her writing on Hepworth by quoting from it in some depth.

Hepworth and Ramsden adopted strikingly different strategies to deal with being women in a world of male creativity, but that each cultivated a strategy is clear. In 1943 Hepworth told her:

> It would be nice if people could abandon the Miss. I should almost prefer to be called Comrade Hepworth. I don't mind my sex as being exposed by my Christian name because the only way for women to get an equal square deal with men is to openly fight as women for the fact that art is 'not biological' as you say. I think nevertheless that you aid the common cause better by being known as a woman. [6]

Appellations are in one way irrelevant—and this is why Hepworth tried to succeed on equal terms—and yet in another way, gender may be more important to understanding Hepworth than has been previously realised. I would suggest that it is significant that the writing most appreciated by Hepworth was by Ramsden and that she particularly welcomed the work of two other female critics—Herta Wescher and Carola Giedion-Welcker [7]. Despite this, Ramsden is not brought into the discussion of those who have written on Hepworth, though her contribution is as great, and as formative. She highlighted Hepworth in three survey books which she wrote between 1940 and 1953, gave space to others to write about Hepworth in her own periodical, and reviewed Hepworth herself. Moreover it was Ramsden who helped Hepworth with fixing and defining titles for her sculptures.

Hepworth and Ramsden shared a common source of inspiration in Rilke. In her 1953 book *Sculpture: Theme and Variations*, Ramsden used Rilke at length, for example quoting Rilke on movement within Rodin's sculpture:

> However great the movement of sculpture may be—it must return to itself, the great circle must complete itself, the circle of solitude that encloses a work of art . . .

One is struck by how well this fits the sculpture to which Ramsden gave the title *Pelagos*, the open sea [8].

In 1943 Ramsden published a review of Hepworth's Temple Newsam exhibition in *Horizon*. She began by quoting from Alfred North Whitehead: 'Our perception to natural events and natural objects is a perception from within nature'. Ramsden continued:

> The achievement of this unity of the many in the one in a perceptible form is the special province of the artist . . . In face of [Hepworth's] achievement one should be drawn both to the contemplation of those cosmic relationships which exist between the order of nature and the mind of man, and to a consideration of the basis and origin of the sculptural instinct itself . . . In the Kantian meaning of the word, these carvings are 'purposive' in 2 ways . . . That is, they induce repose and generate a movement.

Ramsden contrasts Moore's feeling for the organic relationship between man and landscape with Hepworth's interest in the 'idea or intellectual construction which lies beyond it and is, therefore, in the Platonic sense, precedent' [9].

In a 1946 article in *Polemic* Ramsden wrote:

> There is a deepening conviction . . . that it is the modes of interconnectedness of things rather than the things themselves, the evolving curve rather than the completed figure, the process of 'becoming' rather than the state of the 'become' that is ultimately significant. It is therefore inevitable that this consciousness of the 'inbetweenness' of things, this passionate sense that: 'Between the hammers lives on our heart, as between the teeth the tongue . . .' should find expression in plastic art under new and ever more subtle determinations of sculptural form. [10]

Throughout the 1940s Hepworth was deeply grateful for Ramsden's collaboration in explaining her work. In 1941 she writes:

> I liked your article very much. Personally I never believe in simplifying for the general public—but all these men say it's essential. [11]

After the *Polemic* article was published Hepworth sent 'all my thanks for your wonderful work' and described the text as:

> . . . the plane on which idea and action become one movement. If I have done something of what you say then I am content for the first time—because I have contacted the outside world through you. To be intelligible. [12]

Having read Ramsden's article on 'Oval Sculpture' Hepworth declared:

> I am deeply impressed by your article . . . There must be some link or similarity in the way you and I look at things—your ideas on sculpture always seem to put me into a 'world' to strive towards strange unknown forms and space which will resolve what has to be resolved. Or, as you put it so perfectly 'converge towards a point of repose'. I don't find very much in our age which nourishes that sense of 'well-being' which produces a culture—or what you call 'limited within', 'unlimited without' which for me represents the rich relationship of man to the whole. [13]

In May 1950 Ramsden founded a new magazine, *Eidos* [14]. Set up to counter the ethos of wartime, it was 'opposed to all that the words austerity, utility, insularity imply'. Instead Ramsden asserted the magazine's recognition of

> . . . the urgency of the need for a reaffirmation in life of those values, vision, integrity, order, proportion, unity, space, inherent in art—the need in short, for a reintroduction of a sense of form in the fullest meaning of the term.

Around the same time Ramsden began to question a growing anthropomorphism in Hepworth's work. At first Hepworth was surprised and, smoothing away the disjunction, told Hartley:

> Your appreciation of my work has been so important to me and so beneficial that perhaps I expect too much unity in our approach? [15]

However, the gap would not be smoothed away. Hepworth's work became increasingly figurative in the 1950s, and the change did not only alienate Ramsden, it also perturbed Herbert Read. If one refers to Ramsden's aims for *Eidos*, one might discern that where Hepworth wanted to forge a new style out of the war, in keeping with a new spirit of reconstruction, Ramsden wished to turn the clocks back to the pre-war days of complete international abstraction—an abstraction that eschewed the figure and avoided questions of gender. Hepworth's friendship with Read was never brought seriously into question, but she had to let Hartley go.

She was surely right, however, to question Read's priorities as her friend and critic. In 1952 she told Read:

> I am not quite sure from your remark (1) whether you find it difficult, although you like my work, to be objective because I am a woman or (2) whether you like me as a person so much more than you like my work that it puts a strain on your integrity? I don't think either your integrity or my work should be penalised on account of my sex. I do admit that it is difficult, though, to assess objectively especially as there is an ever growing masculine protest from a new generation of critics—some have come very much out into the open very recently about the validity of women's creative faculties. [16]

Hepworth identified a masculine backlash which was coming to dominate critical discourse and which was out of tune with her work. Though Hepworth had been well-served by the male critics of the pre-war era—Bernal, Read, Stokes, etc.—she lost their voices after the war. Ramsden's post-war efforts were soon overwhelmed. The absence of any critic ready to take on the mantle thereafter has borne its legacy in terms of our continuing inability to talk about Hepworth's post-war work.

NOTES AND REFERENCES

1 The catalogue which accompanied the exhibition was limited in its range; the four texts, by the two curators, followed a broadly chronological survey of the artists's life and work. It was designed to stand also as a book with a long shelf life for a more general public. It was always the gallery's intention to broaden the debate through the vehicle of the Critical Forum and its subsequent publication. I discussed the content of the Critical Forum with Lisa Tickner (who chaired it), Catherine Orbach (T.G.L.) and Anne MacPhee (Critical Forum Coordinator). Our principal aim was to encourage new voices on the artist. The diverse backgrounds of invited contributors was thought desirable, but also recognised as inevitable due to the relatively uncoordinated nature of research on the artist. It seemed obvious, therefore, to arrange the programme around a series of loose groupings: the personal/biographic (Edwin Mullins; Sally Festing), the critical (myself; Katy Deepwell), the scientific context (Anne Barlow; Christina Lodder and Martin Hammer) and psychoanalytic/feminist readings of Hepworth's work through the writings of Adrian Stokes (Anne Wagner; Alex Potts). Though the absence of any single agenda for the Critical Forum initially seemed problematic, it did mean that it was free to function as a more genuine catalyst of research, and in fact allowed for a more open-ended exchange of information and opinions.

2 Written from Chy-an-Kerris in Carbis Bay (and thus between July 1942 and 1949), Hepworth's letters to Herbert Read in the Sir Herbert Read Archive, Special Collections, University of Victoria, B.C., Canada are numbered HR/BH 1–314. She discusses Herbert Read's book on children's art, and asks him why he does not discuss their 'plastic' work, as in her experience of running a class with 'Paul and SRS and 4 other young children' the 'model is the most fundamental and secret expression of all' (HR/BH 68). 'I have used all the drawings as a guide to health and happiness in SRS and I could write reams . . . about Sarah and Rachel and my theories about women . . .' In HR/BH 18 Hepworth writes: 'I hope to do a book sometime (with

an analyst) on children's drawings under five years old'. In another letter (HR/BH 24) she describes drawings of 'egg forms within eggs, folded again and again into a purse and hidden in a secret place . . .', and in HR/BH 41 'I'm most particularly interested in Gestalt phsychology [sic]'. For Hepworth sculpture was reality, whereas painting was an illusion. She had a deep-rooted belief in the significance of forms on the collective unconscious. After the galleries of the British Museum reopened, Hepworth went to see the 'fetishes, gods from the 3 millennium onwards' and noted that 'something very deep is stirred up—things "felt" and not seen, which have their own intrinsic shapes'.

3 HR/BH-145 18 January 1953.

4 HR/BH-55 written 12 January (1943) (datable by Hepworth's reference to her recent 40th birthday).

5 15 December 1949 (Arts Council of Great Britain)

6 Tate Gallery Archive (T.G.A. 9310) Eates/Ramsden correspondence from Hepworth, n.d.; written from Chy-an-Kerris [1943?]. Margot Eates and E. H. Ramsden worked as a creative partnership; in discussing their loan to the British Council for Hepworth's Venice exhibition, Margot Eates asked that they be credited as 'Collection E. H. Ramsden and Margot Eates', lending 'on one condition only and that is that the word "Miss" never enters into any reference to us' (Public Records Office BW2/420 British Council Records). Ramsden is perhaps best known for her work on Michelangelo, but also contributed to *This Changing World* with J. R. Brumwell (1944); *Herbert Read: an Introduction to his Work*, edited by H. Treece (1948); and *Paul Nash* with Margot Eates (1948).

7 In HR/BH 199 Hepworth writes, 'Herta Wescher is staying with me this weekend. I'm glad to meet her quietly at last', and in her correspondence with the British Council over coverage of her Venice Biennale, Hepworth asked (31 July 1950) 'I should like to know whether Carola Giedion Welcker [sic] wrote'.

8 RAMSDEN, E. H. (1953) *Sculpture: Theme and Variations: Towards a Contemporary Aesthetic* (London, Lund Humphries). Hepworth also mentioned Rilke in her letters to Read, and in HR/BH 55 told him that the drawing she had sent him was 'very much a part of my reading of Rilke's First Elegy'. In HR/BH 71 Hepworth wrote that of the things which had been most comforting to her she numbered Rilke alongside Read's poetry.

9 RAMSDEN, E. H. (1943) 'Barbara Hepworth—Sculptor', *Horizon* Vol. 7, No. 42, June, pp. 418–20.

10 RAMSDEN, E.H. (1946) 'The Sculpture of Barbara Hepworth, *Polemic* No. 5, Sept.–Oct., p. 33.

11 T.G.A. 9310 64. From Dunluce 25 June 1941.

12 T.G.A. 9310 n.d. [1946?] From Chy-an-Kerris.

13 T.G.A. 9310 n.d. From Chy-an-Kerris.

14 *Eidos* was a bimonthly publication: 'a journal of painting, sculpture and design'. Under Ramsden as editor was an advisory committee comprising William Gibson, Bernard Ashmole, Sir Leigh Ashton and John Rothenstein. In *Eidos* Ramsden brought together a variety of other writers, and for instance on Hepworth she published texts by Read, Cooper and David Lewis. Note also that Hepworth made a piece called *Eidos* in 1946–47.

15 T.G.A. 9310 from Carbis Bay; n.d.

16 19 July 1952 from Trewyn Studio (HR/BH 134). Though this letter was written in relation to Read's introduction, about which she had a number of criticisms, Hepworth went on (in HR/BH 135): 'You, on the contrary, have always been both fair and free—like Adler for instance—allowing full and equal growth to both male and female attributes. You state it, most objectively, in the earlier part of the Introduction and for that, Herbert, I am deeply grateful—for it removes a very great weight, which has at times, been oppressive and given me free air to breathe.' In HR/BH 149 (10 January 1953) Hepworth wrote: 'I seem to be the special bane of critics these days'. On 12 August 1961 (HR/BH 233) she wrote again of the 'dislike of my work which exists among many of the younger writers'.

CLAIRE DOHERTY

The Essential Hepworth? Re-reading the Work of Barbara Hepworth in the Light of Recent Debates on 'the Feminine'

> The retrospective is both an opportunity and a command. The very gathering together of an *oeuvre* seems to require that all the industry and expense of the assembly be concerted to some useful end. It is thus an opportunity to be seized—an occasion for revision, reassessment, re-evaluation—and a failure to put this chance to use feels like an opportunity wasted. [1]

The institution of the retrospective and its concomitants—the conference, publications and media-generated debates—are channels through which Modernist myths of genius, authenticity and the masterpiece, inherent in the fiction of an '*oeuvre*', have been deconstructed. To avoid reinvestment in the values of patriarchal society, which have been grafted onto the work of the artist under scrutiny, we may investigate how their practice was shaped by and participated in the reinforcement of notions of colonialism, gendered difference and primitivism; we might question the role of the spectator in the production of meaning; and we might also expose the ways in which the institutions of the gallery, critic and art historian perpetuated modern myths of creative genius through the fabricated persona of that artist.

Using these critical tools, we search for a new language with which to articulate the significance of that artist's work to the contemporary field. It is an on-going process which challenges the values of our consumer culture and notions of heritage and is enriched by continual revision and scrutiny.

The same opportunities prevail here in the reconsideration of Barbara Hepworth's sculpture, though they are undermined to some degree by the rarity of her solo exhibitions. One of the primary tasks is to dismantle the fiction of 'Hepworth', the sign onto which Modernist liberal ideals have been projected and through which we have read her work for over fifty years. Yet there is a dilemma which lies at the very heart of this undertaking, integral to such a process of re-evaluation. Barbara Hepworth is a phenomenon—a woman who received exceptional recognition world-wide as a member of the avant-garde, and yet she is an artist who now falls between notoriety and obscurity.

Whilst Hepworth is championed by the agencies of British culture as a primary figure in the grand narrative of modern British art, she has received little serious critical attention since her death in 1975. Her achievement is still undermined in veiled references to the superiority of Henry Moore and her work is judged inferior according to an ascribed feminine essence. Yet though these details constitute a classic case of how a historical woman artist has been assigned a secondary status, she is conspicuous by her absence in key feminist survey texts [2]. Despite the fact that the moment of her death fell at the very awakening of feminist art historical research in this country, it would seem that Hepworth could never be embraced as a heroine of the modern women's art movement.

The reason is two-fold. Firstly, Hepworth was a Modernist, the tradition against which feminist art practice has set itself. She literally became 'one of the boys' through her engagement with groups such as *Unit One* and *Abstraction-Création*. She did not assume the identity of a transgressive role model, but rather made work that was successfully promoted by Herbert Read, Adrian Stokes and Paul Nash, as evidence of a significant British abstract movement. Her practice was legitimated by a lineage of male forebears, including Jacob Epstein and Hans Arp, thus the importance of her gender was simply ruled out. Consequently her achievements were seen to be removed from the endeavours of other women and therefore she could only be accepted as exceptional to women. She was never celebrated as an example of what women are able to achieve given equal opportunities.

Despite her seemingly effortless rise to stardom, however, Hepworth's career was fraught with professional and personal challenges, primarily due to the fickle nature of the Modernist promise. As Griselda Pollock has recently noted, Modernism offered women artists

> a delusive freedom . . . access to equality and the chance to be just an artist, but, without any serious deconstruction of the masculine power it had sustained, the liberal ideal reinscribed that gender's privilege . . . [3]

Consequently the artistic achievements of those women involved in the Modernist project were seriously compromised.

Though Modernism appeared to offer Hepworth an ideological freedom from the restrictions of her gender, recent work has revealed that she was subject to prejudice throughout her career, from her near exclusion from *Unit One* to the subversion of her success at the Venice Biennale in 1950 [4]. The transfer of Hepworth's papers to the Tate Gallery Archive in 1996 should at last enable us to explore Hepworth's own 'obstacle race'.

Yet there is another deep-seated dilemma, particularly for feminist art historians, which may explain the lack of critical writing on her work. Hepworth became both subject and object of her art and her public profile is still identified with the early interpretations of her sculpture as intuitive, feminine and organic. The critics wrapped 'Hepworth' in metaphors which alluded to motherhood, feminine intuition, warmth, mysticism and ancient rites [5]. In these terms, her work became the product of a biologically determined womanhood, rather than her artistic subjectivity.

The dilemma of Hepworth lies at the very heart of debates surrounding the feminine and creative practice, debates which question: Is there an essential experience of being a woman—and if there is, is it biologically determined or socially and psychically constructed? Does this experience necessarily condition artistic practice? Is creating as a woman recognisably different from creating as a man? In what terms can we analyse women's cultural production, considering the specificity of their gender, without relegating it to a separate sphere? And how do we foreground issues of class, race, age and experience in a discussion of such a catch-all as 'women's art?' [6].

The ambivalence of the debate is revealed in Hepworth's own writings. On the one hand she resisted the term 'woman artist', strongly emphasising her own artistic subjectivity.

> I'm just me [she said]. Sculptors are workmen. They're not female, they're not anything. They're anonymous workmen. [7]

Yet she was intent on articulating the importance of 'the feminine experience':

> I have never understood why the word feminine is considered to be a compliment to one's sex if one is a woman, but has a derogatory meaning when applied to anything else. The feminine point of view is a complementary one to the masculine . . . I think that women will contribute a great deal to this understanding through the visual arts, and perhaps especially in sculpture, for there is a whole range of formal perception belonging to feminine experience. So many ideas spring from an inside response to form; for example, if I see a woman carrying a child in her arms, it is not so much what I see that affects me, but what I feel within my own body. There is an immediate transference of sensation, a response within to the rhythm of weight, balance and tension of the large and small form making an interior organic whole. It may be that the sensation of being a woman presents yet another facet of the sculptural idea. In some respects it is a form of 'being' rather than observing, which in sculpture should provide its own emotional and logical development of form. [8]

The essentialism, inherent in this statement, is deeply problematic. It seems to confirm the sexist notion that the only source of a woman artist's creativity is her biological given—her womb. In proposing that a woman's physical sensibility is a facet of her creative practice, Hepworth sets us on the slippery slope to *l'art féminin*—a nineteenth-century critical category for art by women [9]. This concept was embraced and patrolled by women themselves for it offered recognition for their skills and, in the form of *Salons des Femmes*, spaces in which to exhibit their work. Even so, *l'art féminin* actually classified work according to negative stereotypes—weak, passive, delicate, irrational and ultimately imitative. Thus in the *Salons des Femmes* one found a capacity for feeling, not thinking, and skilled imitation as opposed to originality. *L'art féminin* was the Other of the male *Salon*, in which art was taken 'seriously'.

These are the assumptions which underlie the critical discourse on Hepworth's sculpture and through which she became Moore's 'Other'. Within these parameters, Hepworth was projected out of an art historical time into an eternity of universal femininity. Her work along with Moore's was read through the polemic of a psychoanalytic tradition, personified by Erich Neumann, in which the mother is defined by her lack and woman is identified as an empty vessel, filled and fulfilled only in relation to her child.

Jungian notions of genius informed this view of the artist as modern primitive [10]. Moore, as a male artist, emerged as the manipulator of form or the virile procreator. He possessed the 'feminine' characteristics of genius, but as a man was able to wield them successfully to produce the masterpiece. Hepworth, on the other hand, as a woman, was seen simply to mimic Moore by reinscribing her own lack onto the material of the work. Owing to her lack of phallus, she could never possess the true qualities of a genius [11].

Contemporary women artists, such as Helen Chadwick and Nancy Spero, have encountered similar levels of stereotyping. Speaking in different visual languages which incorporate a notion of the 'feminine', they have been criticised by feminist writers as complicit in the reassertion of the woman/nature–man/culture dichotomy.

> A feminist art devoted to the celebration of an unproblematic biological or domestic femininity [Lisa Tickner has written] runs the risk . . . of being too bound up with the meanings conventionally ascribed to femininity and the female body (the marginal, the hysterical and the 'other'): it produces a reverse discourse that celebrates difference in the terms by which difference has already been laid down. [12]

Either of Hepworth's 1934 versions of *Mother and Child* (Figs 9 and 10), for example, could be read as a reassertion of these dominant values. The figure, identified as female through the notational features of breasts, womb and attached infant, would seem to confirm woman as an anonymous creature of 'instinct and passion, an antagonist rather than a builder of human culture' [13]. Historically, this is the essential Hepworth.

But what if we interpret Hepworth's statement on 'the feminine', mindful of the post-war mentality towards women in which she was speaking, as a positive indication of the possibility of *la sculpture féminine*? Could we employ here a Kristevean notion of writing as a woman? According to her notion of *l'écriture féminine*, the gender of the artist need not be female, but rather the 'feminine' practice works against a phallocentric order to

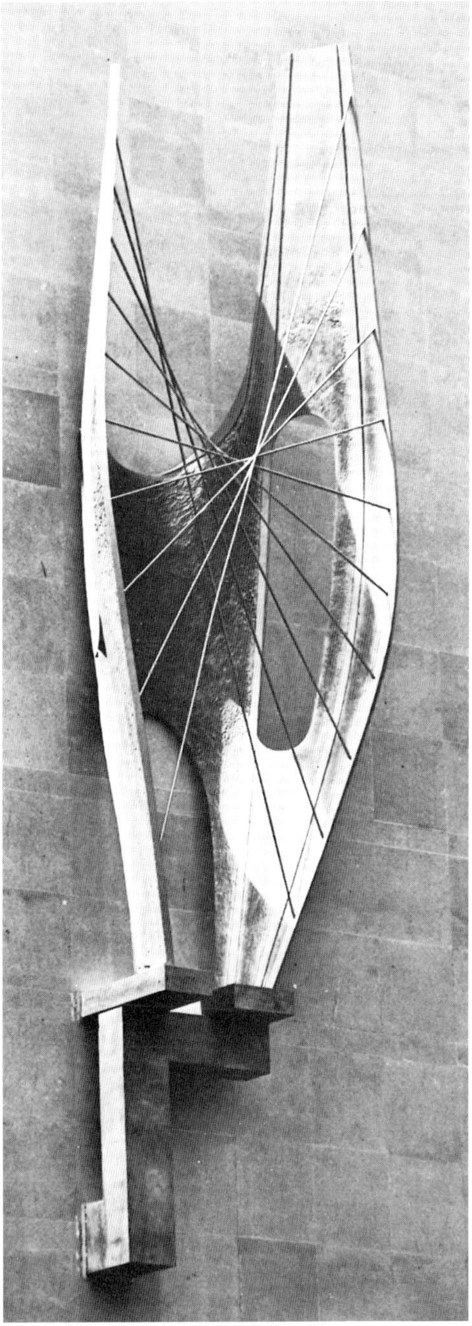

Fig. 43 BARBARA HEPWORTH, *Winged Figure*, 1962 © Trustees of the Barbara Hepworth Estate (published in Bowness, *The Complete Sculpture of Barbara Hepworth 1960–69*, London, Lund Humphries, 1971)

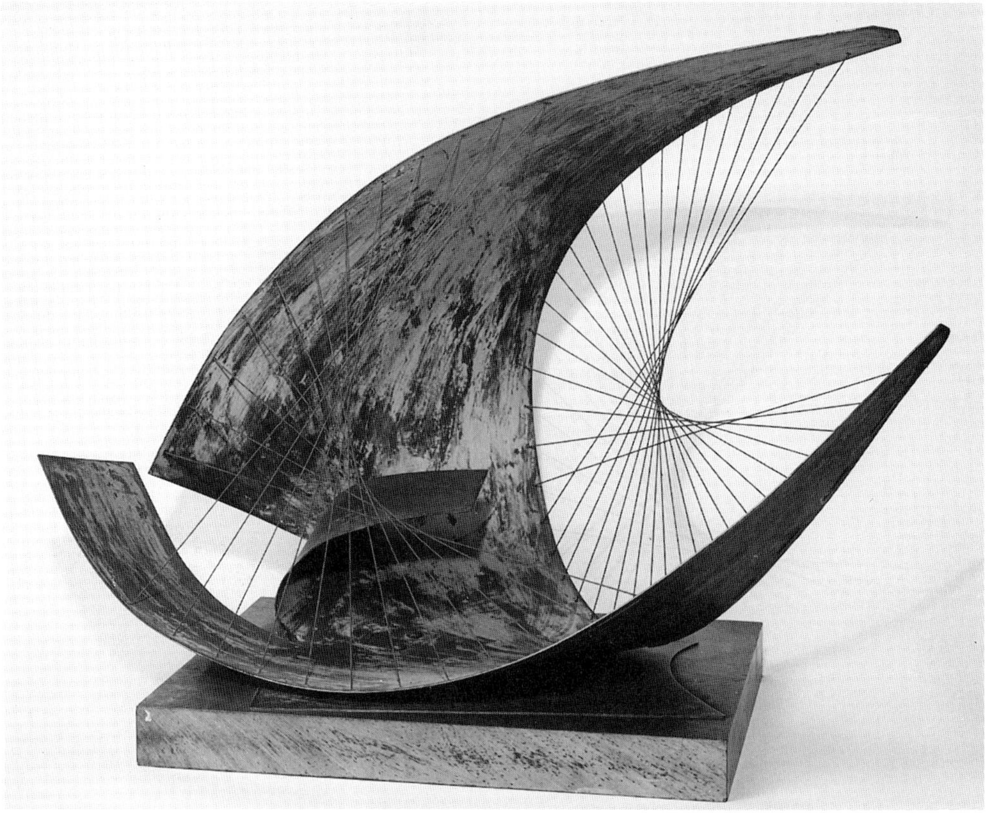

Fig. 44 BARBARA HEPWORTH, *Stringed Figure (Curlew) (Version II)*, 1956 © Trustees of the Barbara Hepworth Estate/Tate Gallery London

> transform the hierarchies and fixities of an existing social order through the ruin and transformation of its cultural practices. [14]

I am not claiming a position for Hepworth which she did not assume—she was not a feminist. And her work cannot and should not be read as radically subversive nor politically motivated. But if 'the feminine' is to be read as a positive, alternative syntax through which patriarchal ways of seeing and thinking are challenged, then Hepworth's *sculpture féminine* proves highly significant to artistic practice today.

Her work after the mid-1930s has few figurative references. Even so, pieces such as *Pelagos*, 1946 (Fig. 29) are still read for their allusions to the womb and to the sheltering, caring function of the mother. What is more astonishing in this sculpture, however, is the exploration of space and volume, the dissection of solid material and the rejection of closed form, through which Hepworth makes a radical statement about an artist's attempt to render the natural process of growth and form. The armatures of *Winged Figure*, 1962 (Fig. 43) or the stringed figures of

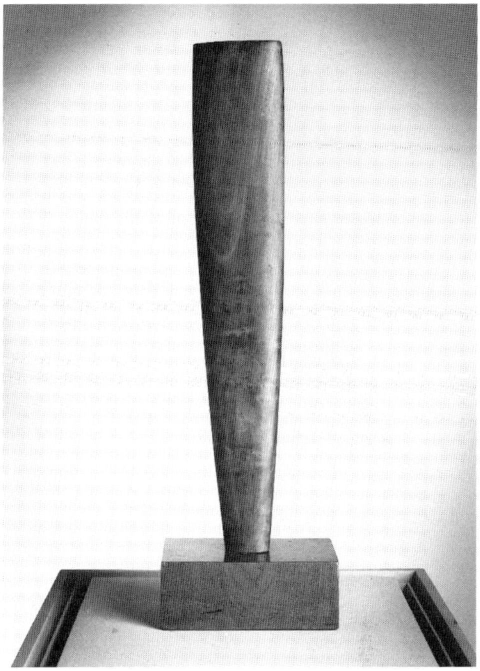

Fig. 45 BARBARA HEPWORTH, *Single Form*, 1937 © Trustees of the Barbara Hepworth Estate/Leeds Museums and Galleries (City Art Gallery)

the 1950s, such as *Stringed Figure (Curlew) (Version II)*, 1956 (Fig. 44), explore the currents and connections in space, rejecting the weight and solidity of the work of her male forebears. In these terms, the femininity of her practice is a bold eversion of sculptural form.

Rather than governed by intuition, in which her biological capacity to have children prescribed the end-result, Hepworth's skill was rigorously intellectual. She did not work from drawings and it is therefore supposed that she felt the form somehow in her physical being. In fact she was an artist who worked closely from the block, fascinated by its integral make-up, developing the form through the material, rather than in plan or section.

Hepworth's more successful single forms are undoubtedly those which move away from the phallic edifice, such as *Single Form*, 1937 (Fig. 45), to the pierced forms of the 1950s, such as *Hieroglyph*, 1953 (Fig. 46). Here endures an illusion to a pre-symbolic order, which suggests an alternative visual language rather than a reassertion of a notion of the 'primitive' or pre-civilised. The symbols of male and female genitalia are fused to evoke a potent essence of sexuality in the block.

Hepworth's practice is enormously rich and diverse in its subversion of the mastery of the gaze. *Porthmeor*, 1958, for example, though rooted to the plinth, appears to strain in a number of directions. In doing so, the form becomes split and fragmented. The spectator's exploration of the sculpture is never prescribed, but variable, motivated and intrigued. The allusions to the landscape of St. Ives are neither delicate nor romantic, but reveal a fascination with the re-creation of a

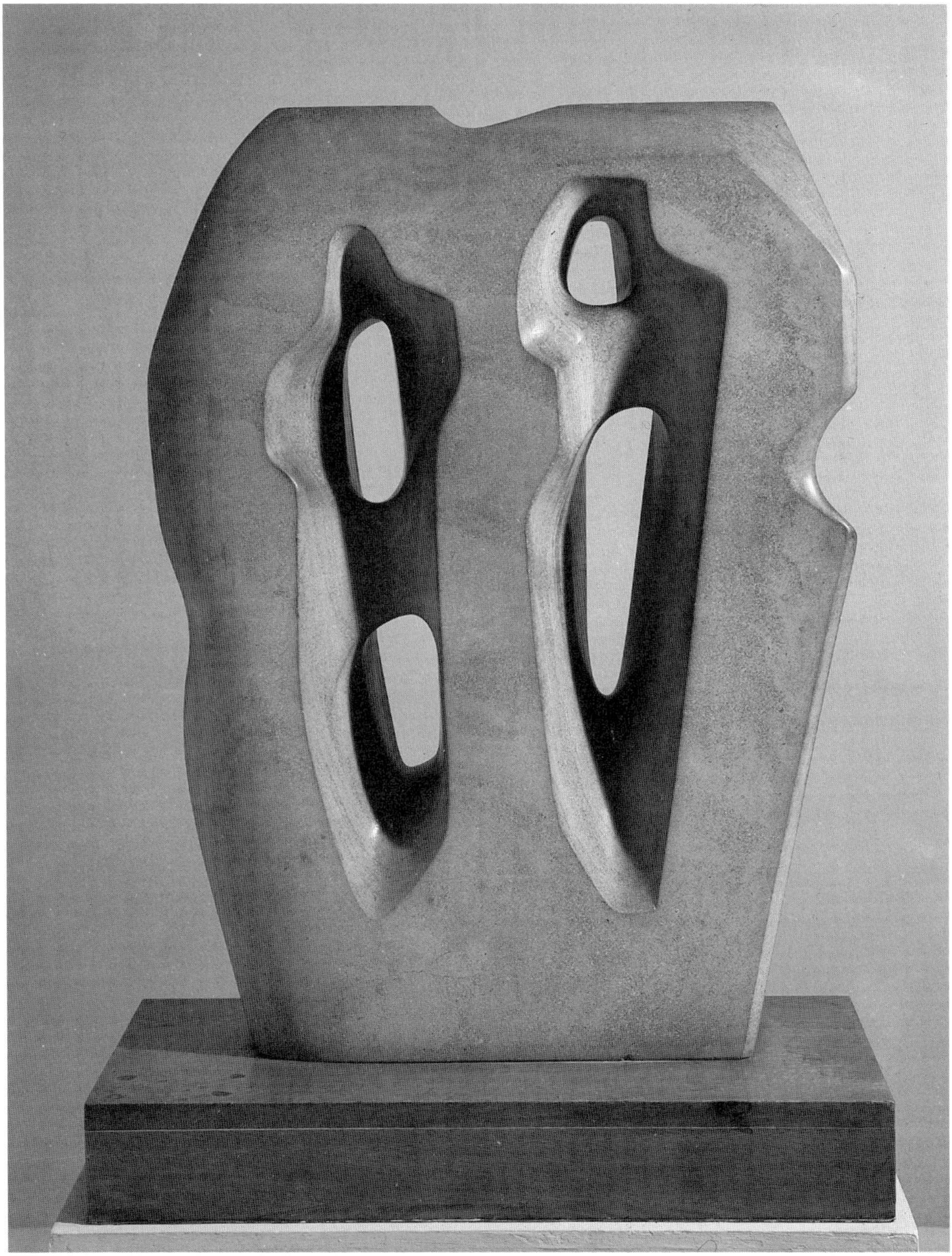

Fig. 46 BARBARA HEPWORTH, *Hieroglyph*, 1953 © Trustees of the Barbara Hepworth Estate/Leeds Museums and Galleries (City Art Gallery)

natural form in sculpture. The viewer is provoked to question: What relationships are initiated in the spaces between the solid forms? What meanings are generated when a natural form is imitated by the mark of the chisel or cast in bronze?

The post-war pieces assume greater significance in the open-air because of these underlying tensions, particularly in the garden or public park, because a double mimesis is in operation. The artificiality of the bronze pieces reflects back onto the manufactured landscaped areas for public recreation. Such a mechanism reveals the British inclination for an ordered natural environment, and more broadly, western man's will to impose order on organic chaos. There is also a Zen-like concentration, revealed in Hepworth's garden in St. Ives, which is fixed on the power of the symbolic. To play the favoured Modernist game of tracing a line of descent, Hepworth here represents the precursor of Richard Long, Barry Flanagan and David Nash.

Hepworth's is neither a cold nor passive practice. In some works, such as *Discs in Echelon*, 1935, it is highly electric, here in the opposition of elements. Though similar, the discs are minutely distinct from each other. The relationship draws the spectator in, willing closer inspection and generating either a desire to eliminate the imperfections or a need to halt the unbearable tension.

The unfixity of the gaze, the polyvalent meanings of the works, the fusion of symbols of sexuality, the play on notions of nature and the natural, the opening up of spaces in between solid forms, the deconstruction of stability and the unusual play on the mythic and Utopian through the manipulation of geometrical forms—this is *la sculpture féminine*. There is no 'essential' Hepworth—no essence of a truly feminine practice—rather, a number of Hepworths. If we employ the recent psychoanalytic reading of the 'feminine' in a re-evaluation of her sculpture, Hepworth emerges as a sculptor who investigated alternative visual languages. She produced multifarious syntaxes, some of which alluded to a pre-symbolic sexuality, some of which required a Zen-like concentration of thought, some exposed the fiction of 'the natural' and others explored the biotechnics of D'Arcy Thompson and Karel Honzig [15].

New critical studies of her work should bring Hepworth's artistic practice into the present, investigating the structure of her career and exposing the fiction of an essential femininity. The dilemma underlying such a critical examination should be exposed and excavated for debate in relation to contemporary art. Most importantly it is vital that Hepworth's sculpture is no longer seen in isolation, but alongside her peers and juxtaposed with the work of contemporary artists who engage with notions of the feminine. Such exhibitions would surely facilitate a re-interpretation of Hepworth as an artist whose contribution to British cultural practice has yet to be measured and will certainly surprise.

NOTES AND REFERENCES

1 KRAUSS, ROSALIND (1980) 'Representing Picasso', *Art in America*, December, p. 91.

2 Hepworth does not appear in NOCHLIN, LINDA and SUTHERLAND HARRIS, ANN (1976) *Women Artists: 1550 - 1950* (Los Angeles, Los Angeles County Museum), nor in PARKER, ROZSIKA and POLLOCK, GRISELDA (1981), *Old Mistresses: Women, Art and Ideology* (London, Pandora Press).

3 POLLOCK, GRISELDA (1992) 'Painting, Feminism and History', in: BARRETT, MICHELLE and PHILLIPS, ANN (Eds) (1992) *Destabilising Theory: Contemporary Feminist Debates* (London, Polity Press), p. 144.

4 See DOHERTY, CLAIRE (1993) *Modernism and the Female Artist: a Feminist Analysis of the Early Career of Barbara Hepworth*, unpublished B.A. thesis, Courtauld Institute of Art (London). See also CURTIS, PENELOPE 'The Artist in Post-War Britain', in: CURTIS, PENELOPE and WILKINSON, ALAN G. (1994) *Barbara Hepworth: a Retrospective* (Liverpool, Tate Gallery Liverpool), pp. 125–149.

5 See HUGHES, ROBERT (1966) 'Hepworth Touch', *Sunday Times*, 29 May; LYNTON, NORBERT (1966) 'A Source of Warmth', *The Guardian*, 4 June; and STOKES, ADRIAN (1978) *The Critical Writings of Adrian Stokes: Volume 1, 1930–1937* (London, Thames & Hudson), pp. 309–10.

6 In the summer of 1994 a scheme was launched to establish a Museum of Women's Art in London. Whilst aiming to celebrate women's artistic achievements, to redress the inequities in the hanging of national collections and to propose a matrilineage of artists for the future, the proposal was criticised owing to the connotations of the expression 'Women's Art', and, like Hepworth, it is caught up in the complex web of debates surrounding the feminine and creative practice.

7 HEPWORTH, BARBARA (1952), in: *Carvings and Drawings* (London, Lund Humphries).

8 *Ibid.*

9 See GARB, TAMAR (1989) 'L'Art Féminin': the Formation of a Critical Category in Late Nineteenth-Century France', *Art History* Vol. 12, No. 1, March, pp. 39–65.

10 See STALLABRASS, JULIAN (1992) 'The Mother and Child Theme in the Work of Henry Moore', in: *Henry Moore: Mother and Child* (Much Hadham, Henry Moore Foundation).

11 See BATTERSBY, CHRISTINE (1989) *Gender and Genius: Towards a Feminist Aesthetics* (London, The Women's Press).

12 TICKNER, LISA (1987) 'Nancy Spero: Images of Women and la Peinture Féminine', in: BLAZWICK, IWONA, FRANCIS, MARK and McGONAGLE, DECLAN (Eds) *Nancy Spero* (London, Institute of Contemporary Arts), p. 7.

13 See Carol Duncan's discussion of this concept in DUNCAN, CAROL (1973) 'Virility and Domination in Early Twentieth-Century Vanguard Painting', *Artforum*, December, pp. 30– 39.

14 Tickner (n. 12), p. 8.

15 See HOLDEN, J. (1987) *Gabo, Hepworth, Nicholson: an Examination of the Influence of Gabo on the Work of Barbara Hepworth and Ben Nicholson with the Objective of Establishing how Artists Learn from Other Artists*, unpublished M.Phil. thesis, University of London, where there are full discussions of HONZIG, KAREL (1937) 'Notes on Biotechnics', in: MARTIN, J. L., NICHOLSON, BEN and GABO, NAUM (Eds) *Circle: International Survey of Constructive Art*; and THOMPSON, D'ARCY W. (1917) *On Growth and Form* (Cambridge, Cambridge University Press).

ALUN R. GRAVES

Casts and Continuing Histories: Material Evidence and the Sculpture of Barbara Hepworth

The sculpture of Barbara Hepworth forms a sizeable body of work, yet one which is essentially coherent. This has much to do with the strong opinions that Hepworth held with regard to the materials and techniques employed in her work. New approaches to authenticity which encourage us to reassess reproductions and give consideration to the continuing histories of objects seem to be particularly relevant to Hepworth in view of the significance of her materials. A central aim of this discussion is to re-emphasise the art object as a physical entity, and to demonstrate how closely our ideas of authenticity and our constructed meanings are dependent upon the nature of that physical form. Correspondingly, this represents a shift in emphasis from seeing works of art primarily as moments in the stylistic development of the artist, to accepting them as objects bearing historical evidence.

Whilst recent studies [1] have suggested the need to reassess what we view as 'authentic', there remains a widespread belief that works of art embody some kind of unique objective reality. There may be evidence that degradation of the physical form of an art object has occurred or that there has been a shift in its function or status, yet this does not generally shake the belief that some 'true' conception of the work exists. This itself reinforces the notion of works of art being static in terms of epistemological meaning. Attention is focused on the moment of creation. This is clearly a fundamental point in the history of the object, yet frequently the boundary between the manufacture and the later life of an object is not one that can be drawn with extreme clarity. Hepworth's *Tides I*, 1946 (Fig. 47) is a case in point. *Tides I* was carved from insufficiently seasoned holly wood and is now characterised by large cracks. This deterioration had occurred during making, and Hepworth abandoned the work unfinished. It is a work without a distinct moment of creation. As Hepworth worked on the piece it simultaneously grew closer to and farther from her conception of how it should be [2]. In terms of the original physical material, the cracks are as authentic as the carved wood. This lack of an ideal moment in the lifetime of the sculpture undermines any concept of restoration of the work. Yet *Tides I* is strangely beautiful; it is appropriately reminiscent of driftwood, and carries the romantic appeal of something lost and regained. The work thus generates responses that are entirely outwith the artist's original intention. Nevertheless, we still find *Tides I* worthy of display; we still venerate it as an art

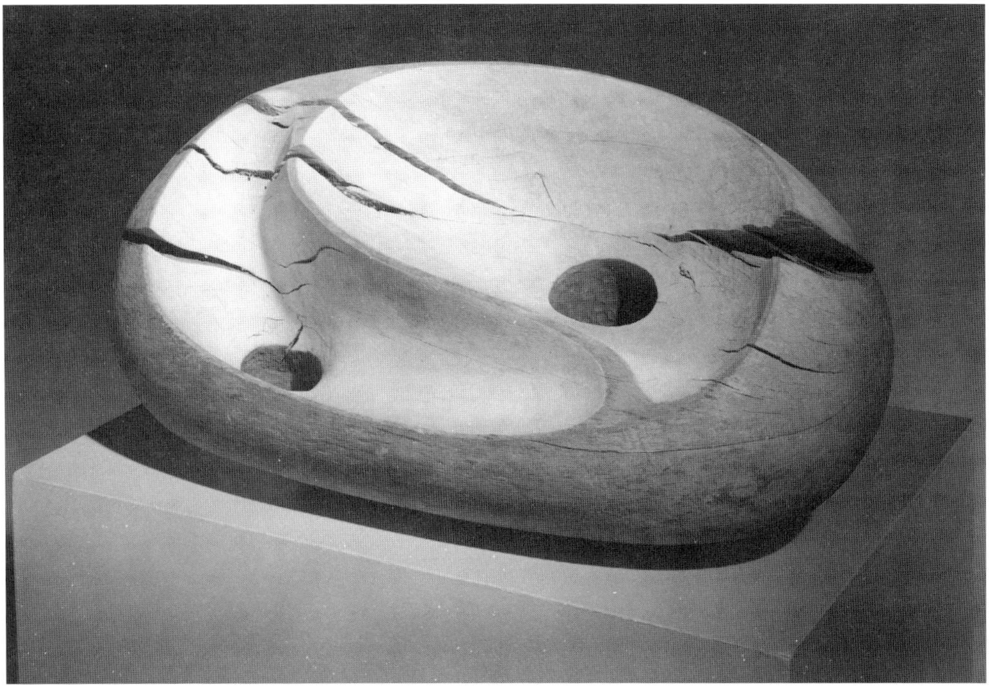

Fig. 47 BARBARA HEPWORTH, *Tides I*, 1946; © Trustees of the Barbara Hepworth Estate/Tate Gallery London

object. In fact it is an especially engaging object: its condition and 'unfinished' tag cause the viewer to ask questions about its history and manufacture. It is an object that can provide a rich and rewarding aesthetic encounter.

Csikszentmihalyi and Robinson's revelatory study of the aesthetic experience, *The Art of Seeing*, offers something of an explanation for this. Here, the content (the initiating factors) of the aesthetic experience was conceptually separated from its structure (the felt quality), allowing it to be seen that:

> While the felt quality of the experience may be the same for every aesthetic encounter, the details that make the experience possible are infinitely varied . . . A major implication is that we are free to be as eclectic as possible in approaching art and in educating people to appreciate it. The criterion for the aesthetic encounter is not the adherence to a canon of essential attitudes—be they formal, historical, religious, sociological, emotional or any other. Any or all of these will do. The criterion for the aesthetic experience is the experience itself, however it is arrived at. [3]

This demonstrates the importance of the full range of evidence embodied in art objects, and by implication, the preservation of this evidence. It also demonstrates the museum's need to make available a wide spectrum of the messages contained in an artefact, so as to enable the viewer to find his or her own pathway to understanding, without meeting too many dead ends.

Whilst the perhaps extreme example of *Tides I* illustrates some of the difficulties of viewing works of art as having a clearly defined moment of creation, the increasing need to acknowledge the continuing histories of art objects further erodes the concept of the unique objective reality. The history of *Wave*, 1943 (Fig. 48) is of particular relevance and illuminates some of the intricacies of authenticity and impermanence. Hepworth had recently moved to a new house and studio overlooking St. Ives Bay, and this landscape is directly reflected in the enclosed form of *Wave*. The interior surface of the carving was painted a pale blue, and a series of strings were added to link the two sides of the form [4].

The significance of colour and strings in works of this type has been explained by Hepworth in what has become one of her most familiar statements:

> The colour in the concavities plunged me into the depth of water, caves, or shadows deeper than the carved concavities themselves. The strings were the tension I felt between myself and the sea, the wind or the hills. [5]

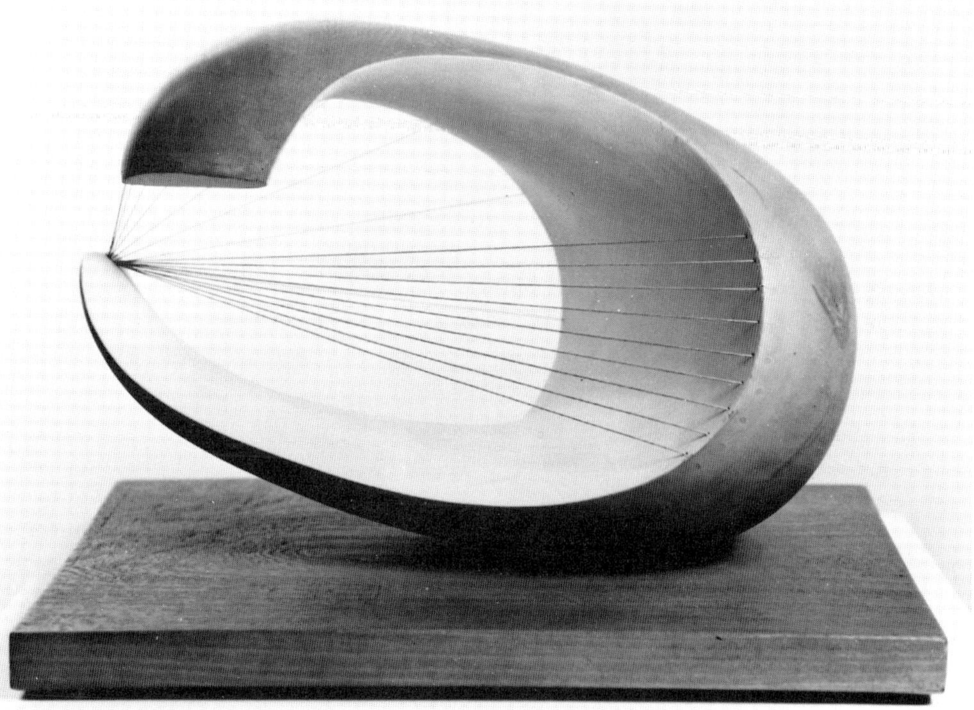

Fig. 48 BARBARA HEPWORTH, *Wave*, 1943 © Trustees of the Barbara Hepworth Estate/Scottish National Gallery of Modern Art

Later, however, Hepworth was to comment:

> I can only think I've been successful in so far as it's [the colour is] seen as part of the form. But in a way my colour has been accepted, but never understood. [6]

Wave, though privately owned, has been on loan to the Scottish National Gallery of Modern Art since 1975. By then significant fading of the painted interior had occurred. A letter from Hepworth to the gallery describes the problem:

> As regards the pale blue—20 years ago I used Ripoline and this lasted superbly, but 10 years ago when I did some restoration due to careless handling I had to resort to Dulux (matt) with a little cobalt pure artists' colour. Alas I have discovered on all sides that this has no staying power and even on big works like the Crucifixion the fading has been absolute. I can't help feeling that a pure white matt ground . . . would not only last but project my point of view. I am much more concerned with the way the colour is applied and the brush strokes than with the actual colour, which used to be pale blue.
>
> I trust your restorer absolutely and am so thrilled that these works [*Figure: Ascending Form*, 1956; *Myloe*, 1962–63; and *Wave*] have come into your hands, I do hope perhaps forever, that would make me really happy. [7]

The other works to which Hepworth makes reference were loaned along with *Wave*, though are no longer at the gallery. No attempt has since been made to return the interior of *Wave* to its original pale blue, and now only the palest hint remains.

How might this fading affect our response to the work and our view of its integrity? The visual surface has been altered and if we were to view authenticity purely in terms of the aesthetic surface we would have to see the work as less authentic. It would not be inconceivable to assume a naturalistic link between the colour and the marine subject, yet Hepworth in 1975 clearly did not think that the colour change would diminish our appreciation of the piece. Her approval of a change in colour rather substantiates the validity of the work's current condition and reduces the conflict between the colouration of the work as made and the faded version which we have inherited. The sense of the object's continuing history has taken on a definite importance. Distinct phases within the life of the object become evident: an initial phase; a period following Hepworth's own restoration characterised by the fading of the paint; and perhaps finally a phase of relative stability. It is interesting to note again that Hepworth's own involvement with the piece was a continuing one and so the concept of a distinct moment of completion has once again been blurred. *Wave* as originally created, and our various historically evolved versions all stand as valid 'realities' of the work. In view of this the only reasoned conservation approach would seem to be one of minimum intervention, sensitive to the combined evidence of the past held within the object.

The role of the artist in subsequent treatments is, in fact, a difficult area. Whilst the artist may be the person most intimate with the technical aspects of the work, there is often resistance to their involvement in practical conservation work. The artist may lack objectivity or re-work the object using their current styles and techniques [8]. Hepworth's suggestion that a complete change of colour from pale blue to white would 'project my point of view', now of course seems highly controversial.

Despite the fact that art objects are evidently not static in terms of physical form or constructed meaning, this aspect of works of art tends to be denied by art museums; from the information provided we might assume that there is only one event in the life of an object, that being its acquisition by the museum. For the art historian too, such questions of object history are of secondary importance and interest in provenance is most often motivated by the possibility of establishing authorship. In reality, art objects have complex histories both before and after they enter the museum. However, the tendency of museums is to regularise artefacts by stripping away the vestiges of their passage through the outside world [9]. For example, the evidence of a sculpture's early life in the open air may be removed without hesitation when the object later comes to rest in a museum.

There are, however, a number of serious problems associated with such an approach. First it assumes that evidence of the object's history is somehow less important than other evidence embodied in the object. The implication is that physical changes occurring after manufacture do not contribute to the object's physical integrity. Second, it assumes that works of art can be returned to their original appearance, and once this is achieved, that we at our point in time will be able to respond to them in at least a very similar way to those for whom they were made. Third, it assumes that the work's cultural value is necessarily greater after treatment than before. Finally, it assumes a lack of awareness, on the part of the artist, that the object was being sent on a long and complex journey during which physical changes might be acceptable, beneficial, or even, in the case of some later twentieth century artists, planned for.

Fortunately, the validity of the object's own history is increasingly being recognised:

> Now a new concept of authenticity is emerging which encourages us to accept that objects have a continuing history, that they are damaged and repaired, cleaned and restored, and that their present state records not only the moment of creation but also a whole subsequent sequence of events. [10]

This viewpoint is in accord with today's preference amongst conservators for minimum treatment, with emphasis on reversibility as a guiding principle. Derek Pullen, head of Sculpture Conservation at the Tate, states:

> Our approach, in brief, is to provide storage and display conditions which slow down the rate of change as much as is practical and to document

> condition and changes, but to avoid interfering with the actual work through treatment other than maintenance. [11]

Such an approach shows sensitivity to the variety of evidence and related meaning which is held within all works of art.

A further aspect of the 'new concept of authenticity' of particular relevance to Hepworth is the need to reassess casts and reproductions. Hepworth's shifting attitude towards casting is of great importance in understanding her work, and is bound up with her approaches to materials and to the reproduction of her forms in different media. Materials themselves have always played an important role in Hepworth's sculpture. When she began exhibiting mature work in the late 1920s, her commitment to direct carving in wood or stone clearly set her apart from the dominant sculptural tradition of modelling. The 'truth to materials' ethic with its moral overtones relates instead to the ideas of Eric Gill and earlier to the Arts and Crafts Movement. In the catalogue foreword for Hepworth and Ben Nicholson's show at Tooth's in 1932, Herbert Read writes:

> The revival of the art [of sculpture] in our own time is due to nothing so much as the re-assertion of this vital connection between the artist and his material. [12]

Speaking at the time of this same exhibition, Hepworth herself states:

> An idea for carving must be clearly formed before starting and sustained during the long process of working; also there are all the beauties of several hundreds of different stones and woods, and the idea must be in harmony with the qualities of each one carved. [13]

The significance of the materials goes beyond the formal qualities of the work and they also carry historical and technological connotations. The historical significance of her work was noted by J. D. Bernal in his catalogue introduction to her solo exhibition at Lefevre of 1937 [14]. In this he related Hepworth's sculpture to neolithic menhirs in a statement which Hepworth later described as 'prophetic' [15].

Throughout her life Hepworth remained committed to the technique of carving; very few of her works do not involve carving to some degree. Even when working on the plaster models for the numerous cast bronzes of the 1960s she would apply large amounts of wet plaster, allow it to dry and then carve it down to the desired surface [16]. Working in bronze enabled Hepworth to expand upon her range of forms, but perhaps more importantly it allowed her to work on a more public scale and in greater quantities. Scale seemed to be almost an obsession of Hepworth's in her later years. Her disappointment with Gimpel Fils over the showing of three small works at the 1959 *Documenta II: Art since 1945* has been noted by Curtis [17]. In her *Pictorial Autobiography* Hepworth reflects:

> I had between 1934 and 1937 achieved three large works over 10ft high (all damaged in the war). [18]

Hepworth's largest pre-war work in fact seems to have been the *Monumental Stela*, 1936, which stood at 6ft (1830 mm) and was indeed destroyed during the war. These attitudes seem to some extent to contradict her statement in *Circle*:

> Scale is not physical size, because a very small thing can have good scale or a very large thing poor scale . . . [19]

Certain of Hepworth's forms and in particular the single standing form seem to have crossed the boundaries of materials. One of the tulipwood *Forms in Echelon*, 1938, appears ultimately to have been resurrected in the gigantic bronze *Single Form* which stands outside the United Nations headquarters in New York. The obvious importance of material to the vitality of a work clearly makes the development of a sculptural idea in a different material problematic. Charles Harrison has commented on the series of single standing forms carved in wood in the late 1930s and destroyed in the war:

> To assess these in terms of surviving bronze casts is to judge them as enterprises of a qualitatively different kind from what was originally envisaged and made. [20]

As well as developing a particular form from one work in one material to another work in another, Hepworth has in a number of instances 'reproduced' specific carvings in bronze and other materials. In the context of Hepworth's commitment to 'truth to materials' this raises certain difficulties. The inevitably dramatic changes to the aesthetic surface of a work which result from such transpositions in media are essentially self-evident and, in the context of the uncontrolled editioning of modern sculpture, have increasingly been a cause for concern [21]. Nevertheless, the direct comparison of versions is unlikely to be favourable to a later conception, and fails fully to realise the significance of the 'reproduction'.

Hepworth's *Discs in Echelon* has a complex history and has appeared in a variety of different materials. The work was first executed as a carving from Padouk wood in 1935. It sees Hepworth working at her most severely geometrical. At this point in her development 'the work was more formal and all traces of naturalism had disappeared' [22]. Subsequently her forms became more complex, being either increasingly organic or sharply crystalline [23]. Yet despite the simple forms and precise spatial arrangement of *Discs in Echelon*, it should not be seen purely as an exercise in geometry. The discs themselves are not perfectly regularised. Apart from the minor irregularities inherent in hand-carving, the discs are in fact drop-shaped in cross section. This imbues the forms with an earthly quality; they are to be perceived as concrete and as such subject to the natural laws. This, in conjunction with the natural material used, gives an organic quality to the forms. It is the combination of these organic qualities with the geometrical configuration which gives life and vitality to the work.

Discs in Echelon is an important work in Hepworth's *oeuvre*, marking the extreme of her geometrical abstraction. Appropriately it was included in the last '7 & 5 Society' exhibition, held at the Zwemmer Gallery in London in 1935. This was considered to be the first all-abstract exhibition in England. Hepworth, Nicholson and Moore dominated the show, which itself was viewed as a coherent body of work [24]. The following year Hepworth took the unusual step of casting the discs in plaster and then, twenty years before fully embracing metal as a medium for her sculpture, produced a unique cast of the work in aluminium. In 1937 the plaster version (which remains in the artist's estate) was included in Hepworth's exhibition at Lefevre, by which time the original wood carving had been acquired by the Museum of Modern Art, New York [25]. After the war the aluminium version was bought from Hepworth by her dealers at the time, Gimpel Fils, in whose collection the work remains.

In the late 1950s when Hepworth was regularly casting new work in bronze, she was encouraged to produce bronze casts of some of her earlier carvings due to the cracking which had occurred in certain pieces [26]. In 1959 *Discs in Echelon* became one of the first of Hepworth's forms to be reproduced in bronze, in this case in an edition of four, one of which remained in the artist's estate and has now entered the collections of the Tate Gallery.

Rather than being inferior 'reproductions' these various metal casts are in fact fascinating objects in their own right. Hepworth's cast in aluminium is a visually stunning, though largely forgotten, work. A singular departure from carving, it sits rather uncomfortably with the rest of her output of the 1930s. Of the nature of aluminium, Kay Gimpel recalls Hepworth describing it as a 'cruel material' [27]. The aluminium of *Discs in Echelon* is itself a potent symbol of modernity [28]. Its significance could not have contrasted more sharply with that of bronze, with its overtones of tradition and the establishment. Hepworth's motivation for this unique work perhaps derives from the sense of social relevance that such a material could offer. It was, after all, produced at the time when she was undertaking work on *Circle* along with Nicholson and Gabo, and the idea of the 'artist in society' was of great importance:

> By placing this work side by side we hope to make clear a common basis and to demonstrate, not only the relationship of one work to the other but of this form of art to the whole social order. [29]

We can therefore argue a case for the aluminium cast on the grounds of its clear historical and social significance. Nevertheless, the formal qualities of the work have clearly altered. The move from carved wood to cast metal diminishes the organic nature of the forms. They seem more static, and the emphasis falls on the rigid geometrical nature of the work. Viewed out of context it could lead to a misunderstanding of Hepworth's principal concerns of the 1930s. The edition of four bronze casts of 1959, suffering from similar formal deficiencies yet lacking the inherent interest of the material, at first seem more problematic. These casts are representative of the unease felt with editioned sculpture previously noted [30].

Hepworth's own dissatisfaction with 'deviations in casting' has also been noted [31]. Some of the problems may however lie more with our critical approach than with the casts themselves.

These casts of 1959 cannot fit at all comfortably into our received view of Hepworth's stylistic development; the forms could not come from any other period than the mid-1930s, whilst the materials would not have been used prior to the mid-1950s. Indeed, during the 1930s Hepworth would have been quite opposed to the use of bronze. Thus the 'history of style' seems rather unsatisfactory for coming to an understanding of the piece [32]. To apprehend its significance it is necessary to have a knowledge of the originating circumstances of the object and the motivation behind its production.

As already mentioned, deteriorations occurring in her works seem to have encouraged Hepworth to cast earlier carvings in bronze. This adds to the functional dimension of such casts, though in a way which invests them with a certain emotional resonance. It illustrates the artists's desire for her work to be preserved; we are reminded of Hepworth's obvious joy at the prospect of her works entering the Scottish National Gallery of Modern Art 'perhaps forever' [33]. In addition, it reflects the theme of endurance, which is so strongly evoked in her often monolithic late work. The editioning of *Discs in Echelon* in 1959 is also clearly bound up with Hepworth's great concern at that time with the promotion and distribution of her work. As such they are supremely relevant to the artist's concerns of the late 1950s, and make sense in the context of her work from that period.

In many ways this is of course obvious; they are pieces of late 1950s material culture and should be seen as such. As Pearce notes:

> They [objects] have the power, in some sense, to carry the past into the present by virtue of their 'real' relationship to past events, and this is just as true for casts, copies and fakes as it is for more orthodox material, for all such copies bear their own 'real' relationship to the impulse which created them. [34]

And further:

> . . . the sign [the work of art itself] which carries meaning is able to do so because, unlike we ourselves who must die, it bears an 'eternal' relationship to the receding past, and it is this that we experience as the power of 'the actual object'. [35]

The direct comparison of a later cast to an earlier carving can therefore be seen as an artificial exercise; a hollow comparison of formal qualities which is inevitably to the detriment of the cast. In doing so it attempts to relate the cast to a time period and creative impulse with which it bears no 'real' relationship. If we are not to devalue such works we must see them as objects carrying different meaning and from a different time to that of the original carvings, even though these are clearly their source.

The sculptures of Barbara Hepworth are rich bearers of evidence. To apprehend fully their significances a wider view needs to be taken than that which seeks to find a single 'true' conception related to a specific moment of creation. Later editions of works should be evaluated as objects in their own right. The continuing histories of objects also need fuller acknowledgment. All evidence of an object's past should be seen as valid. For the fullest understanding we must embrace the widest range of material evidence.

NOTES AND REFERENCES

1 See in particular JONES, M. (1990) *Fake? the Art of Deception* (London, British Museum).

2 In BOWNESS, ALAN (Ed) (1971) *The Complete Sculpture of Barbara Hepworth 1960–69* (London, Lund Humphries), p. 7, Hepworth states: 'I always know from the beginning what a work is going to look like'.

3 CSIKSZENTMIHALYI, M. and ROBINSON, T. (1990) *The Art of Seeing: an Interpretation of the Aesthetic Encounter* (Los Angeles, J. Paul Getty Museum and Getty Centre for Education in the Arts), pp. 177–78.

4 BOWNESS, ALAN (1961) 'Catalogue of Sculptures', in: HODIN, JOSEF P. (1961) *Barbara Hepworth* (London, Lund Humphries), p. 165.

5 HEPWORTH, BARBARA (1952) *Barbara Hepworth: Carvings and Drawings* (London, Lund Humphries), Section 4.

6 *Complete Sculpture* (n. 2), p. 14.

7 HEPWORTH, BARBARA, letter to D. Hall, 13 March 1975, Scottish National Gallery of Modern Art.

8 BARCLAY, M. H. (1990) 'An Art Gallery Conservator: Roles and Responsibilities', in: RAMSAY-JOLICOEUR, B. A. and WAINWRIGHT, I. N. M. (Eds) (1990) *Shared Responsibility: Proceedings of a Seminar for Curators and Conservators* (Ottawa, National Gallery of Canada). See also SMITH, B. (1990) 'Shared Responsibility: Welcome and Introduction', *ibid.*

9 SAUMAREZ SMITH, C. (1989) 'Museums, Artefacts and Meanings', in: VERGO, P. (Ed) (1989) *The New Museology* (London, Reaktion Books). The conspicuous nature of Rysbrack's statue of the Saxon god Thuner was observed by Saumarez Smith when, prior to conservation, the work was first installed in the sculpture courts of the Victoria and Albert Museum. Lichen covered from its sojourn in the gardens of Stowe and the grounds of a Hampshire prep school (where it had been used as a cricket stump), the work had not yet been absorbed and accommodated by its museum environment.

10 Jones (n. 1), p. 14.

11 PULLEN, D. (1993) letter to the author, 4 August.

12 READ, HERBERT (1932) 'Foreword', *Carvings by Barbara Hepworth, Paintings by Ben Nicholson* (London, Arthur Tooth & Sons Galleries).

13 Interview with Barbara Hepworth in: (1932) 'The Aim of the Modern Artist: Barbara Hepworth, Ben Nicholson', *The Studio* Vol. 104, December, p. 332.

14 BERNAL, J. D. (1937) 'Foreword', *Sculpture by Barbara Hepworth* (London, Alex Reid and Lefevre Ltd.), pp. 1–3.

15 HEPWORTH, B. (1993) *A Pictorial Autobiography* (London, Tate Gallery), p. 41.

16 Complete Sculpture (n. 2), p. 15.

17 CURTIS, P. (1994) 'The Artist in Post-war Britain', in: CURTIS, PENELOPE and WILKINSON, ALAN G. (1994) *Barbara Hepworth: a Retrospective* (Liverpool, Tate Gallery Liverpool), p. 143.

18 Hepworth (n. 15), p. 41.

19 HEPWORTH, BARBARA (1937) 'Sculpture', in: MARTIN, J. L., NICHOLSON, B.

and GABO, N. (Eds) *Circle: International Survey of Constructive Art* (London, Faber), p. 114.

20 HARRISON, CHARLES (1981, 1994) *English Art and Modernism 1900–1939* (London and Bloomington, Allen Lane/Indiana University Press), p. 270.

21 See for example (1994) 'Editorial: Connoisseurship, Bronze Casts and Transpositions between Media', *Journal of Museum Management and Curatorship* Vol. 13, pp. 3–8. This focused on the aesthetic deficiencies of some of Picasso's cast bronzes.

22 *Carvings and Drawings* (n. 5), Section 3.

23 JENKINS, D. F. (1982) 'Introduction', *Barbara Hepworth: a Guide to the Tate Gallery Collection at London and St Ives, Cornwall* (London, Tate Gallery), p. 12.

24 Harrison (n. 20), p. 271.

25 *Sculpture by Barbara Hepworth* (n. 14), p. 7.

26 *Hepworth Guide* (n. 23), p. 17. The original wood carving of *Discs in Echelon* has suffered to an extent from cracking. It is, however, not known to the author whether this was the case in 1959, nor whether Hepworth was aware of its condition.

27 GIMPEL, KAY (1995) conversation with the author, January.

28 (1950) *Metals in the Service of Mankind* (London, Science Museum). Aluminium is very much a material of the 20th Century; it could not be produced on a commercial scale until the 1890s, yet by 1950 its world production ranked next to that of iron and steel.

29 'Editorial', in: *Circle* (n. 19), p. vi.

30 'Bronze casts' (n. 21).

31 Curtis & Wilkinson (n. 17), p. 141.

32 PANOFSKY, E. (1939) *Studies in Iconology: Humanistic Themes in the Art of the Renaissance* (New York, Oxford University Press). In Panofsky's influential model, the History of Style was seen as the first controlling principle for the interpretation of a work of art.

33 Letter to Hall (n. 7).

34 PEARCE, S. M. (1992) *Museums, Objects and Collections: a Cultural Study* (Leicester, Leicester University Press), p. 24.

35 PEARCE, S. M. (1990) 'Objects as Meaning: or Narrating the Past', in: *New Research in Museum Studies, Vol. 1: Objects of Knowledge* (London, Athlone), p. 135.

EMMA E. ROBERTS

Barbara Hepworth Speculatively Perceived within an International Context

For many years, probably due to the popularity (both critically and generally) of Henry Moore, Barbara Hepworth has been neglected by art historians. She has continually been compacted into a classical, English paradigm which has denied her a just proportion of serious research. It is my aim here to argue that Hepworth is of much greater international significance than is usually acknowledged, and that in some respects she parallels one of the most important of her American contemporaries. Such comparison must necessarily be largely speculative, though there are many reasons—geographical, psychological, intellectual and visual—which lead me to my conclusions. The profusion of these reasons make it surprising that the issues I raise seem not to have been approached by other critics.

A problem that one encounters early in a study of Hepworth is the ill-considered paradigm which exists in nearly every critical source. Many, many writers accept the convention that she is a 'classical' artist. For example, we are said to feel

> . . . a little abashed by such an austere form of art. In this calmness any desire for romantic excitement, any interest in fragile, contradictory, silly ephemeral humanity seems mere frivolity. [1]

This sort of review is simply a judgment on the external appearance of the sculptures, without any consideration that in twentieth century art the concept is as important as the visual characteristics of the works. Rather than attempting an exploration of Hepworth's inspirations and hopes for the impact of her art, writers simply perceive her use of marble and the smooth surfaces to mean that she was not in a state of emotional excitement during production, and that she expects the viewer to connect the formalism of her work with coldness, austerity and purity. There is rarely any attempt to penetrate 'beneath' the surface appearances of Hepworth's art in order to understand any of the emotions or experiences she has projected into the most appropriate—usually abstract—forms. No-one since Herbert Read has noted that

> . . . 'geo' in 'geometrical' means 'earth', and that a square or a circle is also a natural phenomenon. The universe itself is a geometrical design. [2]

In order to reassess those paradigms which are commonly applied to Hepworth, some discussion of the classical is at first necessary. I maintain that Hepworth may indeed be classical in some senses, particularly in relation to other artists, yet there is a strong sense in which she is inefficiently termed so. As Stanley Casson has said, 'sculptors are not painters; restraint is or should be the very essence of their best work', yet many writers perceive the obvious restraint of Hepworth as a quality which makes her peculiarly classical. They do not take into consideration the requirements of sculpture, particularly carving, and they believe an outwardly inexpressive exterior to be literally inexpressive.

However, it is surely not in doubt that Hepworth has a full understanding of the requirements of carving; her forms are the natural result of the processes that she employs because she does not impose forms which would be a distortion of her materials and methods. She is outwardly restrained because it is impossible to work quickly in wood or stone. Therefore it is also in this sense that she is an organic sculptor—working *with* the material instead of *against* it has to be organic. As Seuphor says:

> It is an art in itself to be able to impose narrow limits upon oneself, to play on a small number of notes, making use of the silences that enable the sound to carry. [3]

Here Seuphor has utilised the metaphor of music in order to clarify what he means by restrained art, and it is partly music which may aid the reassessment of Hepworth's use of the classical, as will be suggested later.

Writers perceive Hepworth to be 'typically English' because she transcribes her experiences of nature into art. They consider her to be 'lyrical', affirmative and socially restorative, and while she may be seen to exemplify all of these qualities, the richer, more mysterious elements in her style and philosophy are ignored. Occasionally, a writer may glimpse what I perceive to be significant in Hepworth and produce vocabulary such as 'mysterious'. For example Hammacher says:

> . . . the caverns that Hepworth opens up . . . have the fascination of an eye or a mouth in a magic mask. [4]

Bowness contributes the suggestion that certain of Hepworth's forms

> . . . assume the character of an icon or a totem . . . it involves us in the whole idea of magic and metamorphosis. [5]

Whilst these quotations do lean towards what I believe is the true intentionality of the sculptor, the concepts are never explored and the reader is simply left with an occasional phrase which does not concur with the main body of criticism.

The central problem, I believe, is a particular reading of 'the classical'. Nietzsche may here be of some assistance. He has perceived two strands to be running through the classical consciousness:

> . . . in the Apollonian state . . . we take delight in 'beautiful appearances', appearances in which 'all forms speak to us [and] there is nothing unimportant or superfluous' [while] . . . 'intoxication', 'rapture', 'ecstasy', 'frenzy'—stands for the Dionysian. [6]

This may be of real value both in perceiving Hepworth anew and also reclaiming her from the traditionally narrow limits of given criticism. If this is legitimate, it may become possible to relate her positively to those of her avant-garde contemporaries with whom she has not been critically associated—even (perhaps surprisingly) the American Abstract Expressionists.

The problem is not confined to the study of Hepworth—it is recognisable, for example, in Hammacher's grappling with Arp:

> . . . his plastic creations seem classic because of their uncomplicated and harmonious external aspect. His talent is, rather, romantic; his is not an expressive but an introverted, tranquil, poetic romanticism. We can never be satisfied with the term 'romantically classic'. [7]

These same words may as easily be spoken of Hepworth, and I suggest that it is this problem that causes her to be considered an unlikely subject for criticism; it is much easier to assimilate her into a narrow and tired paradigm. Instead, if one explores the problem of the duality of Hepworth's classicism, which Hammacher unearths, then she evidently becomes a lively subject capable of many new assessments.

As Nietzsche maintained, there are two elements to the classical, and although they may interrelate, they can be basically classified as opposites. However, to most critics of Hepworth there is only one sort of classicism, and that is the Apollonian. This means that they fail to discover a vast area of richness in her works, which consequently affects the general level of criticism. Nietzsche perceives the person with the Apollonian consciousness to be aware of the 'apotheosis of the *principium individuationis*'—the painful awareness of (besides the beauty) the 'separateness' of one's own being from the rest of humanity. This is in contrast to critics who believe the Apollonian to be the beautiful, the harmonious and the untroubled—as Hepworth's work may appear to the insensitive observer.

It is then easy to see what forces Hepworth's art into 'English' and 'classical' paradigms: the obvious lyricism of the curved forms and openings in works such as *Pelagos* of 1946, and the aesthetic pleasure that one obtains from the exquisite craftsmanship and the conventional beauty of the forms, all lead one to connect her to Wilson, Leighton and early Claudian Turner. It is tempting and sometimes valuable to interpret Hepworth in this manner because her natural forms are indeed the translations of her experiences in particular environments, as well as stereognostic reaction to the structure of the landscape. She internalises her feelings and presents them to the viewer in the only possible manner—abstractly. This is of course something firmly associated with British artistic traditions, and it might perhaps be considered a twentieth century consequence of the eighteenth and nineteenth centuries' elevation of the British landscape and nature as acceptable subject-matters.

However, to ascribe only this positioning for Hepworth is a serious negation of the vitality, mysticism and human and social concerns which are also evident in her art. She is at times revolutionary in her ideas about society and art appreciation, for she believes that if art were to become part of *life*—and not just an arena for specialist knowledge and consumption by the wealthy—then social, mental and psychological problems would be healed. This concurs almost exactly with what Nietzsche and Jung also say on the subject of art, which allows me to believe there is a good chance that Hepworth also rebels against not only a consistently Apollonian judgment of her art but also a misunderstood Apollonian idea. As she herself is heard to say in the voice-over of a film:

> I have often been called puritanical or cold or geometrical, but it is the significance of human and spiritual responses to the world around us that obsesses me at all times. [8]

This is not what one could define as a traditional 'classical' attitude.

It becomes evident that it is a distorted interpretation to perceive Hepworth as Apollonian when one realises, as was mentioned above, that this state of consciousness involves the painful awareness of (as well as the beauty) the 'separateness' of one's own being from the rest of humanity. It appears to me that one of the most noticeable features of Hepworth's writings is the proposal that people should co-operate, interrelate and commune. She herself always attaches to groups and communities—in the 1930s she was a member of many groups, including the 'Seven and Five Society' and 'Unit One':

> . . . suddenly, England seemed alive and rich—the centre of an international movement . . . the co-operation between the five of us was most exciting . . . [9]
>
> I have felt compelled to meet the all-round problem of living in a comprehensible community . . . if the sculptor himself can find personal integration with his surroundings and his community his work will stand a greater chance of developing the poetry which is his free and affirmative contribution to society. [10]

These typical comments, and also certain sculptures she has produced, such as *Group III Evocation* (which is about the relationship of beings to one other, to architecture and to the landscape) illustrate that Hepworth is not Apollonian but is indeed Dionysian. In her creative ecstasy she feels at one with all, and truly at one with the primordial being. As Young says:

> . . . the Dionysian impulse . . . offers . . . an exuberant affirmation of one's supra-individual identity . . . 'the conception of individuation as the primal cause of evil' but also 'the joyous hope that the spell of individuation may be broken in augury of a restored oneness'. [11]

It is interesting to note that Polcari believes the roots of the Abstract Expressionists' art to be in 1920s and 1930s American life, in which:

> . . . the continuity, survival, and triumph of Americans, of the family, and of the community become almost a mythic, symbolic, Utopian dream. [12]

I believe that it is Hepworth's aim for society (and particularly for her art) to encourage a general sense of 'oneness' in order to prevent racism, sexism and nuclear war. This was evident even in brief newspaper articles—for example:

> . . . she has retained a passionate interest in world affairs, and has been quick to support such causes as racial equality, political freedom (she recently refused to exhibit in Portugal) and nuclear disarmament. [13]

It appears, therefore, that Barbara Hepworth's art is not as easily understood and assimilated as is usually believed. There are elements which are vital to her style but which, because they are not overt, have not been thought relevant. These elements associate Hepworth with parallel American movements of the 1940s and 1950s. She is constantly stressing how aware she is of the primeval, and of magical and mystical forces, and this is an interest which is intense during Hepworth's lifetime and explored consistently by the American avant-garde. Polcari stresses it as a major impetus for the rise of Abstract Expressionism:

> . . . cultures had psyches and varied psychological configurations dominated different cultures. These ideas, which were not limited to anthropology, were essential to American thought in the 1930s. [14]

Just as James Frazer's *The Golden Bough* was instrumental in inspiring artists such as Mark Rothko and Barnett Newman, the ideas expressed in it (if, however, stimulated by different sources) were permeating Hepworth's aesthetic.

Frazer's book dealt with issues such as how magicians in so-called 'primitive' cultures influenced society; for example:

> . . . magic has claimed to control the great forces of nature for the good of man. If that has been so, the practitioners of the art must necessarily be personages of importance and influence in any society. [15]

That Hepworth saw herself in this light is clear:

> In all the arts let us become pure spirits, not only liberators but necessarily and before all: liberated. [16]

She attempts, like Nietzsche, to stimulate a social cohesion which is representative of ancient times. As Young says:

> . . . there is a lack of both artistic and political unity, for only the sharing of an 'unconscious metaphysics' can . . . help modern, mythless man . . . Only a state in possession of the 'unwritten laws' of a 'mythical foundation that guarantees its connection with religion and growth from mythical notions' can achieve genuine cohesion. [17]

Hepworth realises that through her carving she may introduce modern people to the healing experience of early humanity's consciousness and spirit; sculpture (or rather, carving):

> . . . presupposes the direct, highly sensual and primitive, in the sense of basic instinct—reaction to form, shape and volume. [18]

She often dwells in her writings or interviews about how she 'listens' to the stone or wood, how her left hand is her 'thinking hand' while her right is a 'motor' hand. She 'lives' with her stones until they become familiar in every respect and she is then able to sense the forms that the blocks suggest. This is what the artist experiences, and yet it is comparable to the viewer's reaction to the finished form: one is invited to touch, and break out from the restraint and politeness of twentieth century life. What she feels whilst carving is conveyed directly through sensations of touch; the marks left by chisels and hammers are then obvious, and it is possible to realise how she was induced to make each mark because one can feel how the form of the wood or stone led her in that direction. It is evident from marks and indentations when Hepworth was carving in a composed, slow rhythm, or when she was excited and therefore worked with powerful, grand movements.

Once the viewer's senses are projected into the work by empathy, if one 'lives with it' for long enough, it:

> . . . may become a mandala, an object which in contemplation confers on the troubled spirit a timeless serenity . . . which is . . . that apprehending consciousness or cosmic awareness upon which life itself finally depends. [19]

Thus Read's statement serves to explain what Hepworth means when she so often states that sculpture is essential to life—it is shown to help the spectator become aware of what makes life worth living.

Here again there is cause for asserting that Hepworth's consciousness is of the Dionysian rather than the Apollonian, which is my main means of liberating her from English and classical paradigms, and of placing her in an international context. A large part of Nietzsche's argument about the Dionysian is that it is based on contemplation rather than action. He asserts that the 'solution' [to the problems of life] 'is not to be found in action': humans are offered, through art:

> . . . a transcendence of their humanity, an escape from individuality into a feeling of absorption into the Primal One. [20]

Inducing contemplation in the viewer of the work of art is a healing act which allows him or her to have a brief sensation of what it is like to be 'near God', to experience the freedom of being 'not of this world'. This is exactly what Mark Rothko does in his spare, non-representational paintings. Unlike the so-called 'action painters'—for example, Jackson Pollock or Willem de Kooning—Rothko turns to 'colour-field' painting which often stimulates the act of contemplating a mandala, as Hepworth's forms and rhythms do. It may be apparent that both Rothko and Hepworth reject the action and tortuousness of their respective contemporaries, Pollock and Moore, in favour of much gentler, healing objectives. Perhaps they were each aware that violent action is no remedy to the problems of the world they were both trying to counter. As Young states:

> . . . self-deception is at the heart of the Apollonian solution . . . action requires the veil of illusion [whereas] Dionysian man knows both the futility of action—that it can change nothing 'in the eternal nature of things'—and the joy of a higher, non-Apollonian state. [21]

It is ironic, but perhaps inevitable, that the profound, gentler and less dynamic works of Rothko and Hepworth are overshadowed by the more spectacular but (I suggest) shallower works of Pollock and Moore.

It may seem bizarre to juxtapose Rothko and Hepworth, and yet I believe that it only seems so because Hepworth has been relegated for so long. It is consistently surprising to perceive the—what now seem obvious—comparisons between the two contemporaries. For example, music is essential to both. As Nietzsche said:

> . . . music represents the metaphysical world directly, the non-musical arts represent it, at best, only indirectly. [22]

But surely, had he been writing after the appearance of non-representational art, he probably would have included 'abstract' art as a way to affect people at the deepest level. Hepworth and Rothko are inspired by music and it is my opinion that they produce 'music-like' effects in their works in order that the viewer might sense the Primal One. Hepworth recognises this, for she states:

> . . . the thought process [of carving] is nearer to musical composition [than any other type of art]. [23]

In fact, Hepworth uses music in order to help her to reach back to the primitive sensibility, whilst also ensuring that her work is relevant to modern needs. This factor helps to place her within a new paradigm and connects her to Rothko and the larger international scene. As she herself says:

> I think Brancusi's understanding of these timeless elements of sculpture is very close to Stravinsky's understanding of rhythm—they are the elements which belong to the primeval forces activating man's sensibilities; but they are, at the same time, sophisticated in the sense that they apprehend contemporary needs and passions and reaffirm the continuity of life. [24]

Obviously Rothko and Hepworth delight in music because they enjoy the fact that it is abstract in the same sense that their works are abstract—necessarily affecting people on an intuitive and primitive level, as well as appealing to contemporary sensibilities in the sophistication and profundity of form and technique. In the 1933 *Abstraction-Création* publication, Hepworth makes clear her affinity with music, and this clearly differentiates her from Moore at a time when they were regularly perceived as interdependent. This is where the two sculptors first definitely diverge, and is indicative that Hepworth and Moore belong to two different paradigms—the former to the Dionysian, and the latter to the Apollonian. In conventional critiques it would be Moore who belongs to the Dionysian because of the excited surfaces of his works and his frank engagement with the grotesque, and it would be Hepworth who belongs to the Apollonian. However, the truth seems to be the reverse, as the Apollonian consciousness seems to offer little hope of release to a higher realm, and to be laden with the burden of superficiality.

It is apparent that Hepworth's interest in music projects her beyond the English avant-garde even in the pre-war years. This interest, together with the extreme abstraction of her forms (again when the very 'English' Moore was happy to return to the figurative) evokes certain concerns of the Bauhaus. In this strict sense she is particularly compatible with Wassily Kandinsky. He based much of his art on complex musical theories, and attempted to make a visual equivalent to the notes and rhythms of music; he was inspired by ancient and diverse cultures, and tried to revive awareness of the spirituality which the potent geometrical symbols of earlier times contained. It must be significant that Hepworth, Kandinsky and Rothko all found such concepts so vitally important.

Perhaps the most striking visual factor which binds the three (I think irrevocably) is their respective pioneering uses of colour. Hepworth was ground-breaking in her employment of colour—something which has not been fully explored in criticism and yet is very noticeable:

> . . . the first impression . . . within the generally familiar context of this artist's world . . . is not of coldness or austerity, but of colour. [25]

Similarly Kandinsky and Rothko are important colourists—the former by suggesting a transcendental, correlative language of shapes and colours; the latter for painting really *only* with colour, thus overwhelming the spectator with an intense, and therefore also transcendental, effect.

However tenuous may seem the links between these figures, I believe they are nonetheless real. Firstly Hepworth had tangible connections with the Bauhaus; she knew Gropius when he resided in Hampstead after he left Germany and before she herself went to live in Cornwall. He went on to found, with Moholy-Nagy, the Bauhaus in Chicago as well as to head the Harvard School of Architecture and occasionally teach at the Black Mountain College in North Carolina. Charles Harrison seems to relate Hepworth and Nicholson to the Bauhaus, though not in so many words:

> . . . the implicit association which Nicholson here makes between a move into abstraction in art and a quasi-religious experience of nature is consistent with that tendency towards 'theosophical' idealism in modernist

> art which can be traced back, via the pseudo-philosophical self-justifications of Mondrian or Kandinsky or the romantic 'transcendental socialism' of the Bauhaus in its early days at Weimar . . . The vaunted pursuit of 'innocence' and 'sincerity' amongst the painters of the Seven and Five during the 1920s can be accommodated within the margins of this development. [26]

Thus the concepts being addressed in European abstraction, including at the Bauhaus, would have been familiar to Hepworth through her contacts with Gropius, with Naum Gabo (whom I exclude from the present survey only because of lack of space) and with Piet Mondrian in the 1930s. One has only to glance at her work entitled *Sculpture With Colour (Deep Blue And Red)*, 1940 (Fig. 25) to perceive how she was affected by Mondrian's art and personality. As Hepworth said:

> I . . . began to take in the power and force of this astonishing creative show of colour and form . . . we discussed the experience and said that this was not the end of anything—it was the beginning of something. [27]

Hepworth and Nicholson encouraged Mondrian to go to St. Ives with them in order to be further away from the atrocities of war. The mysticism of Mondrian's squares, verticals and horizontals, resonant with absolutist colour and architectonic geometry, must have prepared Hepworth for the ideas pregnant in discussions with Gabo (although the latter repudiated any comparability with Mondrian [28]). It is therefore quite reasonable to link Hepworth to contemporary European avant-gardes, and in a much greater sense than her simply being in day-to-day contact with major Europeans in London and St. Ives. However, I am proposing to go beyond the merely reasonable and to suggest comparisons with the post-war American avant-garde and, in particular, with Mark Rothko. This is much more contentious if I suggest, as I intend to do, that the 'connectivity' of Hepworth and Rothko is based on rather more than their mutual interests in Europeans of the pre-war generation.

Firstly, however, it is undeniable that such mutual interests were real. There have been several studies on the migration of European artists to the United States who have stayed for a period in Great Britain, and indeed, many outstanding twentieth century figures did live in this country—sometimes for several years. These include Gabo, Erich Mendelsohn, László Moholy-Nagy, Mondrian and Gropius. London in the 1930s may indeed be perceived as a melting-pot of many avant-garde movements, and it is something of a convention now to maintain that these movements affected British art beneficially, before their representatives moved on to the U.S.A. where they performed a similarly-beneficial service. What I wish to propose, however, is that the effects promulgated in the U.S.A. by the Europeans—such as Mondrian, Gropius (through his contributions to the Black Mountain College curriculum), and Moholy-Nagy (through his foundation of the Chicago Bauhaus)—may well have been characterised by their contact with the British avant-garde as much as by their previous enterprises. It is apparent, for example, that Gropius might have performed the function of transmitting mystical and colourists' ideas from the German Bauhaus to Hepworth [29], whilst then forging a link in America between Hepworth's fecund primitivism, social and philosophical concerns, and the similar preoccupations of the Bauhaus's descendant institutions there. Such interests might easily have transferred to the likes of Mark Rothko and Barnett Newman via Black Mountain College, with which they came into contact on several occasions.

However, a more concrete means of assuring the speculative comparability of Hepworth and Rothko is given by the fact that Rothko made a special effort to visit St. Ives. While there, he was intrigued by the menhirs and ancient 'presence' of the place, and found the light and huge expanses of sea to be inspirational as well as concordant with the colourful and meditative spirit of his own work. There is good reason for assuming that it was on this visit that Rothko met Hepworth, in which case a juxtaposition of them is aided, because the case becomes one of more than mutual awareness. A letter to Hepworth from Rothko includes the phrases:

> My love to you and yours. Thank you so much for your beautiful and gracious letter . . . My love for your work and you are always there.
> Mark Rothko. [30]

This confirms that Rothko appreciated Hepworth's work and suggests that he knew her personally. Terry Frost recalls meeting Rothko, Clement Greenberg and Robert Motherwell in St. Ives and believes it highly unlikely that Rothko and his companions would have missed visiting Hepworth and Nicholson at their studio.

It is not surprising that Rothko would have desired to experience the same impetus as Hepworth in the mythical, the spiritual and deeply historic. He would have been intrigued, like Gropius, by the standing stones and the 'presences' of ancient humanity in Cornwall. Hepworth and Rothko create in a manner which connects them to the process of faith and the workings of religion: they purge and exclude, they concentrate on the absolute, they connect to the inner workings of the spiritual.

It is common that viewers of Rothko's works experience what are considered to be 'religious' sensations. As he said:

> . . . the people who weep before my pictures are having the same religious experience as I had when I painted them. [31]

He seems acutely conscious of the mesmerising potency of certain marks and factures. For example, his loose brushwork and overlapping colours at the edges of his rectangles affect the observer's peripheral vision, giving rise to the impression that the rectangles are roughly tearing themselves away from the ground and are partly floating towards the viewer and partly held down.

One is reminded here of Kandinsky's text *Point and Line to Plane*, which tends to confirm my belief in a pedigree shared by Rothko and Hepworth. Kandinsky says:

> . . . on approaching the boundary of the basic plane, a form increases its tension, until, at the moment of contact with the boundary, the tension suddenly ceases. [32]

It is apparent that similar concerns were of fascination to Hepworth also, for in *Sea Form (Porthmeor)* she finds expression for the immense tension which exists between the upper and lower lips of a wave which is about to crash in on itself.

In justification of my belief that Hepworth and Rothko produce contemplative art, which is linked to the fact that their styles are serene and 'predictable', Jung expresses how predictable and ancient shapes are the most profound and mystical. He states:

> . . . geometrical figures such as the circle, the wheel and the square, and anything fourfold . . . [are] often known as 'mandalas' . . . meaning magic circles . . . In the East the mandala . . . is used ritualistically in shamanistic and Tantric yoga as an aid to contemplation. [33]

It is consistent with this proposal that Rothko, Kandinsky and Hepworth discover shape, colour and meaning to be actually indistinguishable: colour-forms evoke emotions or states of mind in the observer. Each of these artists recognises that colour opens up an eternal universe in which the individual's mind recognises itself. The morality and humanism of these artists is expressed through the medium of colour: the viewer is allowed an insight into his/her psyche and becomes liberated.

A criticism of my attempt to 'internationalise' Hepworth may be based on the common assumptions that she was a provincial artist, showing rarely in America, and that she did not travel widely in the United States. However, from an early stage in her career, and before she won her prize at the São Paulo Bienal in 1959 (which really confirmed her reputation), Hepworth was showing fairly regularly in America. For example, she was invited to lend works to the 'Abstract Artists Exhibition in America', at the Riverside Museum, New York, 1951. Hepworth was aware of the significance of this exhibition: she wrote:

> I am very glad that the committee are including 'Rhythmic Form 1949' and I should be very pleased to lend 'Pendour' which will be returning from the [Venice 1950] Biennale . . . I agree that this exhibition is important. [34]

It is interesting that Hepworth's representational as well as abstract works were popular in America, whereas in Britain the public could not cope easily with her moving effortlessly between abstraction and figuration. It is also apparent that Americans were keen to collect her work generally:

> . . . the Western Association of Art Museum Directors in the U.S. have sent in so many enthusiastic requests for this exhibition that it is hoped to arrange a tour of a year . . . this exhibition will introduce British art to a

> new public, and also ensure that these museums will have the opportunity of purchasing only works of fine quality to represent British art in their collections. [35]

This ground-breaking show would have been of the greatest interest to Rothko and the others: Hepworth's included works—*Pendour* and *Rhythmic Form*—were painted works, which probably would have been a revelation to American eyes at that time.

Of comparable importance would have been the Tate Gallery, London, exhibition of 1964, entitled '54/64'. Here British and American art was exhibited together, confirming transatlantic comparability of the avant-garde. Hepworth and Rothko were both represented, and it is apparent that Hepworth was extremely aware of having a 'presence' in the American *milieu*. It is surprising that Hepworth's position in relation to contemporary American art should not have been examined before. To her British dealers she writes:

> I have been feeling desperately depressed about my American contract—it is one year and three months since I finished with Martha Jackson, and very many months since you were in America. It is really essential that I should have a New York exhibition arranged for say October 1959. [36]

Later she adds:

> I suggested October, but as soon as I had rung off, I realised that a far better date would probably be June or thereabouts for U.S. visitors. [37]

One might assume that this was simply good business sense, but I believe that Hepworth appreciated the fact that American critics seemed capable of interpreting her work more effectively than those of her own country. The criticism she gratefully received from American writers such as Dore Ashton (a prolific writer on Rothko) was invigorating after the (misguided) formalist analysis she often had to cope with in Britain. Ashton in particular sensed the need for an examination of the 'inner necessity' of Hepworth's productions. For example, discussing the Dag Hammarskjöld memorial, she wrote:

> . . . in Hepworth's stones, and in her bronzes too, there is the interior vision which transforms a simple circular opening into an apprehensible symbol. My allegiance to 'Single Form' then, is based on my instinctive awareness of the meaning embodied there—a meaning which surpasses its physical lineaments. [38]

Ashton considers the exterior of Hepworth's sculptures to be simply the start of an intense experience for the observer: one must examine the use of symbols and the acute reliance upon the primordial response. Here Hepworth's close relationship to Rothko is again exemplified. The critic is also aware of the magical and spiritual aspects of Hepworth's *oeuvre* which I consider to have been under-examined, and she makes specific references to this:

> Hepworth has closely pondered the simple configurations of magical societies . . . This conversation with the past is mythic, but it is not a myth . . . With such an aspiration toward universality, Hepworth could hardly narrate a specific myth . . . These two ancient themes—the earth and the upright man—thread through Hepworth's life work. [39]

Perhaps it may finally be said that the prime weakness in an interpretation which figures Rothko, Hepworth and the other artists I have mentioned, is that most of those I consider significant were painters. How could they relate closely to Hepworth, noted as she was for her 'sculptural' attributes, particularly her direct carving? The answer to this seems to me to be twofold. Firstly they shared a common devotion to colour-form. As Bryan Robertson has written of Hepworth:

> in the late thirties and forties Barbara Hepworth in England began to explore the use of colour in sculpture, never descriptively, always abstractly, and applied colour to carvings in wood and stone in ways which appear to deny the solidity of her materials and to pierce through to a new space. [40]

Secondly, they were non-conformists. The prevailing myth of Hepworth is that she was fundamentally a carver, whereas she regularly drew and painted, and occasionally took a hacksaw or sledgehammer to plaster structures which then became bronzes. In the twentieth century this is not to be regarded as deviant artistic behaviour, but it certainly *is* deviant in relation to our received image of Hepworth. All those I have mentioned may be perceived as in some sense deviant artists—Hepworth because she was a classicist and yet insisted on being celebrated for her romanticism; Kandinsky because he found it difficult to reconcile his mystical and humanistic concepts with the Bauhaus style; and Rothko because his 'art utters a single word, insistently', and his meditative paintings did not fit in with the actively gestural expressions of the 'action painters'.

There is an insistent need for re-examination of these artists. It seems reasonable that if they do not fit easily into other paradigms, and if they correlate, then they should be brought together in a sympathetic critique. As has been noted:

> Barbara Hepworth does not stand in the great central humanist tradition of Europe. Rather she is one of those who has opened up fresh avenues and helped to forge the new consciousness of the twentieth century. [41]

It may be inevitable that those who are not directly situated within the dominant tradition become inexpertly assessed and even neglected. It is my aim here to have provided some slight stimulation for a dedicated critique embracing Hepworth and Rothko, and perhaps Kandinsky.

NOTES AND REFERENCES

1 BONE, STEPHEN (1952) 'London, Thursday', *Manchester Guardian*, 3 October.
2 READ, HERBERT (1956) *Ben Nicholson: Work since 1947* Volume Two (London, Lund Humphries), p. 2.
3 SEUPHOR, MICHEL (1959) *Sculpture of this Century: Dictionary of Modern Sculpture* (London, A. Zwemmer Ltd.), p. 172.
4 HAMMACHER, ABRAHAM MARIE (1969) *The Evolution of Modern Sculpture: Tradition and Innovation* (London, Thames & Hudson), p. 256.
5 BOWNESS, ALAN (1967) *Modern Sculpture* (London, Studio Vista), p. 70.
6 YOUNG, JULIAN (1993) *Nietzsche's Philosophy of Art* (Cambridge, Cambridge University Press), p. 33.
7 Hammacher (n. 4), p. 254.
8 HEPWORTH, BARBARA (1968) speaking on the film *Barbara Hepworth at The Tate*, an Arts Council film made by the British Film Institute in 1968 to coincide with the major Hepworth exhibition at the Tate Gallery from 3 April to 16 May 1968. It was directed and photographed by Bruce Beresford.
9 READ, HERBERT and HEPWORTH, BARBARA (1952) *Barbara Hepworth, Carvings and Drawings: Section 3: 1934–1939* (London, Lund Humphries).
10 Read (n. 9) *Section 6: 1949–1952.*
11 Young (n. 6), p. 46. Quotations from *The Birth of Tragedy*.
12 POLCARI, STEPHEN (1993) *Abstract Expressionism and the Modern Experience* (Cambridge, Cambridge University Press), p. 9.
13 ANON (1962) 'In the Picture: Barbara Hepworth', *The Observer*, 13 May.
14 Polcari (n. 12,) p. 5.
15 FRAZER, JAMES (1993) *The Golden Bough: a Study in Magic and Religion* (Hertfordshire, Wordsworth Reference), p. 83. There is much evidence for Rothko, in particular, being very influenced by this book, for example 'Frazer tried to show that a universal theme underlies all mythological traditions . . . Rothko embraced the notion of the universality of mythological themes.' In: CHAVE, ANNA C. (1989) *Mark Rothko: Subjects in Abstraction* (New Haven, Yale University Press), pp. 96–97.
16 HEPWORTH, BARBARA (1933) *Abstraction-Création Cahier*. It may seem expansive to suggest that the artist is an 'artist-magician', but what I mean by this is a leader of society and a creative being in the sense that ancient magicians were. Herbert Read seems to justify my concept for he says: 'It is as if the artist were a demi-god, capable of creating a new satellite, a world dependent on this world but not of it; a new world.' In: Read (n. 9), p. x.
17 Young (n. 6), p. 49. Quotations from *The Birth of Tragedy*.
18 ROBERTSON, BRYAN (1961) 'Introduction', *Sculpture 1961*. Catalogue for a travelling Welsh Arts Council exhibition from 15 July–26 November. It is interesting to note that the founder of the concept of the 'collective unconscious', and the philosopher who took much interest in primitive and ancient cultures, Carl Gustav Jung, also found carving and collecting stones to be healing and a method of 'tapping' the primitive within himself: 'Our social organisation . . . civilises [man] outwardly, while leaving what is primitive in him untamed . . . the method [Jung] evolved [to solve this] depended on the acceptance of irrational impulses later evolved into carving in stone, an activity he found very satisfying and which usually opened the door to new ideas and intellectual discoveries.' In: FORDHEIM, FRIEDA (1966) *An Introduction to Jung's Psychology* (Harmondsworth, Penguin), p. 61.
19 Read (n. 9), pp. x–xi.
20 Young (n. 6), p. 54.
21 *Ibid.*, pp. 44, 47 and 46 respectively.
22 *Ibid.*, p. 36.
23 HEPWORTH, BARBARA (1964) interview with Nevile Wallis. See WALLIS, NEVILE (1964) 'The Hepworth Way', *The Observer Weekend Review*, 12 July.
24 Read (n. 9).
25 'OUR ART CRITIC' (1962) 'Ten Years of Sculpture by Miss Barbara Hepworth', *The Times*, 16 May.
26 HARRISON, CHARLES (1981) *English Art and Modernism 1900–1939* (London, Allen

Lane; Bloomington, Indiana University Press), p. 261.

27 Notes Hepworth made after first experiencing Mondrian's work in his studio in Paris in the early 1930s. HEPWORTH, BARBARA (n.d.) Unpublished notebook on display at the Barbara Hepworth Museum, St. Ives, pp. 2–3.

28 'I do not share Mondrian's metaphysics at all and never did . . .' Letter GABO, NAUM to Herbert Read, dated 8 September 1947. 48/44 Vict, Sir Herbert Read Archive, University of Victoria, B.C. See THISTLEWOOD, DAVID (1984) *Herbert Read: Formlessness and Form* (London, Routledge & Kegan Paul), p. 90.

29 It is especially interesting to note that in the publication *Circle*, at the end of Hepworth's contribution entitled 'Sculpture' is a page of photographs of Stonehenge which were taken by Walter Gropius. This is no accident as there still exists a postcard by an organiser of the book's layout, which reads: 'Photo to come at end of Hepworth article on sculpture'. It is therefore apparent that the similarities in interests and philosophies between Hepworth and Gropius were recognised by their contemporaries.

30 Letter ROTHKO, MARK to Barbara Hepworth dated 6 December 1968; Barbara Hepworth Museum, St. Ives.

31 ROTHKO, MARK (1947–48) 'The Romantics were Prompted', *Possibilities I*, p. 84. Reprinted in (1987) *Mark Rothko 1903–1970* (London, Tate Gallery).

32 KANDINSKY, WASSILY (1926 [1979]) *Point and Line to Plane* (New York, Dover Press), p. 137.

33 Fordheim (n. 18), p. 65.

34 Letter HEPWORTH, BARBARA to Lilian Somerville dated 1 November 1950, British Council Archive, London.

35 Copy letter [SOMERVILLE, LILIAN?] to Barbara Hepworth dated 4 October 1950, British Council Archive, London.

36 Letter HEPWORTH, BARBARA to Peter Gimpel of Gimpel Fils, London, dated 4 December 1958 Gimpel Fils Archive. Indeed, Hepworth had her way because one of her most successful shows was arranged for precisely that time—at Galerie Chalette, New York.

37 Letter HEPWORTH, BARBARA to Charles Gimpel of Gimpel Fils, London, dated 8 June 1959. Gimpel Fils Archive.

38 ASHTON, DORE (1974) 'Barbara Hepworth: an Appreciation' in catalogue of the exhibition *Barbara Hepworth: 'Conversations'* (New York, Marlborough-Gerson Gallery), March–April, p. 5.

39 *Ibid.*

40 ROBERTSON, BRYAN (1994) 'Caro and the Twentieth Century' in catalogue of the exhibition *Anthony Caro: Sculpture through Five Decades: 1955–1994* (London, Annely Juda Fine Art,) 8 March–7 May, p. ix.

41 MULLALLY, TERENCE (1968) 'Sculptor's Talent Confirmed', *The Daily Telegraph*, 8 April.

Index

MEG DUFF

Barbara Hepworth: Bibliography

This does not claim to be a complete bibliography, although it is extensive. It is recommended that readers also consult the bibliographies published in the monographs by J. P. Hodin, 1961, and Alan Bowness, 1971. The bibliography is divided into seven sections:

1. Monographs;
2. Writings by the artist, statements and interviews;
3. Selected books, containing articles or references;
4. Solo exhibition catalogues;
5. Group exhibition catalogues;
6. Articles from periodicals;
7. An index of authors and editors.

All sections are in chronological order. Sections 3, 5, and 6 are selective. In particular, articles from newspapers have been restricted to those which seem most useful or accessible. Permanent collection catalogues have not, in general, been included, with the exception of catalogues published by the Tate Gallery. The Tate Gallery Library is the major source of Hepworth published material. Useful lists of permanent collections will be found in the bibliographies already cited, and in the solo exhibition catalogues from the Marlborough Gallery, New York, 1979, and the Yorkshire Sculpture Park, West Bretton, 1980. Square brackets indicate information supplied from sources other than the publication itself. The great majority of items listed here have been seen by the compiler.

1. MONOGRAPHS

Where publications appear in more than one edition, they are listed under the date of the earliest edition. It has not always been possible to see every edition of a publication.

1 *Barbara Hepworth: Sculptress*; with an introduction by William Gibson; collected and edited by Lillian Browse. London: Faber and Faber, 1946 (1947 reprint) (Ariel books on the arts). 65 pp., ill.

2 *Barbara Hepworth: Carvings and Drawings*; with an introduction by Herbert Read. London: Lund Humphries, 1952. xvi pp., 160 plates.

3 A. M. Hammacher. *Barbara Hepworth*. London: A. Zwemmer, 1958 (Modern sculptors series). [19] pp., 32 plates. Text in English; captions in English, French, German, Dutch. Original Dutch ed. published Amsterdam: Albert de Lange, 1958. German ed. published Cologne; Berlin: Kiepenheuer & Witsch, 1958. Also published New York: Universe Books, 1959.

4 J. P. Hodin. *Barbara Hepworth* [catalogue of works by Alan Bowness]. London: Lund Humphries; Neuchâtel: Editions du Griffon, 1961. 171 pp., ill.

5 Michael Shepherd. *Barbara Hepworth*. London: Methuen, 1963 (Art in progress). [48] pp., ill.

6 *The Unveiling of 'Single Form' by Barbara Hepworth, Gift of Jacob Blaustein after a Wish of Dag Hammarskjöld*. New York: United Nations, 1964. 22 pp., ill. Published on occasion of the unveiling ceremony, 11 June 1964.

7 *Barbara Hepworth: Drawings from a Sculptor's Landscape*; with an introduction to the drawings by Alan Bowness. London: Cory, Adams & Mackay, 1966. 32 pp., 76 plates.

8 A. M. Hammacher. *Barbara Hepworth*. London: Thames and Hudson, 1968 (World of art library: artists). 216 pp., ill. Rev. ed. published London: Thames and Hudson, 1987.

9 *Barbara Hepworth: a Pictorial Autobiography*. Bath: Adams and Dart, 1970. 128 pp., ill. Also published New York: Praeger, 1970 (Books that matter). New and extended ed., prepared under the direction of Alan Bowness, published Bradford-on-Avon: Moonraker Press, 1978; reprinted London: Tate Gallery, 1985.

10 *The Complete Sculpture of Barbara Hepworth 1960–69*, edited by Alan Bowness. London: Lund Humphries, 1971. 222 pp., ill.

11 Alan Bowness. *A Guide to the Barbara Hepworth Museum*. St. Ives: Trewyn Studio and Garden, 1976 (reprinted 1984). Leaflet, [8] pp.

12 *Barbara Hepworth: a Guide to the Tate Gallery Collection at London and St. Ives, Cornwall*; introduction by David Fraser Jenkins. London: Tate Gallery, 1982. 48 pp., ill.

13 Margaret Gardiner. *Barbara Hepworth: a Memoir*. Edinburgh: Salamander Press, 1982. 63 pp., ill. Reprinted, with foreword by Sir Alan Bowness, London: Lund Humphries, 1994.

14 Sally Festing. *Barbara Hepworth: a Life of Forms*. London: Viking, 1995. 343 pp., ill.

2. WRITINGS BY THE ARTIST, STATEMENTS AND INTERVIEWS

15 'The Aim of the Modern Artist: Barbara Hepworth, Ben Nicholson'. *Studio* Vol. 104, Dec. 1932, pp. 332–33. Includes interview with Hepworth, p. 332.

16 [Statement by Barbara Hepworth.] In *Unit One: the Modern Movement in English Architecture, Painting and Sculpture*; edited by Herbert Read. London: Cassell, 1934, pp. 17–25. Reprinted in book *Voicing our Visions*, 1991.

17 'Sculpture'. In *Circle: International Survey of Constructive Art*; edited by J. L. Martin, Ben Nicholson, N. Gabo. London: Faber and Faber, 1937 (reprinted 1971), pp. 113–16, plates pp. 78–81, 127. Reprinted in book *Voicing our Visions*, 1991.

18 'Approach to Sculpture'. *Studio* Vol. 132, No. 643, Oct. 1946, pp. 97–101. Reprinted in books *Voicing our Visions*, 1991, and *Modern Arts Criticism: Volume 2*, 1992.

19 [Autobiographical text in six sections.] In monograph *Barbara Hepworth: Carvings and Drawings*, 1952.

20 [Notes by the artist.] In solo exhibition catalogue *Barbara Hepworth: a Retrospective Exhibition of Carvings from 1927 to 1954*. London: Whitechapel Art Gallery, 1954, pp. 10–11, 12, 13–14, 16, 20–21, 26–27, 29.

21 [Short statement.] In group exhibition catalogue *Barbara Hepworth, Ben Nicholson*. Newcastle upon Tyne: Hatton Gallery, 1956, [1] p.

22 [Poem.] In group exhibition catalogue *Statements*. London: Institute of Contemporary Arts, 1957, [1] p.

23 [Short statement.] In group exhibition catalogue *Moments of Vision*. Rome: Rome-New York Art Foundation, 1959, [1] p.

24 Eduard Roditi. 'Barbara Hepworth'. In *Dialogues on Art*. London: Secker & Warburg, 1960, pp. 90–102. Interview. Reprinted in book *Modern Arts Criticism. Volume 2*, 1992.

25 'Two conversations with Barbara Hepworth: Art and Life; The Ethos of Sculpture'. In monograph J. P. Hodin. *Barbara Hepworth*, 1961, pp. 23–24.

26 'Statement by the artist'. In solo exhibition catalogue *Barbara Hepworth: an Exhibition of Sculpture from 1952–1962*. London: Whitechapel Art Gallery, 1962, [2] pp.

27 Mervyn Levy. 'Impulse and Rhythm: the Artist at Work—9' *Studio* Vol. 164, No. 833, Sept. 1962, pp. 84–91. Includes interview.

28 Tom Greenwell. 'Barbara Hepworth: Talking Freely'. *Yorkshire Post* (Leeds), 13 and 14 Nov. 1962. Interview appearing in two consecutive issues.

29 'Artist's notes on technique'. In monograph Michael Shepherd. *Barbara Hepworth*, 1963, [2] pp.

30 Warren Forma. 'Barbara Hepworth'. In *5 British Sculptors (Work and Talk)*. New York: Grossman, 1964, pp. 7–27. Interview/statement. See also group exhibition of same title, New York, March–April 1965.

31 Nevile Wallis. 'The Hepworth Way'. *Observer Weekend Review*, 12 July 1964. Interview.

32 'Greek Diary: 1954–1964'. In *J. P. Hodin, European Critic: Essays by Various Hands*, edited by Walter Kern, and published as a tribute on his 60th

birthday. London: Cory, Adams and Mackay, 1965, pp. 19–24. Reprinted in book *Voicing our Visions*, 1991.

33 'Tribute and reminiscence'. In *Michael Tippett: a Symposium on his 60th Birthday*, edited by Ian Kemp. London: Faber and Faber, 1965, pp. 58–59.

34 'The Artist and his Work—4: Sculpture: an Act of Praise'. *Christian Science Monitor*, 13 July 1965, p. 8.

35 'A Sculptor's Landscape'. In monograph *Barbara Hepworth: Drawings from a Sculptor's Landscape*, 1966, pp. 7–13.

36 'A Sculptor's Landscape: Excerpts from an Autobiographical Essay'. *Studio International* Vol. 171, No. 878, June 1966, p. 257. Reprinted from monograph *Barbara Hepworth: Drawings from a Sculptor's Landscape*, 1966.

37 Winifred Nicholson, Barbara Hepworth *et al*. 'Reminiscences of Mondrian'. *Studio International* Vol. 172, No. 884, Dec. 1966, pp. 286–92. Text by Hepworth pp. 288–89.

38 Edwin Mullins. 'Scale and Monumentality: Notes and Conversations on the Recent Work of Barbara Hepworth'. *Sculpture International*, No. 4, 1967, pp. 18–27. Issue No. given as No. 4 on cover, No. 1 on title page.

39 Susan Puddefoot. 'A Totem, a Talisman, a Kind of Touchstone'. *Times*, 3 April 1968. Interview.

40 Sue Dunkley. 'A Famous Woman Sculptor'. *Gibraltar Chronicle*, 4 June 1968. Interview.

41 [Autobiographical text.] In monograph *Barbara Hepworth: a Pictorial Autobiography*, 1970.

42 Edwin Mullins. 'Barbara Hepworth'. In solo exhibition catalogue *Barbara Hepworth Exhibition 1970*. Hakone: Hakone Open-Air Museum, 1970, [11] pp. Includes quotations by Hepworth from various printed sources, and also from letters to and conversations with Mullins. A reduced version of this text appears in solo exhibition catalogue *Barbara Hepworth*. Plymouth: City Art Gallery Plymouth, 1970.

43 'Alan Bowness: Conversations with Barbara Hepworth'. In monograph *The Complete Sculpture of Barbara Hepworth 1960–69*, 1971, pp. 7–16.

44 'The Times Diary: Keeping up the Fight and the Work'. *Times*, 9 Jan. 1973. Interview on occasion of Hepworth's 70th birthday.

45 Judith Rich. 'Barbara Hepworth'. *Guardian*, 17 Jan. 1973, p. 8. Interview.

46 Cindy Nemser. 'Conversation with Barbara Hepworth'. *Feminist Art Journal* (U.S.A.) Vol. 2, No. 2, Spring 1973, pp. 3–6, 22. Reprinted in book *Art Talk*, 1975.

47 Cindy Nemser. *Art Talk: Conversations with 12 Women Artists*. New York: Charles Scribner's Sons, 1975, pp. 12–33. Originally published in *Feminist Art Journal* Vol. 2, No. 2, Spring 1973.

48 Susan Bradwell. 'Barbara Hepworth'. *Arts Review* Vol. 27, No. 11, 30 May 1975, p. 308. Obituary. Includes account of interview with Hepworth shortly before her death.

49 R. A. C. Cobbe. 'Examination of Modern Paintings: Technical Information Received from Artists'. *Studies in Conservation* Vol. 21, No. 1, Feb. 1976, pp. 25–33. Includes explanation by Hepworth of materials and techniques used for 'Prelude I' (in Birmingham Museum and Art Gallery), p. 27.

50 *Some Statements by Barbara Hepworth*. St. Ives: Barbara Hepworth Museum, 1977. Booklet, [8] pp. containing 10 short statements reprinted from other sources.

51 [Quotations from letters to Margaret Gardiner.] In monograph Margaret Gardiner. *Barbara Hepworth: a Memoir*, 1982. Quoted throughout the text.

52 Corinne Miller. 'Introduction'. In solo exhibition catalogue *Barbara Hepworth: Early Life*. Wakefield: Wakefield Metropolitan District Council, 1985, pp. 6–23. Includes quotations by Hepworth from various printed and archival sources.

3. SELECTED BOOKS CONTAINING ARTICLES OR REFERENCES

This section contains a variety of material, from general surveys to short but specific references. In the earliest publications the references to Hepworth are often not extensive, but are interesting for placing her in context. Items marked + are either distinct articles on Hepworth, or contain substantial portions of text devoted to a discussion of her work. Where a book appears in more than one edition, it is listed under the earliest edition.

53 Stanley Casson. *XXth Century Sculptors*. London: Oxford University Press, 1930, pp. 19–20, 126, 127–28.

54 R. H. Wilenski. *The Meaning of Modern Sculpture*. London: Faber and Faber, 1932, p. 130, plate 5a.

55 Frank Rutter. *Art in my Time*. London: Rich & Cowan, 1933, pp. 196, 231.

56 Herbert Read. *Art Now: an Introduction to the Theory of Modern Painting and Sculpture*. London: Faber and Faber, 1933, plate 86.

57 Eric G. Underwood. *A Short History of English Sculpture*. London: Faber and Faber, 1933, p. 173, plate 47.

58 *The Arts Today*, edited with an introduction by Geoffrey Grigson. London: John Lane, The Bodley Head, 1936, pp. 101, 105.

59 Carola Giedion-Welcker. *Modern Plastic Art: Elements of Reality: Volume and Disintegration*; English version by P. Morton Shand. Zürich: H. Girsberger, 1937, pp. 12, 155, plates pp. 112–13.

60 E. H. Ramsden. *An Introduction to Modern Art*. London; New York; Toronto: Oxford University Press, 1940, pp. 20–21, 23, plate XI.

61 Kathleen Raine. *Stone and Flower: Poems 1935–43*; with drawings by Barbara Hepworth. London: Nicholson and Watson, 1943. 4 plates (1 coloured) by Hepworth.

62 Leo Walmsley. *So Many Loves*; with an introduction by Stephanie Walmsley. London: Collins, 1969, pp. 214–17, 227–29, 234–39, 247–49, 253, 256–58, 269. Reminiscences of friendship with Hepworth, Moore, Skeaping. First published 1944.

63 Eric Newton. *British Sculpture 1944–1946 = La sculpture britannique 1944–1946*. London: John Tiranti, 1947, pp. viii, x, plates 32–33. Parallel English/French text.

64 Herbert Read. *The Meaning of Art*. Rev. ed. London: Penguin, 1949 (A Pelican book), pp. 181–84, plate 61.

65 E. H. Ramsden. *Twentieth Century Sculpture*. London: Pleiades Books, 1949, pp. 20–22, 36, plates 9–10.

66 + Eric Newton. 'The Sculptor Returns'. In *In My View*. London; New York; Toronto: Longmans, Green, 1950, pp. 210–13. Reprint of review of exhibs. of Moore and Hepworth, first published Oct. 1946.

67 Herbert Read. *Contemporary British Art*. London: Penguin, 1951 (reprinted 1954) (A Pelican book), pp. 31, 32, 42, plate 56. Rev. ed. published 1964.

68 Herbert Read. *The Philosophy of Modern Art: Collected Essays*. London: Faber and Faber, 1952. pp. 98–99, 202, 223, plates 13–14.

69 E. H. Ramsden. *Sculpture: Theme and Variations: Towards a Contemporary Aesthetic*. London: Lund Humphries, 1953, pp. 6, 41–42, 48, 52, plates pp. 90–93.

70 Andrew Carnduff Ritchie. *Sculpture in the Twentieth Century*. New York: Museum of Modern Art, 1953, pp. 35, 197, 228.

71 + Patrick Heron. *The Changing Forms of Art*. London: Routledge & Kegan Paul, 1955, pp. 215–21.

72 Ulrich Gertz. *Contemporary Plastic Art = Plastik der Gegenwart*. 2nd enl. ed. Berlin: Rembrandt-Verlag, 1955, p. 257, plates pp. 238–39. Parallel English/German text.

73 Eduard Trier. *Moderne Plastik: von Auguste Rodin bis Marino Marini*. Frankfurt am Main: Büchergilde Gutenberg, 1955, pp. 64–65, 88–89, plate 72.

74 Herbert Read. *The Art of Sculpture: the A. W. Mellon Lectures in the Fine Arts, 1954, National Gallery of Art, Washington*. London: Faber and Faber, 1956, p. 102, plate 213.

75 Carola Giedion-Welcker. *Contemporary Sculpture: an Evolution in Volume and Space*. London: Faber and Faber, 1956, pp. 138–41, 170, 268–69. Published New York: George Wittenborn, and Stuttgart: Gerd Hatje, under title *Plastik des XX. Jahrhunderts*.

76 + J. P. Hodin. 'Barbara Hepworth: the Meaning of Abstract Art'. In *The Dilemma of Being Modern: Essays on Art and Literature*. London: Routledgc & Kegan Paul, 1956, pp. 128–34.

77 + Herbert Read. *The Tenth Muse: Essays in Criticism*. London: Routledge & Kegan Paul, 1957, pp. 228–39. Reprint of introduction to *Barbara Hepworth: Carvings and Drawings*, 1952.

78 Victor Pasmore. 'Abstract Painting and Sculpture'. In *The World of Abstract Art*, edited by the American Abstract Artists. London: Alec Tiranti, 1957, pp. 9–15. Published in New York by Wittenborn, Schultz.
79 Herbert Read. 'Great Britain'. In *Art since 1945*. London: Thames and Hudson, 1958, pp. 222, 228, 230, 243.
80 J. P. Hodin. 'La sculpture anglaise'. In *Encyclopédie de l'art international contemporain*, edited by Waldemar George *et al.* Paris: Editions d'Art et Industrie; Prisme des Arts, 1958, p. 47.
81 *Modern Art: a Pictorial Anthology*, edited by Charles McCurdy. New York: Macmillan, 1958, p. 234.
82 Agnes Allen. *The Story of Sculpture*. London: Faber and Faber, 1958, p. 197, plate 30.
83 + Michel Seuphor. 'Moore and Hepworth'. In *The Sculpture of this Century: Dictionary of Modern Sculpture*. London: A. Zwemmer, 1960, pp. 91–100. Originally published Neuchâtel: Editions du Griffon, 1959, pp. 90–100. Also published New York: Braziller, 1960.
84 'Barbara Hepworth'. In *A Dictionary of Modern Sculpture*; general editor Robert Maillard. London: Methuen, 1962, pp. 134–36. First published as *Dictionnaire de la sculpture moderne*. Paris: Fernand Hazan, 1960.
85 Eduard Trier. *Form and Space: the Sculpture of the Twentieth Century*. London: Thames and Hudson, 1961, pp. 160, 221, 284, plate 137. First published in German, Berlin: Mann, 1960. Rev. and enl. ed. published London: Thames and Hudson, 1968.
86 *The Tate Gallery: Report of the Trustees for the Year 1 April 1959 to 31 March 1960*. London: HMSO, 1960, p. 19. 1 work by Hepworth acquired by the Gallery.
87 *The Tate Gallery: Report of the Trustees for the Year 1 April 1960 to 31 March 1961*. London: HMSO, 1961, pp. 21–22, plate 12. 2 works by Hepworth acquired by the Gallery.
88 + Herbert Read. 'To Barbara Hepworth'. In *A Letter to a Young Painter*. London: Thames and Hudson, 1962, pp. 120–27.
89 John Rothenstein. *British Art since 1900: an Anthology*. London: Phaidon Press, 1962, pp. 22, 33, 173, plate 118.
90 Herbert Read. *A Concise History of Modern Sculpture*. London: Thames and Hudson, 1964 (The world of art library: History of art), pp. 112, 192–97, 199, 202, 204, 219.
91 Dennis Farr. *British Sculpture since 1945*. London: Tate Gallery Publications, 1965 (Tate Gallery little books), plates 2, 4, 12.
92 Alan Bowness. *Modern Sculpture*. London: Studio Vista, 1965 (reprinted 1967) (Dutton pictureback), pp. 2, 70–74, 118–23.
93 + Bryan Robertson, John Russell and Lord Snowdon. *Private View*. London: Nelson, 1965, pp. 42–45.
94 Alan Bowness. 'British Art Today'. In *Art of our Time: Painting and Sculpture*

throughout the World, edited by Will Grohmann. London: Thames and Hudson, 1966, pp. 107–36.

95 G. A. Jellicoe. *Studies in Landscape Design. Volume II*. London; Toronto; New York: Oxford University Press, 1966, pp. 5, 7, 12, plate 12.

96 + *The Tate Gallery Report 1964–65*. London: HMSO, 1966, pp. 39–42. 9 works by Hepworth acquired by the Gallery.

97 George Heard Hamilton. *Painting and Sculpture in Europe 1880 to 1940*. London: Penguin Books, 1967 (Pelican history of art), pp. 214, 234–36, 381, plate 141. Rev. ed. published 1972.

98 A. M. Hammacher. *Modern English Sculpture*. London: Thames and Hudson, 1967.

99 Jack Burnham. *Beyond Modern Sculpture: the Effects of Science and Technology on the Sculpture of this Century*. London: Allen Lane, The Penguin Press, 1968, pp. 73, 80, 93–94, 150–51. Also published in U.S.A.

100 + *The Tate Gallery 1967–8*. London: Tate Gallery Publications, 1968, pp. 26, 27, 61–63. 9 works by Hepworth acquired by the Gallery.

101 H. H. Arnason. *A History of Modern Art: Painting, Sculpture, Architecture*. London: Thames and Hudson, 1969, pp. 344, 514, 519–20, 534, 565. 2nd rev. ed. London: Thames and Hudson, 1977. 3rd rev. ed. New York: Abrams, 1986.

102 *The Tate Gallery: Acquisitions 1968–9*. London: Tate Gallery Publications, 1969, p. 13. 1 work by Hepworth acquired by the Gallery.

103 + Wyndham Lewis. *Wyndham Lewis on Art: Collected Writings 1913–1965*, edited and introduced by Walter Michel and C. J. Fox. London: Thames and Hudson, 1969, pp. 365, 406, 407, 467, 471. Includes reprints of reviews first published in *Listener*, 17 Oct. 1946, 16 Feb. 1950.

104 A. M. Hammacher. *The Evolution of Modern Sculpture: Tradition and Innovation*. London: Thames and Hudson, 1969, pp. 246, 248–57. Enl. ed. published under title *Modern Sculpture: Tradition and Innovation*. New York: Harry N. Abrams, 1988.

105 + Mervyn Levy. 'Barbara Hepworth 1903 —'. In *Drawing & Sculpture*. Bath: Adams & Dart, 1970, pp. 130–41.

106 Michel Seuphor. *L'art abstrait: 2. 1918–1938*. Paris: Maeght, 1972, pp. 97, 98, 99, 190, 208.

107 Michel Ragon and Michel Seuphor. *L'art abstrait: 3. 1939–1970 en Europe*. Paris: Maeght, 1973, pp. 41, 130, 132, 135.

108 + Hilton Kramer. *The Age of the Avant-garde: an Art Chronicle of 1956–1972*. London: Secker & Warburg, 1974, pp. 166–68, 507. Includes reprint of review first published in *New York Times*, 16 March 1966.

109 Hugo Munsterberg. *A History of Women Artists*. New York: Clarkson Potter, 1975, pp. 90–95.

110 Karen Petersen and J. J. Wilson. *Women Artists: Recognition and Reappraisal from the Early Middle Ages to the Twentieth Century*. New York; Hagerstown;

San Francisco; London: Harper & Row, 1976. (Harper colophon books), pp. 120–21, 123, 124.

111 + John Skeaping. *Drawn from Life: an Autobiography*. London: Collins, 1977, pp. 69–76, 81–82, 90–95, 98–99, 247.

112 J. P. Hodin. 'In the Studio of Barbara Hepworth'. In *John Milne: Sculptor: Life and Work*. London: Latimer New Dimensions, 1977, pp. 79–83.

113 + *The Tate Gallery 1974–6: Illustrated Catalogue of Acquisitions*. London: Tate Gallery Publications, 1978, pp. 105–07. 3 works by Hepworth acquired by the Gallery.

114 + Adrian Stokes. *The Critical Writings of Adrian Stokes. Volume I: 1930–1937*, edited by Lawrence Gowing. London: Thames and Hudson, 1978, pp. 307, 309–10. Includes reprint of review first published in *Spectator*, 3 Nov. 1933.

115 Elsa Honig Fine. *Women & Art: a History of Women Painters and Sculptors from the Renaissance to the 20th Century*. Montclair (N.J.): Allanheld & Schram; London: Prior, 1978, pp. 180–83.

116 Donna G. Bachmann and Sherry Piland. *Women Artists: an Historical, Contemporary and Feminist Bibliography*. Metuchen (N.J.); London: Scarecrow Press, 1978, pp. 253–54.

117 Jörg Krichbaum and Rein A. Zondergeld. *Künstlerinnen: von der Antike bis zur Gegenwart*. Cologne: DuMont, 1979 (DuMont Taschenbücher, 82), pp. 17, 29, 76, 184–85, 252, 273.

118 + *The Tate Gallery 1976–8: Illustrated Catalogue of Acquisitions*. London: Tate Gallery Publications, 1979, pp. 80–90. 4 works by Hepworth acquired by the Gallery.

119 *Catalogue of the Print Collection: Complete Acquisitions to April 1978, with Supplement for May 1978 to March 1980: Modern Collection Tate Gallery 1980*. London: Tate Gallery Publications, 1980, pp. 46–47. Lists 43 prints by Hepworth.

120 Charles Harrison. 'Sculpture and the New "New Movement" '. In *British Sculpture in the Twentieth Century*, edited by Sandy Nairne and Nicholas Serota. London: Whitechapel Art Gallery, 1981, pp. 103–11. Published on occasion of group exhibition. Whitechapel Art Gallery, Sept. 1981–Jan. 1982.

121 Richard Calvocoressi. 'Public Sculpture in the 1950s'. In *British Sculpture in the Twentieth Century*, edited by Sandy Nairne and Nicholas Serota. London: Whitechapel Art Gallery, 1981, pp. 135–53. Published on occasion of group exhibition. Whitechapel Art Gallery, Sept. 1981–Jan. 1982.

122 Charles Harrison. *English Art and Modernism*. London: Allen Lane; Bloomington: Indiana University Press, 1981.

123 W. J. Strachan. *Open Air Sculpture in Britain: a Comprehensive Guide*. London: A. Zwemmer; Tate Gallery, 1984. Includes details of 40 works by Hepworth.

124 + Tom Cross. 'Barbara Hepworth, Bernard Leach and Denis Mitchell'. In

Painting the Warmth of the Sun: St. Ives Artists 1939–1975. Penzance: Alison Hodge; Guildford: Lutterworth Press, 1984, pp. 108–22.

125 Peter Davies. *The St. Ives Years: Essays on the Growth of an Artistic Phenomenon*. Wimborne (Dorset): The Wimborne Bookshop, 1984.

126 + *The Tate Gallery 1980–82: Iillustrated Catalogue of Acquisitions*. London: Tate Gallery Publications, 1984, pp. 110–25. 28 works by Hepworth acquired by the Gallery.

127 Michael Williams. *People & Places in Cornwall*. St. Teath, Bodmin (Cornwall): Bossiney Books, 1985, pp. 54–62.

128 + *The Tate Gallery 1982–84: Illustrated Catalogue of Acquisitions*. London: Tate Gallery Publications, 1986, pp. 197–98. 2 works by Hepworth acquired by the Gallery.

129 Edward Lucie-Smith. *Sculpture since 1945*. London: Phaidon, 1987, pp. 22–24, colour plate 6.

130 + *The Tate Gallery 1984–86: Illustrated Catalogue of Acquisitions: Including Supplement to Catalogue of Acquisitions 1982–84*. London: Tate Gallery Publications, 1988, pp. 167–69. 1 work by Hepworth ('Conversation with Magic Stones', 1973) acquired by the Gallery.

131 Whitney Chadwick. *Women, Art and Society*. London: Thames and Hudson, 1990. (World of art), pp. 289–90, 308.

132 Nicholas Hely-Hutchison. 'Skeaping's Association with Hepworth and Moore'. In *John Skeaping 1901–1980: a Retrospective*. London: Arthur Ackermann, 1991, pp. 11–13. Exhibition catalogue.

133 Irene Veenstra and Toos van Kooten. *With Space in Mind: Works on Paper from the Collection in the Kröller-Müller Museum*. Otterlo: Rijksmuseum Kröller-Müller, 1991, pp. 90–91, 317. Details of 6 works by Hepworth.

134 + 'Barbara Hepworth 1903–1975'. In *Voicing our Visions: Writings by Women Artists*, edited by Mara R. Witzling. London: Women's Press, 1991, pp. 271–86. Includes reprints of many of Hepworth's most important statements.

135 + Susan Waller. *Women Artists in the Modern Era: a Documentary History*. Metuchen (N.J.); London: Scarecrow Press, 1991, pp. 339–50. Includes reprint of statements by Hepworth from monograph *Barbara Hepworth: Carvings and Drawings*, 1952.

136 Janet A. Anderson. *Women in the Fine Arts: a Bibliography and Illustration Guide*. Jefferson (N.C.); London: McFarland, 1991, pp. 320–21.

137 Michael Tucker. *Dreaming with Open Eyes: the Shamanic Spirit in Twentieth Century Art and Culture*. [London]: Aquarian/Harper San Francisco, 1992, pp. 274–75, 276–78.

138 *Henry Moore Bibliography*, compiled and edited by Alexander Davis. Much Hadham: Henry Moore Foundation, 1992. 3 volumes. See *Volume 3: Index 1898–1986* for references throughout.

139 + *Modern Arts Criticism: a Biographical and Critical Guide to Painters, Sculptors, Photographers and Architects from the Beginning of the Modern Era to the Present.*

Volume 2, edited by Joanne Prosyniuk. Detroit; New York; London: Gale Research, 1992, pp. 253–76. Includes reprints of interviews with Hepworth and major critical writings on her.

140 *Sculpture in the Rijksmuseum Kröller-Müller: Catalogue of the Collection*, compiled and edited by Marianne Brouwer and Rieja Brouns. 5th English ed. Otterlo: Kröller-Müller Stichting, 1992, pp. 112–14, 233. Includes details of 14 works by Hepworth.

141 Michael Tooby. *Tate Gallery St. Ives: Barbara Hepworth Museum and Sculpture Garden: an Illustrated Companion*. London: Tate Gallery, 1993, pp. 12–13, 41–45, 50–51, 81–84.

142 Marion Whybrow. *St. Ives 1883–1993: Portrait of an Art Colony*. Woodbridge (Suffolk): Antique Collectors' Club, 1994.

143 + Peter Davies. 'Barbara Hepworth'. In *St. Ives Revisited: Innovators and Followers*. Abertillery (Gwent): Old Bakehouse Publications, 1994, pp. 41–52.

4. SOLO EXHIBITION CATALOGUES

144 *Catalogue of Sculpture by Barbara Hepworth*. London: Alex. Reid & Lefevre, 1937. 8 pp., ill. Introd. by J. D. Bernal. 23 works. Exhib. Oct. 1937.

145 *Exhibition of Sculpture and Drawings by Barbara Hepworth*. Wakefield: Wakefield City Art Gallery, 1944. 8 pp. Introd. by Herbert Read. 45 works. Exhib. Feb.–March 1944.

146 *Exhibition of Sculpture and Drawings by Barbara Hepworth*. Halifax: Bankfield Museum, 1944. 8 pp. Introd. by Herbert Read. 45 works. Exhib. March–April 1944. Identical to catalogue for Wakefield, Feb.–March 1944.

147 *Barbara Hepworth: Sculpture and Drawings*. London: Lefevre Gallery, 1946. [8] pp., ill. 70 works. Exhib. Oct. 1946.

148 *Barbara Hepworth*. New York: Durlacher Bros., [1949]. Folded sheet, [4] pp. 39 works. Exhib. Oct. [1949].

149 *New Sculpture and Drawings by Barbara Hepworth*. London: Lefevre Gallery, 1950. [8] pp., ill. 53 works. Exhib. Feb. 1950.

150 *Barbara Hepworth: Sculpture and Drawings*. Wakefield: Wakefield City Art Gallery, 1951. [28] pp., ill. Introd. by Patrick Heron. 114 works. Organised by Wakefield City Art Gallery for Festival of Britain, 1951. Exhib. May–July 1951. Travelling to York and Manchester, to Oct. 1951.

151 *New Sculpture and Drawings by Barbara Hepworth*. London: Lefevre Gallery, 1952. [8] pp., ill. 51 works. Exhib. Oct. 1952.

152 *Barbara Hepworth: a Retrospective Exhibition of Carvings and Drawings from 1927 to 1954*. London: Whitechapel Art Gallery, 1954. 31 pp., ill. Introd. by David Baxandall. Includes texts by Hepworth. 198 works. Exhib. April–June 1954.

153 *Barbara Hepworth: Carvings and Drawings*. [Minneapolis: Walker Art Center],

1955. [16] pp., ill. Introd. by Herbert Read. Notes by the artist (reprinted from monograph *Barbara Hepworth: Carvings and Drawings*, 1952). 31 works. Arranged through the courtesy of the Martha Jackson Gallery, New York. Exhib. April–May 1955. Travelling throughout U.S.A. and Canada to June 1956.

154 *Recent Works by Barbara Hepworth*. London: Gimpel Fils, 1956. [2] pp., ill. 37 works. Exhib. June 1956.

155 *Barbara Hepworth: Sculpture, Paintings, Drawings*. New York: Martha Jackson Gallery, 1956. Folded sheet, [4] pp. Exhib. Dec. 1956–Jan. 1957.

156 *Recent Works by Barbara Hepworth*. London: Gimpel Fils, 1958. [8] pp., ill. 38 works. Exhib. June 1958.

157 *Barbara Hepworth*. London: British Council, 1959. [12] pp., ill. Introd. by J. P. Hodin. Parallel English/Spanish text. 28 works. Organised by British Council. Exhib. at *V Bienal do Museu de Arte Moderna*, São Paulo, Sept.–Dec. 1959. Travelling throughout South America to 1960.

158 *Hepworth*. New York: Galerie Chalette, 1959. [26] pp., ill. Introd. by Herbert Read. 30 works plus drawings. Exhib. Oct.–Nov. 1959.

159 *Barbara Hepworth*. Zürich: Galerie Charles Lienhard, 1960. [40] pp., ill. Text by J. P. Hodin. German text; biography in English. 54 works. Organised in co-operation with Gimpel Fils. Exhib. Oct. 1960.

160 *Barbara Hepworth: an Exhibition of Photographs of Sculpture and Drawings with some Original Bronzes, Arranged by the British Council*. London: British Council, [1961]. [16] pp., ill. Introd. by Alan Bowness. Exhib. 1961. Travelling to Ceylon, New Zealand, Hong Kong, Sarawak, Vietnam, Thailand, Malaya to 1963.

161 *Barbara Hepworth*. London: Gimpel Fils, 1961. [24] pp., ill. 37 works. Exhib. May–June 1961.

162 *Abstract Form and Life: Sculpture by Barbara Hepworth and Biological Models*. Belfast: Queen's University of Belfast Visual Arts Group, [1962]. Folded sheet, [4] pp., ill. 5 works. Exhib. April 1962.

163 *Barbara Hepworth: an Exhibition of Sculpture from 1952–1962*. London: Whitechapel Art Gallery, 1962. [80] pp., ill. Introd. by Bryan Robertson. Includes statement by Hepworth. 76 works. Exhib. May–June 1962.

164 *Barbara Hepworth: Sculpture and Drawings*. London: John Lewis Partnership, 1963. 1 p. duplicated typescript. 21 works. Exhib. John Lewis Auditorium, John Lewis, Oxford Street, London, April 1963.

165 *Barbara Hepworth: Sculpture and Drawings*. Zürich: Gimpel Hanover Galerie, [1963]. [20] pp., ill. German text; catalogue in English. 25 works. Exhib. [Nov. 1963–Jan. 1964].

166 *Barbara Hepworth: Sculpture and Drawings*. London: Gimpel Fils, 1964. [24] pp., ill. 60 works. Exhib. June 1964.

167 *Barbara Hepworth*. [Copenhagen]: Kunstforeningen, 1964. [16] pp., ill. Text by J. P. Hodin. Danish text; catalogue in English. 40 works. Organised by

British Council. Exhib. Sept.–Oct. 1964. Travelling throughout Scandinavia, with variant catalogues and some differences in works exhibited.

168 *Barbara Hepworth*. Stockholm: Moderna Museet, 1964. Folded poster, [16] pp., ill. Text by J. P. Hodin. Swedish text. 45 works. Organised in collaboration with British Council. Exhib. Nov.–Dec. 1964.

169 *Barbara Hepworth: veistoksia ja piirustuksia = skulpturer och teckningar*. [Helsinki]: Ateneum, 1965. [16] pp., ill. Text by J. P. Hodin. Parallel Finnish/Swedish text. 40 works. Organised in collaboration with British Council. Exhib. Jan.–Feb. 1965.

170 *Barbara Hepworth: skulptur og tegninger*. Oslo: Kunstnernes Hus, 1965. [16] pp., ill. Text by J. P. Hodin. Norwegian text. 40 works. Organised by British Council. Exhib. March 1965.

171 *Beeldhouwwerken en tekeningen van Barbara Hepworth*. Otterlo: Rijksmuseum Kröller-Müller, 1965. [40] pp., ill. Text by J. P. Hodin. Dutch text. 68 works. Exhib. Rietveld Pavilion, Rijksmuseum Kröller-Müller, May–July 1965. Enlarged version of British Council exhib. for Scandinavia, subsequently shown in reduced form in Basle and Turin.

172 *Barbara Hepworth*. [Basle: Kunsthalle Basel, 1965.] [40] pp., ill. Text by J. P. Hodin. German text. 47 works. Organised with assistance of British Council. Exhib. Sept.–Oct. 1965. Travelling to Karlsruhe and Essen to June 1966.

173 *Barbara Hepworth*. Turin: Galleria Civica d'Arte Moderna, 1965. 109 pp., ill. Introd. by Giuseppe Marchiori. Includes statement by Hepworth (reprinted from monograph *Barbara Hepworth: Carvings and Drawings*, 1952). Italian text. 46 works. Organised with collaboration of British Council. Exhib. Oct.–Nov. 1965.

174 *Barbara Hepworth*. New York: Marlborough-Gerson Gallery, 1966. [40] pp., ill. Introd. by Herbert Read. 40 works. Exhib. April–May 1966.

175 *Barbara Hepworth*. London: Gimpel Fils, 1966. [28] pp., ill. 35 works. Exhib. May–June 1966.

176 *Barbara Hepworth: mostra fotografica, con disegni e bronzi originali*. Florence: British Council, 1966. 5 pp. duplicated typescript, ill. Text by Alan Bowness. Italian text. 46 works. Exhib. on occasion of La Settimana Britannica, Florence, Oct. 1966.

177 *Barbara Hepworth*. London: Tate Gallery, 1968. 64 pp., ill. Texts by Ronald Alley, Nicolete Gray, R. W. D. Oxenaar. 226 works. Exhib. April–May 1968.

178 *Barbara Hepworth*. New York: Gimpel Gallery, 1969. [32] pp., ill. 24 works plus drawings. Exhib. April–May 1969.

179 *Twelve Lithographs by Barbara Hepworth*. London: Curwen Gallery, [1969]. Folded card, [4] pp., ill. 12 works. Exhib. [June–July] 1969.

180 [*Barbara Hepworth: Lithographs*.] St. Ives: Penwith Gallery, 1969. Exhib. Sept. 1969.

181 *Barbara Hepworth: Sculpture and Lithographs*. London: Arts Council of Great Britain, 1970. [28] pp., ill. Introd. by Ronald Alley. 28 works. Exhib. Abbotsholme, Uttoxeter, Jan.–Feb. 1970. Travelling throughout Britain to Jan. 1971.

182 *Barbara Hepworth: Recent Work: Sculpture, Paintings, Prints*. London: Marlborough Fine Art, 1970. 50 pp., ill. Introd. by Adrian Stokes. 68 works. Exhib. Feb.–March 1970.

183 *Barbara Hepworth*. Plymouth: City Art Gallery Plymouth, 1970. [40] pp., ill. Text by Edwin Mullins. Text includes quotations from Hepworth. 108 works. Exhib. June–Aug. 1970.

184 *Barbara Hepworth Exhibition 1970*. Hakone: Hakone Open-Air Museum, 1970. [116] pp., ill. Text by Edwin Mullins. Text includes quotations from Hepworth. Japanese and English texts. 46 works. Organised by Hakone Open-Air Museum and other institutions, including British Council. Exhib. June–Sept. 1970.

185 *Barbara Hepworth: The Aegean Suite: Nine Lithographs*. London: Curwen Gallery, 1971. [8] pp., ill. Introd. by Stanley Jones. 9 works. Exhib. 1971.

186 *Barbara Hepworth*. New York: Gimpel Gallery, 1971. [34] pp., ill. Text by Joel Hurstfield. 36 works. Exhib. March–April 1971.

187 *Barbara Hepworth: 'The Family of Man': Nine Bronzes and Recent Carvings*. London: Marlborough Fine Art, 1972. 72 pp., ill. Introd. by A. M. Hammacher. 21 works. Exhib. April–May 1972.

188 *Barbara Hepworth*. London: Gimpel Fils, 1972. Leaflet, [4] pp. and 6 photographs in folder. 33 works. Exhib. Oct.–Nov. 1972.

189 *Barbara Hepworth: 'Conversations'*. New York: Marlborough Gallery, 1974. 60 pp., ill. Text by Dore Ashton. 18 works. Exhib. March–April 1974.

190 *Barbara Hepworth*. Zürich: Marlborough Galerie, 1975. 64 pp., ill. Introd. by C. Giedion-Welcker. German text. 27 works. Exhib. Aug.–Oct. 1975.

191 *Barbara Hepworth 1903–1975*. London: Gimpel Fils, 1975. [36] pp., ill. 63 works. Exhib. Oct.–Nov. 1975.

192 *Barbara Hepworth 1903–1975*. London: William Darby, 1975. [24] pp., ill. 10 works. Exhib. Nov. 1975.

193 *Barbara Hepworth: Late Works on Loan from the Trustees of the Barbara Hepworth Estate*. 48 pp., ill. Introd. by Douglas Hall. 14 works. Exhib. on occasion of Edinburgh Festival, held Royal Botanic Garden, Edinburgh, Aug.–Sept. 1976.

194 *Barbara Hepworth*. New York: Gimpel & Weitzenhoffer, 1977. [12] pp., ill. 20 works. Exhib. March–April 1977.

195 *Barbara Hepworth*. Osaka: Gallery Kasahara, 1978. 24 pp., ill. Japanese text. 32 works. Exhib. Feb.–March 1978.

196 *Barbara Hepworth: a Selection of Small Bronzes and Prints*. Edinburgh: Scottish Arts Council, 1978. [20] pp., ill. Introd. by Douglas Hall. 43 works. Exhib.

Scottish College of Textiles, Galashiels, April–May 1978. Travelling throughout Scotland to Dec. 1978.

197 *Barbara Hepworth: Carvings and Bronzes.* New York: Marlborough Gallery, 1979. 72 pp., ill. Introd. by Nicholas Wadley. 61 works. Exhib. May–June 1979.

198 *Barbara Hepworth.* [West Bretton]: Yorkshire Sculpture Park, 1980. 44 pp., ill. Introd. by Peter Murray. Texts by Andrew Causey, R. W. A. (sic) Oxenaar. 28 works. Organised to coincide with Wakefield Festival 80. Exhib. July–Oct. 1980.

199 *Barbara Hepworth: Carvings.* London: Marlborough Fine Art, 1982. 43 pp., ill. Introd. by Moelwyn Merchant. 27 works. Exhib. July–Aug. 1982.

200 *Barbara Hepworth: a Sculptor's Landscape 1934–1974.* Swansea: Swansea City Council, 1982. [22] pp., ill. Introd. by Brian Smith. Text by Douglas Hall. 44 works. Organised by Swansea Museums Service. Exhib. Glynn Vivian Art Gallery and Museum, Swansea, Oct.–Nov. 1982. Travelling to Bangor, Wrexham and Isle of Man to Feb. 1983.

201 *Barbara Hepworth: Early Life.* Wakefield: Wakefield Metropolitan District Council Art Gallery and Museums, 1985. 40 pp., ill. Introd. by Corinne Miller. Text includes quotations from Hepworth. 18 works. One of two complementary exhibs. held simultaneously in Wakefield. Exhib. Wakefield Art Gallery, May–July 1985.

202 *Barbara Hepworth: Late Carvings.* Wakefield: Wakefield Metropolitan District Council Art Gallery and Museums, 1985. 28 pp., ill. Introd. by Alan Bowness. 16 works. One of two complementary exhibs. held simultaneously in Wakefield. Exhib. Elizabethan Exhibition Gallery, May–July 1985.

203 *Barbara Hepworth: Ten Sculptures 1951–1973.* London: New Art Centre, 1987. [24] pp., ill. 10 works. Exhib. Nov. 1987–Jan. 1988.

204 *Barbara Hepworth: the Art Gallery of Ontario Collection*, by Alan G. Wilkinson. Toronto: Art Gallery of Ontario, 1991. 47 pp., ill. 25 works. Organised and circulated by the Art Gallery of Ontario. Exhib. Art Gallery of Algoma, Sault Ste. Marie, Aug.–Sept. 1991. Travelling throughout Canada to May 1992.

205 *Barbara Hepworth: a Retrospective*, by Penelope Curtis and Alan G. Wilkinson. London: Tate Gallery Publications, 1994. 168 pp., ill. 115 works. Organised by Tate Gallery Liverpool and Art Gallery of Ontario. Exhib. Tate Gallery Liverpool, Sept.–Dec. 1994. Travelling to Yale Center for British Art, New Haven, Feb.–April 1995, and Art Gallery of Ontario, Toronto, May–Aug. 1995.

206 *Barbara Hepworth: Lithographs Made at Curwen Studio 1969 and 1971.* London: Curwen Gallery, 1994. Folded card, [4] pp., ill. Text by Stanley Jones. Exhib. Oct. 1994.

5. GROUP EXHIBITION CATALOGUES

In this section, the number of works listed refers to works by Hepworth, and the inclusion of an illustrations statement indicates that her work is illustrated. Please note that catalogues for the Penwith Society of Arts have been omitted for the most part. Hepworth exhibited in the opening exhibition, Summer 1949, and regularly throughout her life. Her work continued to be exhibited in the Society's exhibitions after her death in 1975. The catalogues are too numerous to list individually.

207 *Exhibition of Sculpture, Engravings and Drawings by Barbara Hepworth, William Morgan and John Skeaping*. London: Beaux Arts Gallery, 1928. [6] pp., ill. 23 works. Exhib. June 1928.

208 *Exhibition of Sculpture, Drawings and Drypoints by John Skeaping and Barbara Hepworth Skeaping, and Engravings and Drawings by William E. C. Morgan*. Glasgow: Alex. Reid & Lefevre Ltd., 1928. [10] pp., ill. 6 works. Exhib. Sept. 1928.

209 *An Exhibition of Sculpture by John Skeaping and Barbara Hepworth*. London: Arthur Tooth & Sons' Galleries, 1930. [8] pp., ill. 16 works. Exhib. Oct.–Nov. 1930.

210 *Catalogue of the 11th Exhibition of the Seven and Five Society*. London: Leicester Galleries, 1932. 7 pp. 3 works. Exhib. Feb. 1932.

211 *Carvings by Barbara Hepworth, Paintings by Ben Nicholson*. London: Arthur Tooth & Sons' Galleries, 1932. [8] pp., ill. Introd. by Herbert Read. 12 works. Exhib. Nov.–Dec. 1932.

212 *Catalogue of the 12th Exhibition of the Seven and Five Society*. London: Leicester Galleries, 1933. 8 pp. 4 works. Exhib. Feb. 1933.

213 *Artists of Today*. London: Zwemmer Gallery, [1933]. 7 pp. 5 works. Exhib. May–June [1933].

214 [*Art Now*.] London: Mayor Gallery, 1933. [12] pp. Introd. by Herbert Read. 1 work. On occasion of publication of book *Art Now*, by Herbert Read. Exhib. Oct. 1933.

215 *Barbara Hepworth, Ben Nicholson*. London: Alex. Reid & Lefevre Ltd., 1933. [7] pp., ill. 23 works. Exhib. Oct.–Nov. 1933.

216 *Unit 1*. London: Mayor Gallery, 1934. [3] pp. 4 works. Exhib. April 1934. Travelling to Liverpool, Manchester, Hanley, Derby, Swansea and Belfast to April 1935.

217 *Unit 1*. Liverpool: Walker Art Gallery, 1934. [7] pp. 4 works. Exhib. May–June 1934. A slightly different version of this exhib. previously at Mayor Gallery, London, April 1934.

218 *7 & 5*. London: Zwemmer Gallery, 1935. Poster, ill. 1 work. Exhib. Oct. 1935.

219 *Abstract & Concrete: an Exhibition of Abstract Painting & Sculpture 1934 & 1935*.

[4] pp. 2 works. Organised by Nicolete Gray in co-operation with AXIS. Exhib. 41 St. Giles, Oxford, Feb. 1936. Travelling to Liverpool School of Architecture, March 1936, Gordon Fraser's Gallery, Cambridge, May–June 1936. See also exhib. at Lefevre Gallery, London.

220 *Abstract & Concrete: an International Exhibition of Abstract Painting & Sculpture Today*. London: Alex. Reid & Lefevre Ltd., [1936]. [8] pp. Introd. by Nicolette (sic) Gray. 3 works. Organised by Nicolete Gray and AXIS in conjunction with Alex. Reid & Lefevre Ltd. Exhib. [April] 1936. See also exhib. at 41 St. Giles, Oxford.

221 *Modern Pictures for Modern Rooms: an Exhibition of Abstract Art in Contemporary Settings*. London: Duncan Miller Ltd., 1936. [6] pp., ill. Introd. by S. John Woods. 1 work. Organised by S. John Woods and Duncan Miller. Exhib. April 1936.

222 *Abstract Art: Sculpture, Paintings, Reliefs: Barbara Hepworth, Arthur Jackson, Henry Moore, Ben Nicholson, John Piper*. [4] pp., ill. Text by S. John Woods. Exhib. Everyman Cinema, Hampstead, London, Nov. [1936?].

223 *Constructive Art*. London: London Gallery, 1937. [8] pp. Texts by J. L. Martin and Siegfried Giedion. 4 works. Exhib. July 1937.

224 *Tentoonstelling abstracte kunst*. Amsterdam: Stedelijk Museum, 1938. 16 pp., ill. Introd. by H. Buys. Dutch text. Exhib. April 1938.

225 *Living Art in England*. Catalogue printed in *London Bulletin*, No. 8–9, Jan.–Feb. 1939, pp. 8–44, 57–58. Text by Herbert Read, pp. 5–7. 2 works. Exhib. London Gallery, London, Jan.–Feb. 1939.

226 *Yorkshire Artists' Exhibition 1939*. Leeds: Leeds City Art Gallery, 1939. 9 pp. 2 works. Exhib. Jan.–March 1939.

227 *Abstract and Concrete Art*. Catalogue printed in *London Bulletin*, No. 14, May 1939, pp. 2–4, 21–22. Preface by [Wassily] Kandinsky. 2 works. Exhib. Guggenheim Jeune, London, May 1939.

228 [*Exhibition of Paintings and Sculpture*.] London: Redfern Gallery, 1941. [1] p. 5 works. Exhib. Oct.–Nov. 1941.

229 *New Movements in Art: Contemporary Work in England: an Exhibition of Recent Painting and Sculpture*. London: London Museum, [1942]. [6] pp. Introd. by E. H. R[amsden]. 3 works. Exhib. March–May 1942.

230 *Exhibition of Paintings, Sculpture and Drawings by Paul Nash and Barbara Hepworth*. Leeds: Temple Newsam, 1943. 23 pp. Introd. by Philip Hendy. 62 works. Exhib. April–June 1943.

231 *Saint Ives Society of Artists Summer Collection 1946*. St. Ives: Saint Ives Society of Artists, 1946. [6] pp. 2 works. Exhib. New Gallery, Norway Square, St. Ives, Summer 1946.

232 *Sculpture in the Home*. London: Arts Council of Great Britain, 1946. [12] pp. Introd. by Frank Dobson. 1 work. Exhib. Wakefield City Art Gallery and Museum, Oct.–Nov. 1946. Travelling to Manchester, Hull, Canterbury, Newcastle upon Tyne to March 1947.

233 *Saint Ives Society of Artists Summer Collection 1947*. St. Ives: Saint Ives Society of Artists, 1947. [4] pp. 2 works. Exhib. New Gallery, Norway Square, St. Ives, Summer 1947.

234 *Barbara Hepworth, Peter Lanyon, Ben Nicholson, John Wells*. Printed by Guido Morris, St. Ives. [5] pp. 7 works. Exhib. Bookshop of G. R. Downing, St. Ives, July 1947.

235 *2ème Salon des Réalités Nouvelles: art abstrait, concret, constructivisme, non figuratif, orphisme*. Paris: [Comité du 2ème Salon des Réalités Nouvelles], 1947. 32 pp. 2 works. Exhib. Palais des Beaux-Arts de la Ville de Paris, July–Aug. 1947.

236 *3ème Salon des Réalités Nouvelles*. Paris: [Comité du 3ème Salon des Réalités Nouvelles], 1948. Exhib. 1948.

237 *Forty Years of Modern Art 1907–1947: a Selection from British Collections*. London: Institute of Contemporary Arts, [1948]. 2 publications: [12] pp. 2 works; [32] pp., ill. Introd. by Herbert Read. Exhib. Academy Hall, Oxford Street, London, Feb.–March 1948.

238 *Paintings by Barbara Hepworth; Paintings by L. S. Lowry*. London: Lefevre Gallery, 1948. [10] pp., ill. Introd. by 'a surgeon'. 64 works. Exhib. April 1948.

239 *Open Air Exhibition of Sculpture*. London: London County Council, 1948. 12 pp. Introd. by R. R. Tomlinson. Also souvenir catalogue, 44 pp., ill. Text by Eric Newton. 1 work. Organised by London County Council in association with Arts Council of Great Britain. Exhib. Battersea Park, London, May–Sept. 1948.

240 *Saint Ives Society of Artists Summer Collection 1948*. St. Ives: Saint Ives Society of Artists, 1948. [4] pp., 1 work. Exhib. New Gallery, Norway Square, St. Ives, Summer 1948.

241 *40,000 Years of Modern Art: a Comparison of Primitive and Modern*. London: Institute of Contemporary Arts, 1948. 54 pp. Essays by W. G. Archer and Robert Melville. 1 work. Exhib. Dec. 1948–Jan. 1949.

242 *Penwith Society of Arts in Cornwall First Exhibition*. St. Ives: Penwith Society of Arts, 1949. [2+] pp. 3(?) works. Exhib. Public Hall, Fore Street, St. Ives, Summer 1949. Information from incomplete catalogue.

243 *4ème Salon des Réalités Nouvelles*. Paris: [Comité du 4ème Salon des Réalités Nouvelles], 1949. 31 pp. 2 works. Exhib. Palais des Beaux-Arts de la Ville de Paris, July–Aug. 1949.

244 *6 English Moderns: Piper, Sutherland, Hepworth, Tunnard, Moore, Nicholson*. Cincinnati: Cincinnati Modern Art Society, 1950. [16] pp., ill. 9 works. Exhib. Cincinnati Art Museum, Feb. 1950.

245 *XXV Biennale di Venezia: catalogo*. Venice: Alfieri, 1950. 442 pp., ill. Text on Hepworth by David Lewis. Italian text. 59 works. Exhib. June–Oct. 1950.

246 *Exhibition of Works by John Constable, Matthew Smith, Barbara Hepworth*. London: British Council, 1950. Folded leaflet, [6] pp. Text on Hepworth by

David Lewis. 59 works. Organised by British Council for Venice Biennale, 1950. Exhib. June–Oct. 1950.

247 *Sculpture in the Home: Second Exhibition 1950–51*. London: Arts Council of Great Britain, 1950. [16] pp., ill. Introd. by Philip James. 2 works. Exhib. New Burlington Galleries, London, Aug.–Sept. 1950. Travelling throughout Britain to Aug. 1951.

248 *The Penwith Society of Arts in Cornwall: an Exhibition of Painting, Drawing, Sculpture and Crafts*. [Bristol]: Arts Council of Great Britain Western Region, 1950. [10] pp. Introd. by D. L. [David Lewis]. 2 works. Exhib. [Penwith Society of Arts, St. Ives, Nov.–Dec.] 1950.

249 *1950: Aspects of British Art*. London: Institute of Contemporary Arts, 1950. [4] pp. Introd. by Peter Watson. 2 works. Exhib. Dec. 1950–Jan. 1951.

250 *Ten Decades: a Review of British Taste 1851–1951*. London: Institute of Contemporary Arts, 1951. [68] pp. Introd. by Geoffrey Grigson. 1 work. A Festival of Britain exhib. organised by the Institute of Contemporary Arts by arrangement with the Arts Council of Great Britain. Exhib. 1951.

251 *Twenty-one Modern British Painters*. [London: British Council?], 1951. 17 pp. Introd. by Doris Shadbolt. 1 work. Organised by British Council in conjunction with Vancouver Art Gallery. Exhib. Vancouver Art Gallery, 1951. Travelling in U.S.A. and Canada.

252 *Some Recent Purchases of the Contemporary Art Society*. London: Arts Council of Great Britain, 1951. [18] pp. Introd. by Raymond Mortimer. 1 work. Exhib. Plymouth City Art Gallery, May–June 1951. Travelling throughout England to Dec. 1951.

253 *Sculpture: an Open Air Exhibition*. London: London County Council, 1951. [72] pp., ill. Introd. by Nikolaus Pevsner. Also condensed version, [16] pp. 1 work. Organised by London County Council and Arts Council of Great Britain. Exhib. Battersea Park, London, May–Sept. 1951.

254 *Penwith Society of Arts in Britain: Festival of Britain 1951*. St. Ives: Penwith Society of Arts, 1951. Folded leaflet, [4] pp. 5 works. Exhib. Fore Street, St. Ives, Summer 1951.

255 *Sculpture of the Twentieth Century*. New York: Museum of Modern Art, 1952. 47 pp. Introd. by Andrew Carnduff Ritchie. 1 work. Exhib. Philadelphia Museum of Art, Fairmount Park Art Association, Philadelphia, Oct.–Dec. 1952. Travelling to Art Institute of Chicago, Jan.–March 1953, Museum of Modern Art, New York, April–Sept. 1953. See also book of same title, 1953.

256 *International Sculpture Competition: The Unknown Political Prisoner: British Preliminary Exhibition*. London: Institute of Contemporary Arts, 1953. Leaflet, [4] pp. Introd. by A. J. T. Kloman. 1 work. Sponsored by Institute of Contemporary Arts. Exhib. New Burlington Galleries, London, Jan. 1953.

257 *International Sculpture Competition: The Unknown Political Prisoner: Internatio-*

nal Exhibition of Grand Prize Winner and Other Prize-winning Entries and Runners-up. London: Institute of Contemporary Arts, 1953. [24] pp., ill. Introd. by Anthony J. T. Kloman. 1 work. Sponsored by Institute of Contemporary Arts. Exhib. Tate Gallery, London, March–April 1953. (Hepworth, one of four runners-up, won prize of £750.)

258 *Sculpture in the Home: Third Exhibition 1953*. London: Arts Council of Great Britain, 1953. [16] pp., ill. Introd. by Philip James. 3 works. Exhib. Gloucester College of Art, May 1953. Travelling throughout Britain to May 1954.

259 *St. Ives Festival, Cornwall, of Music and the Arts*. [St. Ives: St. Ives Festival Council], 1953. 48 pp., ill. Text on art by David Lewis. Programme book for musical events, etc. Includes exhib. at Penwith Society of Arts. Organised in association with Arts Council of Great Britain. Festival held June 1953.

260 *2e biennale voor beeldhouwkunst*. Antwerp: Stad Antwerpen, 1953. 32 pp. Introd. by F. Baudouin. Dutch text. 1 work. Also separate French ed. Organised by City of Antwerp. Exhib. Middelheimpark, Antwerp, June–Sept. 1953.

261 *Sculpture in the Open Air: London County Council Third International Exhibition of Sculpture*. London: London County Council, 1954. [54] pp., ill. Introd. by Kenneth Clark. 1 work. Exhib. Holland Park, London, May–Sept. 1954.

262 *3 British Artists: Hepworth, Scott, Bacon*. New York: Martha Jackson Gallery, [1954]. Folded card, [6] pp., ill. 11 works. Exhib. Oct.–Nov. [1954].

263 *Paintings, Drawings and Sculpture: a Selection from the Arts Council Collection*. London: Arts Council of Great Britain, 1955. [36] pp. Introd. by Philip James. 1 work. Exhib. Arts Council Gallery, London, Jan.–Feb. 1955.

264 *Summer Exhibition*. London: Gimpel Fils, 1955. [4] pp. 4 works. Exhib. July–Aug. 1955.

265 *Documenta: Kunst des XX. Jahrhunderts*. Munich: Prestel-Verlag, 1955. [238] pp. Introd. by Werner Haftmann. German text. 3 works. Exhib. Museum Fridericianum, Kassel, July–Sept. 1955.

266 *Exposition internationale de sculpture contemporaine*. Paris: Musée Rodin, 1956. Exhib. 1956.

267 *The Seasons: an Exhibition of Painting and Sculpture Organised by the Contemporary Art Society*. London: [Tate Gallery], 1956. [10] pp. Introd. by Raymond Mortimer. 1 work. Exhib. Tate Gallery, London, March–April 1956.

268 *Some Contemporary British Sculpture*. London: Arts Council of Great Britain, 1956. Folded Card, [6] pp. 1 work. Organised by the Norwich 1956 Exhibition Committee in conjunction with the Aldeburgh Festival. Exhib. Red House, Aldeburgh, June 1956. Travelling to Castle Museum, Norwich, and other venues.

269 *Summer Exhibition*. London: Gimpel Fils, 1956. [4] pp. 2 works. Exhib. July–Aug. 1956.

270 *Barbara Hepworth, Ben Nicholson*. Newcastle upon Tyne: Hatton Gallery, 1956. Folded sheet, [10] pp., ill. Includes short texts by the artists. 21 works. Exhib. Dec. 1956.

271 *Statements: a Review of British Abstract Art in 1956*. London: Institute of Contemporary Arts, 1957. [16] pp. Introd. by Lawrence Alloway. Includes poem by Hepworth. 1 work. Exhib. Jan.–Feb. 1957.

272 *Contemporary British Sculpture*. London: Arts Council of Great Britain, 1957. 16 pp., ill. Introd. by Philip James. 1 work. Open air exhib. Castle Museum, Nottingham, May–June 1957. Travelling to Southampton, Cardiff, Penzance, Cheltenham Festival to Oct. 1957.

273 *Sculpture 1850 and 1950*. London: London County Council, 1957. [64] pp., ill. Introd. by Charles Wheeler. 1 work. Open air exhib. Holland Park, London, May–Sept. 1957.

274 *4e biennale voor beeldhouwkunst*. Antwerp: Stad Antwerpen, 1957. 43 pp., [27] pp. of plates. Introd. by Lode Craeybeckx. Dutch text. 1 work. Organised by City of Antwerp. Exhib. Middelheimpark, Antwerp, May–Sept. 1957.

275 *Henry Moore, Marino Marini, Barbara Hepworth, F. E. McWilliam, Epstein, Leon Underwood*. London: Zwemmer Gallery, 1957. [4] pp. 11 works. Exhib. June 1957.

276 *Summer Exhibition*. London: Gimpel Fils, 1957. [4] pp. 3 works. Exhib. July–Aug. 1957.

277 *The Penwith Society of Arts in Cornwall: a Selection of Paintings, Drawings, Sculpture & Pottery*. London: Arts Council of Great Britain, 1957. [8] pp. Introd. by P. J. [Philip James]. 3 works. Exhib. Laing Art Gallery, Newcastle upon Tyne, Nov.–Dec. 1957. Travelling throughout England to Nov. 1958.

278 *Internationale beeldententoonstelling Sonsbeek*. Arnhem: [Stichting Sonsbeek], 1958. Exhib. 1958.

279 *50 ans d'art moderne*. Brussels: Expositions Internationales des Beaux-Arts 1958, 1958. [122] pp., 220 pp. of plates. Introd. by Emile Langui. 1 work. Exhib. Palais International des Beaux-Arts, Brussels, April–July 1958. Also published in English as a book: *50 Years of Modern Art*, by Emile Langui. London: Thames and Hudson, 1959.

280 *Collectors' Choice VIII*. London: Gimpel Fils, 1958. [20] pp., ill. 1 work. Exhib. May 1958.

281 *Contemporary British Sculpture*. London: Arts Council of Great Britain, 1958. 19 pp., ill. Introd. by Elizabeth Davison. 1 work. Open air exhib. Leamington Spa, May–June 1958. Travelling to Shrewsbury Festival and Cardiff to Aug. 1958.

282 *A Private Exhibition of Contemporary British Paintings, Sculpture and Drawings*. [London: British Council?], 1958. [8] pp. 1 work. Exhib. British Embassy, Brussels, [Summer] 1958.

283 *Modern Sculpture: Kenneth Armitage, Ralph Brown, Barbara Hepworth, Henry*

Moore, Leslie Thornton. Leeds: Leeds City Art Gallery, 1958. 16 pp., 20 pp. of plates. 21 works. Exhib. Oct.–Nov. 1958.

284 *Sculpture in the Home: Fourth Exhibition 1958*. London: Arts Council of Great Britain, 1958. [16] pp., ill. 2 works. Exhib. Arts Council Gallery, Cambridge, Nov.–Dec. 1958. Travelling throughout Britain to July 1959.

285 *The 1958 Pittsburgh Bicentennial Exhibition of Contemporary Painting and Sculpture*. Pittsburgh: Carnegie Institute, 1958. [146] pp. Introd. by Gordon Bailey Washburn. 1 work. Exhib. Department of Fine Arts, Carnegie Institute, Dec. 1958–Feb. 1959.

286 *British Artist Craftsmen*. London: Ambassador Publishing, 1959. [68] pp., ill. 1 work. Exhib. circulated by the Smithsonian Institution, Washington. Travelling throughout U.S.A. 1959–1960.

287 *5e biennale voor beeldhouwkunst*. Antwerp: Stad Antwerpen, 1959. 63 pp., [24] pp. of plates. Parallel Dutch/French/English/German text. 5 works. Organised by City of Antwerp. Exhib. Middelheimpark, Antwerp, May–Sept. 1959.

288 *II. documenta '59: Kunst nach 1945: internationale Ausstellung. Band 2: Skulptur*. Cologne: M. DuMont Schauberg, 1959. 191 pp., ill. Introd. by Eduard Trier. German text. 3 works. Exhib. Orangerie, Kassel, July–Oct. 1959.

289 *Moments of Vision*. Rome: Rome-New York Art Foundation, 1959. [61] pp., ill. Introd. by Herbert Read. Parallel English/Italian text. Includes brief statement by Hepworth. Exhib. July–Nov. 1959.

290 *Paintings by Francis Bacon, Paintings and Etchings by S. W. Hayter, Sculptures and Drawings by Barbara Hepworth*. [London: British Council, 1959.] [33] pp. Text on Hepworth by J. P. Hodin. Parallel English/Portuguese/Spanish text. 35 works. Organised by British Council for Bienal de São Paulo, 1959. Exhib. Museu de Arte Moderna, São Paulo, Sept.–Dec. 1959.

291 *V Bienal do Museu de Arte Moderna de S. Paulo: catlogo geral*. São Paulo: Museu de Arte Moderna, 1959. 552 pp., ill. Introd. by Lourival Gomes Machado. Portuguese text. 35 works. Exhib. Sept.–Dec. 1959.

292 *Sculpture: Ten Modern Masters—Kenneth Armitage, Reg Butler, André Derain, Sir Jacob Epstein, Emilio Greco, Barbara Hepworth, Giacomo Manzu, Marino Marini, Bernard Meadows, Henry Moore*. Toronto: Laing Galleries, 1959. [28] pp., ill. Introd. by Herbert Read. 10 works. Exhib. Nov. 1959.

293 *Beeldententoonstelling Floriade*. Rotterdam: Museum Boymans-van Beuningen, 1960. [48] pp., ill. Dutch text. 2 works. Exhib. March–Sept. 1960.

294 *Contemporary British Sculpture*. London: Arts Council of Great Britain, 1960. [24] pp., ill. Introd. by Ronald Pickavance. 1 work. Open air exhib. Cannon Hill Park, Birmingham, April–May 1960. Travelling throughout Britain to Oct. 1960.

295 *Sculpture in the Open Air*. London: London County Council, 1960. [64] pp., ill. Introd. by Philip James. 1 work. Exhib. Battersea Park, London, May–Sept. 1960.

296 *Recent British Sculpture: Robert Adams, Kenneth Armitage, Reg Butler, Lynn Chadwick, Hubert Dalwood, Barbara Hepworth, Bernard Meadows, Henry Moore, Eduardo Paolozzi.* London: British Council, 1961. [35] pp., ill. Introd. by David Thompson. 12 works. Organised by British Council. Exhib. circulated in Canada by the National Gallery of Canada, Ottawa, 1960. Travelling to Australia and New Zealand to 1963.

297 *Design & Sculpture by Consagra, Hoflehner, Mullen, Perez, Piper, Ramous & Hepworth.* London: MacRoberts & Tunnard, 1961. [7] pp. 6 works. Exhib. Feb.–March 1961.

298 *Contemporary British Sculpture.* London: Arts Council of Great Britain, 1961. [16] pp., ill. Introd. by Ronald Pickavance. 1 work. Open air exhib. Cannon Hill Park, Birmingham, April–May 1961. Travelling throughout Britain to Sept. 1961.

299 *2ème exposition internationale de sculpture contemporaine.* Paris: Musée Rodin, 1961. [190] pp., ill. Introd. by Cécile Goldscheider. French text. 1 work. Exhib. [Summer] 1961.

300 *Sculpture 1961.* Cardiff: Arts Council of Great Britain Welsh Committee, 1961. [38] pp., ill. Introd. by Bryan Robertson. 8 works. Exhib. National Museum of Wales, Cardiff, July–Sept. 1961. Travelling to Swansea, Aberystwyth and Bangor to Nov. 1961.

301 *6e biennale voor beeldhouwkunst.* Antwerp: Stad Antwerpen, 1961. 56 pp., 24 pp. of plates. 3 works. Organised by City of Antwerp. Exhib. Middelheimpark, Antwerp, July–Oct. 1961.

302 *The 1961 Pittsburgh International Exhibition of Contemporary Painting and Sculpture.* Pittsburgh: Carnegie Institute, 1961. [100] pp., ill. Introd. by Gordon Bailey Washburn. 1 work. Exhib. Department of Fine Arts, Carnegie Institute, Oct. 1961–Jan. 1962.

303 *Collectors' Choice XI.* London: Gimpel Fils, 1962. 28 pp., ill. 1 work. Exhib. Jan. 1962.

304 *Contemporary British Sculpture.* London: Arts Council of Great Britain, 1962. [16] pp., ill. Introd. by Ronald Pickavance. 1 work. Open air exhib. Caerphilly Castle, Caerphilly, April–May 1962. Travelling throughout Britain to Sept. 1962.

305 *Small Sculpture.* London: Waddington Galleries, 1962. [15] pp., ill. 7 works. Exhib. July 1962.

306 *Aspects of Twentieth Century Art; Picasso—Important Paintings, Watercolours, and New Linocuts; Henry Moore—Recent Work, Life Drawings.* London: Marlborough Fine Art, 1962. [84] pp., ill. 1 work. Exhib. July–Aug. 1962.

307 *British Art and the Modern Movement 1930–40.* Cardiff: Welsh Committee of the Arts Council of Great Britain, 1962. 40 pp., ill. Introd. by Alan Bowness. 12 works. Exhib. National Museum of Wales, Cardiff, Oct.–Nov. 1962.

308 *International Exhibition and Sale of Contemporary Art.* London: O'Hana

Gallery, 1962. [57] pp. Introd. by Herbert Read. 3 works. Organised by Christian Action. Exhib. Nov. 1962.

309 *British Art Today*. San Francisco: San Francisco Museum of Art, 1962. [51] pp., ill. Introd. by Lawrence Alloway. 3 works. Exhib. Nov.–Dec. 1962. Travelling to Dallas and Santa Barbara to April 1963.

310 *Eröffnungs-Ausstellung*. Zürich: Gimpel & Hanover Galerie, 1962. [88] pp., ill. Parallel German/English text. 2 works. Exhib. Nov. 1962–Jan. 1963.

311 *The VII Tokyo Biennale 1963*. Tokyo: Mainichi Newspapers, 1963. [96] pp., ill. Parallel Janese/English text. 2 works. Exhib. 1963.

312 *Sculpture: Open-air Exhibition of Contemporary British and American Works*. London: London County Council, 1963. [62] pp., ill. Introd. by Herbert Read. 1 work. Exhib. Battersea Park, London, May–Sept. 1963.

313 *1er Salon International de Galeries Pilotes Lausanne*. Lausanne: Musée Cantonal des Beaux-Arts, 1963. 329 pp., ill. Introd. by René Berger. 1 work. Exhib. June–Sept. 1963.

314 *Englische Maler und Bildhauer*. Zürich: Gimpel Hanover Galerie, 1963. [48] pp., ill. 4 works. Exhib. Aug.–Sept. 1963.

315 *Contemporary British Sculpture*. London: Arts Council of Great Britain, 1964. [16] pp., ill. Introd. by Ronald Pickavance. 1 work. Open air exhib. Cannon Hill Park, Birmingham, April–May 1964. Travelling throughout England to Sept. 1964.

316 *54:64: Painting and Sculpture of a Decade*. 2nd rev. ed. London: [Calouste Gulbenkian Foundation], 1964. 276 pp., ill. 3 works. Organised by the Calouste Gulbenkian Foundation. Exhib. Tate Gallery, London, April–June 1964.

317 *Profile III—Englische Kunst der Gegenwart*. Bochum: Städtische Kunstgalerie Bochum, 1964. [86] pp., ill. Introd. by Herbert Read and Roland Penrose. German text. 5 works. Exhib. April–June 1964.

318 *London Group: 1914–1964 Jubilee Exhibition: Fifty Years of British Art*. London: [Tate Gallery], 1964. [36] pp., ill. Texts by Andrew Forge, Dennis Farr and Alan Bowness. 1 work. Exhib. July–Aug. 1964.

319 *1964 Autumn Arts Festival*. Bromsgrove (Worcs.): Stoke Prior Brushworks, 1964. [40] pp., ill. 1 work. Exhib. Oct. 1964.

320 *The 1964 Pittsburgh International Exhibition of Contemporary Painting and Sculpture*. Pittsburgh: Carnegie Institute, 1964. [88] pp. Introd. by Gustave von Groschwitz. 1 work. Exhib. Museum of Art, Carnegie Institute, Oct. 1964–Jan. 1965.

321 *Sculpture from the Arts Council Collection*. London: Arts Council of Great Britain, 1965. [28] pp., ill. Introd. by David Thompson. 1 work. Travelling exhib. 1965.

322 *British Sculpture in the Sixties*. London: [Tate Gallery], 1965. [28] pp., ill. Introd. by James Melvin, Bryan Robertson and Alan Bowness. 5 works.

Organised by the Contemporary Art Society in association with the Peter Stuyvesant Foundation. Exhib. Tate Gallery, London, Feb.–April 1965.

323 *Art in Britain 1930–40 Centred around Axis, Circle, Unit One.* London: Marlborough Fine Art, 1965. 92 pp., ill. Texts by Herbert Read, Jasia Reichardt. Includes statement by Hepworth (from *Unit 1*, 1934). 20 works. Exhib. March–April 1965.

324 *Collectors' Choice XIII.* London: Gimpel Fils, 1965. [32] pp., ill. 3 works. Exhib. March–April 1965.

325 *5 British Sculptors (Work and Talk).* New York: IBM Gallery, 1965. Folded poster, [8] pp., ill. 6 works. Exhib. March–April 1965. See also book of same title by Warren Forma, 1964.

326 *Contemporary British Sculpture.* London: Arts Council of Great Britain, 1965. [16] pp., ill. Introd. by Ronald Pickavance. 1 work. Open air exhib. Cannon Hill Park, Birmingham, April–May 1965. Travelling throughout England to Sept. 1965.

327 *The Marlborough Exhibition Summer 1965.* London: Marlborough Fine Art, 1965. 4 pp. 5 works. Exhib. Summer 1965.

328 *Panathenées de la sculpture internationale: la première exposition internationale de sculpture.* Athens: Office Nationale du Tourisme Hellénique, 1965. [12] pp. 2 works. Exhib. Athens, Sept.–Nov. 1965.

329 *The English Eye.* New York: Marlborough-Gerson Gallery, 1965. 131 pp., ill. Introd. by Robert Melville and Bryan Robertson. 6 works. Exhib. Nov.–Dec. 1965.

330 *Sculpture in the Open Air.* London: Greater London Council, 1966. [56] pp., ill. Introd. by Alan Bowness. 3 works. Exhib. Battersea Park, London, May–Sept. 1966.

331 *5e internationale beeldententoonstelling Sonsbeek '66.* Arnhem: [Stichting Sonsbeek], 1966. 110 pp., ill. Introd. by H. L. C. Jaffé. Dutch text. 4 works. Open air exhib. Sonsbeek, Arnhem, May–Sept. 1966.

332 *Metamorphosis: Figure into Abstract: the Sir Alfred Herbert Centenary Exhibition.* Coventry: Herbert Art Gallery, 1966. 32 pp., ill. Text by Mervyn Levy. 4 works. Exhib. Sept.–Oct. 1966.

333 *Reliefs, Sculpture.* London: Marlborough Fine Art, 1966. [16] pp., ill. 3 works. Exhib. Sept.–Oct. 1966.

334 *Contemporary Sculpture.* London: Gimpel Fils, 1967. [20] pp., ill. 6 works. Exhib. Feb.–March 1967.

335 *Outdoor Sculpture.* London: Arts Council of Great Britain, 1967. [16] pp., ill. Introd. by Andrew Dempsey. 3 works. Exhib. Cannon Hill Park, Birmingham, April–May 1967. Travelling to Norwich and Northampton to July 1967.

336 *Dix ans d'art vivant 1955–1965.* Saint-Paul de Vence: Fondation Maeght, 1967. [96] pp., ill. Introd. by François Wehrlin. 2 works. Exhib. May–July 1967.

337 *Collectors' Choice XIV*. London: Gimpel Fils, 1967. [19] pp., ill. 4 works. Exhib. June 1967.

338 *Sculpture: exposition internationale de sculpture contemporaine = International Exhibition of Contemporary Sculpture*. Montreal: [Expo 67], 1967. [120] pp., ill. Introd. by Guy Robert. Parallel French/English text. Exhib. Expo 67, Montreal, Summer 1967.

339 *Recent Acquisitions*. London: Marlborough Fine Art, 1967. [44] pp., ill. 3 works. Exhib. July–Aug. 1967.

340 *1967 Pittsburgh International Exhibition of Contemporary Painting and Sculpture*. Pittsburgh: Carnegie Institute, 1967. [80] pp., ill. Introd. by Gustave von Groschwitz. 1 work. Exhib. Museum of Art, Carnegie Institute, Oct. 1967–Jan. 1968.

341 *Guggenheim International Exhibition 1967: Sculpture from Twenty Nations*. New York: Solomon R. Guggenheim Museum, 1967. 148 pp., ill. Introd. by Edward F. Fry. 1 work. Exhib. Oct. 1967–Feb. 1968. Travelling to Toronto, Ottawa and Montreal to Aug. 1968.

342 *L'art vivant 1965–1968*. Saint-Paul de Vence: Fondation Maeght, 1968. [140] pp., ill. Introd. by François Wehrlin. 1 work. Exhib. April–June 1968.

343 *British Sculpture/Bristol*. Bristol: City Art Gallery, 1968. [15] pp., ill. 3 works. Exhib. June 1968.

344 *Exhibition of British Sculpture*. [Oxford]: Pergamon Press, 1968. 32 pp., ill. Introd. by Mario Amaya. Text on Hepworth by Edwin Mullins (reprinted from *Sculpture International*, No. 4, 1967). 4 works. Exhib. Coventry Cathedral, June–Aug. 1968.

345 *Sculpture in the City: City of London Festival*. London: City of London Festival Committee, 1968. Folded leaflet, [8] pp. 8 works. Open air exhib. in City of London, 9 July 1968.

346 *Recent Acquisitions 1968*. London: Marlborough Fine Art, 1968. [36] pp., ill. 4 works. Exhib. July–Aug. 1968.

347 *Bernard Leach, Barbara Hepworth*. St. Ives: St. Ives Council, 1968. Folder containing leaflet, [4] pp. ill., and separate exhibition catalogues for Leach and Hepworth, each [20] pp., ill. [53] works. On occasion of conferment of Honorary Freedom of the Borough on Bernard Leach and Barbara Hepworth. Exhibs. Guildhall, Public Library, Penwith Gallery, Parish Churchyard, Trewyn Studios, etc., St. Ives, Sept.–Oct. 1968.

348 *Collectors' Choice*. New York: Gimpel & Weitzenhoffer, 1969. [42] pp., ill. 4 works. Exhib. Gimpel Gallery, New York, March 1969.

349 *A Selection of 20th Century British Art*. London: Marlborough Fine Art, 1969. [96] pp., ill. 3 works. Exhib. Cunard Marlborough London Gallery, on board Queen Elizabeth 2, [May 1969].

350 *St. Ives Group: 2nd Exhibition: 1969 Bath Festival*. Bath: Festival Gallery, 1969. [4] pp. 5 works. Open air exhib. Bath Festival, June 1969.

351 *Open Air Sculpture at Syon Park*. London: Gimpel Fils, 1969. Folded leaflet,

[6] pp., ill. 3 works. Organised by Gimpel Fils. Exhib. Syon Park, London, Summer 1969.

352 *Sculpture and Reliefs.* London: Gimpel Fils, 1969. [24] pp., ill. 3 works. Exhib. June–Aug. 1969.

353 *10e biennale Middelheim Antwerpen.* Antwerp: Stad Antwerpen, Kunsthistorische Musea, 1969. 154 pp., ill. 4 works. Exhib. Openluchtmuseum voor Beeldhouwkunst, Middelheimpark, Antwerp, [June–Oct.] 1969.

354 *An Exhibition of Outdoor Sculpture at Blenheim Palace Garden Centre.* 6 pp. duplicated typescript. [1 work]. Organised by Oxford Gallery, Oxford, in collaboration with Annely Juda Fine Art, London. Exhib. July–Sept. 1969.

355 *The First International Exhibition of Modern Sculpture.* Hakone: Hakone Open-Air Museum, 1969. c.[200] pp., ill. Mainly Japanese text. 2 works. Exhib. Aug.–Oct. 1969.

356 *Yedi Ingiliz heykelstrasi = Seven British Sculptors: Robert Adams, Kenneth Armitage, Lynn Chadwick, Hubert Dalwood, Barbara Hepworth, Bernard Meadows, Henry Moore.* [London: British Council, 1970]? [50] pp., ill. Turkish and English texts. 3 works. Organised by British Council and Turco-British Association. Exhib. Ankara and Istanbul, [1970].

357 *Gallery Choice.* London: Gimpel Fils, 1970. [26] pp., ill. 2 works. Exhib. March–April 1970.

358 *Open Air Sculpture II.* London: Gimpel Fils, 1970. [46] pp., ill. 5 works. Exhib. Syon Park, London, Summer 1970.

359 *Les Ves semaines internationales de la femme.* [Nice]: Salon International de la Femme, 1970. [30] pp., ill. French text. Includes small Hepworth retrospective in honour of the award of Grand Prix International de l'Art Féminin 1970. 10 works. Exhib. on occasion of Ve Salon International de la Femme, Nice, Oct. 1970.

360 *British Painting and Sculpture 1960–1970.* London: Tate Gallery, 1970. 124 pp., ill. Introd. by Edward Lucie-Smith. 1 work. Organised by Tate Gallery and British Council. Exhib. National Gallery of Art, Washington, Nov. 1970–Jan. 1971.

361 *Helen Sutherland Collection: a Pioneer Collection of the 1930s.* London: Arts Council of Great Britain, 1970. 26 pp. Introd. by Nicolete Gray. 7 works. Exhib. Hayward Gallery, London, Dec. 1970–Jan. 1971. Travelling to Newcastle upon Tyne, Cambridge, Cardiff and Kendal to May 1971.

362 *Masters of the 20th Century.* New York: Marlborough Gallery, 1971. 164 pp., ill. 1 work. Exhib. 1971.

363 *A Tribute to Samuel J. Zacks from the Sam and Ayala Zacks Collection.* Toronto: Art Gallery of Ontario, 1971. c.[300] pp., ill. Introd. by Ayala Zacks. Texts by Robert Welsh, Mario Amaya, Theodore Allen Heinrich. 3 works. Exhib. May–June 1971. Travelling to National Gallery of Canada, Ottawa, Aug. 1971.

364 *The Non-objective World 1924–1939.* Milan: Electa, 1971. 167 pp., ill. Introd.

by Eckhard Newman. Parallel English/French/Italian text. 5 works. Exhib. Galerie Jean Chauvelin, Paris, June 1971. Travelling to Annely Juda Fine Art, London, July–Sept. 1971; Galleria Milano, Milan, Oct.–Nov. 1971.

365 *IVe exposition internationale de sculpture contemporaine.* Paris: Musée Rodin, 1971. [126] pp., ill. Introd. by Giuseppe Marchiori. 1 work. Exhib. [Summer] 1971.

366 *Gillian Ayres. . .[et al]: [Graphics from Editions Alecto London].* Athens: Desmos Gallery, 1971. [24] pp., ill. Introd. by Charles Spencer. Parallel Greek/English text. 4 works. Exhib. Nov.–Dec. 1971.

367 *Cent dessins du Musée Kröller-Müller.* Paris: Institut Néerlandais, 1971. [142] pp., ill. Introd. by R. W. D. Oxenaar. Parallel Dutch/French text. 3 works. Exhib. Dec. 1971–Jan. 1972.

368 *Who are You: the Human Form in Primitive and Modern Art.* London: Gimpel Fils, 1972. Folded leaflet, [14] pp. 1 work. Exhib. March–April 1972.

369 *Masters of the 19th and 20th Centuries.* London: Marlborough Fine Art, 1972. 196 pp., ill. 3 works. Exhib. Summer 1972.

370 *The Non-objective World 1939–1955.* [London: Annely Juda Fine Art], 1972. 197 pp., ill. Text by George Rickey. Parallel English/German/Italian text. 1 work. Exhib. Annely Juda Fine Art, London, July–Sept. 1972. Travelling to Galerie Liatowitsch, Basle, Sept.–Oct. 1972, and Galleria Milano, Milan, Nov.–Dec. 1972.

371 *Painting, Sculpture and Drawing in Britain 1940–49.* London: Arts Council of Great Britain, 1972. 51 pp., ill. Introd. by Alan Bowness. 8 works. Exhib. Whitechapel Art Gallery, London, Nov. 1972. Travelling throughout Britain to June 1973.

372 *Master Sculptors of the 20th Century.* London: Gimpel Fils, 1973. [42] pp., ill. 1 work. Exhib. Jan.–March 1973.

373 *Selected European Masters of the 19th and 20th Centuries.* London: Marlborough Fine Art, 1973. 170 pp., ill. 3 works. Exhib. Summer 1973.

374 *The Private Collection of Martha Jackson.* College Park (Md.): [University of Maryland Art Gallery], 1973. 47 pp. Introd. by Elayne H. Varian. 1 work. Exhib. University of Maryland Art Gallery, College Park, June–Sept. 1973. Travelling to Finch College Museum of Art, New York, and Albright-Knox Art Gallery, Buffalo to Feb. 1974.

375 *The Non-objective World 1914–1955.* London: Annely Juda Fine Art, 1973. 191 pp., ill. Introd. by Margit Staber. Parallel English/German text. Exhib. July–Sept. 1973. Travelling to University Art Museum, University of Texas, Austin, Oct.–Dec. 1973.

376 *Henry Moore to Gilbert & George: Modern British Art from the Tate Gallery.* London: Tatc Gallcry, 1973. 143 pp., ill. Text by Anne Seymour. 7 works. Organised for Europalia 73 Great Britain by the Tate Gallery in co-operation with the British Council. Exhib. Palais des Beaux-Arts, Brussels, Sept.–Nov. 1973.

377 *Twelve Views of Mankind.* Stirling: MacRobert Centre Art Gallery, University of Stirling, 1974. [32] pp., ill. Text by Douglas Hall. 1 work. Exhib. March–April 1974.

378 *Art Then: Eight English Artists 1924–1940.* Edinburgh: Scottish Arts Council, 1974. [48] pp., ill. Text by David Baxandall. 11 works. Exhib. Scottish Arts Council Gallery, Edinburgh, Aug.–Sept. 1974.

379 *Twentieth Century Monumental Sculpture.* New York: Marlborough Gallery, 1974. 57 pp., ill. 2 works. Exhib. Oct.–Nov. 1974.

380 *Hampstead in the Thirties: a Committed Decade.* London: Hampstead Artists' Council in co-operation with Arkwright Arts Trust, 1974. 64 pp. Introd. by Jeanette Jackson. Texts by J. P. Hodin *et al.* 6 works. Exhib. Camden Arts Centre, London, Nov. 1974–Jan. 1975.

381 *The Artist and the Book in France: from Matisse to Vasarely; and Barbara Hepworth Sculpture and Lithographs.* Folkestone: New Metropole Arts Centre, [1974]. [18] pp., ill. 20 works. Hepworth works by courtesy of Marlborough Fine Art, London. Exhib. [Dec. 1974–Feb. 1975].

382 *Four British Sculptors: Adams, Hepworth, Meadows and Moore.* New York: Gimpel Weitzenhoffer, 1975. [4] pp. duplicated typescript. 7 works. Exhib. April–May 1975.

383 *Sculptures in a Landscape: Large Abstract Sculptures Selected for their Appropriateness to a Landscape Setting.* London: Greater London Council, [1975]. Folded poster, [8] pp., ill. Introd. by Ellis Hillman. 1 work. Exhib. Marble Hill House, London, Aug.–Sept. 1975.

384 *Masterworks in Wood: the Twentieth Century.* Portland (Or.): Portland Art Museum, 1975. [112] pp., ill. Introd. by Jan van der Mark. 1 work. Exhib. Sept.–Oct. 1975.

385 *The Martha Jackson Collection at the Albright-Knox Art Gallery.* Buffalo (N.Y.): Albright-Knox Art Gallery, 1975. 47 pp., ill. Text by Linda L. Cathcart. 1 work. Exhib. Nov. 1975–Jan. 1976.

386 *Graphics '76: Britain.* Lexington (Ky.): University of Kentucky Art Gallery, 1976. 38 pp., ill. Introd. by Pat Gilmour. 4 works. Exhib. dedicated to late Dame Barbara Hepworth. Exhib. Feb.–March 1976. Travelling throughout U.S.A.

387 *Sculpture for the Blind: an Exhibition for the Blind and Partially Sighted.* London: Tate Gallery, 1976. [8] pp. Introd. by Terry Measham. 1 work. Exhib. Nov.–Dec. 1976.

388 *Artists at Curwen: a Celebration of the Gift of Artists' Prints from the Curwen Studio*, by Pat Gilmour. London: Tate Gallery, 1977. 167 pp., ill. 3 works. Exhib. Feb.–April 1977.

389 *Silver Jubilee Exhibition of Contemporary British Sculpture, Battersea Park, in microcosm.* London: Redfern Gallery, 1977. Card, [2] p. 1 work. Exhib. June–July 1977.

390 *A Silver Jubilee Exhibition of Contemporary British Sculpture.* London: Greater

London Council, 1977. [118] pp., ill. Texts by William Packer, Bryan Robertson, Barry Martin. 1 work. Exhib. Battersea Park, London, June–Sept. 1977.

391 *Englische Kunst der Gegenwart.* Bregenz (Austria): Verein Bregenzer Kunstausstellungen, 1977. 306 pp., ill. Introd. by Norbert Lynton. Parallel German/English text. 9 works. Exhib. Künstlerhaus Bregenz, July–Oct. 1977.

392 *Carved, Modelled, Constructed: Three Aspects of British 20th Century Sculpture.* London: Tate Gallery, 1977. Broadsheet, [6] pp. Text by Sandy Nairne. Exhib. Dec. 1977–Feb. 1978.

393 *Groups.* London: Waddington and Tooth Galleries, 1978. [24] pp. Exhib. April 1978.

394 *Abstraction-création 1931–1936.* Münster: Westfalisches Landesmuseum für Kunst und Kulturgeschichte des Landschaftsverbandes Westfalen-Lippe, 1978. 309 pp., ill. Introd. by Gladys C. Fabre. Parallel German/French text. 2 works. Exhib. April–June 1978. Travelling to Musée d'Art Moderne de la Ville de Paris, June–Sept. 1978.

395 *Masters of Modern Sculpture.* New York: Marlborough Gallery, 1978. 43 pp., ill. 3 works. Exhib. May–June 1978.

396 *Unit 1: Based on the 1934 Unit One Exhibition held at the Mayor Gallery.* Portsmouth: Portsmouth City Museum and Art Gallery, 1978. 37 pp., ill. Introd. by Charles Harrison. Text on Hepworth by Alan Bowness. 5 works. Exhib. May–July 1978.

397 *The Pier Gallery, Stromness Orkney.* Stromness: Pier Arts Centre Trust, 1978. 64 pp., ill. Texts by Patrick Heron, Alan Bowness. 13 works. Works from the collection of the Pier Gallery, Stromness. Exhib. Tate Gallery, London, Sept.–Oct. 1978. Travelling to Aberdeen and Glasgow to Feb. 1979.

398 *Eröffnungs-Ausstellung = Opening Exhibition [Barbara Hepworth, Ben Nicholson, Jürg Altherr].* Zürich: Gimpel-Hanover & André Emmerich Galerien, 1978. Cards and leaflet, [10] pp., ill. German and English text. 9 works. Exhib. Nov. 1978–Jan. 1979.

399 *Groups II.* London: Waddington Galleries, 1979. [32] pp., ill. 2 works. Exhib. Jan.–Feb. 1979.

400 *Modern European Sculpture, 1918–1945: Unknown Beings and Other Realities,* by Albert E. Elsen. New York: Braziller, 1979. 192 pp., ill. 2 works. Exhib. Albright-Knox Art Gallery, Buffalo, N.Y., May–June 1979. Travelling to Minneapolis and San Francisco to Nov. 1979.

401 *Groups III.* London: Waddington Galleries, 1980. [47] pp., ill. 1 work. Exhib. Feb.–March 1980.

402 *Abstraction 1910–1940.* London: Annely Juda Fine Art, 1980. 87 pp., ill. 1 work. Exhib. July–Sept. 1980.

403 *Klassische Moderne = The Classical Moderns.* Cologne: Galerie Gmurzynska,

1981. 272 pp., ill. Text by Hiltrud Jordan. Parallel German/English text. 8 works. Exhib. May–Aug. 1981.

404 *Westkunst: zeitgenössische Kunst seit 1939*, von Laszlo Glozer. Cologne: DuMont, 1981. 524 pp., ill. German text. 1 work. Organised by Museen der Stadt Köln. Exhib. [May–Aug.] 1981.

405 *Sculpture du XXe siècle 1900–1945: tradition et ruptures*. Saint-Paul de Vence: Fondation Maeght, 1981. [226] pp., ill. Introd. by Jean-Louis Prat. 2 works. Exhib. July–Oct. 1981. Travelling to Fundación Juan March, Madrid, Oct.–Dec. 1981.

406 *British Sculpture in the Twentieth Century. Part 1: Image and Form 1901–1950*. London: Whitechapel Art Gallery, 1981. [6] pp. 16 works. Exhib. Sept.–Nov. 1981. See also book of same title, 1981.

407 *British Sculpture in the Twentieth Century. Part 2: Symbol and imagination 1951–1980*. London: Whitechapel Art Gallery, 1981. [8] pp. 4 works. Exhib. Nov. 1981–Jan. 1982. See also book of same title, 1981.

408 *Circle: Constructive Art in Britain 1934–40*. Cambridge: Kettle's Yard Gallery, 1982. 88 pp., ill. Introd. by Leslie Martin. Essays by Jane Beckett *et al.* 3 works. Exhib. Feb.–March 1982.

409 *Sculpture at Margam: Maquettes for Public Sculpture*. Cardiff: Welsh Sculpture Trust, 1982. [8] pp. Text by Shelagh Hourahane. 1 work. Exhib. Margam Sculpture Park, Margam, [Aug.–Oct.] 1982.

410 *Sculpture*. London: Waddington Galleries, 1982. 35 pp. 1 work. Exhib. Sept.–Oct. 1982.

411 *Britain Salutes New York: Paintings and Sculpture by Contemporary British Artists*. New York: Marlborough Gallery, 1983. 24 pp., ill. 2 works. Exhib. April–May 1983.

412 *Masters of the 19th and 20th Centuries*. New York: Marlborough Gallery, 1983. [107] pp., ill. 2 works. Exhib. May–June 1983.

413 *The Nicholsons: Work by Sir William Nicholson, Ben Nicholson, Winifred (Dacre) Nicholson, Dame Barbara Hepworth . . . [et al]*. London: Crane Kalman Gallery, 1983. 28 pp., ill. Introd. by A. K. [Andras Kalman]. 6 works. Exhib. June–July 1983.

414 *Sculpture in a Country Park: an Outdoor Exhibition in the Grounds of Margam*. Cardiff: Welsh Sculpture Trust, 1983. 156 pp., ill. Introd. by Gordon Young. Texts by Moelwyn Merchant and Rudolf W. D. Oxenaar. Parallel Welsh/English text. Exhib. Margam Sculpture Park, Margam, [June 1983–June 1984].

415 *Groups VII*. London: Waddington Galleries, 1984. 80 pp., ill. 1 work. Exhib. Jan. 1984.

416 *Unit One: Spirit of the 30s: an Exhibition to Celebrate the Half Century of the First Unit One Exhibition Held at the Mayor Gallery in Cork Street, April 1934*. London: Mayor Gallery, 1984. 56 pp., ill. Text by Mark Glazebrook. 3 works. Exhib. May–June 1984.

417 *Creation: Modern Art and Nature*. Edinburgh: National Galleries of Scotland, 1984. 112 pp., ill. Introd. by Douglas Hall and Keith Hartley. 1 work. Exhib. Scottish National Gallery of Modern Art, Edinburgh, Aug.–Oct. 1984.

418 *St. Ives 1939–64: Twenty Five Years of Painting, Sculpture and Pottery*. London: Tate Gallery, 1985. 248 pp., ill. Selected by David Brown. Essay by David Lewis. 25 works. Exhib. Feb.–April 1985.

419 *British Artists in Italy 1920–1980: Rome & Abbey Scholars*. [Canterbury]: Kent County Council Education Committee, 1985. 55 pp., ill. Texts by Penelope Curtis, Alan Powers and Roger Mills. 2 works. Organised by Canterbury College of Art for Canterbury Fringe Festival 1985. Exhib. Herbert Read Gallery, Canterbury College of Art, Sept.–Oct. 1985, and travelling.

420 *Sculpture in Britain between the Wars*. London: Fine Art Society, 1986. 157 pp., ill. Introd. by Benedict Read and Peyton Skipwith. Exhib. June–Aug. 1986.

421 *Two Sculptors and Two Potters: [Barbara Hepworth, Henry Moore, Hans Coper, Lucie Rie]*. Middlesbrough: Cleveland County Museum Service, 1986. Folded card, [8] pp., ill. Text by Edward Lucie-Smith. 8 works. Exhib. Cleveland Gallery, Middlesbrough, Oct.–Nov. 1986.

422 *Masters of the 19th and 20th Centuries*. New York: Marlborough Gallery, 1986. [100] pp., ill. 3 works. Exhib. Nov.–Dec. 1986.

423 *Revelation for the Hands*. Leeds: Henry Moore Centre for the Study of Sculpture, 1987. [47] pp., ill. Introd. by Adam White. 1 work. Exhibition for the blind and partially sighted, organised by Henry Moore Centre for the Study of Sculpture. Exhib. Leeds City Art Gallery, Jan.–March 1987. Travelling to Mead Gallery, University of Warwick Arts Centre, April–May 1987.

424 *British Art in the 20th Century: the Modern Movement*, edited by Susan Compton. London: Royal Academy of Arts; Munich: Prestel, 1987. 458 pp., ill. Texts by Dawn Ades *et al.* 8 works. Exhib. Royal Academy, London, Jan.–April 1987.

425 *A Century of Modern Sculpture: the Patsy and Raymond Nasher Collection*, edited by Steven A. Nash. New York: Rizzoli, 1987. 208 pp., ill. Texts by Elizabeth Frank *et al.* 1 work. Exhib. Dallas Museum of Art, April–May 1987. Travelling to National Gallery of Art, Washington, June 1987–Jan. 1988.

426 *A Selection of Important Sculpture*. London: Marlborough Fine Art, 1988. 68 pp., ill. 2 works. Exhib. June–Aug. 1988.

427 *The Non-objective World Revisited*. London: Annely Juda Fine Art, 1988. 103 pp., ill. Introd. by Stephen Bann. 2 works. Exhib. July–Oct. 1988.

428 *Modern British Sculpture from the Collection*. Liverpool: Tate Gallery Publications, 1988. 144 pp., ill. Text by Penelope Curtis. 9 works. Works from the collection of Tate Gallery, London. Exhib. Tate Gallery, Liverpool, Sept. 1988, for 3 years.

429 *100 Years of Art in Britain: an Exhibition to Celebrate the Centenary of Leeds City Art Gallery*. Leeds: Leeds City Art Gallery, 1988. 123 pp., ill. Text by Frances Spalding. 1 work. Exhib. Oct. 1988–Jan. 1989.

430 *Sculptures, Reliefs and Drawings*. London: Gimpel Fils, 1989. [39] pp., ill. 3 works. Exhib. June–Sept. 1989.

431 *A Century of Art in Cornwall 1889–1989*. Truro: Cornwall County Council, 1989. [24] pp. Introd. by John Halkes. 2 works. Organised by Newlyn Orion Galleries, *Part 1: An Historical Perspective*. Exhib. County Hall, Truro, Sept.–Oct. 1989.

432 *British Modernism: Henry Moore and his Circle of Hampstead in the Thirties*. Leeds: [Fine Art Department, Leeds University], 1990. [44] pp. Introd. by Terry Friedman. 1 work. Organised by B.A. Honours students, Fine Art Department, Leeds University. Exhib. Leeds City Art Gallery, Feb.–Aug. 1990.

433 *British Art from 1930*. London: Waddington Galleries, 1991. 73 pp., ill. 1 work. Exhib. Feb.–March 1991.

434 *The Marlborough Gallery Re-opening Exhibition*. London: Marlborough Fine Art, 1991. 48 pp., ill. Exhib. April–May 1991.

435 *International Sculpture*. London: Marlborough Fine Art, [1991]. [15] plates in folder, ill. 2 works. Exhib. [July–Aug. 1991].

436 *Ten Decades: Careers of Ten Women Artists born 1897–1906: Mary Adshead, Eileen Agar, Emmy Bridgwater, Evelyn Gibbs, Barbara Hepworth, Gertrude Hermes, Lilian Holt, Sylvia Melland, Betty Rea, Nan Youngman*. Norwich: Norwich Gallery, Norfolk Institute of Art and Design, 1992. [43] pp., ill. Introd. by Katy Deepwell. 3 works. Exhib. March–May 1992.

437 *Modern Sculpture*. New York: Marlborough Gallery, 1992. [68] pp., ill. 3 works. Exhib. Sept.–Nov. 1992.

438 *Partners*. London: Annely Juda Fine Art, 1993. [79] pp., ill. Introd. by Mel Gooding. 2 works. Exhib. June–Sept. 1993.

439 *Works on Paper and Sculpture*. London: Waddington Galleries, 1993. 108 pp., ill. 2 works. Exhib. Sept.–Oct. 1993.

440 *Herbert Read: a British Vision of World Art*, edited by Benedict Read and David Thistlewood. Leeds: Leeds City Art Galleries in association with Henry Moore Foundation; London: Lund Humphries, 1993. 182 pp., ill. Introd. by Alan Bowness. 6 works. Exhib. Leeds City Art Gallery, Nov. 1993–Feb. 1994.

441 *Modern Paintings*. London: Jonathan Clark & Co., 1994. 38 pp., ill. 1 work. Exhib. Summer 1994.

442 *British & French Paintings, Drawings & Sculpture: 17th Annual Exhibition*. London: Browse & Darby, 1994. [61] pp., ill. 1 work. Exhib. July–Aug. 1994.

6. ARTICLES FROM PERIODICALS

443 'London Exhibitions'. *Drawing & Design* Vol. 4, [No. 6, June] 1928. Includes review of group exhib. with Morgan and Skeaping, Beaux-Arts Gallery, June 1928, p. 199.

444 G. A. Jellicoe. 'Modern British Sculpture'. *Studio* Vol. 99, Jan. 1930, pp. 27–31.

445 John Grierson. 'The New Generation in Sculpture'. *Apollo* Vol. 12, No. 71, Nov. 1930, pp. 347–51.

446 Louise Gordon-Stables. 'London Letter'. *Art News* Vol. 29, No. 6, 8 Nov. 1930. Includes review of exhib. with Skeaping, Tooths' Galleries, Oct.–Nov. 1930, p. 23.

447 F. G. R. 'Let's be Modern!' *Connoisseur* Vol. 86, No. 352, Dec. 1930, p. 413. Review of exhib. with Skeaping, Tooths' Galleries, Oct.–Nov. 1930.

448 Paul Nash. 'A Painter and a Sculptor'. *Week-End Review*, 19 Nov. 1932, p. 613. Review of exhib. with Nicholson, Tooths' Galleries, Nov.–Dec. 1932.

449 'Barbara Hepworth'. *Abstraction-création: art non-figuratif*, No. 2, 1933, p. 6. Illustrations only.

450 Herbert Read. 'Unit One'. *Architectural Review* Vol. 74, Oct. 1933, pp. 125–28.

451 Adrian Stokes. 'Miss Hepworth's Carvings'. *Spectator*, 3 Nov. 1933, p. 621. Review of exhib. with Nicholson, Lefevre Gallery, Oct.–Nov. 1933. Reprinted in book *The Critical Writings of Adrian Stokes*, 1978.

452 'Hepworth 1933'. *Abstraction-création: art non-figuratif*, No. 3, 1934, p. 23. Illustrations only.

453 H. Frankfort. 'New Works by Barbara Hepworth'. *Axis: a Quarterly Review of Contemporary 'Abstract' Painting and Sculpture*, No. 3, July 1935, pp. 14–18.

454 J. M. Richards. 'London Shows: Ben Nicholson at the Lefevre; 7 & 5 at Zwemmer's'. *Axis: a Quarterly Review of Contemporary 'Abstract' Painting and Sculpture*, No. 4, Nov. 1935, pp. 21–24. Includes comments on Hepworth, p. 24.

455 S. John Woods. 'Zwemmer Gallery: 7 & 5 14th Exhibition'. *Decoration*, 7 Nov. 1935, p. 39.

456 Naum Gabo. 'Constructive Art'. *Listener* Vol. 16, No. 408, 4 Nov. 1936, pp. 846–48.

457 William Gibson. 'Art: Barbara Hepworth'. *London Mercury* Vol. 37, No. 217, Nov. 1937, pp. 57–58. Review of exhib. Lefevre Gallery, Oct. 1937.

458 Herbert Read. 'L'art contemporain en Angleterre'. *Cahiers d'art* Vol. 13, Nos. 1–2, 1938, pp. 29–42.

459 Herbert Read. 'Three English Sculptors'. *XXe siècle* Vol. 2, No. 1 (supplement to Vol. 1, Nos. 5/6), 1939, p. 45. English edition. Reprinted in French in new series, Vol. 21, No. 13, Christmas 1959, pp. 42–43.

460 'Art Out-of-Doors'. *Architectural Review* Vol. 85, April 1939, pp. 200–01.

461 E. H. Ramsden. '[Temple Newsam Exhibitions]: II—Barbara Hepworth: Sculptor'. *Horizon* Vol. 7, No. 42, June 1943, pp. 418–22.

462 E. H. Ramsden. 'The Sculpture of Barbara Hepworth'. *Polemic* (London), No. 5, Sept.–Oct. 1946, pp. 33–34 and 4 pp. of plates.

463 Wyndham Lewis. 'Moore and Hepworth'. *Listener* Vol. 36, No. 927, 17 Oct. 1946, pp. 505–06. Reprinted in book *Wyndham Lewis on Art*, 1969.

464 Denys Sutton. 'Femmes peintres'. *Arts, beaux-arts, littérature, spectacles* (Paris) No. 95, 29 Nov. 1946, p. 3. Includes brief review of exhib. Lefevre Gallery, Oct. 1946.

465 William Gibson. 'Art: Two English Sculptors'. *Britain Today* No. 129, Jan. 1947, pp. 30–31.

466 J. P. Hodin. 'Les oeuvres récentes de Barbara Hepworth'. *Les arts plastiques* (Brussels) Nos. 5–6, 1948, pp. 245–47.

467 Herbert Read. 'Barbara Hepworth: a New Phase'. *Listener* Vol. 39, No. 1002, 8 April 1948, p. 592.

468 Patrick Heron. 'Barbara Hepworth, Lawrence Gowing'. *New Statesman and Nation* Vol. 35, No. 894, 24 April 1948, p. 333. Includes review of exhib. with Lowry, Lefevre Gallery, April 1948.

469 Denys Sutton. 'Barbara Hepworth'. *Arts, beaux-arts, littérature, spectacles* (Paris) No. 169, 4 June 1948, p. 3. Review of exhib. with Lowry, Lefevre Gallery, April 1948.

470 J. P. Hodin. 'Ausstellung Lefevre Gallery, London'. *Werk* Vol. 36, April 1949, supplement pp. 43–44.

471 'Reviews and Previews: Barbara Hepworth'. *Art News* Vol. 48, No. 6, Oct. 1949, p. 45. Brief review of exhib. Durlacher Gallery, Oct. 1949.

472 M.B. [Margaret Breuning]. 'Barbara Hepworth in American Debut'. *Art Digest* Vol. 24, No. 2, 15 Oct. 1949, pp. 20–21. Review of exhib. Durlacher Gallery, Oct. 1949.

473 J. P. Hodin. 'Cornish Renaissance'. *Penguin New Writing* No. 39, 1950, pp. 113–24.

474 Perspex. 'Current Shows and Comments'. *Apollo* Vol. 51, No. 300, Feb. 1950. Includes brief review of exhib. Lefevre Gallery, Feb. 1950, p. 35.

475 J. P. Hodin. 'Portrait of the Artist, No. 27: Barbara Hepworth'. *Art News and Review* Vol. 2, No. 1, 11 Feb. 1950, pp. 1, 6.

476 Nevile Wallis. 'Sculptor and Painter'. *Observer*, 12 Feb. 1950. Review of exhib. Lefevre Gallery, Feb. 1950.

477 Wyndham Lewis. 'Round the London Galleries'. *Listener* Vol. 43, No. 1099, 16 Feb. 1950, p. 298. Includes review of exhib. Lefevre Gallery, Feb. 1950. Reprinted in book *Wyndham Lewis on Art*, 1969.

478 Lawrence Dame. 'Regarding Europe'. *Art Digest* Vol. 24, No. 12, 15 March 1950, p. 6.

479 'Exhibitions'. *Architectural Review* Vol. 107, No. 640, April 1950. Includes brief review of exhib. Lefevre Gallery, Feb. 1950, p. 279.

480 A. M. Hammacher. 'Aantekeningen bij het werk van Barbara Hepworth'. *Kroniek van Kunst en Kultuur* (Amsterdam) Vol. 11, No. 4, April 1950, pp. 90–92.

481 J. P. Hodin. 'Barbara Hepworths lastste werkstukken'. *Kroniek van Kunst en Kultuur* (Amsterdam) Vol. 11, No. 4, April 1950, pp. 93–94.

482 David Lewis. 'Sculptures of Barbara Hepworth'. *Listener* Vol. 44, No. 1122, 27 July 1950, pp. 120–22.

483 J. P. Hodin. 'Barbara Hepworth'. *Les arts plastiques* (Brussels) Vol. 4, No. 3, July–Aug. 1950, pp. 199–208.

484 David Lewis. 'The Sculptures of Barbara Hepworth'. *Eidos* (London) No. 2, Sept.–Oct. 1950, pp. 24–[31].

485 Herbert Read. 'Barbara Hepworth'. *La Biennale di Venezia* No. 3, Jan. 1951, pp. 12–14. Italian text.

486 Denys Sutton. 'Living Art for Britain's Festival'. *Art News* Vol. 50, No. 4, Summer 1951, pp. 26–27, 54–55.

487 David Baxandall. 'Some Recent Carvings by Barbara Hepworth'. *Apollo* Vol. 56, No. 332, Oct. 1952, pp. 116–18. Review of exhib. Lefevre Gallery, Oct. 1952.

488 Stephen Bone. ['Review of exhib. Lefevre Gallery, Oct. 1952'.] *Manchester Guardian*, 3 Oct. 1952.

489 M. H. Middleton. 'Art'. *Spectator*, 10 Oct. 1952. Review of exhib. Lefevre Gallery, Oct. 1952.

490 P. H. [Patrick Heron]. 'Barbara Hepworth at the Lefevre'. *New Statesman and Nation* Vol. 44, No. 1128, 18 Oct. 1952, p. 450.

491 Robert Melville. 'Exhibitions'. *Architectural Review* Vol. 112, No. 672, Dec. 1952. Includes review of exhib. Lefevre Gallery, Oct. 1952, pp. 412–13.

492 G. S. Whittet. 'London Commentary'. *Studio* Vol. 145, No. 718, Jan. 1953. Includes review of exhib. Lefevre Gallery, Oct. 1952, p. 28.

493 '*Barbara Hepworth: Carvings and Drawings*'. *Listener* Vol. 49 No. 1249, 5 Feb. 1953, pp. 231–32. Book review.

494 [Book review of *Barbara Hepworth: Carvings and Drawings*.] *Werk* Vol. 40, Sept. 1953, supplement p. 158.

495 'Constructive Autobiography'. *Art News* Vol. 52, No. 6, Oct. 1953, p. 62. Book review of *Barbara Hepworth: Carvings and Drawings*, 1952.

496 Robert Melville. 'Geometry and Grace'. *Architectural Review* Vol. 114, No. 683, Nov. 1953, p. 333. Book review of *Barbara Hepworth: Carvings and Drawings*, 1952.

497 Christopher Small. 'Barbara Hepworth'. *Spectator*, 16 April 1954, p. 457. Review of exhib. Whitechapel Art Gallery, April–June 1954.

498 John Berger. 'Sculptural Vacuum'. *New Statesman and Nation* Vol. 47, No. 1206, 17 April 1954, p. 498. Review of exhib. Whitechapel Art Gallery, April–June 1954. Reprinted in book *Modern Arts Criticism. Volume 2*, 1992.

499 Lawrence Alloway. 'Art News from London'. *Art News* Vol. 53, No. 3,

May 1954. Includes review of exhib. Whitechapel Art Gallery, April–June 1954, p. 45.

500 Robert Melville. 'Vertical Forms Evolving: Barbara Hepworth and Reg Butler'. *Art News and Review* Vol. 6, No. 7, 1 May 1954. Includes review of exhib. Whitechapel Art Gallery, April–June 1954, p. 2.

501 'Woman's Place'. *Time* Vol. 63, No. 18, 3 May 1954, pp. 80, 83. Review of exhib. Whitechapel Art Gallery, April–June 1954.

502 Reyner Banham. 'Object Lessons'. *Architectural Review* Vol. 115, No. 690, June 1954, pp. 403–06. Discusses 'Figures in a Landscape' (film about Hepworth, directed by Dudley Shaw Ashton for British Film Institute).

503 G. S. Whittet. 'London Commentary'. *Studio* Vol. 148, No. 736, July 1954. Includes review of exhib. Whitechapel Art Gallery, April–June 1954, p. 28.

504 'Bacon, Hepworth, Scott'. *Art News* Vol. 53, No. 6, Oct. 1954, pp. 51–52. Review of group exhib. Martha Jackson Gallery, Oct.–Nov. 1954.

505 H. K. [Hilton Kramer?]. 'British Trio'. *Arts Digest* Vol. 29, No. 2, 15 Oct. 1954, p. 22. Review of group exhib. Martha Jackson Gallery, Oct.–Nov. 1954.

506 'Barbara Hepworth Retrospective'. *Arts Digest* Vol. 29, No. 14, 15 April 1955, p. 31. Announcement of exhib. Walker Art Center, Minneapolis, April–May 1955.

507 Patrick Heron. 'Barbara Hepworth—Carver'. *Arts Digest* Vol. 29, No. 15, 1 May 1955, pp. 8–9, 30. Review of exhib. Walker Art Center, April–May 1955.

508 David Lewis. 'Moore and Hepworth: a Comparison of their Sculpture'. *College Art Journal* Vol. 14, No. 4, Summer 1955, pp. 314–19.

509 Klaus J. Fischer. 'Vier Bildhauerinnen der Gegenwart'. *Das Kunstwerk* Vol. 9, No. 1, 1955–56, pp. 40–41, 43–46.

510 David Lewis. 'B. Hepworth'. *Arti Visive* (Rome), new series Nos. 3–4, [1956], pp. [5, 20]. English text.

511 'Barbara Hepworth'. *Konstrevy* (Stockholm) Vol. 31, Nos. 5–6, 1956, p. 198. Swedish text.

512 Pierre Rouve. 'Maturity of Barbara Hepworth'. *Art News and Review* Vol. 8, No. 11, 23 June 1956, p. 2. Review of exhib. Gimpel Fils, June 1956.

513 Isabel Batcheller. 'Barbara Hepworth, Sculptor'. *Canadian Art* Vol. 13, No. 2, Winter 1956, pp. 225–27.

514 'Reviews and Previews'. *Art News* Vol. 55, No. 9, Jan. 1957. Includes review of exhib. Martha Jackson Gallery, Dec. 1956–Jan. 1957, p. 21.

515 Pierre Rouve. 'Maturité de Barbara Hepworth'. *Prisme des arts* (Paris), No. 8, Jan. 1957, pp. 27–28.

516 'Barbara Hepworth'. *Arts* Vol. 31, No. 5, Feb. 1957, p. 54. Review of exhib. Martha Jackson Gallery, Dec. 1956–Jan. 1957.

517 Lawrence Alloway. 'Art News from London'. *Art News* Vol. 56, No. 4,

Summer 1957, p. 62. Includes discussion of Hepworth's commissioned sculpture for Mullard's Electronic Centre.

518 Pierre Rouve. 'Carver of Space'. *Art News and Review* Vol. 10, No. 11, 21 June 1958, p. 8. Review of exhib. Gimpel Fils, June 1958.

519 Jean Yves Mock. 'Barbara Hepworth at Gimpel Fils'. *Apollo* Vol. 68, No. 401, July 1958, pp. 22–23.

520 F.-C. L. [Francine-Claire Legrand]. 'Ve biennale de sculpture à Middelheim (Anvers)'. *Quadrum* (Brussels), No. 7, 1959, pp. 159–61.

521 Herta Wescher. 'Barbara Hepworth'. *Cimaise* Series 6, No. 5, June–Aug. 1959, pp. 9–17. Parallel French/English text.

522 'Barbara Hepworth'. *Art News* Vol. 58, No. 7, Nov. 1959, p. 15. Review of exhib. Galerie Chalette, Oct.–Nov. 1959.

523 'People in the Arts'. *Arts* Vol. 34, No. 2, Nov. 1959, p. 11. Includes brief announcement that Hepworth won grand international prize at fifth São Paulo Bienal.

524 M. S. [Martica Sawin]. 'Barbara Hepworth'. *Arts* Vol. 34, No. 3, Dec. 1959, p. 58. Review of exhib. Galerie Chalette, Oct.–Nov. 1959.

525 Herbert Read. 'Trois sculpteurs anglais'. *XXe siècle*, new series Vol. 21, No. 13, Christmas 1959, pp. 42–43. With English translation at end of issue. Reprinted from original series, Vol. 2, No. 1 (supplement to Vol. 1, Nos. 5–6), 1939, p. 45.

526 J. P. Hodin. 'Barbara Hepworth: a Classic Artist'. *Quadrum* (Brussels) No. 8, 1960, pp. 75–84. French summary p. 191.

527 Gillo Dorfles. 'La quinta biennale de San Paolo'. *Domus* No. 362, Jan. 1960, pp. 43–48.

528 John Russell. 'London Letter: Artist and Dealer'. *Art in America* Vol. 48, No. 1, Spring 1960, pp. 100–02, 104.

529 G. S. Whittet. 'London Commentary'. *Studio* Vol. 159, No. 806, June 1960. Includes comments on 'Meridian', State House, Holborn, pp. 215, 222.

530 John Russell. 'London Letter: Sculpture Renaissance'. *Art in America* Vol. 48, No. 2, Summer 1960, pp. 106–08.

531 Denys Chevalier. 'Les expositions à l'étranger. Zurich: Barbara Hepworth'. *Aujourd'hui* Vol. 5, No. 29, Dec. 1960, p. 52. Review of exhib. Galerie Charles Lienhard, Oct. 1960.

532 'Ausstellung in Zürich'. *Werk* Vol. 47, Dec. 1960, supplement p. 253.

533 J. P. Hodin. 'Artist and Architect: Recent Monumental Works Produced in England'. *Quadrum* (Brussels) No. 10, 1961, pp. 11–26. Includes section on Hepworth, pp. 24–26. French summary p. 188.

534 J. P. Hodin. 'La sculpture anglaise depuis Moore'. *XXe siècle*, new series, Vol. 23, No. 16, May 1961, supplement, pp. [1–4]. Includes comments on Hepworth, p. [1].

535 Norbert Lynton. 'Barbara Hepworth, Gimpel Fils'. *Arts Review* Vol. 13, No. 11, 17 June 1961, pp. 11, 13.

536 Michel Strauss. 'Current and Forthcoming Exhibitions: London'. *Burlington Magazine* Vol. 103, No. 700, July 1961. Includes review of exhib. Gimpel Fils, May–June 1961, pp. 327, 329.

537 'Brave New Patrons'. *Architectural Review* Vol. 130, No. 775, Sept. 1961, pp. 206–07. Includes references to 'Meridian', State House, Holborn.

538 J. P. Hodin. 'Englische Bildhauerei bei Gimpel Fils'. *Werk* Vol. 48, Dec. 1961, supplement p. 278.

539 E. Lovell Andrews. 'The Work of Barbara Hepworth: "Barbara Hepworth", by J. P. Hodin'. *Apollo* Vol. 76, new series No. 2, April 1962, pp. 154–55. Book review.

540 Christopher Salvesen. 'Barbara Hepworth'. *Arts Review* Vol. 14, No. 9, 19 May 1962, p. 10. Review of exhib. Whitechapel Art Gallery, May–June 1962.

541 Edwin Mullins. 'The Ecole de Paris'. *Apollo* Vol. 76, new series No. 4, June 1962. Includes: 'The Vitality of English Sculpture', pp. 301–02.

542 Anita Brookner. 'Coming and Forthcoming Exhibitions: London'. *Burlington Magazine* Vol. 104, No. 711, June 1962. Includes review of exhib. Whitechapel Art Gallery, May–June 1962.

543 ' "Barbara Hepworth", by J. P. Hodin'. *Burlington Magazine* Vol. 104, No. 712, July 1962, pp. 309–10. Book review.

544 Edwin Mullins. 'The Open-air Vision: a Survey of Sculpture in London since 1945'. *Apollo* Vol. 77, new series No. 6, Aug. 1962, pp. 455–61. Includes discussion of Hepworth's work, pp. 458–60.

545 G. S. Whittet. 'You Can't Write Off the British: London Commentary'. *Studio* Vol. 164, No. 832, Aug. 1962. Includes review of exhib. Whitechapel Art Gallery, May–June 1962, pp. 72, 75.

546 Herbert Read. 'A Nest of Gentle Artists'. *Apollo* Vol. 77, new series No. 7, Sept. 1962, pp. 536–38. Reminiscences of Hampstead and its artists in the 1930s.

547 Norbert Lynton. 'London Letter'. *Art International* Vol. 6, No. 7, Sept. 1962. Includes review of exhib. Whitechapel Art Gallery, May–June 1962, pp. 46–47.

548 [Book review of *Barbara Hepworth*, by J. P. Hodin.] *Werk* Vol. 49, Sept. 1962, supplement p. 220.

549 Michael Williams. 'Barbara Hepworth'. *Guardian*, 17 April 1963, p. 6.

550 G. S. Whittet. 'May Days for the Moderns: London Commentary'. *Studio* Vol. 166, No. 843, July 1963. Includes brief comments on 'Winged Figure', John Lewis Building, pp. 11–13.

551 G. S. Whittet. 'Battersea Power Sculpture'. *Studio* Vol. 166, No. 844, Aug. 1963, pp. 48–53. Review of group exhib. Battersea Park, May–Sept. 1963.

552 'Ausstellung in Zürich'. *Werk* Vol. 51, Jan. 1964, supplement p. 17.

553 Vivien Raynor. ' "Barbara Hepworth", by J. P. Hodin'. *Arts Magazine* Vol. 38, No. 5, Feb. 1964, pp. 73, 75. Book review.

554 James Burr. 'Round the London Galleries: the Severe Forms of Serenity'. *Apollo* Vol. 79, new series No. 28, June 1964. Includes review of exhib. Gimpel Fils, June 1964, pp. 508–09.

555 Kenneth Coutts-Smith. 'Barbara Hepworth'. *Arts Review* Vol. 16, No. 11, 13 June 1964, p. 8. Review of exhib. Gimpel Fils, June 1964.

556 'In Abstract Memoriam'. *Time* Vol. 83, No. 25, 19 June 1964, p. 68. On Hammarskjöld memorial.

557 Keith Roberts. 'Current and Forthcoming Exhibitions: London'. *Burlington Magazine* Vol. 106, No. 736, July 1964. Includes review of exhib. Gimpel Fils, June 1964, pp. 352–53.

558 'Dag Hammarskjöld Memorial'. *Foundry Trade Journal*, 16 July 1964, pp. 84–85.

559 G. S. Whittet. 'Movement and Repose in Contemporary Work: London Commentary'. *Studio International* Vol. 168, No. 856, Aug. 1964. Includes review of exhib. Gimpel Fils, June 1964, p. 78.

560 'Modern Art: Scottish National Gallery of Modern Art, Edinburgh'. *Burlington Magazine* Vol. 106, No. 741, Dec. 1964. Includes brief discussion of 'Dyad', p. 600, plate 57.

561 J. P. Hodin. 'Barbara Hepworth and the Mediterranean Spirit'. *Marmo* (Milan) No. 3, [Dec. 1964], pp. 58–65.

562 J. P. Hodin. 'Quand les artistes parlent du sacré'. *XXe siècle*, new series Vol. 26, No. 24, Dec. 1964, pp. 17–27. Quotes Hepworth pp. 23–24. English translation at end of issue.

563 'Barbara Hepworth's Gift of Sculpture to the Tate Gallery'. *Illustrated London News* Vol. 245, 5 Dec. 1964, p. 907.

564 J. P. Hodin. 'The Avant-garde of English Sculpture and the Liberation from the Liberators'. *Quadrum* (Brussels) No. 18, 1965, pp. 55–70. French summary p. 182.

565 Charles S. Spencer. 'The Phenomenon of British Sculpture'. *Studio International* Vol. 169, No. 863, March 1965, pp. 98–105.

566 J. P. Hodin. 'Barbara Hepworth, Kröller-Müller Museum, Otterlo'. *Arts Review* Vol. 8, No. 10, 29 May 1965, p. 5. Review of exhib. May–July 1965.

567 J. P. Hodin. 'Barbara Hepworth et la tradition classique'. *XXe siècle*, new series Vol. 27, No. 25, June 1965, pp. 100–04. English translation at end of issue.

568 G. S. Whittet. 'Art contemporain britannique: la guérilla de l'avant-garde'. *Aujourd'hui* Vol. 9, No. 50, July 1965, pp. 58–59. French text with English summary.

569 Cyril Barrett. 'London Commentary'. *Das Kunstwerk* (Baden-Baden) Vol. 19, No. 1, July 1965, pp. 11–15. Reviews of group exhibs. *British Sculpture in the Sixties*, Tate Gallery, Feb.–April 1965, and *Art in Britain 1930–40*, Marlborough Fine Art, March–April 1965. English text.

570 Marjorie Bruce-Milne. 'Dame Barbara Looks Back'. *Christian Science Monitor*, 13 July 1965, p. 10(?).
571 John Fitzmaurice Mills. 'Barbara Hepworth at the Rietveld Pavilion, Kröller-Müller Museum'. *Connoisseur* Vol. 159, No. 642, Aug. 1965, pp. 242–43.
572 'Acquisition of Works of Art by Museums and Art Galleries: Rijksmuseum Kröller-Müller, Otterlo: Barbara Hepworth, "Square with Two Circles" '. *Burlington Magazine* Vol. 107, No. 752, Nov. 1965. pp. 596, 598.
573 'Ausstellung in Basel'. *Werk* Vol. 52, Dec. 1965, supplement p. 285.
574 Myfanwy Piper. 'Back in the Thirties'. *Art and Literature*, No. 7, Winter 1965, pp. 136–50. Personal reminiscences.
575 C. Carter. 'Modern Sculpture in Aberdeen'. *Scottish Art Review* Vol. 10, No. 3, 1966, pp. 4–5.
576 'Barbara Hepworth: London Exhibition'. *Sculpture International* No. 2, [1966], pp. 54–57. Review of exhib. Gimpel Fils, May–June 1966.
577 Hilton Kramer. 'Barbara Hepworth: Vanguard to the Establishment'. *New York Times*, 13 March 1966. Review of exhib. Marlborough-Gerson Gallery, April–May 1966. Reprinted in book *The Age of the Avant-garde*, 1974.
578 J. P. Hodin. 'Vom Stil der Barbara Hepworth'. *Die Kunst und das Schöne Heim* (Munich), April 1966.
579 James Burr. 'London Galleries'. *Apollo* Vol. 83, new series No. 51, May 1966. Includes brief reference to exhib. Gimpel Fils, May–June 1966, pp. 387, 389.
580 A. H. [Anne Hoene]. 'Barbara Hepworth'. *Arts Magazine* Vol. 40, No. 7, May 1966, pp. 58–59. Review of exhib. Marlborough-Gerson Gallery, April–May 1966.
581 Edwin Mullins. 'Hepworth at Home'. *Daily Telegraph Magazine*, 20 May 1966, pp. 32–35.
582 E. Bridgeman. 'Barbara Hepworth at Gimpel Fils'. *Arts Review* Vol. 18, No. 10, 28 May 1966, p. 241.
583 Gene Baro. 'Barbara Hepworth in her Times'. *Studio International* Vol. 171, No. 878, June 1966, pp. 252–56.
584 Norbert Lynton. 'A Source of Warmth'. *Guardian*, 4 June 1966, p. 6. Review of exhib. Gimpel Fils, May–June 1966.
585 'Recent Museum Acquisitions: Sculpture and Drawings by Barbara Hepworth (The Tate Gallery); Barbara Hepworth's "Oval Form (Trezion)" (National Art Gallery, Wellington, New Zealand)'. *Burlington Magazine* Vol. 108, No. 761, Aug. 1966, pp. 424–27.
586 Alistair Gordon. 'Barbara Hepworth: Four Drawings, Four Masterworks'. *Connoisseur* Vol. 163, No. 655, Sept. 1966, pp. 24–27.
587 Diane Kirkpatrick. ' "Sphere with Colour (Grey & White)" by Barbara Hepworth'. *University of Michigan Museum of Art Bulletin* (Ann Arbor) Vol. 2, new series Nos. 1 and 2, 1966–67, pp. 28–32.

588 G. S. Whittet. 'Sculpture & Architecture: the Uncertain Partnership'. *Sculpture International* No. 5, 1967, pp. 12–21. Includes brief discussion of 'Meridian', State House, Holborn, p. 20.

589 Bryan Robertson. 'A Sculptor through her Drawings'. *Studio International* Vol. 173, No. 887, March 1967, supplement, pp. 4, 6. Book review of *Barbara Hepworth: Drawings from a Sculptor's Landscape*, 1966.

590 Charles Harrison. 'Abstract Painting in Britain in the Early 1930s'. *Studio International* Vol. 173, No. 888, April 1967, pp. 180–91.

591 J. P. Hodin. 'Influences européennes et américaines en Angleterre'. *XXe siècle*, new series Vol. 29, No. 28, June 1967, pp. 22–26.

592 ' "Drawings from a sculptor's landscape", by Barbara Hepworth'. *Connoisseur* Vol. 166, No. 667, Sept. 1967, pp. 52–53. Book review.

593 Jay Jacobs. 'Figures, Fads and Fatuities'. *Art in America* Vol. 55, No. 5, Sept.–Oct. 1967. Includes book review of *Barbara Hepworth: Drawings from a Sculptor's Landscape*, 1966, pp. 114–15.

594 Bryan Robertson. 'Hepworth at the Tate'. *Spectator*, 5 April 1968, p. 448.

595 Christopher Neve. 'Holes in a Sculptor's Landscape: Barbara Hepworth at the Tate'. *Country Life* Vol. 143, No. 3710, 11 April 1968, pp. 886–87.

596 Robert Melville. 'Creative Gap'. *New Statesman* Vol. 75, No. 1935, 12 April 1968, p. 494. Review of exhib. Tate Gallery, April–May 1968. Reprinted in book *Modern Arts Criticism. Volume 2*, 1992.

597 Guy Burn. 'Hepworth'. *Arts Review* Vol. 20, No. 7, 13 April 1968, pp. 184–85. Review of exhib. Tate Gallery, April–May 1968.

598 Paul Overy. 'Inflations'. *Listener* Vol. 79, No. 2038, 18 April 1968, p. 517. Includes review of exhib. Tate Gallery, April–May 1968.

599 James Burr. 'London Galleries: Carving a Place in History'. *Apollo* Vol. 87, new series No. 75, May 1968. Includes review of exhib. Tate Gallery, April–May 1968, p. 384.

600 Keith Roberts. 'Current and Forthcoming Exhibitions: London'. *Burlington Magazine* Vol. 110, No. 782, May 1968. Includes review of exhib. Tate Gallery, April–May 1968, pp. 299, 301.

601 Robert Lebel. 'L'irruption des femmes dans la sculpture'. *XXe siècle*, new series, Vol. 30, No. 30, June 1968, supplement pp. [3–12].

602 Barbara M. Reise. 'Friendly Biography'. *Studio International* Vol. 176, No. 902, July 1968, p. 56. Book review of *Barbara Hepworth*, by A. M. Hammacher, 1968.

603 John Fitzmaurice Mills. 'Art at the United Nations Headquarters'. *Connoisseur* Vol. 169, No. 682, Dec. 1968, pp. 262–66. Includes references to Hammarskjöld memorial, p.264.

604 L. R. Rogers. ' "Barbara Hepworth", by A. M. Hammacher'. *British Journal of Aesthetics* Vol. 9, No. 2, April 1969, pp. 209–10. Book review.

605 'Barbara Hepworth'. *Art News* Vol. 68, No. 3, May 1969, p. 21. Review of exhib. Gimpel Gallery, New York, April–May 1969.

606 Cindy Nemser. 'Barbara Hepworth'. *Arts Magazine* Vol. 43, No. 7, May 1969, p. 59. Review of exhib. Gimpel Gallery, New York, April–May 1969.

607 Jerrold Lanes. 'Current and Forthcoming Exhibitions: New York'. *Burlington Magazine* Vol. 111, No. 795, June 1969. Includes review of exhib. Gimpel Gallery, April–May 1969, p. 406.

608 Stanley Jones. 'Twelve Lithographs by Barbara Hepworth'. *Studio International* Vol. 177, No. 912, June 1969, pp. 300–01.

609 'Barbara Hepworth, Curwen Gallery'. *Arts Review* Vol. 21, No. 12, 21 June 1969, p. 407.

610 Norman Capener. 'Concourse'. *Annals of the Royal College of Surgeons of England* Vol. 45, July 1969, pp. 46–49.

611 James Burr. 'London Galleries'. *Apollo* Vol. 90, new series No. 89, July 1969. Includes review of exhib. Curwen Gallery, [June–July] 1969, p. 74.

612 Robert Thomas. 'Graphics'. *Art and Artists* Vol. 4, No. 4, July 1969, p. 66. Includes brief review of exhib. Curwen Gallery, [June–July] 1969.

613 James Burr. 'London Galleries'. *Apollo* Vol. 91, new series No. 96, Feb. 1970. Includes review of exhib. Marlborough Fine Art, Feb.–March 1970, p. 151.

614 William Packer. 'London Exhibitions'. *Art and Artists* Vol. 4, No. 11, Feb. 1970. Includes review of exhib. Marlborough Fine Art, Feb.–March 1970, p. 30.

615 Robert Melville. 'Little Girls'. *New Statesman* Vol. 79, No. 2033, 27 Feb. 1970, p. 305. Includes brief review of exhib. Marlborough Fine Art, Feb.–March 1970.

616 'Hepworth on Site'. *Arts Review* Vol. 22, No. 4, 28 Feb. 1970, p. 104. Includes details of four public sculptures by Hepworth.

617 Pierre Rouve. 'Barbara Hepworth'. *Arts Review* Vol. 22, No. 4, 28 Feb. 1970, pp. 105, 119. Review of exhib. Marlborough Fine Art, Feb.–March 1970.

618 Bernard Denvir. 'London Letter'. *Art International* Vol. 14, No. 4, April 1970. Includes review of exhib. Marlborough Fine Art, Feb.–March 1970, pp. 61–62.

619 Keith Roberts. 'Current and Forthcoming Exhibitions: London'. *Burlington Magazine* Vol. 112, No. 805, April 1970. Includes brief review of exhib. Marlborough Fine Art, Feb.–March 1970, p. 263.

620 David Jolley. ['Acquisition by the Whitworth Art Gallery of Barbara Hepworth's "Sphere with Inner Form", 1963'.] *Burlington Magazine* Vol. 112, No. 809, Aug. 1970, pp. 562–63, 568.

621 'Barbara Hepworth'. *Art News* Vol. 70, No. 3, May 1971, p. 15. Brief review of exhib. Gimpel Gallery, New York, March–April 1971.

622 Marianne Hancock. 'Barbara Hepworth'. *Arts Magazine* Vol. 45, No. 7, May 1971, pp. 58–59. Review of exhib. Gimpel Gallery, New York, March–April 1971.

623 'Hepworth Sculpture in Dulwich'. *Studio International* Vol. 181, No. 933, May 1971, pp. 197–98.
624 James Burr. 'London Galleries'. *Apollo* Vol. 94, new series No. 113, July 1971. Includes brief review of exhib. Curwen Gallery, 1971, p. 69.
625 Ron Lusker. 'New York: the Season in Sculpture'. *Craft Horizons* (New York) Vol. 31, No. 4, Aug. 1971. Includes brief review of exhib. Gimpel Gallery, March–April 1971, p. 65.
626 Pat Gilmour. 'Barbara Hepworth: Aegean Suite Lithographs'. *Connoisseur* Vol. 178, No. 715, Sept. 1971, p. 72. Review of exhib. Curwen Gallery, 1971.
627 Edwin Mullins. 'Barbara Hepworth's "Family" '. *Daily Telegraph Magazine*, 7 April 1972, pp. 28–29, 31–32.
628 William Gaunt. 'The Family of Man'. *Times*, 15 April 1972, p. 12.
629 Richard Walker. 'The Family of Man'. *Arts Review* Vol. 24, No. 8, 22 April 1972, p. 227. Review of exhib. Marlborough Fine Art, April–May 1972.
630 Marina Vaizey. 'Marlborough Fine Art: Barbara Hepworth'. *Financial Times*, 28 April 1972, p. 3.
631 James Burr. 'London Galleries: Symbols from St. Ives'. *Apollo* Vol. 95, new series No. 123, May 1972. Includes review of exhib. Marlborough Fine Art, April–May 1972, p. 409.
632 Keith Roberts. 'Current and Forthcoming Exhibitions: London'. *Burlington Magazine* Vol. 114, No. 831, June 1972. Includes brief review of exhib. Marlborough Fine Art, April–May 1972, pp. 424, 427.
633 Marina Vaizey. 'In the Galleries: Barbara Hepworth'. *Connoisseur* Vol. 180, No. 724, June 1972, p. 161. Review of exhib. Marlborough Fine Art, April–May 1972.
634 William Feaver. 'London Letter: April'. *Art International* Vol. 16, Nos. 6–7, Summer 1972. Includes review of exhib. Marlborough Fine Art, April–May 1972, pp. 120–21.
635 Noel Welch. 'Barbara Hepworth: a Personal View'. *Cornish Review* (Penzance) No. 25, Winter 1973, pp. 23–36.
636 Jane Bell. 'Barbara Hepworth at Marlborough'. *Arts Magazine* Vol. 48, No. 8, May 1974, p. 75. Review of exhib. Marlborough Gallery, New York, March–April 1974.
637 Phyllis Derfner. 'New York Letter'. *Art International* Vol. 18, No. 6, Summer 1974. Includes review of exhib. Marlborough Gallery, March–April 1974, pp. 47, 51.
638 Jeanne Siegel. 'Barbara Hepworth'. *Art News* Vol. 73, No. 6, Summer 1974, p. 125. Review of exhib. Marlborough Gallery, New York, March–April 1974.
639 Lawrence Alloway. ['Comments on "Single Form" '.] *Nation* (New York) Vol. 219, No. 8, 21 Sept. 1974, p. 254. Reprinted in book *Modern Arts Criticism. Volume 2*, 1992.

640 Fenella Crichton. 'London Letter'. *Art International* Vol. 18, No. 9, Nov. 1974. Includes review of group exhib. *Art Then*, Scottish Arts Council Gallery, Aug.–Sept. 1974, pp. 38–39.

641 F. Portela Sandoval. ['Obituary'.] *Goya*, No. 126, May 1975, p. 399.

642 'Barbara Hepworth Dies in Fire at Cornwall Studio'. *New York Times*, 21 May 1975, p. 46. Two obituaries: 'A sense of flow', by Alden Whitman; 'Spirit of 30s sculpture: Dame Barbara's abstracts reflected ferment of time of emerging creation', by Hilton Kramer.

643 'Barbara Hepworth: Sculptor who Led the Way'. *Daily Telegraph*, 22 May 1975, p. 7. Obituary.

644 Terence Mullaly. 'Heroic Phase Comes to a Close'. *Daily Telegraph*, 22 May 1975, p. 7(?).

645 Caroline Tisdall. ['Obituary: Barbara Hepworth'.] *Guardian*, 22 May 1975, p. 10.

646 'Obituary: Dame Barbara Hepworth: a British Exponent of Abstract and Monumental Forms'. *Times*, 22 May 1975, p. 18.

647 Patrick Heron. 'Hepworth: a Singular Passion'. *Observer*, 25 May 1975, p. 11. Obituary.

648 Michael Shepherd. 'Bright, Still Beauty of Hepworth'. *Sunday Telegraph*, 25 May 1975. Obituary.

649 Henry Moore. 'The Shaping of a Sculptor'. *Sunday Times*, 25 May 1975, p. 27. Obituary.

650 Frank Davis. 'Substance and Shadow: a Tribute to Dame Barbara Hepworth, who Died Recently'. *Art and Antiques*, 14 June 1975, pp. 16–17.

651 J. P. Hodin. 'Barbara Hepworth'. *Studio International* Vol. 190, No. 976, July–Aug. 1975, p. 72. Obituary.

652 Tadayasu Sakai. 'Barbara Hepworth's Death'. *Mizue*, No. 845, Aug. 1975, pp. 50–51. Japanese text with brief English summary.

653 Gordon Brown. 'Four British Sculptors'. *Arts Magazine* Vol. 50, No. 1, Sept. 1975, p. 24. Brief review of group exhib. Gimpel Weitzenhoffer, April–May 1975.

654 James Burr. 'Immortality in Marble, Wood and Bronze'. *Apollo* Vol. 102, new series No. 164, Oct. 1975, p. 297. Review of exhib. Gimpel Fils, Oct.–Nov. 1975.

655 'Galeries'. *L'oeil* No. 243, Oct. 1975, p. 62. Includes review of exhib. Marlborough Galerie, Zürich, Aug.–Oct. 1975.

656 Oswell Blakeston. 'Barbara Hepworth, Gimpel Fils'. *Arts Review* Vol. 27, No. 22, 31 Oct. 1975, p. 630.

657 David Lewis. 'Barbara Hepworth 1903–1975'. *Carnegie Magazine* (Pittsburgh) Vol. 49, No. 9, Nov. 1975, pp. 398–405. Obituary.

658 Charles McCorquodale. 'Barbara Hepworth: Gimpel Fils'. *Art International* Vol. 19, No. 10, Dec. 1975, pp. 26–27.

659 Marina Vaizey. 'London'. *Art News* Vol. 74, No. 10, Dec. 1975. Includes brief review of exhib. Gimpel Fils, Oct.–Nov. 1975, p. 101.
660 William Packer. 'Trewyn Studio St. Ives: the Barbara Hepworth Museum'. *Financial Times*, 21 April 1976.
661 'Two New Museums in Cornwall'. *Arts Review* Vol. 28, No. 9, 30 April 1976, p. 209. Includes details of newly opened Hepworth Museum, St. Ives.
662 J. P. Hodin. 'From Cornwall'. *Art and Artists* Vol. 11, No. 3, June 1976, pp. 16–21.
663 Ann Hills. 'Barbara Hepworth Museum Opens'. *Burlington Magazine* Vol. 118, No. 879, June 1976, pp. 451–53.
664 Nicholas Hills. 'Hepworth Museum'. *Architectural Review* Vol. 160, No. 954, Aug. 1976, p. 119.
665 Edward Gage. 'Art at the Edinburgh Festival'. *Arts Review* Vol. 28, No. 18, 3 Sept. 1976. Includes review of exhib. Royal Botanic Garden, Aug.–Sept. 1976, p. 449.
666 John Tancock. 'Nineteenth- and Twentieth-century Sculpture'. *Connoisseur* Vol. 193, No. 777, Nov. 1976, pp. 238–40. Discusses sculpture in Norton Simon collection, including Hepworth and Moore.
667 Richard Calvocoressi. 'Edinburgh Festival 1976'. *Connoisseur* Vol. 193, No. 777, Nov. 1976, p. 250. Includes review of exhib. Royal Botanic Garden, Aug.–Sept. 1976.
668 Alan Bowness. 'The Barbara Hepworth Museum, St. Ives, Cornwall'. *Museums Journal* (London) Vol. 76, No. 4, March 1977, pp. 148–49.
669 Malcolm Quantrill. 'London Letter'. *Art International* Vol. 21, No. 4, July–Aug. 1977. Includes review of group exhib. *A Silver Jubilee Exhibition of Contemporary British Sculpture*, Battersea Park, June–Sept. 1977, pp. 70–72.
670 Malcolm Quantrill. 'From London: Some Anglo-Saxon Intentions and Responses'. *Art International* Vol. 22, No. 2, Feb. 1978. Includes comments on 'Family of Man', p. 88.
671 Vivien Raynor. 'Art: the Sculpture of a Perfectionist'. *New York Times*, 8 May 1979. Review of exhib. Marlborough Gallery, New York, May–June 1979.
672 David Thistlewood. 'Herbert Read's Aesthetic Theorizing 1914–1952: an Interpretation of the "Philosophy of Modern Art" '. *Art History* Vol. 2, No. 3, Sept. 1979, pp. 339–54.
673 Diane Kirkpatrick. 'Modern British Sculpture at the University of Michigan Museum of Art'. *Bulletin, Museums of Art and Archaeology, The University of Michigan* (Ann Arbor) Vol. 3, 1980, pp. 64–76, and frontispiece. Includes discussion of 'Sphere with Colour (Grey & White)', pp. 69–71.
674 Waldemar Januszczak. 'The Seed of Art that Flowered on Stony Ground: the Barbara Hepworth Museum in St. Ives is to be Given to the Nation'. *Guardian*, 7 Jan. 1980, p. 9.

675 John Spurling. 'Sunlight and Soap'. *New Statesman*, 25 April 1980. Includes comments on Barbara Hepworth Museum, St. Ives, pp. 640–41.

676 Michael Young. 'Hepworth's Studio Still Vibrant'. *Times*, 17 July 1980, p. 13.

677 Frances Spalding. 'Barbara Hepworth, Yorkshire Sculpture Park, Bretton Hall'. *Arts Review* Vol. 32, No. 18, 12 Sept. 1980, pp. 401–02.

678 Peter Davies. 'St. Ives: the Creative Emergence in Cornwall 1940–1960'. *Fine Art Letter* (Winchester School of Art) Vol. 3, May 1981, pp. 3–5.

679 N. Cusick. '3 in Washington D.C.'. *Women Artists News* (U.S.A.) Vol. 7, No. 3, Fall 1981, pp. 9–10.

680 Judith Zilczer. 'The Theory of Direct Carving in Modern Sculpture'. *Oxford Art Journal* Vol. 4, No. 2, Nov. 1981, pp. 44–49. Includes discussion of Moore and Hepworth, pp. 46–48.

681 Alan Gouk. 'Subject to Stones: British Sculpture at the Whitechapel 1: 1901–1950'. *Artscribe*, No. 32, Dec. 1981, pp. 24–30.

682 Peter Davies. 'St. Ives in the Forties'. *Artscribe*, No. 34, March 1982, pp. 55–57.

683 John Russell Taylor. 'Galleries: Giving Substance to the Silly Season'. *Times*, 13 July 1982, p. 8. Includes review of exhib. Marlborough Fine Art, July–Aug. 1982.

684 Max Wykes-Joyce. 'Barbara Hepworth, Marlborough Fine Art'. *Arts Review* Vol. 34, No. 16, 30 July 1982, pp. 400–01.

685 'Barbara Hepworth Carvings'. *Art and Artists* [No. 191], Aug. 1982, p. 34. Review of exhib. Marlborough Fine Art, July–Aug. 1982.

686 Naomi Mitchison. 'Big Stones'. *Spectator*, 7 Aug. 1982, p. 23. Book review of *Barbara Hepworth: a Memoir*, by Margaret Gardiner, 1982.

687 Kay Larson. 'Humanism in No-Man's-Land'. *New York* Vol. 15, No. 34, 30 Aug. 1982, pp. 58–60. Review of exhib. Storm King Art Center, Mountainville, N.Y., June–Oct. 1982. (No catalogue traced for this exhib.)

688 Frances Spalding. 'The Nail at Work'. *Times Literary Supplement*, 17 Sept. 1982, p. 997. Book review of *Babara Hepworth: a Memoir*, by Margaret Gardiner, 1982.

689 Peter Davies. 'The Significance of St. Ives'. *Art and Artists* No. 222, March 1985, pp. 14–17. Review of group exhib. *St. Ives 1939–64*, Tate Gallery, Feb.–April 1985.

690 Christopher Reid. 'Something in the Air'. *Crafts* No. 73, March–April 1985, pp. 28–34. Review of group exhib. *St. Ives 1939–64*, Tate Gallery, Feb.–April 1985.

691 William Feaver. 'Down to the Sea'. *Art News* Vol. 84, No. 5, May 1985, pp. 111–12. Review of group exhib. *St. Ives 1939–64*, Tate Gallery, Feb.–April 1985.

692 Jeremy Lewison. 'The Early Prints of Ben Nicholson'. *Print Quarterly* (U.K.)

Vol. 2, No. 2, June 1985, pp. 105–24. Includes discussion of influence of Hepworth.

693 Peter Murray. 'Barbara Hepworth'. *Arts Review* Vol. 37, No. 13, 5 July 1985, p. 331. Review of exhibs. *Early Life* and *Late Carvings*, Wakefield, May–July 1985.

694 Paul Bowness. 'Operation Drawings of Dame Barbara Hepworth'. *British Medical Journal*, 21–28 Dec. 1985, pp. 1788–89(?).

695 Peter Fuller. 'Against Internationalism'. *Art Monthly* No. 100, Oct. 1986, pp. 12–14.

696 Liv Kavanagh. 'Fine Art and Textiles: the Ascher Head Squares and Wall Panels'. *Apollo* Vol. 125, new series No. 303, May 1987, pp. 331–37.

697 Mary Rose Beaumont. 'Barbara Hepworth, New Art Centre'. *Arts Review* Vol. 39, No. 24, 4 Dec. 1987, pp. 845–46.

698 Jacqueline Herald. 'Limited Editions on Silk'. *Antique Collector* Vol. 59, No. 1, Jan. 1988, pp. 58–65.

699 Peyton Skipwith. 'Drawings by British Sculptors 1918–1939'. *Drawing* (New York) Vol. 10, No. 1, May–June 1988, pp. 1–4. Includes brief reference to Hepworth, p. 3.

700 Catherine Ferbos. 'La sculpture anglaise: sculptures 'in-between'—le paysage'. *Artstudio* No. 10, Autumn 1988, pp. 20–25. Mainly about the sculpture of the 1980s, with references to the earlier work of Hepworth and Moore.

701 Peyton Skipwith. 'Background Notes to Henry Moore's "Time-Life Screen" '. *Burlington Magazine* Vol. 131, No. 1038, Sept. 1989, pp. 637–41. Includes discussion of consideration of Hepworth for the project, pp. 639–41.

702 Ann Sutherland Harris. 'Entering the Mainstream: Women Sculptors of the 20th Century, Part One—Barbara Hepworth and Louise Nevelson'. *Gallerie: Women's Art* (Canada) Vol. 2, No. 2, Fall 1989, pp. 8–13.

703 Cynthia Rose. 'Cambridge: Ede's Corner'. *Art News* Vol. 88, No. 9, Nov. 1989, pp. 103–04.

704 Charles Hall. 'Barbara Hepworth, Ben Nicholson'. *Arts Review* Vol. 42, No. 15, 27 July 1990, p. 416. Review of exhib. *Ben Nicholson: Major Works; Barbara Hepworth: Carvings*, Gimpel Fils, London, June–Sept. 1990. (No catalogue traced for this exhib.)

705 Alastair Grieve. 'Towards an Art of Environment: Exhibitions and Publications by a Group of Avant-garde Artists in London, 1951–55'. *Burlington Magazine* Vol. 132, No. 1052, Nov. 1990, pp. 773–81. Mainly about the younger generation of abstract and constructionist artists.

706 Sophie Bowness. 'Mondrian in London: Letters to Ben Nicholson and Barbara Hepworth'. *Burlington Magazine* Vol. 132, No. 1052, Nov. 1990, pp. 782–88.

707 Deanna Petherbridge. 'Ten Decades: Careers of Ten Women Artists born

1897–1906'. *Women's Art Magazine*, No. 46, May–June 1992, pp. 16–17. Review of group exhib. Norwich Gallery, March–May 1992.

708 William Packer. 'Le monde de Moore'. *Beaux-Arts Magazine* No. 102, June 1992, pp. 61–65. Includes comments on Moore's attitude to Hepworth, p. 62.

709 Penelope Dening. 'Carving her Name with Ruthlessness'. *Sunday Telegraph*, 16 May 1993, Reviews p. 5.

710 Brian Wall. 'Wall's Eye'. *Art Review* Vol. 46, Sept. 1994, pp. 51–54. Reminiscences of former assistant to Hepworth.

711 Rachel Barnes. 'On Good Form'. *Guardian*, 12 Sept. 1994, Arts pp. 4–5.

712 William Packer. 'A Firm Commitment to Abstraction'. *Financial Times*, 20 Sept. 1994, p. 19. Review of exhib. Tate Gallery Liverpool, Sept.–Dec. 1994.

713 William Feaver. 'Who Shaped the Hole of Modern Art?'. *Observer*, 25 Sept. 1994, Review p. 11. Review of exhib. Tate Gallery Liverpool, Sept.–Dec. 1994.

714 Richard Cork. 'A Woman's Place is in the Stone'. *Times*, 27 Sept. 1994, p. 39. Review of exhib. Tate Gallery Liverpool, Sept.–Dec. 1994.

715 Penelope Curtis. 'Through Thick and Thin'. *Women's Art Magazine* No. 60, Sept.–Oct. 1994, pp. 12–14.

716 Bryan Robertson. 'Barbara Hepworth'. *Modern Painters* Vol. 7, No. 3, Autumn 1994, pp. 51–55.

717 Andrew Lambirth. 'Hepworth and Dobson Shows'. *R A Magazine* No. 44, Autumn 1994, p. 23.

718 Lynn MacRitchie. 'Thinking through the Sense of Touch'. *Independent*, 4 Oct. 1994, p. 23. Review of exhib. Tate Gallery Liverpool, Sept.–Dec. 1994.

719 Martin Gayford. 'An All-Feminine, Natural-Born Nurturer'. *Daily Telegraph*, 5 Oct. 1994, p. 22. Review of exhib. Tate Gallery Liverpool, Sept.–Dec. 1994.

720 Clare Henry. 'Centre Stage for First Lady of Abstract'. *Herald* (Glasgow), 10 Oct. 1994. Review of exhib. Tate Gallery Liverpool, Sept.–Dec. 1994.

721 'Barbara Hepworth: Gimpel Fils'. *Time Out*, 2–9 Nov. 1994, p. 49. Brief review of exhib. Gimpel Fils, London, Oct.–Nov. 1994. No catalogue published for this exhib.

722 Andrew Causey. 'Liverpool and New Haven: Barbara Hepworth'. *Burlington Magazine* Vol. 136, No. 1101, Dec. 1994, pp. 860–61. Review of exhib. Tate Gallery Liverpool, Sept.–Dec. 1994.

723 Richard Cork. 'On Growth and Form'. *Tate: the Art Magazine*, No. 4, Winter 1994, pp. 38–43.

724 Penelope Curtis. 'Signing Off'. *Tate: the Art Magazine*, No. 4, Winter 1994, p. 80.

Index of authors and editors

Where no author or editor is credited in exhibition catalogues, the museum, gallery or, occasionally, the exhibiting organisation is cited.